HUGO GROTIUS AS APOLOGIST
FOR THE CHRISTIAN RELIGION

STUDIES IN THE HISTORY
OF
CHRISTIAN THOUGHT

FOUNDED BY HEIKO A. OBERMAN †

EDITED BY

ROBERT J. BAST, Knoxville, Tennessee

IN COOPERATION WITH

HENRY CHADWICK, Cambridge
SCOTT H. HENDRIX, Princeton, New Jersey
BRIAN TIERNEY, Ithaca, New York
ARJO VANDERJAGT, Groningen
JOHN VAN ENGEN, Notre Dame, Indiana

VOLUME CXI

J.P. HEERING

HUGO GROTIUS AS APOLOGIST
FOR THE CHRISTIAN RELIGION

HUGO GROTIUS AS APOLOGIST FOR THE CHRISTIAN RELIGION

A STUDY OF HIS WORK
DE VERITATE RELIGIONIS CHRISTIANAE
(1640)

BY

J.P. HEERING

TRANSLATED BY J.C. GRAYSON

BRILL
LEIDEN · BOSTON
2004

Grateful acknowledgement is made to the Nederlandse Organisatie voor Wetenschappelijk Onderzoek (NWO) for the financial support that made this publication possible.

This book is printed on acid-free paper.

Library of Congress Cataloging-in-Publication Data

Heering, Jan-Paul.
  [Hugo de Groot als apologeet van de christelijke godsdienst. English]
  Hugo Grotius as apologist for the Christian religion : a study of his work De veritate religionis Christianae, 1640 / by Jan-Paul Heering ; translated by J.C. Grayson.
    p. cm. — (Studies in the history of Christian thought ; v. 111)
  Includes bibliographical references and index.
  ISBN 90-04-13703-3
  1. Grotius, Hugo, 1583-1645. De veritate religionis Christianae. 2. Apologetics—History—17th century. I. Title. II. Series.

BT1103.G763H4413 2003
239—dc22

                                                                              2003069558

ISSN   0081-8607
ISBN   90 04 13703 3

Coverdesign: Thorsten's Celine Ostendorf

PRINTED IN THE NETHERLANDS

Dedicated to Monique

'Meaning is a kind of constant flickering of presence and absence together.'

T. Aegerton

CONTENTS

FOREWORD

Paci christianorum studentis officium et hoc est, demoliri dogmata, quae pacem civilem perturbant. Prius est bonum civem esse quam bonum christianum.—So said Hugo Grotius in one of his last polemical works against the theologian André Rivet (*Rivetiani Apologetici pro schismate contra Votum pacis facti discussio*, in *Opera Theologica*, 1732, IV, p. 701). This is just one example of a statement of Grotius, which as a theologian when I wrote the Dutch version of this study I could not fully comprehend (especially not the last sentence meaning: it's more important to be a good citizen than a good christian), but which more than ten years later as a lawyer I now feel that I understand rather better.

In 1987, when I began to study Grotius' apologetic work, encouraged by my promotor Prof. Dr Hans Posthumus Meyjes, I could not have suspected that this study would turn my life into another course. The first result of this study was my dissertation, which I defended at Leiden in 1992. The thesis was written in Dutch and therefore only accessible to a relatively small public. Once again it was Hans Meyjes who urged an English translation. That plan, however, hung fire for a long time, because very soon after my promotion all my time was taken up by my legal studies and later by my work as a lawyer. It was in fact Hugo Grotius who had led me to this, for it was his work that aroused my interest in juridical thought. In the meantime Hans Meyjes continued to urge an English translation of the thesis, which I had almost forgotten. After overcoming some hesitation I decided to apply to NWO for a translation subsidy, which was granted.

I am very grateful to Hans Meyjes for the way in which he initiated me into Grotius' thought, for his friendly encouragement from the beginning of my studies, and especially for the patience with which time and again he urged on my dilatoriness.

My promotor also recommended me to Chris Grayson, who had translated several Leiden studies, including Hans Meyjes's own thesis. I was therefore particularly pleased that Mr Grayson was willing to undertake the translation of my work. I thank him for the prompt and expert way in which he acquitted himself of his task.

The result is entirely to my satisfaction, for his English is certainly smoother than the Dutch original.

Since research on Grotius has not stood still between 1992 and 2003, the text has been slightly modified and the notes have been supplemented on a number of points. Errors have been corrected and omissions filled in as far as possible. Dr Henk Nellen was my Virgil in this. I thank him for the expert and friendly way in which he kept me informed of the latest developments. His critical remarks also led to a few necessary corrections in chapter 5, especially on the work of Socinus on which Grotius drew.

Dr Arthur Eyffinger was kind enough to make available to me a selection of his impressive collection of illustrations, which have helped to bring this book alive. My thanks are due to him for his generosity and helpfulness.

I thank NWO for the subsidy for both my doctoral research and this translation. I am also grateful to my publishers, Brill (in particular Irene van Rossum), for their willingness to publish this work and for the agreeable cooperation which has resulted in a book that is at least attractive externally.

This book is dedicated to my wife Monique, who patiently bore long periods of (at least mental) absence on my part and who with unwearied energy ensured that our daily life continued to run smoothly.

J.P. Heering   Voorburg, September 2003

LIST OF ABBREVIATIONS

App.	Appendix.
ARA	Algemeen Rijksarchief, The Hague.
Bergman, 'Suppl. Annot'	J.T. Bergman, 'Supplementum Annotationis', in H. Grotius, *De veritate religionis christianae*, ed. J.T. Bergman, Leiden 1831 [= *BG* nᵒ 1000], pp. 246–80.
BG	J. Ter Meulen/P.J.J. Diermanse, *Bibliographie des écrits imprimés de Hugo Grotius*, The Hague 1950, facsimile reprint, Zutphen 1995.
BL	*Biografisch Lexicon voor de Geschiedenis van het Nederlands Protestantisme*, Kampen 1978 . . .
Brandt-Cattenburgh	C. Brandt and A. van Cattenburgh, *Historie van het leven des heeren Huig de Groot, beschreven tot den aanvang van zijn Gezantschap wegens de Koninginne en Kroone Van Zweeden aan 't hof van Vrankrijk*, 2nd ed. Dordrecht/Amsterdam 1732
BsG	J. ter Meulen and P.J.J. Diermanse, *Bibliographie des écrits sur Hugo Grotius imprimés au XVIIᵉ siècle*, The Hague 1961.
BW	*Briefwisseling van Hugo Grotius*, ed. P.C. Molhuysen, B.L. Meulenbroek, P.P. Witkam, H.J.M. Nellen and C.M. Ridderikhoff, 17 vols. [RGP], The Hague 1928–2001.
BWNG	B. Glasius, *Godgeleerd Nederland. Biographisch Woordenboek van Nederlandsche Godgeleerden*, Bois-le-Duc 1851–6.
BWPGN	J.P. de Bie and J. Loosjes (ed.) *Biographisch Woordenboek van Protestantsche Godgeleerden in Nederland*, 6 vols., The Hague [1903–1949].
ca.	circa.
Comment.	commentary/commentaire.
DBF	*Dictionnaire de Biographie française*, Paris 1933.
DHGE	*Dictionnaire d'histoire et de géographie ecclésiastique*, Paris 1912 . . .

DNB	*Dictionary of National Biography from the Earliest Times to 1900*, London 1885–1900.
DTC	A. Vacant/E. Mangenot/E. Amann, ed. *Dictionnaire de théologie catholique*, 15 vols., Paris 1899–1972.
e.a.	et alii.
ed.	edidit/ediderunt.
EJ	*Encyclopaedia Judaica*, 16 vols., Jerusalem [1971–2].
etc.	et cetera.
Eyff, *Handschr.*	A. Eyffinger, *De handschriftelijke nalatenschap van Hugo de Groot. Inventaris van de papieren in Nederlandse openbare collecties*, The Hague 1985 [unpublished].
fol.	folio.
Fruin, *Verhooren*	R. Fruin (ed.), *Verhooren en andere bescheiden betreffende het rechtsgeding van Hugo de Groot*, [Werken uitgegeven door het Historisch Genootschap gevestigd te Utrecht, New Series n° 14], Utrecht 1871.
Haag	E. Haag/E. Haag (ed.), *La France Protestante ou vies des protestants français*, 10 vols., Paris 1849–59.
Ibid.	Ibidem.
Introd.	Introduction.
JE	*The Jewish Encyclopaedia*, 12 vols., New York/London 1901–06.
Molhuysen, 'Bibliotheek'	P.C. Molhuysen, 'De bibliotheek van Hugo de Groot in 1618', *Mededeelingen der Nederlandsche Akademie van Wetenschappen, Afdeeling Letterkunde*, new series 6.3, Amsterdam 1943.
Ms.	manuscript.
n.	note
NBW	*Nationaal Biografisch Woordenboek*, Brussels 1964 . . .
n.d.	no date.
NNBW	P.C. Molhuysen and P.J. Blok (ed.), *Nieuw Nederlandsche Biografische Woordenboek*, 10 vols., Leiden 1911–37.

n°   number.
n°s   numbers.
NS   new series.
NTT   *Nederlands Theologisch Tijdschrift*, 1 (1946)– . . .
p.   page.
Petit   L.D. Petit, *Bibliografische lijst der werken van Leidsche hoogleeraren van de oprichting der hoogeschool tot op onze dagen. Faculteit der godgeleerdheid*, eerste aflevering (1575–1619), Leiden 1894.
prol.   prolegomena.
red.   redactor.
RGG³   *Die Religion in Geschichte und Gegenwart, Handwörterbuch für Theologie und Religions-wissenschaft*, Dritte Auflage, 6 vols., Tübingen 1957–62.
RGP   Rijks Geschiedkundige Publicatiën, The Hague.
SC   Sources chrétiennes, Paris 1941.
sc.   scilicet.
sqq.   sequentes.
s.v.   sub voce.
TRE   G. Krause/G. Müller (ed.), *Theologische Realenzyklopädie*, Berlin etc. 1977– . . .
VRC   Hugo Grotius, *De veritate religionis christianae*, ed. J.T. Bergman, Leiden 1831.
WNT   *Woordenboek der Nederlandscher Taal*, The Hague/Leiden/Arnhem 1864– . . .

INTRODUCTION

Hugo Grotius is one of the few figures of the seventeenth century Dutch Golden Age who can still claim worldwide fame. Even during his lifetime Grotius was called 'Erasmus redivivus', 'the Delft oracle' or 'the Phoenix of learning'. The lustre of his name has not yet faded, but his works are no longer as well known as they were. It is true that Grotius' oeuvre was very extensive and many-sided, and included, apart from his legal writings, many literary, philological, historical, biblical and theological works; but it is just as true that nowadays they are virtually unread outside a small circle of specialists.

In fact the only one that is still generally known is his great legal work *De iure belli ac pacis* (1625), which was described some time ago as 'the book that just cannot die'.[1] The same cannot be said for any other work of Grotius. But in earlier centuries this juridical treatise was less well-known, or at least less frequently reprinted and trans-lated, than his defence of the faith: *De veritate religionis christianae* (1640). This is the Latin version of a Dutch poem that Grotius wrote while imprisoned in the castle of Loevestein and published in 1622 under the title *Bewijs van den waren godsdienst* (Proof of the true religion). The book offers a defence of or apology for the Christian religion against atheism, paganism, Judaism and Islam. It was already famous in the author's lifetime, especially in the Latin version. Huizinga remarked, not unjustly, that 'for his own century, Grotius was without doubt more the author of *De veritate religionis christianae* than of *De iure belli ac pacis*'.[2]

Grotius' contemporaries praised the work by calling it 'a golden booklet'. As a typical production of late humanistic classicism it was characterised above all by its conciseness and simplicity.[3] Busken Huet regarded Grotius' apologetic work as the epitome of the religious

---

[1] C. van Vollenhoven, 'Het boek van 1625', in *Verspreide Geschriften*, I, Haarlem 1934, p. 225.

[2] J. Huizinga, 'Grotius' plaats in de geschiedenis van den menschelijken geest', in *Tien Studiën*, Haarlem 1926, p. 118.

[3] *BW* III, n° 1238 (to C. Sarravius, 10 March 1628), p. 263: "Quare cognoscen-dum tibi adfero libellum hunc nostrum [= *VRC*] argumenti magni et a non uno tractati, in quo, si nihil aliud, brevitatem cum perspicuitate aut praestiti aut praestare conatus sum."

civilisation of the seventeenth century.[4] One can better say the epitome of a *part* of that civilisation, for many orthodox Calvinists
abhorred it. Grotius' work bears witness to a broad religious faith,
which can also be described as moderate or 'Arminian'.[5] As such it
forms a perfect counterweight to the well-known, ponderous and
dogmatic Canons laid down by the Synod of Dordt in 1619. Over
against this 'labyrinth of dogma', the product of a constricting Calvinist
confessionalism, Grotius put his undogmatic defence of the faith at
the service of Christians of every confession.[6] He was more successful than any other author, certainly in the seventeenth and eighteenth centuries, in gaining the approval of every Christian who
inclined to moderation or latitudinarianism.

Grotius' apologetic work has already been the subject of five mono-
graphic studies. The first was by J.C. Koecher, *Historia libri Grotiani
de veritate religionis christianae* (1739).[7] This work is certainly not without merit. Koecher gave a brief account of the origin of Grotius'
defence of the faith and a summary of the various editions and translations, as well as an inventory of the commentaries and criticisms
devoted to it, but he omitted to pass a historical judgement on
Grotius' work.

The most detailed monograph to follow Koecher was written by
T.C.L. Wijnmalen, *Hugo de Groot als verdediger des christendoms beschouwd*
(Hugo Grotius considered as defender of Christendom) (1869).[8] This
study must be described as simply unsatisfactory. Wijnmalen confined
himself to an examination of the first version, the *Bewijs van den waren
godsdienst*, while the significance of Grotius' defence of the faith lies
essentially in the Latin version, which differs from the Dutch didactic poem in several respects. Wijnmalen's choice prevented him from
giving a complete description of the origin and reception of the work
and a full analysis of its contents. The author barely considered the
important question of the sources, and treated the work in complete

---

[4] C. Busken Huet, *Het land van Rembrand. Studien over de Noordnederlandsche beschav-
ing in de zeventiende eeuw*, 5th edition, Haarlem [n.d.], II, 1, p. 83.
    [5] See E.J. Kuiper, 'Hugo de Groot en de remonstranten', *NTT*, 37 (1983), 111–25.
    [6] Cf. W.J.M. van Eysinga, *Huigh de Groot. Een schets*, Haarlem 1945, p. 73.
    [7] J.C. Koecher, *Historia libri Grotiani de veritate religionis christianae*, in Hugo Grotius,
De veritate religionis christianae. Variis dissertationibus illustratus, opera ac studio Io. Chr. Koecheri,
Halle 1739, pp. 1–192.
    [8] T.C.L. Wijnmalen, *Hugo de Groot als verdediger des christendoms beschouwd. Eene lit-
terarisch-apologetische proeve*, Utrecht 1869.

isolation from the rest of Grotius' oeuvre. His approach limited him to a superficial consideration, and made it impossible for him to judge Grotius' defence of the faith on its real merits.

The other monographs are no more than sketches: C. Roy, *Hugo Grotius considéré comme apologète* (1855), C. Looten, *De Grotio christianae religionis defensore* (1889) and C.W. Roldanus, *Hugo de Groot's Bewijs van den waren godsdienst* (1944).[9] We can pass over the studies by Roy and Looten, which offer little more than a summary of the contents of Grotius' work. More thorough and better documented is the monograph by Roldanus. Apart from an introduction and analysis of the contents it also offers a brief historical consideration of Grotius' defence of the faith. Unfortunately Roldanus confined herself, as the title of her study indicates, largely to the Dutch version of the work. She dealt briefly with the question of Grotius' sources, but went no further than noticing several agreements with Duplessis Mornay and Vives. On Grotius' debt to his predecessors and his intentions in the work, however, Roldanus left her readers no wiser.

In view of the shortcomings of these studies there is reason enough to investigate Grotius' apologetic writings anew, all the more so since much new material by and about Grotius has come to light in recent decades, which allows a more comprehensive judgement of his works. It is sufficient to cite a few editions of special importance for the study of Grotius' *De veritate religionis christianae.*

The monumental edition of Grotius' correspondence in seventeen substantial volumes is of incalculable value for everyone who wishes to go deeply into the life and works of the author.[10] This edition means that we are now much better equipped than before to form a precise picture of Grotius' relations with his contemporaries, the history of the origin of his works and the reactions they provoked.

In 1984 G.H.M. Posthumus Meyjes discovered an unknown work by Grotius entitled *Meletius sive de iis quae inter christianos conveniunt epistola.*[11] This work, which is presumed to date from 1611, resembles

---

[9] C. Roy, *Hugo Grotius considéré comme apologète*, Colmar 1855; C. Looten, *De Grotio christianae religionis defensore*, Insulis [= Lille] 1889; and C.W. Roldanus, *Hugo de Groot's Bewijs van den waren godsdienst*, Arnhem 1944.

[10] *Briefwisseling van Hugo Grotius*, ed. P.C. Molhuysen et al., 17 vols [Rijks Geschiedkundige Publicatiën], The Hague 1928–2001.

[11] Hugo Grotius, *Meletius sive de iis quae inter christianos conveniunt epistola*, Critical edition with translation, commentary and introduction by G.H.M. Posthumus Meyjes [Studies in the History of Christian Thought, 40], Leiden etc. 1988.

the *De veritate religionis christianae* in offering a concise proof of the truth of the Christian religion, and deals at length with religion in its theoretical and practical aspects. A comparison between the two works makes it possible to gain a new insight into the continuity and development of Grotius' theological thought.

Some years ago F. Laplanche made an important contribution to a better understanding of Grotius' defence of the faith in his rich study of Christian apologetics in the age of late humanist classicism: *L'Évidence du Dieu chrétien. Religion, culture et société dans l'apologétique protestante de la France classique (1576–1670)*.[12] Laplanche investigated a group of apologetic texts from this period, one of them being Grotius' *De veritate religionis christianae*. He placed them in a broad social and cultural historical perspective, so that he was able to paint a subtle and complex picture of their historical significance. He demonstrated convincingly that Protestant defenders of the faith in this period reached back to the achievements of patristics, humanism and the Reformation. These apologists opposed a division between faith and reason, and stressed the importance of a natural, that is a rational, knowledge of God. They also employed the argument from historical proof developed in the primitive Church. Unlike Roman Catholic apologists they could not appeal to a fixed and authorised tradition, for they saw the Bible as the only source of divine revelation. The method followed by Laplanche necessarily meant that his treatment concentrated on the structures that these Protestant apologetics had in common. This did rather less than justice to the distinctive features of Grotius' text, so that we have an opportunity to add detail to certain parts of Laplanche's picture.

It is the intention of this study to give a new analysis of the historical importance of Grotius' apologetic works. The two chief questions that we wish to answer are: what motives and intentions led him to write his defence of the faith; and what sources did he use? Before we can solve these problems we need to go into the complicated history of the book and analyse its contents. Some other aspects also demand our attention, among them the history of the reception of Grotius' defence of the faith.

This study is made up of seven chapters, broadly as follows. The first chapter discusses the history of the origin of this defence of the

---

[12] F. Laplanche, *L'Évidence du Dieu chrétien. Religion, culture et société dans l'apologétique protestante de la France classique (1576–1670)*, Strasbourg 1983.

faith. Grotius composed his Dutch didactic poem in 1620 as a prisoner in the castle of Loevestein. Initially he presented this work as an introduction to the faith. The title of one of the first versions, of which a manuscript has been preserved, is *Geloofs Voorberecht*. He published his poem in 1622 under the title *Bewijs van den waren godsdienst*. The work was dedicated to the people of Holland, whose sympathy the author wished to gain for his miserable fate, first as a prisoner and later as an exile.

In the second chapter we deal with the complicated history of the Latin version in which Grotius recast his Dutch poem. The first edition of this version appeared in 1627 under the title *Sensus librorum sex quos pro veritate religionis christianae scripsit Hugo Grotius*. Two years later the author published a second, enlarged and improved edition under the simplified title *De veritate religionis christianae*, which he retained in subsequent impressions. The last authorised edition of the work appeared at Paris in 1640. The greatest difference from the earlier editions was that it was provided with extensive notes.

The third chapter summarises the contents of the apologetic work.

The fourth chapter gives an analysis of the intentions that must have been in Grotius' mind as he wrote it, and of his method of proof. The motives that led him to write his defence of the faith seem to have been largely eirenic. As early as his first theological work, the *Meletius*, he had revealed that he was deeply troubled by the internal divisions of Christianity. Grotius regarded this division as a disease, which in his view was caused above all by his contemporaries' excessive preoccupation with dogma. In his *De veritate* he wished to prove the truth of the Christian faith using exclusively rational arguments and historical testimonies, that is the means of proof generally accepted in humanist dialectic. That left no room for the treatment of specific doctrines of the Christian faith, such as the trinity or the divinity of Christ.

The fifth chapter raises the question of the sources of Grotius' apologetic work. It is our firm conviction that Grotius drew his material chiefly from three humanist apologists, namely Juan-Luis Vives (1492–1540), Fausto Sozzini (1534–1604) and Philippe Duplessis Mornay (1549–1623). Here and there he enriched his borrowings from them with material found in older philosophical and apologetic literature. It is not unlikely that he also had his youthful work *Meletius* close at hand while he was writing the *De veritate*.

The sixth chapter gives an overall view of the structure of the

apparatus of notes that Grotius added to the text of his defence in
1640. The notes do not appear to tell the reader anything about
the sources of his text, but in fact they contribute new evidence in
the form of a series of historical testimonies, which merely served to
buttress the argument.

The seventh and last chapter is devoted to the reception that Grotius'
apologia encountered, particularly in its author's lifetime. Immediately
after it appeared in a Latin version the work won much support
from both Protestants and Catholics. The only criticism came from
the contra-remonstrants, especially Voetius, Schoockius and Rivet,
but these theologians scarcely elaborated their criticism, and in fact
confined themselves to taunts and jeers, though their charge of
Socinianism is not without foundation. In Grotius' lifetime his apologetic work went into two German and two French translations, as
well as an English version. We give only a summary survey of the
enormous number of posthumous editions and translations.

It remains for us to say that—unless otherwise indicated—we give
references to and cite from the last critical edition of Grotius' *De
veritate religionis christianae* (Leiden, 1831), edited by J.T. Bergman.[13]
This edition was based on the last edition authorised by Grotius
(Paris, 1640). Though Bergman's edition can still be described as
acceptable, a new critical edition is certainly desirable. For the sake
of readability the punctuation and spelling of the citations have been
slightly modernised and the use of capital letters reduced. For references
to the poem *Bewijs van den waren godsdienst* we use, unless otherwise
stated, the last edition edited by J. de Vries (Amsterdam, 1844).[14]

[13] Hugo Grotius, *De veritate religionis christianae*, Editionem novam curavit et selecta
annotatione instruxit Jo. Theod. Bergman, Vol. I, Leiden 1831.
[14] Hugo Grotius, *Bewijs van den waren godsdienst, met zijn overige Nederduitsche gedichten*.
Uitgegeven door Jeronimo de Vries, Amsterdam 1844, pp. 1–167.

1. Hugo Grotius at age fifteen, proudly showing the medal he received from
the French King Henry IV in 1598. Drawing by Jacques de Gheyn II (1599).
Coll. Fodor, Historical Museum, Amsterdam.

2. Loevestein Castle. Engraving by C.J. Visscher. Coll. Atlas v. Stolk, Rotterdam.

Op de WAAG-SCHAAL.

GOMMAR en ARMIJN te Hoof Leyd' den rock van d'Advocaet, GOMMARS seyd' die boven lingh,
Dongen om het recht geloof, En de kussens van den Raedt, Trooste met sijn stale kling,
Yeders ingebracht bescheyt End' het brein dat geensins schveen Die soo swaar was van gewicht
In de Waegschael wort geleyt, T'del van gesonde re'en, Dat al 't ander viel te licht,
Doctor GOMMAR arme knecht Brieven die vermelden plat, Doen aanbadt elk GOMMARS pop,
Hadd' het met ten eersten slecht, 't Heylich recht van elcke Stadt: End' ARMIJN die kreeg de schop,
Midts den schranderen ARMIJN GOMMAR sagh vast hier en gins, Oock PELAEGS leer BELLARMIJNS
Tegen BESAM en CALVIJN, Tot soo lang mijn Heer de Prins. En de Kettery SOCIJNS.

E. ISRAELS.

3. "Op de Waagschaal". Anonymous caricature (1618). Printed in F. Muller, *De Nederlandsche Geschiedenis in Platen. Beredeneerde beschrijving van Nederlandsche Historieplaten, zinneprenten en historische kaarten. Eerste deel* (Amsterdam 1863-1870), nr. 1333 sub e. Vondelmuseum, Amsterdam.

4. Hugo Grotius, Engraving by W. Delff (1632), after a portrait by Mierevelt (1631).
Printed in J.F. van Someren, *Beschrijvende Catalogus van gegraveerde portretten van Neder-landers*, deel 2 (Amsterdam 1891), S. 2139c.

5. The Execution of Oldenbarnevelt at the Binnenhof on 13 May, 1619. Engraving by C.J. Visscher (1619). Coll. Atlas v. Stolk, Rotterdam.

INLEIDING TOT
DE HOLLANDSCHE
RECHTS-GELEERTHEYD.

Befchreven by
Hugo De Groot

IN 'GRAVEN-HAGE
By de Weduwe van Hillebrant
Jacobfz. van Wou. 1631.

6. Frontispiece of the first edition of *Inleiding tot de Hollandsche Rechts-Geleertheyd* (1631). Coll.
Peace Palace Library, The Hague. Photo: D-Vorm, Leidschendam.

7. Johannes Wtenbogaert (1557-1644). Etching by Rembrandt, with Latin poem by Grotius. Rijksmuseum, Amsterdam, inv. nr. B 279.

8. Portrait of Erasmus. By H. Holbein (1530). Öffentliche Kunstsammlung, Basel.

CHAPTER ONE

THE GENESIS OF THE POEM
BEWIJS VAN DEN WAREN GODSDIENST
(PROOF OF THE TRUE RELIGION)

a. *Background*

The political fall of Hugo Grotius

After it had concluded a truce with Spain in 1609 the Republic of the United Netherlands experienced a period of serious internal unrest that led to the famous coup of prince Maurice in 1618.[1] On 29 August 1618, acting on the authority of the States-General, the prince arrested Johan van Oldenbarnevelt, the Advocate of Holland, with his most important political associates, Hugo Grotius and Rombout Hogerbeets. The States-General declared that these politicians had put the country in grave danger and had to be arrested to preserve national unity.[2]

The arrested politicians, according to this statement, were officially suspected of disturbing the public order of the country. Stubborn rumours were also circulating that Oldenbarnevelt had carried on a secret correspondence with the king of Spain and that he had had to make considerable concessions to obtain a good peace with the arch-enemy. To accommodate Spain Oldenbarnevelt was supposed to have attempted to impose restrictions on the East India Company, the nation's pride, and to nip the development of the West India

---

[1] See I. Schöffer, 'De crisis van de jonge Republiek, 1609–1625', in *Algemene Geschiedenis der Nederlanden*, vol. 6, Utrecht-Antwerp 1953, pp. 1–51; H. Gerlach, *Het proces tegen Oldenbarnevelt en de 'Maximen in den staet'*, Haarlem 1965; J. den Tex, *Oldenbarnevelt*, 5 vols, Haarlem 1960–72; S. Groenveld, 'De loop der gebeurtenissen, 1609–1650', in *De bruid in de schuit. De consolidatie van de Republiek, 1609–1650*, Zutphen 1985, pp. 1–45.

[2] The text of the declaration that the States-General caused to be printed and distributed is in Groenveld, 'Bruid in de schuit', p. 39.

Company in the bud. These rumours fed a second suspicion of the trio, far more serious than the first: high treason.[3]

They were also accused of having acted in the interest of the 'remonstrants'. This was the name given to the followers of the professor of theology at Leiden, Jacobus Arminius, who had entered into a lengthy and profound discussion with his colleague Franciscus Gomarus on divine predestination. This discussion was the occasion of a widespread and far-reaching conflict in the church, which played an important part in the struggle for political power between Oldenbarnevelt and prince Maurice. The remonstrants were supporters of greater intervention by the government in ecclesiastical affairs, and for that reason they had the backing of Oldenbarnevelt. Prince Maurice, on the other hand, sided with the 'contra-remonstrants', who pleaded for the sovereignty of the church and for years had been urging the calling of a national synod, only to be repeatedly thwarted by Oldenbarnevelt and his right hand man Grotius. With these powerful political opponents out of the way, the national synod could be opened at Dordrecht on 13 November 1618. During the synod a third suspicion against the captive politicians could be formulated: namely, disturbing the religious order of the state.[4]

Hugo Grotius tried to save himself by writing a submissive and pleading letter to prince Maurice from his prison cell in The Hague, in an attempt to exculpate himself from the three suspicions.[5] He defended the policy of tolerance he had followed during the disputes that divided the church and the country, but distanced himself from both parties.[6] He explained his point of view on the national synod as follows: provincial synods should be held first, then a national synod, and after that a 'general' or international synod ought to be called, which would be less partisan and would enjoy more authority. He referred emphatically to his love for and services to the country, to which both his writings and his actions bore witness. At the same time he pleaded for the continuance of the East India Company

---

[3] The combined charges were also characterised as *perduellio* or *crimen laesae majestatis in summo gradu*. See Gerlach, *Het proces*, p. 675.

[4] An antiquated offence, *crimen laesae majestatis divinae*, from the time of the Inquisition. See Den Tex, III, p. 742.

[5] *BW* II, n° 583 (to prince Maurice, 13 September 1618), pp. 4–12.

[6] *BW* II, n° 583, p. 4: "Wat my aengingh ick vonde my soo in myn gemoet, dat ick van de twee opiniën, die inde kercken wierden gedisputeerd, nochte d'eene nochte d'ander nyet t'eenemael en conde toestaen, maar hadde myn eygen bedencken."

and the creation of the West India Company. Finally, he asked to be released from all further proceedings.[7]

On 6 February 1619 the preliminary investigation of the suspects was completed, and the trial could begin. The judges could not find sufficient evidence of treason against the state, nor is the charge of disturbing public order actually mentioned in so many words in the verdicts, but it is clearly suggested.[8] The punishments also correspond to the crime of disturbing the public order. The charge of disturbing religion is explicitly included in the verdicts.[9] The sentences were unusually harsh. Oldenbarnevelt was sentenced to death on 12 May 1619, and lost his head on the scaffold the next day. Grotius and Hogerbeets heard their sentences on 17 May: "perpetual" (lifelong) imprisonment and the forfeiture of their property.

Grotius refused to acknowledge his guilt, and listened to his sentence with his face averted. He is supposed to have remarked to his servant that "he did not think any sentence perpetual but Hell".[10]

In prison

Grotius spent more than eight months in preliminary arrest at The Hague. At first he often felt ill.[11] In the beginning, his wife Maria van Reigersberch was not allowed to visit him. The prisoner put his trust in God's aid.[12] Every day he fortified himself with prayer, read intensively in the Bible and consoled himself with the thought that the Almighty knew of the wrong done to him.[13] After the first hearing his pen and ink were taken from him, but he was not left empty-handed,

---

[7] *BW* II, n° 583, p. 11.

[8] The official charge was *crimen laesae majestatis*, that is injuring the honour of the supreme authority, i.e. the States-General. See Groenveld, 'Bruid in de schuit', p. 40.

[9] Fruin, *Verhooren*, 'Sententie', p. 337.

[10] See Fruin, *Verhooren*, 'Memorie', p. 72.

[11] Fruin, *Verhooren*, Memorie, p. 37: "Voor mijne detentie was ick gestadig zyeckelick geweest, insonderheyt swak van mage, waerdoor ick oock nae mijne detentie dickmaels in swaere syeckte ben vervallen, bij wijlen de spijs niet wel connende inhouden."

[12] *BW* II, n° 54 (to Maria van Reigersberch, 21 September 1618), p. 12: "Godt Almachtigh die ons to noch toe soo genaedelick bygestaean heeft sal ons niet nalaten te helpen ende te vertroosten."

[13] Fruin, *Verhooren*, 'Memorie', p. 38: "Godt weet dat my hyerin ongelijck geschiet."; cf. *BW* II, n° 650 (to N. van Reigersberch, 8 October 1620), pp. 34–5: "Godt heeft mi door dit middel zeer krachtelijck geroepen—zo ik vertrouwe—tot meerder kennis en betrachting zyner heilige wille. Ik hoop my met ernst daartoe te begeven, om den tyd van myne bezoeking niet te verzuimen."

for he had laid in a stock of writing materials.[14] Maria van Reigersberch spared no effort to bring about an improvement in her husband's situation. She saw to it that Grotius regularly received books from such good friends as Petrus Scriverius, Thomas Erpenius and Gerard Vossius, so that he could devote his scanty leisure to study.

Grotius afterwards related that he had spent the hours in his prison cell in The Hague chiefly in reading the Bible and the annotations and paraphrases on it of such famous scholars as Erasmus, Beza, Drusius and Casaubon. He had also made a study of the early Christian authors, including Eusebius of Caesarea, Clement of Alexandria and Tertullian. He had begun to draft a number of works, some of which, however, had been confiscated by his gaolers.[15]

In the night of 5 to 6 June 1619 Grotius was transferred to the castle of Loevestein near Gorinchem, where he was to serve the remainder of his prison sentence. Conditions in this castle were less unpleasant for him than those in his cell in The Hague, and he was also allowed to have his wife and daughter Cornelia with him. He could lead an extremely regular life here, almost entirely devoted to study.

Grotius regularly received chests full of books from his friends, above all from Vossius.[16] In these books he found the material for the works he was to write in Loevestein, among them a number of poems in Dutch.

---

[14] Fruin, *Verhooren*, 'Memorie', p. 50.
[15] Fruin, *Verhooren*, 'Memorie', p. 70: "Mijne occupatien geduyrende den voorn. tijdt waren het lesen van Godts woord, insonderheyt van het Nieuwe Testament, daer ick by heb gelesen Paraphrasin ende Annotationes Erasmi, Annotationes Bezae, Drusii et Casauboni, oock bij wijlen yet uyt Harmonia Calvini. Ick heb ock gelesen veel in Eusebiii Historia ende in Epiphanio adversus Hereses, Clementem Alexandrinum ende Tertullianum heel uyt; gelijck mede scriptores Augustae. Ick heb oock bij wijlen wat gelesen in Plutarcho. In' t aldereerste heb ick oock bij geschrifte gestelt in 't Latijn mijne bedenckingh op onse kerckelijke differenten [perhaps *Disq.*]; 't welck bij mijnen dyenaer zijnde uytgeschreven, ick socht te senden aen d'Heer Hogerbeets, maer de Heeren hebben het Schrift onder haer gehouden, doch onder mij is de minuyte gebleven nevens eenige projecten de satisfactione Christi, de justa defensione, vi gladii et bello [perhaps a preliminary study for *IBP*]. Ick heb oock getransleert de versen dye staen in Stobaei Physicis ende en goet deel in Eclogis Ethicis [= Stob., *Dicta Poetarum*], alsoock Phoenissas Euripidis [= Eur. *Trag.*], doch hyervan is het eerste deel mijnen dyenaer ontvallen door een spleet in mijn camer, comende op de audientie van den Provincialen Raedt; dit stuck is opgeraept ende in handen van de Heeren geraeckt."
[16] C.S.M. Rademaker, 'Books and Grotius at Loevestein', *Quaerendo*, II (1972), 2–29; idem, *Life and Work of Gerardus Joannes Vossius (1577–1649)*, Assen 1981.

Dutch poems

Before his imprisonment Grotius' published poems had been exclusively in Latin. He had been composing poetry in that language since his childhood, and as a student at the University of Leiden and shortly afterwards he developed into a leading neo-Latin poet with a command of many genres. His most productive period of poetic composition (1600–05) coincided with his friendship with Daniel Heinsius, who like Grotius combined exceptional scholarly and literary talents.[17] Heinsius and Grotius had met in the small circle of pupils around the famous French scholar Joseph Scaliger, who may be called the prince of Leiden humanists.[18] Scaliger's prize pupils developed an intensive cooperation and a close friendship, based on mutual admiration and competition. But in the conflicts during the Truce they became estranged from each other because Grotius displayed a clear sympathy for the remonstrants while Heinsius chose to side with the contra-remonstrants.

A collection of Grotius' Latin poems appeared in 1617,[19] not on his own initiative but on that of his youngest brother Willem. Grotius had been reluctant, declaring that he had passed the age at which he could publish such *jeux d'esprit*. "At a man's age it is better to be silent than to stammer."[20] At that time he had quite other things than poetry on his mind. As pensionary of Rotterdam he was wholly absorbed in his work and the cares that it brought. The golden years of his fame as a poet laid far behind him. His share in the theological controversies and his laborious efforts to mediate in the politics of the ecclesiastical conflict had made him suspect to many of his former admirers. He hoped that the publication of his youthful poems would revive his reputation, and wrote to a friend:

---

[17] For biographical information on Heinsius (1580/1–1655) see P. Sellin, *Daniel Heinsius and Stuart England*, Leiden-London 1968, pp. 3–69, and J.H. Meter, *The Literary Theories of Daniel Heinsius*, Assen 1984, pp. 5–276.

[18] For Scaliger see A. Grafton, *Joseph Scaliger. A Study in the History of Classical Scholarship*, 2 vols., Oxford 1983–93. For more literature on Scaliger see A. Grafton and H.J. de Jonge, *Joseph Scaliger. A Bibliography (1852–1982)*, The Hague 1983.

[19] H. Grotius, *Poemata collecta & magnam partem nunc primum edita a fratre Guilielmo Grotio*, Leiden 1617 [= *PC*].

[20] *BW* I, n° 441 (to W. de Groot, 15 December 1650), p. 455: "Praecipuum scriptionis patrocinium seritas editionis decoquet [...] At viro silere quam balbutire est satius."

tired by manly cares I go back to my youth, to see if an edition of
these trifles will bring me more thanks and less envy than my more
serious works.[21]

During Grotius' imprisonment poetry made an unexpected return to
his life. Though he had bidden farewell to this Muse several times
in earlier years, composing poetry gave him much pleasure and consolation in his confinement. In a letter to Vossius he said that the
Muses were now much kinder to him than ever before.[22] As early
as his youthful work *Parallelon* he had called the art of poetry the
best method of intellectual relaxation.[23]

In The Hague and Loevestein Grotius composed a number of
religious poems in Dutch. His choice of Dutch was remarkable. In
his youth he had produced some poems in the vernacular, but they
were not intended for publication.[24] The Dutch poems written in
prison, on the other hand, were published on the author's initiative.

In their poetry of the first decade of the seventeenth century
Heinsius and Grotius had imitated the great classical authors of
Roman antiquity, writing almost exclusively Latin poems bound by
strict literary rules. The current literature in Dutch, such as the
poems of the 'rhetoricians', was a long way from meeting these strict
classical requirements, and therefore in the eyes of the humanists it
was impure and inferior. The hegemony of neo-Latin verse kept
Dutch poetry in the shadows for a long time, but that situation was
to change when a collection of Dutch poems by Heinsius was published in 1616.[25]

---

[21] *BW* I, n° 477 (to G.M. Lingelsheim, 24 September 1616), p. 530: "Ad pueri-
tiam redeo, fessus virilibus curis, experturus an maiore cum gratia et invidia minore
ioca quam seria edere liceat."

[22] *BW* II, n° 596, to G.J. Vossius (15 December 1619), p. 26: "Mihi fortunae
huius levamentum sunt illae, ut nosti, tunc etiam cum negotiis pene opprimerer,
"dulces ante omnia Musae"; nunc vero multo quam ante dulciores, cum experior
quam hoc sit prae ceteris rebus ἀναφαίρετον."

[23] *Parall.*, II 17, 57: "Si quid ego recte judico, etiam mediocriter doctis in Poesi
optime interquiescit animus."

[24] Apart from the anonymously published epigrams on prince Maurice, of which
his authorship is doubtful (see *BG*, n° 396), Grotius probably composed a few Dutch
poems in his youth. Cf. *BW* I, n° 143 (to N. van Reigersberch, 18 August 1608),
p. 126: "Multa quoque alia Gallice et Batavice lusi quae in iuvenum ac virginum
manibus sunt, adeo bene nobis cessit nostra insania."

[25] D. Heinsius, *Nederduytsche poemata*. Bij een vergadert en uytgegeven door P.[etrus]
S.[criverius], Amsterdam 1616.

This edition marked a decisive turning point in the esteem in which poetry in Dutch was held. Petrus Scriverius, who supervised the publication of Heinsius' poems, wrote an interesting introduction, holding up Heinsius' poems as models of an ideal poetic art in which the vernacular equalled classical poetry.[26] This publication may have spurred Grotius to write and publish his own poems in Dutch. The old rivalry with his former brother in arts may have played a part in this. The poems that Grotius wrote in his cell are in form and technique very close to the classicising poems of Heinsius.[27]

A few months after his arrest Grotius wrote a baptismal catechism in Dutch verse for his daughter Cornelia.[28] He sent this edifying didactic poem to his wife when it was completed.[29] In this work he discussed virtually all the Christian doctrines and institutions that were to be found in the authoritative 'Formulas of Unity', as they were called (the Netherlands Confession and the Heidelberg Catechism).[30] The poem appeared in the same year, 1618, and was enthusiastically received: at least eight separate editions of the little work appeared in the following year.[31] In 1619 Grotius wrote some more Dutch poems, including a rhymed version of the Lord's Prayer.[32]

---

[26] For this see P. Tuynman, 'Petrus Scriverius: 12 januari 1576–30 April 1660', *Quaerendo*, VII (1977), 5–37, especially 13–20; and *Bacchus en Christus. Twee lofzangen van Daniël Heinsius. Opnieuw uitgegeven door L.Ph. Rank, J.D.P. Warners en F.L. Zwaan* [Zwolse drukken en herdrukken voor de Maatschappij der Nederlandse Letterkunde te Leiden], Zwolle 1965, p. 14.

[27] Grotius' *Bewijs* is a typical classicising poem. It is strongly rhetorical in character and bears the stamp of the *poeta doctus*. Grotius' poem, like those of Heinsius, is composed in French alexandrines. For this classicist poetry see Tuynman, 'Petrus Scriverius', 13–20, and Th. Weevers, *The Poetry of the Netherlands in its European Context: 1170–1930*, London 1960, pp. 73–80.

[28] H. Grotius, *Vraghe en antwoordt over den doop. Ghestelt in zijn gevanckenisse voor zijn dochter Cornelia de Groot* (1618).

[29] *BW* II, n° 587, p. 14: "Allerliefste, Ik zend u de Duitsche veerzen voor onze Cornelia. Zy slachten myne gevangenis. Zy zyn langer gevallen dan ik wel meende. Gy en Grootvader moet Cornelia de veerzen wat uitleggen, alzoo ik het niet doen en kan. Zijt hiermede Gode bevolen."

[30] Immediately after his arrest he found a catechism in his cell: Fruin, *Verhooren*, 'Memorie', p. 35: "Ick ben eerst geleyt op een camer, daer ick bewaert wyerd door twee hellebardiers. Op de tafel vond ick daer leggen een Catechismus, [. . .] off die boecken daer op voorraedt geleydt waren en weet ick niet."

[31] *BG*, n°ˢ 60–7.

[32] H. Grotius, *Uytlegginghe van het Gebedt ons Heeren Iesu Christ, ghenaemt het Vader-ons* (1619).

b. *The writing of the apologetic work* (Bewijs)

It did not escape Gerard Vossius that the poems his friend had written in Dutch had been favourably received. On 6 June 1619 he
wrote to Maria van Reigersberch:

> You are sufficiently aware with what joy and admiration that which
> your husband wrote for his daughter Cornelia about Baptism has been
> read by everyone. I know several people who have not only read the
> same with hearty edification, but moreover, although they were oth-
> erwise very impassioned and ill-disposed towards your husband, have
> nevertheless admitted that it must be a sign of no bad conscience and
> a Christian mind and great knowledge of divine things, to have such
> striking meditations in such places; and to express them so sweetly and
> with such skill and art in rhyme. I therefore wish that your husband
> would again write something similar; either of the love we owe Christ
> our Saviour, and the imitation of him; or of the true signs of God's
> children; or of eternal life or the like: which will be salutary and
> profitable not only to the learned but to the unlearned also; and more-
> over will also serve to bring it about that even the common man will
> more and more have a great and good feeling for your husband.[33]

Maria received another letter from Vossius a month and a half later,
in which he again stressed that it would be a good thing if the prisoner would write something else to edify the common man and
enhance his own reputation.[34]

Grotius was rather reluctant to comply with Vossius' exhortation.[35]
Though he found it easy to write poetry in the vernacular, he felt
it would be very difficult not to give offence and arouse suspicion,
with the times as they were. He recalled the difficulties his latest
theological publication, *De satisfactione*, had caused him, yet he was
willing to think about something on the love of Christ or a commentary
on the Sermon on the Mount.[36] He thanked Vossius for the books

---

[33] The letter is included in the latest edition of the *Bewijs* [= *BG*, n° 151], Bijl.
I, pp. 309–11.

[34] For this letter of Vossius to Maria (23 August 1619) see *Bewijs*, Bijl. II, pp. 311–14.

[35] See *BW* II, n° 590, to G.J. Vossius (August/September 1619), pp. 15–16.
Molhuysen incorrectly dated this letter to July 1619, but Grotius' references to
Vossius' suggestions show that it is a reply to Vossius' letter to Maria van Reigersberch
of 23 August 1619, and thus cannot have been written long after it.

[36] *BW* II, n° 590, p. 16: "Lingua nostrate facile sit aliquid moliri, sed hoc tempore
offensas et suspiciones evitare perquam difficile. Meministi ut nobis cesserit quod pro
satisfactionis doctrina pio studio erat a nobis laboratum. Cogitabo tamen, dum tu
quoque cogites, quid quale quantumque esse debeat quod non odio, non fastidio sit
futurum. Ex omnibus maxime arrideat argumentum de Christi adversus nos amore."

on Christian apologetics, but had to confess that he was making slow progress with them, because he gave priority to other studies, leaving only Sundays and a few leisure hours to profit from them.[37]

Undoubtedly Grotius read the books mentioned with an eye to the composition of his own defence of the Christian faith. His letter does not make it clear if he was already planning to compose such a work in Dutch verse, but we do know that the idea of writing an apologetic work had taken hold of him some time earlier, since his brother Willem mentioned it in a letter to Gerard Vossius on 14 June 1619. In this letter Willem was emphatic in asking Vossius to continue sending books to the prisoner, because he could make good use of them in defending the Christian faith against atheists, Jews, heathens and Muslims, as well as against the no less dangerous internal enemies of Christianity.[38]

For the time being Grotius himself did not give much hint of his intentions in his letters. On 15 December 1619 he wrote to Vossius, rather non-committally, that he would think further about a short book against unbelievers and Jews.[39] He must have begun work on his apologetic book some time in the following months. On 4 March 1620 he was able to report to Vossius that it would be a short work in Dutch verse. He had finished the first three books, and briefly summarised them for his friend. The other three books had still to be written. He promised to send Vossius the whole work on completion.[40]

---

[37] *BW* II, n° 590, p. 16: "Libris tuis qui ad firmanda christianismi dogmata pertinent adhuc utor; tarde lectio procedit, quia quae iam affecta habeo isti labori studeo antevertere; nisi quod dictos Domino dies et quod horarum succisivum est huc traho."

[38] Rademaker, 'Books', App. 3 (letter of Willem de Groot to G.J. Vossius, 14 June 1619: Rawlinson Letters, vol. 80, fol. 1031), pp. 18–19: "Id si feceris non tantum a fratre nobisque omnibus maximas inibis gratias, sed quod majus est etiam de ecclesia bene poteris mereri, supportando illi arma qui causam eius adversus atheos, gentes, judaeos, mahumetistas defendendam suscepit. Et horum quidem librorum quos iam petit acies adversus atheos instruitur praecipue, iis victis ac propulsatis ad reliquos hostes gressum faciet, ut iis quoque copiis fusis, internos ecclesiae hostes qui tectius grassantur sed saepe incautos opprimunt aggressurus. Faveat his eius coeptis quae ad divini nominis gloriam suscipiuntur Deus omnipotens, cujus favori te tuosque commendo."

[39] *BW* II, n° 596, p. 26: "De commentatione maiore in Sermonem in monte deque libello adversus impios et iudaeos cogitabo etiamnum."

[40] *BW* II, n° 598, p. 29: "Libellus est Belgicis versibus complectens argumenta de Deo, eius unitate et proprietatibus praecipuis, de creatione, providentia et spe vitae alterius. Deinde ea testimonia quibus doctrinae christianae in genere consideratae veritas probatur. Sequentur alia quae libris Novi et Veteris Testamenti suam auctoritatem vindicant. Hucusque processit impetus, superest refutatio quorumdam

We can establish that the work, or at least the first version, must have been finished before 2 April 1620. That was the date of a letter from Willem de Groot to his brother Hugo, which is almost entirely devoted to discussion of the apologetic work.[41] Willem began by paying his brother a compliment: no one could have dealt with the topic better or more clearly. The arguments were powerful and well chosen, the order was clear and the choice of words excellent. Moreover, the author had succeeded in adding something new to the existing literature. But it was to be feared, Willem added, that the work would not be appreciated by everybody, even though the author tried to present himself as an intermediary between all Christian parties.[42]

Grotius replied to his brother that he was happy to have devoted his time to the poem, for poetical composition had allowed his mind a beneficial freedom that was denied to his body. He remarked that no one had ever managed to please everyone, and he certainly could not hope to do so in such disastrous times. He was very well aware that objections would be raised, but he was convinced that his work would not need much defence before fair judges or critics.[43]

The title of the work was clearly not yet definite, but it is obvious that Grotius originally presented his work as an introduction to

---

quae ab ethnicis, hebraeis et sarracenis obiici solent. De vitae alterius felicitate, quam materiam mihi commendaveras, hic aliquid dicendi fuit locus, cum christianae doctrinae perfectio ex finis propositi perfectione esset demonstrata. Mittam ad te poema totum simulatque absolutum erit."

[41] A copy of this letter is to be found in the Algemeen Rijksarchief at The Hague: ARA, 1911, XXII, n° 32. I do not know the whereabouts of the original.

[42] ARA, 1911, XXIII, n° 32 (W. de Groot to H. Grotius, 2 April 1620), [fol. 1]: "Vidi Roterodami, sed raptim vidi, tua de initiis fidei carmina et judicium quidem meum in re tam ardua apud te praesertim exponere vix audeo. Hoc tamen dicam a nemine materiam istam solidius tractari et dilucidius explicari posse, nam et argumenta sunt firma, imo selecta, et ordo perspicuus et verba aptissima. Omitto iam elegantissimas descriptiones, quae hic illic infarciuntur; omitto poeticos spiritus et reliqua, quae in omnibus tuis carminibus miramur. Certe hoc opus aliquid amplius sibi arrogata, quia plurimum ab incepti novitate, quod nemo adimpleri posse hactenus credidi, commendatur. Vereor tamen, ut omnibus hoc tuo laudabili instituto satifacias, praecipue iis, qui nimio contendi studio laborant, dum ea quae ab omnibus conceduntur persequendo medium te inter varias christiani orbis divisiones et schismata interponis."

[43] BW II, n° 600, (to W. de Groot, 12 April 1620), pp. 30–1: "Carmina mea, mi frater, satis habent si suo tempore excusentur. Unde enim mihi iste spiritus, quem poësis supra omne scripti genus desiderat, cui ne libera quidem aura frui datur. [. . .] Omnibus placere nemini hactenus concessum est: nedum ego id sperem in tanto calumniae regno. Caeterum quae putas obiici posse et obiectum iri non nego, apud aequos iudices non egent magno patrocinio."

the faith. Willem described his brother's poem as *de initiis fidei carmina*.[44] Grotius himself repeatedly used the term *Isagoge fidei* in his letters.[45] It is certain that for a time the poem bore the title *Geloofs Voorberecht* ('Introduction to the Faith').[46]

Geloofs Voorberecht

The Bibliothèque Nationale in Paris owns a manuscript bearing this title, which appears to contain a preliminary version of Grotius' *Bewijs van den waren godsdienst* ('Proof of the True Religion').[47]

The text is written in a regular and legible hand, which is certainly not that of Grotius himself but probably of his secretary.[48] Here and there we find sentences and phrases that have been immediately deleted—sometimes before they were fully written out—and replaced by entirely new sentences on the following lines. This suggests that the work was dictated, with the accompanying improvisations. The manuscript also contains a number of notes that must have been added at a later period and are unmistakeably in the hand of Grotius himself. Besides corrections and additions they include marginal titles of the sections. Finally we can make out notes by Grotius, written in another ink (light brown in colour), making minor corrections to the text and indicating the page numbers and closing epigraphs of the six books. The manuscript is not easy to date. We do not know how many versions Grotius drafted between the conception of the work (March 1620) and its printing (May 1622). Since the text of this manuscript differs in many points from the printed version, we must assume that the printed text was based on a later

---

[44] See ARA, 1911, XXIII, n° 32, [fol. 1]. Willem de Groot referred to the work in his diary as 'Inleydinge van het geloof' (introduction to the faith). *Broeders gevangenisse. Dagboek van Willem de Groot betreffende het verblijf van zynen broeder Hugo op Loevestein.* Uit echte bescheiden aangevuld en opgehelderd door mr. H. Vollenhoven, The Hague 1842, p. 111.

[45] Cf. *BW* II, n°s 601, p. 32, 609, p. 39 and 612, p. 41.

[46] The word 'voorberecht' means an introduction or introductory teaching (*prolegomena*). See *WNT*, XXIII, Leiden 1986, s.v.

[47] *Geloofs Voorberecht* [= *GV*]. See G. Huet, *Catalogue des manuscrits néerlandais de la Bibliothèque nationale*, Paris 1886, n° 34: 'Manuscrit non signé, copie contemporaine avec des notes marginale et une partie des corrections de la main de l'auteur, 1620.' There is a very poorly legible copy of this manuscript in the library of the Peace Palace at The Hague [Y4513 n° 517].

[48] C.J. Gellinek recognised the hand of Grotius' clerk Willem Corneliszoon van de Velde: see a note (dated 22 February 1980) in the Hague copy of the ms.

transcript. *Geloofs Voorberecht* appears to be one of the first versions from the year 1620 or 1621. Presumably our manuscript is the copy of January 1621 to which Grotius refers in a letter to his brother Willem.[49] The manuscript reveals about four hundred corrections, either directly made by the first hand, or added later by Grotius himself. Sometimes we find two or three successive variant texts of one and the same passage. The great majority of the corrections (about 95 per cent) are technical and consist of improvements to spelling or syntax. Some changes of textual content appear, as we shall see, to have been inspired by the criticism of Grotius' friends. More than half of all the changes are found in the first book.

Comparison between *Geloofs Voorberecht* and the *Bewijs* shows that Grotius paid much attention to his friends' criticism. The most detailed reaction to the work came from the leading remonstrant theologian Simon Episcopius.[50]

Episcopius expressed his admiration for Grotius' clear and elegant style, but added a number of critical remarks. He had problems in particular with the first book of the work. He pointed out, for example, that Grotius had fallen into a *petitio principii* by proving God's uniqueness from his necessity, for God and necessity are by definition equivalent, at least in Aristotelian philosophy. Episcopius advised his friend to provide more support for this part of his argument.[51] The passage in *Geloofs Voorberecht* to which he referred read:

> If then divinity is common to many [gods], each god is neither self-existent nor necessary, but this one and that one acquires his distinctiveness from some other being. And that is simply at odds with God's being, for that which is self-existent cannot suffer the action of others, and that which is necessary cannot be casually marked off as a part of the whole. From this I conclude that it is certain that God of his own nature is necessarily unique.[52]

---

[49] *BW* II, n° 612 (10 January 1621), p. 41: "Isagoge nostra iam describitur."

[50] See *BW* II, n° 759 (from S. Episcopius), pp. 216–18. Since the close of the letter has been lost, its date is not known. Grotius incorporated Episcopius's comments in his *Bewijs*, but there are no traces of them in *GV*. It appears plausible that this letter was written in late 1621 or early 1622, when Grotius was probably in possession of a new copy of his poem.

[51] *BW* II, n° 759, p. 217: "Argumentum quo probatur, fol. 4 et 5, Deum unum esse, quia palmarium, cui non pauca alia in sequentibus superstruuntur, paulo magis adstringendum videtur, aut fortius suffulciendum. Videtur enim fere in eo principium peti; idem enim est quaerere, an Deus unus sit, et an id quod a se est, sive τὸ ἄναρχον καὶ ἀναίτον, unum tantum sit: Deum enim esse, et a se esse, synonyma sunt, uti ex antedictis patet."

[52] *GV*, I, pp. 7–8: "Indien aan velen dan de Godheid is gemeen/Zo is niet ieder

Grotius did not dismiss the advice of his remonstrant friend, and replaced the above passage in the *Bewijs* with the following:

> Now he who supposes many gods, if he considers it aright, will not
> find any necessity in each god. No reason compels us to suppose many
> gods, no reason to count ten or more or less. The fertility of the cause
> is the only origin of multiplicity that we can see, but God has no
> cause. Nothing can be imagined by which this god or that could be
> distinguished from another god. Wherever one looks, one finds noth-
> ing that would suggest more than one god to us.[53]

The manuscript also contains a brief paragraph, which forms part
of the proof that God is the cause of all things, entitled 'that matter is not eternal':

> From what has just been said, that there can only be one [God], it
> follows as a certainty that matter is not a self-existent thing, but it too
> is God's work. And if you wish me to give further reasons: that which
> is self-existent must be the best of all, [but] matter is formless, wild,
> savage and without force, and therefore it cannot be regarded as self-
> existent.[54]

This passage too provoked criticism from Episcopius, who pointed
out to Grotius that he was trapped in a circular chain of reasoning,
in which the argument from necessity was again the culprit. The
remonstrant stressed that the passage lacked any philosophical foundation and could easily be refuted.[55] The whole paragraph was omitted

---

God bij hem zelve een./ Noch ook noodzakelijk, maar krijgt zo die als deze,/ Zijn
onderscheidenheid uit enig ander wezen./ Het welke 't eenemael met Godes wezen
strijdt,/ Want 't geen zelfwezig is van and'ren niet en lijdt,/ En't geen noodza-
keiejk is en kan niet bij gevalle/ Als afgetekend zijn tot enkel uit het alle./ Hieruit
besluit ik dan voor zeker en gewis/ Dat God uit eigen aard noodzaak'lijk enkel is."

[53] *Bewijs*, p. 7: "Wie nu veel Goden stelt, indien hij 't wel verzint,/ In ieder God
gans geen noodzakelijkheid en vindt./ Geen reden ons en dwingt om vele Goon
te stellen,/ Geen reden om of tien of min of meer te tellen./ Des oorzaaks vrucht-
baarheid zien wij alleen dat geeft/ De menigvuldigheid: nu God geen oorzaak
heeft./ Geen ding kan zijn bedacht waar door zo die als deze/ Van ene andere
God zou onderscheiden wezen./ Waar men 't oog op slaat, men vindt der zaken
geen,/ Die ons zou wijzen aan meerder Goon dan een."

[54] *GV*, I, pp. 14–15: "Dat nu de stof mee niet bij haar zelve is,/ Maar ook is
Godes werk volgt zeker en gewis,/ Op 't geen nu is gezegd, dat zulks maar een
kan wezen./ Wilt gij dat ik u dit met naarder reden vest:/ " 'T geen bij hem zelve
is moet wezen 't allerbest,/ De stof is ongedaan, wild, woest en zonder krachten,/
Daarom en kan men die niet voor zelfwezig achten."

[55] See *BW* II, n° 759, p. 217: "Eadem est ratio argumenti, quo probatur materiam non esse aeternam, fol. 6, praeterquam quod fundamento careat, materiam
actu non esse, sed potentia, [. . .]. Fortasse a se esse non dicit magnam profec-
tionem, sicut neque esse singularem perfectionem dicit: quid enim singulare habet

from the *Bewijs*. Episcopius also objected to two sections of the proof
of God's providence, but that criticism did not lead Grotius to make
any changes in his text.[56]

In the second book of *Geloofs Voorberecht* Grotius argued that
Christians ought to refrain from all swearing of oaths, with the reser-
vation that "the same should be saved for God's affairs".[57] Episcopius
wrote that he did not see why oaths must be reserved exclusively
for God's affairs, and not for the wellbeing of our neighbours, and
in particular the public good.[58] It was probably this remark that led
the author to revise the phrase cited to "that the same be saved for
the highest need."[59]

Episcopius also objected to Grotius' characterisation of the Jewish
conception of sacrifice. In the fifth book of *Geloofs Voorberecht* Grotius
made the following comment on the Jewish sacrifice:

> the use of which is ancient, but it too first sprang from men's minds
> and not from God's word.[60]

Episcopius wondered if it could indeed be maintained that sacrifices
had been instituted, not by God, but by man.[61] Vossius too criticised this
point, and warned the author that his assertion could expose him to
the charge of Socinianism.[62] Grotius modified the lines quoted above to

---

rudis, indigesta, bruta moles supra nihilum? Sed a se esse cum tali perfectione ut
agere possit in omnia alia, et a nullo pati necesse habeat, id perfectionem veram
quin dicat extra dubium est."

[56] Cf. *BW* II, n° 759, pp. 217–18.

[57] *GV*, II, p. 26.

[58] *BW* II, n° 759, p. 218: "Videtur nimis generaliter asseri, iuramentum omne
prorsus prohibitum esse, aut saltem, immo obiter indicari Deum illud reservatum
velle, cum de causa tantum sua agitur: salus enim proximi, et imprimis publica cur
isti accenseri non debeat, aut saltem possit, nulla ratio esse videtur."

[59] *Bewijs*, p. 54: "dat tot de hoogste nood de zelve zij gespaard."

[60] See *GV*, V, p. 9: "Waarvan 't gebruik is oud, doch evewel kwam 't voort/ Eerst
uit der mensen hoofd en niet uit Godes woord."

[61] *BW* II, n° 759, p. 218: "Indicatur sacrificia non esse primitus a Deo profecta,
sed ab hominibus adinventa. Videndum est utrum hoc verum sit, utrum tuto dicatur.
Si ex ipsis iudaeorum libris evinci possit id ab ipsorum magistris adsertum olim
fuisse, tum id optime adhibetur ad retundendum argumentum, quod pro aeterno
eorum sacrificiorum ritu confirmando adferre solet; aut saltem ad indicandum religionem messiae perfectissimam esse posse, quae sacrificiis istis careat."

[62] See *BW* II, n° 608 (to G.J. Vossius, [November 1620]), p. 37: "De sacrificiis
non memini apud Socinum legere; sed videtur mihi ea esse sententia Iustini Martyris
quem et alii sequuntur, tum vere et inter Hebraeos Maimonidae et Albonis. Scio
sententiam esse probabilem tantum, nam ἀποφατικῶς ex sacris literis in rebus eiusmodi nihil valide colligitur. Tu non quid censoribus placiturum sit, sed quid verum
maxime putes tecum et cum aliis cogita." Vossius' previous letter has been lost.

You even doubt if this usage sprang first from men's minds or first from God's word.[63]

Geloofs Voorberecht shows two variants of the closing lines of the poem. The first variant, which is deleted, reads:

If I have missed the mark here or there, do not take it ill, I am a man, not old, and will learn better in time. Excuse it rather than taking it bitterly, and think, Oh Lord, it was written in Loevestein.[64]

In September 1621 Gerard Vossius informed the author that some of his friends were dissatisfied with this passage, in which Grotius excused himself on the grounds of his age and declared that he was willing to learn better. In the eyes of his friends these words were an unworthy cliché, not at all befitting a man of such heavenly understanding and outstanding learning.[65]

Grotius, clearly sensitive to these flattering words, replaced the offending lines by a new variant that was to be included in the printed version:

If I have missed the mark here or there, remember with compassion what a cloud obscures human eyes. Excuse the work rather than taking it bitterly, and think, Oh Lord, it was written in Loevestein.[66]

c. *Editions*

On 21 March 1621 Grotius managed to escape from Loevestein in a chest of books. Six months later he considered his apologetic work ready for publication. In October he sent it to Antwerp, hoping to

---

[63] *Bewijs*, p. 124: "De uwen twijf'len zelf of dit gebruik kwam voort,/ Eerst uit der mensen hoofd, of eerst uit Godes woord."

[64] *GV*, VI, p. 14: "Is hier of daar gemist, wilt het ten beste keren,/ Ik ben een mens, niet oud, en wil nog beter leren,/ Verschoon het liever wat, dan dat gij 't bitter laakt/ En denkt, ach Heer, het is te Loevestein gemaakt."

[65] *BW* II, n° 691 (from G.J. Vossius, [September 1621],) p. 137: "De quo quia mentio incidit, praeterire illud non possum, versum antepenultimum, vel illi proximum, minus probari amicis quibusdam tuis. Ais sicubi minus satisfacias, ob aetatem excusari debere, et paratum esse discere veriora. Protritum hoc illis videtur, et illis etiam usitatum, quibus imperant τῶν παίδων βασιλέες. At minime convenire viro coelestis ingenii, et eximiae adeo eruditionis. Dixi ego primam hanc Christiani laudem esse, humilitatem: et summi magistri hanc esse voluntatem, ut pueri similes simus. Sed satisfacere eo non potui. Tu cogitabis."

[66] Cf. *GV*, VI, p. 14; *Bewijs*, p. 167: "Is hier of daar gemist, herinnert met meedogen/ U zelve wat een wolk bedwelmt der mensen ogen:/ Verschoon veel liever 't werk dan dat gij 't bitter laakt/ En denkt, ach Heer, het is te Loevestein gemaakt."

hear from a friend about the possibility of having it published in that city.[67] But Grotius was soon disappointed by this friend, the exiled remonstrant preacher Nicolaas Grevinchoven, and then tried to have the work published in the northern Netherlands.[68] He instructed his brother Willem to arrange for its publication.[69]

On 15 December the same year Willem de Groot sent a report on his findings to the author. Three weeks earlier Grevinchoven had already sent the six books to Grotius' parents, because the work could not be printed in Antwerp. Willem had consulted Grevinchoven and Wtenbogaert about Hugo's plan to apply to the States-General for permission to publish. Both the remonstrants advised against this, because the risk of rejection was too great. Moreover, the work would become known as a result, and might fall into the hands of the contra-remonstrants. In their opinion the work ought to be printed in Holland as soon as possible, but without anyone knowing of it. Henricus Slatius, another remonstrant preacher, advised against asking for permission to print the book in Brabant, because it might be just as easy to publish it secretly in Holland.[70]

Clearly Grotius was hoping for authorisation from the States-General, so that the appearance of his work could form a sort of official rehabilitation. But his remonstrant friends dispelled his dream. Over the following months, as the author realised that his work could not be published immediately, he grew impatient. He wrote to his family that its printing could not be delayed any longer.[71] But it did

---

[67] *BW* II, n° 703 (to N. van Reigersberch, 29 October 1621), p. 149.

[68] *BW* II, n° 707 (to N. van Reigersberch, 23 November 1621), p. 156: "'s Geloofs voorbericht meen ick dat myn broeder tot Antwerpen sal vinden ende vandaer mede brengen."

[69] *BW* II, n° 707, p. 157: "Van de ses boucken heb ick mijn broeder de Groot last gegeven om met UE. te spreecken."

[70] *BW* II, n° 711 (from W. de Groot, 15 December 1621), p. 162: "Interea Grevinchovium de tuis sex libris conveni, quos ille iam tribus ab hinc septimanis ad parentes nostros transmiserat; non posse hic eos imprimi et causas cur non possint iam ad te perscripsit ipse. Egi cum Wtenbogardo de tuo consilio, egi et cum Grevinchovio, uterque putat non petendam ab Ordinibus veniam, sed opus illud quamprimum insciis omnibus praelo in Hollandia committendum. Negant tanti sibi videri eam veniam ut repulsae praesentaneum periculum aequet. Affirmant tam commode haec clam quam palam impressa in manus hominum non malorum etiam contraremonstrantium posse pervenire. Slatius eadem de re mecum locutus est, negabat ille veniam imprimendi in Brabantia petendam fuisse, sed clam impressoribus tradendum; id enim tam facile hic quam in Batavia fieri potuisse; [. . .]."

[71] *BW* II, n° 717 (to W. and J. de Groot, 14 January 1622), pp. 167–8: "De Hexabiblo commendo vobis ne diutius protrahatur, exeat quo poterit modo."

not prove easy to find a publisher who was willing to have the work printed in secret.[72] Grotius urged his brother Willem to persevere and if necessary to have the book published without permission.[73]

In May 1622 the apologetic work was finally printed. Grotius was eager to see the proofs, and said that there was to be no further change to the title.[74] This suggests that there had been some discussion about it, but we do not know precisely what it involved. In any case the result shows that the author finally preferred to presenting his poem as a defence of the faith and not as an introduction to it. On 1 June 1622 Vossius reported to Grotius that the work had been published.[75]

First edition (BG *n° 143*)

The work appeared under the title *Bewijs van den waren godsdienst*, but without naming any publisher or place of publication.[76] It was in fact printed secretly. The edition is provided with an introductory poem, entitled 'Admonition to peace to all Christians'. This poem is signed with the phrase 'Who does good?', a motto of Willem de Groot, and its argument is as follows. If the rough sailors on a ship come to blows with one another, the fight can grow violent, but when someone sights a pirate ship they will cease their quarrels and turn with one mind against the enemy. In the same way the author of this work wishes to admonish divided Christians towards unity by pointing out their common enemies: heathens, Jews and Muslims. The message of the work is that Christians must steer their course by the Scriptures and not be arrogant and intolerant if they differ in their opinions, but ought to bear with one another in love.[77]

---

[72] *BW* II, n° 722 (to N. van Reigersberch, 17 February 1622), p. 173: "De ses boecken moeten yemant gegeven werden om heymelick te doen drucken. Het profijt is soo cleyn, dat daerop niet en staet te letten."

[73] *BW* II, n° 729 (11 March 1622), p. 179: "De Hexabiblo nolite quaeso diutius ampliare. Prodeat permissu publico si is paratus iam est; sin minus, sine illo."

[74] *BW* II, n° 758 (to W. de Groot, 27 May 1622), p. 215: "Hexabiblon meum videre aveo. In titulo nihil mutandum."

[75] *BW* II, n° 761, p. 220: "Gaudeo sex tuos de vera religione libros in lucem prodiisse."

[76] *Bewys van den waren godsdienst. In ses Boecken gestelt By Hugo de Groot. Gedruckt in 't Iaer onses Heeren MDCXXII* [= *BG*, n° 143]. The typeface and paper used indicate that the printer had done everything he could to conceal his identity, in the opinion of Dr R. Breugelmans, Head of the Department of Western Printed Books in the University Library, Leiden.

[77] *Bewys* [*BG*, n° 143], 'Vermaninge tot vrede aen alle Christenen', [fols 2–4].

But this first edition also included, without the author's knowledge, a second anonymous foreword with the title 'Warning to simple Christians'. Its unknown author opposed the eirenic tendency of Grotius' defence of the faith and Willem's 'Admonition'. The leading idea of this foreword is that the primary aim should not be peace but religious truth. Peace and tolerance mean nothing if they are not founded on truth. What would become of religion if everything were to be tolerated, even the errors of papists, Arians and Mennonites? And what is the Romish idolater but a heathen, the Christian who denies the divinity of Christ but a Jew, and the Mennonite who denies Christ's humanity but a Muslim? The unknown writer advises readers to view Grotius' work from this perspective, and closes his warning with these words:

> See, we have sought to warn the simple Christian briefly and simply, and to admonish him, by distinguishing, to draw even more profit from this book, hoping that the author too is of such an opinion and mind. Amen, vale. *Veritas superat onnia.*[78]

It was clear that this foreword was contra-remonstrant in its inspiration. The fears of Grevinchoven and Wtenbogaert that the Gomarists would interfere in the printing appeared to be justified. It is impossible to say for certain who was the author of this foreword, but Gerard Brandt mentioned Henricus Rosaeus as a possible candidate.[79]

When Grotius received the first edition of his defence of the faith he wrote to his brother that he had discovered a number of printer's errors, which he had noted for a possible corrected edition.[80] A few days later he noticed the anonymous foreword. He found the pas-

---

[78] *Bewys* [*BG* n° 143], 'Waerschouwinghe aen de eenvoudighe Christenen' [fol. 6].

[79] G. Brandt, *Historie der Reformatie en andre kerkelyke geschiedenissen in en omtrent de Nederlanden*, vol. 4, Rotterdam 1704, p. 819: "Het Bewijs van den waeren godsdienst, 't welk de Heer de Groot op Loevestein over twee jaeren hadt gerijmt, wierdt ook te deser tijdt gedruckt, met een Voorreden of Waerschouwing, die iemant der contraremonstranten, men houdt dat het Rosaeus was, daer by voegde, en met het ooghmerk des boeks niet over een quam, jae streedt. Dit was een groote ontrouwigheit van den drukker, die de gemelde waerschouwing daer voor stelde buiten weten van de geenen, die hem 't boek lieten drukken." Brandt does not say what grounds he had for the attribution to Rosaeus. The foreword may have been an initiative of the printer, who wanted to cover himself by this antidote against punitive measures if he were detected.

[80] *BW* II, n° 767 (to W. de Groot, 20 June 1622), p. 225: "Hexabiblon nostra prodiise et esse quibus placeat sane gaudeo. Sunt in editione menda nonnulla, quae annotabimus et alio tempore ad te mittemus, ut si forte distrahantur huius editionis exemplaria adornemus meliorem alteram, [. . .]."

sage entirely at odds with his own intentions, and feared that it would deter many, above all remonstrants, from reading his work. He suggested that reliable booksellers ought to be warned to cut out the undesirable foreword, and felt that it might be useful if Puppius or another remonstrant were to compose a new foreword.[81] To Hogerbeets he confided "I am very dismayed about the preface written for my six books, since it will without doubt detract from the value of the book."[82]

It is remarkable that neither Vossius nor Grotius noticed this foreword when they first read the book. We can hardly imagine that these philologically trained readers simply missed it. Presumably the printer left the foreword out of the copies intended for Grotius and his friends, and the author only noticed it in a copy that was not intended for his eyes.[83]

Second edition (BG n° 144)

The second edition of the *Bewijs* probably appeared in October or November of the same year (1622).[84] On 25 November Grotius wrote to his brother Willem that he wished to see this edition.[85] The second edition includes the 'Admonition' by Willem de Groot but not the 'Warning' by the unknown contra-remonstrant, nor the remonstrant foreword to which Grotius alluded. Once again the publisher and the place of publication are not stated on the title page, but it is impossible to be certain if this second edition was printed by the same printer as the first.[86] The list of printer's errors included at the end of the previous edition is omitted, because these errors are corrected in the text of the second edition. It is not known if the printer's

---

[81] *BW* II, n° 771 (to W. de Groot, 24 June 1622), p. 229: "Praefationem ad Hexabiblon vidi a meo instituto alienissimam et quae a lectione multos rei gnaros absterrebit. Moneri possent librarii boni ut eam exscindant; forte expediet et aliam praefationem fieri a Remonstrantium aliquo. Posset moneri Puppius."

[82] *BW* II, n° 775 (28 July 1622), p. 233.

[83] The 'Waerschouwinghe aen de eenvoudighe Christenen' is inserted as a loose gathering in the first edition of the *Bewijs*, so that it could easily be extracted.

[84] *Bewys van den waren godsdienst. In ses Boecken gestelt By Hugo de Groot. Ghedruckt in't Jaer onses Heeren Duysent ses hondert XXII* [= *BG*, n° 144].

[85] *BW* II, n° 801 (to W. de Groot, 25 November 1622), p. 260: "Audio secundam editionem Hexabibli prodiisse. Velim eius exemplar videre."

[86] In the opinion of Dr Breugelmans another setting was used for the second edition.

errors that Grotius mentioned in his letter to Willem are incorporated. Otherwise the text of the apologetic work remained unchanged. We can assume that the author himself gave the order for a new edition, because of his dissatisfaction with the anonymous foreword in the first edition. We do not know what judgement Grotius passed on this edition, but the absence of a third edition during his lifetime makes it entirely plausible to assume that it had the author's full support.

d. *Dedication*

Grotius dedicated his *Bewijs* to the people of Holland. The work opens with an 'Admonition to the Hollanders', the first lines of which read:

> True-hearted Hollanders, renowned for many an age, who now make the Lion flag fly far and wide wherever the wind can bear it, and spread your name both where the dawn breaks and where the evening rises, yea, who have gone farther than the sun's path takes him.[87]

He calls the people of Holland 'true-hearted', a compliment he undoubtedly did not pay to their government. He refers to the old-established fame of Holland, but at even greater length to the province's more recent glory, which it had won above all by its feats of seamanship, and describes enthusiastically how Holland's name has become renowned all over the world on the seas.[88]

Grotius then turns to the Dutch seamen, admonishing them that seafaring must serve not merely the pursuit of gain, but the dissemination of the Christian faith.[89] Finally the author relates this

---

[87] *Bewijs* [BG n° 151], p. 1: "Trouwhartig Hollandsch volk, vermaert van meenig eeuw,/ Die nu al over langh de vlagge van de Leeuw/ Doen vliegen hebt soo verr' de wind heeft konnen dragen/ En Uwen naem verbreyd, soo daer 't begint te dagen/ Als daer den avond rijst, jae wyder zijt gegaan/ Dan hem de zon wel strekt door synen dwerschen baen."

[88] A few years earlier Grotius had supplied juridical backing for the expansionist policy of the Dutch East India Company with the publication of his *Mare liberum sive de iure quod Batavis competit ad Indicana commercia dissertatio*, Leiden 1604.

[89] Both the national government and the directors of the East India Company had often urged the seafarers to spread the Christian faith in exchange for the great material profits. Cf. C.R. Boxer, *The Dutch Seaborne Empire 1600–1800*, London 1965, pp. 132–54. As early as his juvenile work *Oratio in laudem navigationis* Grotius had linked seafaring with the spreading of the Christian faith. See J. Soutendam, 'Een onbekend werk van Huigh de Groot uit zijn vroege jeugd (Hugonis Grotii oratio in laudem navigationis), *Oud-Holland. Nieuwe Bijdragen*, 7 (1889), 293–7.

general goal of Christian propaganda to the specific content of his work, and reminds the seafarers that in their voyages they will meet unbelievers and followers of other religions: the present work can be of service in persuading these people of the error of their ways, and if possible in converting them to the true faith.[90]

At the close of his *Bewijs* Grotius again addresses the Hollanders directly:

> Do not take this work of my hands unworthily, o marketplace of the earth, flower of the Netherlands, fair Holland. Let it take my place with you, my queen: I show as best I can the love I have always borne for you, and still bear and shall bear for the rest of my days.[91]

The author follows the rules of eloquence by displaying his emotions at the end of his work, in order to win his public definitively for his cause.[92] Grotius describes his fatherland in lyrical terms. He offers the Hollanders his work with a pathetic gesture: "let it take my place with you". The whole tragedy of his political fall, imprisonment and exile echoes in this line. The famous last line of the work is a further allusion to his sad fate and thereby a covert appeal for a degree of sympathy: "and think, Oh Lord, it was made in Loevestein".

Fatherland

Grotius was emphatic in his appeal to his fatherland. This was not false pathos. The conception of the 'fatherland' did indeed play an important part in his life and thought. When he left university in 1599, at his father's insistence, to become an advocate, he put his life at the service of Holland and thereby of his fatherland.[93] Holland

---

[90] *Bewijs*, p. 3: 'Om desen allegaer haer dwalingh t'overtuigen/ En waer't dat God het gaev' tot het gelooff te buigen/ Heeft meenich edel geest seer wel besteed zyn tijd./ Ik raed u dat gij dan haer bladren naerstigh slijt,/ Maer voor al dat gy leest de boeken ons gegeven/ By mannen, die gy kent van God te zijn gedreven./ Wilt gy ook sijn gedient van mijn gering verstand?/ Seer garen sal ik u gaen stellen hier te hand/ Een kort gedenkschrift: maer soo dan mijnen schoeren/ Haer toonden wat te swak om dit werk uit te voeren/ Neemt my ten beste af de vlyt naer mijne maet,/ En denkt dat God ook self het hart neemt voor de daed.'

[91] *Bewijs*, p. 167.

[92] See H. Lausberg, *Handbuch der literarischen Rhetorik*, 2nd ed., Munich 1970, p. 236.

[93] Grotius regarded Holland as his fatherland: see W.J.M. van Eysinga, 'Iets over De Groots jongelingsjaren', *De Gids*, 105, 4 (1941), 54. In the seventeenth century the name Holland denoted not only the province of that name and its inhabitants but the whole of the Dutch Republic. Cf. E.H. Kossmann, 'The Dutch case: a national or regional culture', *Transactions of the Royal Historical Society*, 29 (1979), 155–69.

patriotism found its most fertile soil in the struggle for freedom against
Spain. After the successful campaigns of prince Maurice, which were
crowned by the battle of Nieuwpoort (2 July 1600), feelings of national
self-confidence and solidarity flourished in the Republic. It was in
these years of growing patriotism and nationalism that Grotius wrote
his first historical work, at the instigation of the States-General, his
Parallelon.[94] This work is penetrated by a glowing love of his fatherland.
In his opening verses the author calls it a duty to do his country
a service, and regards himself as an example of devotion (*pietas*) to
his fatherland.[95] There is a clear religious connotation in the Latin
word *pietas*.

   Grotius seems to have been inspired by the great French jurist and
historian Jacques de Thou, the leading figure among the *politiques*.[96]
Grotius kept up a regular correspondence with De Thou, whose work
was dominated by the concept of the *patria*. The French scholar invested
the fatherland in the first place with a legal significance, describing
it as the whole body of laws that govern a state.[97] But at the same time
the fatherland was for him "a second God".[98] De Thou deliberately
maintained the religious element, which had been important in
defining the *patria* in the middle ages, albeit adapting it to the political
goal of national unity.[99] In a letter to De Thou Grotius admitted

[94] This wide-ranging historical study, which Grotius probably wrote between 1600
and 1602, has largely been lost. Only the third and last part has survived: Hugo
Grotius, *Parallelon rerumpublicarum liber tertius; De moribus ingenioque populorum Atheniensium,
Romanorum, Batavorum. Vergelijking der gemeenebesten door Hugo de Groot. Derde Boek: over de
zeden en den inborst der Athenienseren, Romeinen en Hollanderen. Uit een echt Handschrift uit-
gegeeven, in't Nederduitsch vertaald, en met Aanmerkingen opgehelderd door Mr. Johan Meerman,
Heer van Dalem en Vuren*, 3 vols., Haarlem 1801–03: *BG* nº 750 [= *Parall.*]. Recent
literature on the *Parallelon*: Wolfgang Fikenscher, *De fide et perfidia—Der Treugedanke
in den Staatsparallelen des Hugo Grotius aus heutiger Sicht*, Munich 1979; A. Eyffinger,
'Some marginal notes', *Grotiana*, NS, 2 (1981), 116–22.
[95] *Parall.* I, 4: *Commendat suam patriae pietatem*: "Non ego doctrinae, non duro Marte
probati Roboris exemplum, sed pietatis ero".
[96] For this see R. Schnur, *Die französischen Juristen im konfessionellen Bürgerkrieg des
16. Jahrhunderts. Ein Beitrag zur Entstehungsgeschichte des modernen Staates*, Berlin 1962,
pp. 29 sqq.
[97] See C.G. Dubois, *La Conception de l'histoire de France au XVI* siècle (1560–1610)*,
Paris 1977, pp. 172–85.
[98] J.A. de Thou, *Historiarum sui temporis pars prima*, Paris 1604, Praefatio: "[. . .]
sic enim mihi semper fuit persuasissimum, patriam juxta veterum sententiam alterum
Deum, et leges patrias alteros Deos esse, quas qui violant, quantumvis se quaesito
pietatis colore defendant, sacrilegii ac paricidii poena teneri." Cited from Dubois,
p. 175.
[99] Cf. E.H. Kantorowicz, *The King's Two Bodies. A Study in Medieval Political Theory*,
Princeton 1970, p. 249.

that he would not dare to measure himself against the Frenchman, but could claim to be similarly inspired by love of his country.[100]

Patriotism in the sixteenth century had come to have an increasingly clear political content, and had inspired many authors to exalt their own nationality.[101] To legitimise such nationalist propaganda several humanist scholars drew arguments from history. The Florentine Niccolo Machiavelli had set the example of such political historiography. He felt that history ought to be directly useful to contemporary political life, and that preference ought therefore to be given to the study of those ages that had most in common with one's own.[102] This view of history as a mirror was extremely attractive to such humanist authors as Lipsius and Grotius. The idea of a similarity of times (*similitudo temporum*) encouraged historians to write the political history of their own times, imitating historians of ancient Rome such as Tacitus.[103]

Grotius' *Parallelon* offers a fine example of history as a mirror.[104] As the title of his work indicates, the young author compares the Athenian and Roman republics of ancient times with modern Batavia, that is Holland. In Grotius' opinion neither the Greeks nor the Romans could stand up to the comparison with the illustrious Hollanders of the first years of the seventeenth century. Just as French humanists sought refuge in the Gallic myth, Grotius and other Holland humanists cherished the Batavian myth, according to which the people of Holland were believed to descend from the ancient Batavians.[105]

---

[100] *BW* I, n° 315 (5 February 1614), p. 295: "Ego quoque, impar sane oneri, sed magno patriae amore accensus simile opus molior, tanto autem minus tuo, quanto minor est Batavia, non dicam Gallia vestra, sed toto orbe."

[101] See J. Huizinga, *Patriottisme en nationalisme in de Europeesche geschiedenis tot het einde der 19e eeuw*, Haarlem, 1940, pp. 43–77.

[102] N. Machiavelli, *Discorsi sopra la prima deca di Tito Livio*, I, 39: "E si conosce facilmente, per chi considera le cose presenti e le antiche, come in tutte le città ed in tutti i popoli sono quegli medesimi desiderii e quelli medesimi omori, e come vi furono sempre. In modo que gli è facil cosa, a chi esamina con diligenza le cose pasate, prevedere in ogni republica le future, e farvi quegli rimedi che dagli antichi sono stati usati; o, non ne trovando degli usati, pensarne de' nuovi, per la similitudine degli accidenti." Cited from N. Machiavelli, *Tutte le opere*, a cura di Mario Martelli, Florence 1971, p. 122.

[103] See E.L. Etter, *Tacitus in der Geistesgeschichte des 16. und 17. Jahrhunderts*, Basel 1966, pp. 16–17.

[104] See A. Droetto, 'Il "Tacitismo" nella storiografia Groziana', in *Studi Groziani*, Turin 1968, pp. 101–53 (for the agreement between Machiavelli and Grotius see pp. 146–53).

[105] Cf. H. Grotius, *Liber de antiquitate reipublicae Batavicae*, Leiden 1610.

This myth allowed their compatriots to share in the glory of antiquity, and gave the concept of the fatherland an almost religious content.[106]

Grotius had to leave his fatherland after his arrest and sentence, if he was not to remain in prison to the end of his days. These events did not extinguish his patriotism; rather, they fanned its flames. In a letter to Caspar Barlaeus he relates how during his imprisonment he had experienced the wonderful power of both religion and love of his fatherland, which had cost him so dear.[107] Very soon after his escape from Loevestein he wrote to the States-General:

> but all the wrong done to me, and which may yet be done to me, shall never turn me away from the love that I have always borne and, to the best of my modest capacity, demonstrated, for my fatherland.[108]

He experienced the early years of his exile as a personal tragedy. In a letter to his father he sighed: "now love for my ungrateful fatherland everywhere stands in the way of my interests".[109]

For a long time he continued to hope for repatriation, but he also wanted to be completely rehabilitated. This proved to be asking too much. His fatherland was to remain a distant dream. Once the hope of an honourable return to Holland had vanished, his love of his fatherland was at an end. In 1641 he wrote these embittered words to his brother Willem: "Holland is a republic with which no reasonable person ought to have anything to do, for he would harm himself or his fatherland thereby."[110]

---

[106] This myth was based on the description of the Batavians by the ancient historian Cornelius Tacitus. For this see I. Schöffer, 'The Batavian myth during the sixteenth and seventeenth centuries', in P.A.M. Geurts and A.E.M. Janssen (eds), *Geschiedschrijving in Nederland*, II, The Hague 1981, pp. 85–109.

[107] *BW* III, n° 1333 (10 October 1628), p. 401: "Primum enim quod me tam longus carcer docuit, vim habent mirificam adversus calamitates erigendi animi sacra dogmata, [. . .]. Proximus huic affectui est patriae amor, quem penitus imbibisse tanti mihi constat et tamen ne nunc quidem eum excutere possum."

[108] *BW* II, n° 626 (30 March 1621), p. 62: "Maer al het quaet dat my aenghedaen is, ende noch soude moghen aengedaen werden, en sal mij nimmer van de liefde die ick altijdt hebbe gedraghen en nae mijn kleyn vermoghen betuyght tot mijn Vaderlandt."

[109] *BW* III, n° 1102 (27 October 1626), p. 75: "Nunc amor ingratae patriae ubique commodis meis obstat."

[110] *BW* XII, n° 5458 (to W. de Groot, 9 November 1641), p. 617: "Hollandorum, ut ex tuis et aliorum literis cognosco, ea respublica est, cui nemo mediocriter sapiens miscere se debeat; nam aut sibi nociturus est aut patriae."

Summary

Grotius was caught up in the political downfall of Oldenbarnevelt, brought about by the coup staged by prince Maurice in 1618. His sentence put an abrupt end to a very promising political career. He went to prison, where he carried on an intensive scholarly and literary activity, writing Dutch religious poems, including a rhymed baptismal catechism that was particularly warmly received. Vossius encouraged the author to write more in this style, to win the sympathy of the Hollanders. In the first months of 1620 Grotius wrote a poem that he originally presented to his friends and confidants as an introduction to the faith. A manuscript of one of the early versions, entitled *Geloofs Voorberecht*, has been preserved. Comparison of this manuscript with the printed text shows that Grotius took to heart the criticism of his friends. The work was printed secretly and appeared in May 1622 under the title *Bewijs van den waren godsdienst*. The first edition included, apart from the text by Hugo and a short poem by Willem de Groot, a contra-remonstrant foreword added without the author's knowledge. A second edition without this unwanted foreword was published in November the same year. Grotius dedicated his work to the people of Holland, whom he tried to convince of his well-intentioned love of his fatherland.

CHAPTER TWO

DE VERITATE RELIGIONIS CHRISTIANAE

a. *Latin editions*[1]

Translation

After his escape from the castle of Loevestein Grotius arrived in Paris
in April 1621. Here he met Franciscus Junius junior, son of the well
known Leiden professor of theology in whose house he had lived for
a time as a student. In 1619 Junius junior had given up his post as
a preacher to devote himself, as a private citizen, to philology.[2]
Grotius valued his meeting with Junius and hoped the former preacher
would soon have some work in hand.[3] A few months later he even
tried to provide for this by inviting Junius to enter his service as his
secretary. Junius, however, declined the honour, preferring a career
with more independence and opportunity for study in England.[4]

On 15 December 1621 Grotius asked Junius to undertake the
Latin translation of his apologetic work.[5] A few months later he
reported to his brother Willem that Junius had promised him the

---

[1] R. Breugelmans, 'Maire's editions of Grotius' *De veritate religionis christianae* from
1627 to 1640', *Quaerendo*, 22 (1992), 191–6.

[2] On Franciscus Junius senior (1542–1602): C. de Jonge, *De irenische ecclesiologie
van Franciscus Junius (1542–1602)*. Onderzoek naar de plaats van het geschrift *Le
Paisible Chrestien* (1593) in zijn theologisch denken, Nieuwkoop 1980. On Franciscus
Junius junior (1598–1677): *NNBW*, IX, col. 483; *BWPGN*, IV, pp. 616–18; *BL*, II,
pp. 278–9.

[3] *BW* II, n° 633 (to G.J. Vossius, 23 April 1621), p. 67: "Inter eos quos cum
summa mea voluptate vidi est Franciscus tuus Junius, tibi simillimus tum caetera
tum hoc quoque quod nos constanter ac fideliter amat. Spero tam felix ingenium
tanta diligentia excultum, tanta probitate ornatum, non diu fore ab usu sepositum."
Vossius was Junius' brother in law.

[4] Cf. *BW* II, n° 708 (from Junius, 27 November 1621), pp. 158–9, and *BW* II,
n° 712 (to F. Junius, 15 December 1621), p. 163. Junius became librarian of Thomas
Howard, Earl of Arundel.

[5] *BW* II, n° 712, p. 164: "Sex libros meos pro christiana religione conscriptos
prodituros propediem arbitror. Multi optant eorum librorum sensus Latino sermone
exprimi, quod scio a nemine quam a te rectius praestari posse. Sed an res tuae et
tempora id ferant, tu rectius iudicabis."

Latin paraphrase.[6] When he received the Dutch edition, he instructed his brother to urge Junius to make haste with the Latin paraphrase, adding that he would have no objection to the work being printed in England.[7] But Grotius was too optimistic in his calculations. When Junius arrived in England in August 1622 he told the author that he had particularly enjoyed his apologetic work and hoped to be able to justify the expectations placed in him, but he admitted that it was not entirely in his power to perform this task, because there were many demands on his time.[8] At that time Junius was clearly still intending to translate the work, but later cried off the undertaking, presumably because of the lack of time.

It is remarkable that Grotius had already taken various initiatives for a Latin translation of his apologetic work even before the Dutch edition appeared. After the publication of *Bewijs* the author hardly appeared to concern himself any longer with the fate of his poem, at least in its Dutch form. In Paris his eye was no longer on a Dutch public but on an international circle of readers. In the first half of the year 1626 Grotius himself recast his apologetic work as a Latin prose treatise. He sent his translation to his brother Willem on 10 July that year, telling him that his friends in Paris were strongly urging him to publish this Latin version. He asked his brother to consult Vossius about the possibility of publishing his Latin translation together with his baptismal catechism in Leiden.[9]

The idea of a combined publication of the two works had been put forward a few years earlier by Vossius.[10] Grotius did not indicate

---

[6] *BW* II, n° 737 (8 April 1622), p. 191: "Hexabiblus ubi prodierit, fac quaeso ut Vossius exemplum sibi habeat et alterum quod statim ad Franciscum Iunium transmittat, qui paraphrasin Latinam pollicitus est."

[7] *BW* II, n° 767 (to W. de Groot, 20 June [1622]), p. 225: "Franciscum Iunium incitari velim ut properet nobis dare Latinam liberiorem paraphrasin. Puto nihil obstiturum quominus ea in Anglia edatur."

[8] *BW* II, n° 782 (from F. Junius, [end of August] 1622), p. 241: "Dici vix potest quantopere taedium itineris mei sublevaverit tua ad christianam religionem introductio, quam triduo antequam Londinio discederem cum gratissimis fratris tui litteris recte accepi; utinam vestrae expectationis aliqua saltem ex parte respondere possem! Sed de his imposterum; nunc praecipiti nimis festinatione, prae nuntii abiturientis importunitate, litteris hisce finem video imponendum."

[9] *BW* III, n° 1088, pp. 61–2: "Mitto simul ad te versionem latinam sex librorum de Veritate christiana, quam a me hic amici impetrarunt et urgent, ut edam. Sed pauca quaedam hic theologis non satis probantur. Consule Vossium, an sine offensa et sine ulla mutatione Lugduni edi possit at addi Latina catechesis mea, quam ibidem ex Belgica versam habere vos arbitror."

[10] *BW* III, n° 761 (from G.J. Vossius, 1 June 1622), p. 220. In 1623 Grotius had

which of his friends in Paris were urging him to publish.[11] Presumably he was thinking of the circle around Jerôme Bignon, to whom he dedicated the Latin version.[12] Bignon was a member of the 'Cabinet Dupuy', the most prominent group of scholars in Paris at the time, with which, apart from the brothers Dupuy, such famous men as Peiresc, De Cordes and Sarrau were associated.[13] Grotius became known to this prestigious society almost as soon as he arrived in Paris, and formed friendly ties with many of its learned members.

On 21 July 1626 he asked his brother to discuss with Vossius the possibility of publication by the Leiden publisher Jean le Maire. The work must be sent back to Paris immediately if Le Maire proved unexpectedly unwilling to print it.[14] Earlier that year Grotius had had a work published by Le Maire, and had been satisfied with that edition.[15] The author was in great haste and eager to have his Latin apologetic work printed as soon as possible. In the meantime he continued to make corrections to his text, and passed them on to Willem.[16] It was disappointing that after three months he had still heard nothing from Vossius. He told his brother Willem that he had hoped his friend would not find it too much trouble to read the work. He suspected that Vossius feared being held responsible for

translated his *Vraghe* written in his cell in The Hague, into Latin: see *BW* II, nᵒ 817 (to B. Aubéry du Maurier, 26 January 1623), p. 276. This translation later appeared as a separate publication: *Baptizatorum puerorum institutio alternis interrogationibus et responsionibus. Ex Belgicis rhythmis quos in carcere Hagiensi Hugo Grotius fecerat, ab autore Latina reddita. Amsterdam 1635.*

[11] It should be recalled that publication of a work with the argument that this was "at the urging of others" was a very common topos among the ancients and humanists. See Lausberg, *Rhetorik*, I, p. 102.

[12] Cf. *BW* III, nᵒ 1163 (to W. de Groot, 13 August 1627), p. 154: "Placet quod de libris scribis de Veritate religionis christianae. Exemplaria exspectant hic amici, praesertim is, cujus gratia operam hanc suscepi, Bignonus."

[13] On the Cabinet Dupuy see R. Pintard, *Le Libertinage érudit dans la première moitié du XVIIᵉ siècle*, Paris 1983 [unrevised reprint of the first edition, Paris 1943], pp. 90–101.

[14] *BW* III, nᵒ 1089 (21 July 1626), p. 62; "Rogo simulatque acceperis explores sententiam Vossii, an sine offensa ibi edi possit et, si potest, an Mairius curam velit suscipere elegantis editionis; alioqui quamprimum remitti scriptum ad me velim."

[15] *BW* II, nᵒ 1071 (to W. de Groot, 25 April 1626), p. 45: "Venit ad nos Mairius, attulit Lucanum, ejusque exemplaria mihi dedit. Placet editio; pro cura suscepta tibi ac D. Vossio gratias ago." Grotius alludes to Lucan, *Pharsalia* [= *BG* nᵒ 425]. On the publisher Jean le Maire see *NNBW*, VII, cols. 834–5.

[16] *BW* III, nᵒ 1093 (17 August 1626), p. 66. See also *BW* III, nᵒ 1145 (1 May 1627), p. 127; nᵒ 1156 (10 July 1627), p. 142.

the publication. Nevertheless he attached great importance to his friend's opinion, which he was anxious to receive.[17]

In January 1627 he asked his brother to send the work back to Paris, if it could not be published immediately.[18] When the impatient author had still heard nothing from Vossius a month later, he decided to write to his friend himself with a request to correct the work in collaboration with his Leiden colleague Jacchaeus.[19] A few months later he had second thoughts about his decision to have the Latin catechism printed in the same volume as the defence of the faith, because he feared that certain things in the catechism might restrict the sale of the other work.[20] He was probably alluding to the Christian doctrines he had dealt with in the catechism but not in the defence of the faith.

In August 1627 Vossius informed him that the edition was ready, and admitted that while reading the work he had felt as if he were at a heavenly banquet, dining with the gods themselves. He had personally supervised the printing and had done his very best to achieve a good result, even though he had been unable to prevent a few errors, because of his absence.[21]

---

[17] *BW* III, n° 1105 (to W. de Groot, 2 November 1626), p. 78: "Speraveram Vossio non grave futurum Hexabiblon perlegere. Veretur auctor nominari editionis apud eos, qui nobis male volunt. Sed fide silentii data poterit ipsius securitati prospici. Magni facio ejus judicium et omnino velim siquid est minus rectum ab eo moneri." Since 1622 Vossius had been professor at Leiden, where the contra-remonstrants ruled the roost, and for that reason he was cautious in his involvement in Grotius' work.

[18] *BW* III, n° 1120 (9 January 1627), p. 95: "Hexabiblos si non statim ibi publicari potest, rogo ad me remittatur, nam urgent amici."

[19] See *BW* III, n° 1136 (to G.J. Vossius, 22 February 1622), pp. 115–16; n° 1135 (to G. Jacchaeus, 22 February 1622), p. 115.

[20] *BW* III, n° 1145 (to W. de Groot, 1 May 1627), p. 127: "Scripseram antehac putare me addendam Catechesin latinam, sed rem reputans vereor, quaedam in eo libello sint, quae obstent, quominus ubique caetera vendantur, cujus rei nobis imprimis habenda cura est."

[21] *BW* III, n° 1167 (from G.J. Vossius, 23 August 1627), p. 161: "Excusus jam liber tuus de religionis christianae veritate. Quem cum lego in coelesti coenaculo cum dis mihi epulari videor. Ut quam correctissime ederetur curavi, ut potui et debui. Sed cum semel Ultrajectum, iterum mihi Hagam excurrendum esset, nec persuadere possem typothetis, ut absente me alia praelo subjicerent, filiis curam committere sum coactus. Ita factum ut tribus quatuorve pagellis quaedam compareant negligentius edita, ea imprimis, unde errorem spissum ad calcem annotavi." Cf. *BW* III, n° 1169 (from Maria van Reigersberch, [4 September 1627]), p. 166.

First edition (BG n° *944*)

The first Latin edition bears on the title page the words *Sensus librorum sex quos pro veritate religionis christianae Batavice scripsit Hugo Grotius. Lugduni Batavorum. Ex officina Iohannis Maire MDCXXVII.*[22] The work was dedicated to Jerôme Bignon, advocate-general of the Parlement of Paris.[23]

Bignon was considered one of the greatest scholars of his age, and was in many respects the equal of Grotius. He was a child prodigy, who excelled in learning, mastering philology, philosophy, history, theology and law.[24] A dazzling legal and political career took him to the highest offices. In the year when Grotius recast his defence of the faith in Latin (1626) Bignon became advocate-general of the Parlement. Grotius explicitly refers to this post in the dedication of his work, so that we may assume that it was his way of congratulating his friend. After his flight from Loevestein Grotius developed a warm friendship with Bignon in Paris. The two scholars often discussed religion, which was close to their hearts, and were generally in agreement, even though Bignon was a Roman Catholic and Grotius a Protestant.[25] They shared a humanist outlook that was characterised by an eirenic-Erasmian orientation to the old Church and a striving for *docta pietas*.

Bignon thanked Grotius profusely for the dedication, and praised the work, which in his eyes was the product of great learning and piety, and which above all displayed a rare combination of conciseness, completeness and clarity.[26]

---

[22] *BG* n° 944.

[23] *Sensus*, p. 1: "Ad virum amplissimum Hieronymum Bignonum, Advocatum Regium in summo auditorio Parisiensi. Quaerere identidem ex me soles, vir et de patria tua et de literis et, si id adjici pateris, de me quoque optime merite, Hieronyme Bignone, quod argumentum sit eorum librorum, quos pro religione christiana patriae meae sermone scripsi. Neque id quaerere te miror. Non enim ignoras, ut qui omnia legi digna, et quidem tanto cum judicio legeris, quantum excoluerint istam materiam philosophica subtilitate Raemundus Sebundus, dialogorum varietate Ludovicus Vives, maxima autem tum eruditione, tum facundia vestras Philippus Mornaeus."

[24] On Jerôme Bignon (1598–1656) see G.L.C. Pérau, *Vie de Jerôme Bignon, advocat général et conseiller d'état*, Paris 1757; *DBF*, X, pp. 438–9; M. Fumaroli, *L'Age de l'éloquence. Rhétorique et 'res literaria' de la Renaissance au seuil de l'époque classique*, Geneva 1980, pp. 551–8.

[25] See Pérau, pp. 291–2.

[26] *BW* II, n° 1190 (from J. Bignon, 23 October 1627), p. 188: "Quas tibi agere possim gratias, vir amplissime, non video. Ita magnitudine beneficii effecisti, ut verba huic officio deessent [. . .] Non aliud quippe esse potuit nobilius argumentum, in quo ad publicam utilitatem pietas scriptoris et omnis generis profunda eruditio pari momento spectarentur. Certe omnia quamquam in eo genere commode dicta sunt, tam brevi spatio inclusisse adeoque dilucide et valide digessisse indicatis etiam nobilium auctorum locis prope supra fidem est."

Grotius himself, however, was not satisfied with the first edition, and told his brother Willem that on rereading it he had discovered a great many printer's errors, which he had corrected in his own hand in the copies intended for his friends. He said that he would welcome it if the printer would take over this task from him.[27] A week later he wrote to his brother in law Nicolaas van Reigersberch that he would appreciate it if his work were published in England, which could be done through the mediation of Vossius and Junius junior.[28] He repeated this suggestion a few months later in a letter to Willem, but as far as we know he never referred to it again.[29]

On 5 March 1628 Grotius reported to Van Reigersberch that one of his acquaintances had received an edition that gave Paris and not Leiden as the place of publication. Grotius, who was clearly unaware of this, assumed that it was a malicious trick of Heinsius or someone else who wanted to make it appear that the book had been written to benefit the papists, or to show that the author was still out of favour in Holland. He asked his brother in law to investigate the matter.[30] Grotius alluded to an 'issue', the title page of which read: *Sensus librorum sex quos pro veritate religionis christianae Batavice scripsit Hugo Grotius. Parisiis, apud Iacobum Ruart MDCXXVII.*[31] This does

---

[27] *BW* II, n° 1194 (6 November 1627), p. 195: "Dum eum librum [= *VRC*] relego, inveni praeter annotata magnum mendorum numerum. In iis quae distribui exemplaribus correxi mea manu. Velim in caeteris tantundem typographus fieri curet. Sunt enim, quae sensum vitiant. Cognosces ex hoc indice." In the Leiden University library there is a copy of *Sensus* (shelf mark 188 G27) which is provided with a list of printer's errors ('errata minora'). This list was probably inserted as a loose gathering in the remaining copies of the first impression. It is not clear if the list was made by Grotius or the printer.

[28] *BW* II, n° 1195 (13 November 1627), p. 197: "Ick soude wel goedvinden, dat mijn bouck de Veritate religionis christianae in Engelant werd naegedruckt. Vossius soude dat door Junium connen bestellen."

[29] *BW* III, n° 1216 (29 January 1628), p. 229: "Ex usu nostro mihi videatur fore, si in Anglia nostri libelli de Veritate religionis christianae—quorum exemplaria reliqua et ego et alii impatienter exspectamus—recudantur; quod forte per Iunium peragi poterit." The first English edition did not appear until 1639, without the author's knowledge: *BG* n° 939.

[30] *BW* III, n° 1235 (to N. van Reigersberch), p. 259: "Boutard, secretaris van d'Espesse, heeft aen een van mijn kennisse gesonden een exemplaer van mijn bouck de Veritate religionis christianae. Maer in plaets van Lugduni Batavorum is daerop gedruckt Lutetiae Parisiorum, soo ick achtte door Heinsius belast ofte yemant anders om to doen geloven, dat dit bouck tot voordeel van de papisten is gemaeckt, ofte omdat men toonen soude, dat mijn naem in Hollant niet duldelick en is. Wilt hyer wat nae vernemem ende met mijn broeder de Groot daerover spreecken?"

[31] *BG* n° 945. Apart from the title page and the format, this edition barely differs from the first impression by Le Maire. The printer's errors of the first edition are not corrected in this reprint. The list of 'Errata minora' was omitted from the reprint.

not seem to be a separate edition but an 'issue' which, apart from the
title page, did not differ from the first Le Maire edition. The setting
unmistakeably points to Le Maire. Probably Le Maire and Ruart had
made an agreement to share the print run. This was a normal procedure among publishers. Grotius' suspicion that ill-wishers in Leiden
had tampered with the title page therefore appears to be unfounded.

Second edition (BG *n° 946*)

In the meantime Grotius himself was at work on an improved and
enlarged version, which he completed in July 1628 and sent to his
brother Willem. He impressed on Willem the need to make sure
that no new errors crept in when the old ones were corrected.[32]

The second edition appeared in July or August 1629: *De veritate
religionis christianae. Editio secunda, priore auctior et emendatior. Lugduni
Batavorum. Ex officina Ioannis Maire MDCXXIX.*[33] Grotius had clearly
distanced himself from the long winded title of the previous edition,
which made the relationship with the Dutch poem explicit, and now
presented the Latin version as an independent work.

It did not escape the author that the second edition teemed with
printer's errors.[34] Vossius felt obliged to offer a justification, and
related his experiences with the Leiden publisher. As soon as he had
heard that Le Maire was preparing a new edition, he had volun-
teered his services to correct the errors. But the publisher did not
think this help necessary, because he did not need to work from a
manuscript, but from an earlier edition, which greatly simplified matters. Vossius was not satisfied with this answer, and continued to
press Le Maire until the publisher admitted that he would be using
the assistance of Caspar Barlaeus. Grotius' friend had been reassured
by this at first, but later heard that Le Maire had made use of the
perfunctory services of some 'hireling' (probably a student). All this
proved once more, Vossius concluded, how little publishers cared for
the quality of their work.[35]

---

[32] *BW* III, n° 1289 (27 July 1628), pp. 347–8: "Mitto ad te, mi frater, ita ut
nuper promiseram meum opus de Veritate religionis christianae, emendatum et auc-
tum nonnullis in locis. Tuum et amicorum erit videre, ne dum vetera corriguntur,
nova admittantur menda. Sane nuper res satis negligenter acta fuit."

[33] *BG* n° 946.

[34] *BW* IV, n° 1418 (to G.J. Vossius, 18 August 1629), p. 88: "De typothetis quam
juste queraris, vel ex nova librorum de Veritate christianae religionis editione agnosco."

[35] *BW* IV, n° 1490 (from G.J. Vossius, 6 April 1630), p. 180: "Libros tuos de

Third edition (BG *n° 947*)

Grotius was in Holland in January 1632, hoping to be repatriated and fully rehabilitated. He wrote to Wtenbogaert that at the request of his French friends he was working on a third edition of his Latin defence of the faith. He believed the Amsterdam publisher Blaeu would be better able to produce a handsome edition than Le Maire, but he would have no objection if Le Maire too were to bring out a new edition.[36] A month later he reported to his French friends that his defence of the faith was to be printed for the third time.[37] For reasons that are not clear Blaeu dropped out of the project, but Le Maire proved willing to undertake the new edition. Grotius, however, insisted that the Leiden publisher should use better paper than the poor stuff on which the earlier edition had been printed.[38] If Le Maire could not guarantee an improvement and was unwilling to accept the help of Vossius, the work must be taken from him, the author stipulated.[39] On 8 October Vossius reported that the Leiden

---

religionis christianae veritate altera hac editione tot mendis obsitos prodiisse, sane doleo. Simulac cognoram Lamerium novam editionem cogitare, obtuleram sponte ei operam meam ad corrigenda typothetae sfalmata. Sed negavit ea sibi nunc opus esse, quia non manuscriptum quicquam excuderet, quod molestius procedere solet, sed jam semel excusum. Cum ne sic quidem satisfaceret, iterum institi, usque dum significaret se in isto usurum opera clarissimi Barlaei. Tum demum mihi acquiescendum putavi. Sed postmodo cognovi contentum fuisse perfunctoria opella mercenarii cuiusdam. Scis autem, quam parum hoc hominum genus sollicitum esse soleat, utrum emendate an inemendate prodeant."

[36] *BW* V, n° 1729 (14 January 1632), pp. 8–9: "Belangende 't boecxke de Veritate religionis christianae; uyt Vrancrijck heb ick schrijven ontfangen, dat ick het soude laeten drucken met beter letter. Ick meen sulcx oock oirboir sal zijn soo voor oude luyden als voor andere luyden van qualiteyt, dye garen een schoonen druck hebben. Dit vertrouw ick, dat Blaeu beter sal [doen] dan La Maire. Doch wil La Maire evenwel en nyettegenstaende eenen beteren druck oock dye cleynen aenleggen, ick heb daer nyet tegen; eene overlesing ende verbetering sal voor beyde dyenen."

[37] *BW* V n° 1742 (to J. de Cordes, 12 February 1632), p. 23; n° 1747 (to P. Dupuy, 23 February 1632), p. 26.

[38] *BW* V, n° 1753 (to J. de Groot, 15 March 1632), p. 34: "Monendus est per fratrem aut per amicum aliquem, Lugduni qui vivat, librarius Lamairius, ut libelli pro veritate religionis christianae exemplaria si non omnia saltem aliquam multa excudat charta meliore. Nam illa prioris editionis sordida est. Id ex Gallia viri praestantes me rogant."

[39] *BW* V, n° 1766 (to G.J. Vossius, 31 May 1632), p. 47: "Quando Lamairius, vir optime atque eruditissime, novam pro veritate religionis christianae editionem nec praestat hoc mercatu qui Francofurti fuit, nec in sequentem promittit ad tuam opem, quam mihi salutarem toties expertus sum, confugio teque oro, ut si habes—habere autem te puto—exemplum eorum, quae correxeram aut addideram—ut erat quibusdam in locis non poenitenda accessio-, ne patiaris perire et hunc prope dixerim novi carceris fructum."

publisher was printing the new improved and enlarged edition in a larger typeface.[40]

The third edition appeared in 1633. The title page bore the words: *De veritate religionis christianae. Editio tertia, prioribus auctior, et emendatior. Lugduni Batavorum. Ex officina Ioannis Maire MDCXXXIII.*[41] A reprint of this edition appeared in the same year, also printed by Le Maire.[42] As far as we know Grotius gave no reaction to this third edition or the reprint in 1633. Probably no copies of these editions reached the author, who spent much of that year in Hamburg. Not until September 1634 did the author give any sign of being aware of the third edition.[43] But he was forced to admit that though this new edition was an improvement in some places, the printer's negligence had once again allowed countless new errors to creep in.[44]

In 1639 two 'issues' of a pirate edition of *De veritate* appeared. Both were presented as the fifth enlarged and improved edition. Only the title pages differed: the first issue purported to be published at Oxford and the second at Leiden, by Le Maire.[45] These statements are probably fictitious; nothing in this issue betrays the hand of Le Maire. Everything suggests that both issues were produced by the same printer at Oxford. Perhaps the name of Le Maire was used to promote sales on the continent. There is no trace of the alleged additions and corrections in this pirate edition. Presumably the publisher wished to create the impression of an authorised edition. The text of the pirate edition does not differ from that of the third edition of Le Maire. The author was—as far as we know—completely unaware of this edition.

---

[40] *BW* V, n° 1792 (from G.J. Vossius, 8 October 1632), p. 72: "Lamerius jam dudum a me habet tuum pro veritate christiana codicem, in quo pluscula et correxeras et addideras, et jam majusculis excudere literis coepit."

[41] *BG* n° 947.

[42] Hugo Grotius, *De veritate religionis christianae. Editio tertia, prioribus auctior, et emendatior. Lugduni Batavorum. Ex officina Ioannis Maire MDCXXXIII.* There is a copy of this reprint in the library of the University of Utrecht [shelf mark: E oct. 1375]. The differences between the two editions are extremely slight.

[43] *BW* V, n° 1952 (to J. de Cordes, 19 September 1634), p. 279.

[44] *BW* V, n° 1959 (to J. de Cordes, 30 October 1634), p. 287: "In libro de Veritate religionis christianae, quem tertium vulgavit Mairius, ut quaedam sunt a me addita, emendata loca nonnulla, ita ipsius negligentia nova irrepserunt menda non pauciora prioribus."

[45] Hugo Grotius, *De veritate religionis christianae. Editio Quinta, prioribus auctior et emendatior. Oxoniae. Excudebat L.L.* [= Leonard Lichfield] *Jmpensis G. Webb 1639* [= *BG* n° 948]; Hugo Grotius, *De veritate religionis christianae. Editio Quinta, prioribus auctior et emendatior. Quibus accessit ejusdem Tractatus de unitate et pace concordiae ecclesiae. Lugduni Batavorum. Ex officina Ioannis Maire, 1639* [= *BG* n° 949].

The making of the Notes

In the same year (1639) Grotius compiled an apparatus of notes for a new edition of his apologetic work, something which his friends and family had been pressing him to do for some time. Willem de Groot had pointed out the desirability of explanatory notes to his brother soon after the conception of the work in 1620, but at that time Hugo had been unwilling to follow his advice. He acknowledged that certain things in the work would undoubtedly not be clear to everyone, but said that even such complicated authors as Lucretius and Virgil were read without commentaries. He also claimed that it was difficult to decide what needed further explanation and what did not, and that a commentary could perhaps be added later.[46]

Vossius remarked that when the *Bewijs* appeared his wife could only enjoy the valuable work because she had someone in her house who could explain the difficult descriptions and allusions to less well known parts of history. That led him to ask if it would not be useful to less learned readers to add explanatory notes in the margin or beneath the text. Such secondary work need not be done by Grotius himself; it could be entrusted to Willem de Groot or someone else, his learned friend suggested.[47]

Grotius promptly passed this suggestion to his brother, who did not react to it.[48] In October 1628 Willem again reminded the author of the desirability of notes. Grotius explained that producing an apparatus of notes did not fit in with his other activities. He was busy going through literature for his juridical work, and he pointed out that writing notes was no sinecure, because some would be needed to give

---

[46] *BW* II, n° 601 (to W. de Groot, 17 April [1620]), p. 32: "Verum est quod scribis esse quaedam in Fidei Isagoga non omnibus aperta. Sed meminisse debemus et Lucretium et Virgilium solere sine commentariis legi. Deinde quid explicandum sit, quid non, vix distingui potuit ob ingeniorum diversitatem. Videtur mihi posse prima editio, nisi aliud impediat, sine commentariis procedere; ut et Bertasii Hebdomas, in quam postea commentarii satis luculenti non ab ipso, sed a Simone Goulartio pastore, ni fallor, Genevensi, accesserunt."

[47] *BW* II, n° 761 (from GJ Vossius, 1 June 1622), p. 220: "Gaudeo sex tuos de vera religione libros in lucem prodiisse. Sunt illae unicae deliciae multorum, et eos inter coniugis meae, cui eo impensius placent, quod domi suae habet intepretem eorum, quae circumlocutione quadam dicuntur a te, vel etiam ubi alludis ad historiam minus in vulgus notam. Dubitavi interdum, an non in gratiam imperitiorum utile foret, declarationem talium ad oram verbo annotari, vel ad calcem adiungi. Quod iam alios scis in hymnis suis praestitisse. Nec tamen minutum adeo laborem subiri a te velim, sed fratre, vel alio."

[48] *BW* II, n° 767 (20 July 1622), p. 225.

explanations while others must provide corrections and supplementary arguments to remove every trace of unclearness. He did, however, promise his brother that he would think about it when he had the time.[49]

It was clear that Grotius was only willing to produce the notes if he could fit them in with his plans for his work. The opportunity presented itself in 1639. On 28 May that year he wrote to Willem that he had finished the notes to *De iure belli,* and was collecting testimonies for the notes to his apologetic work.[50] Grotius had already collected so much literature for his legal masterwork that it was now quite easy for him to compile the much smaller apparatus of notes for his defence of the faith in one operation. In many cases he could use the same material. Three months later he had already completed the notes for the new edition. On 28 August he sent the apparatus to Bignon for his judgement, pointing out the value of his testimonies as legally convincing proofs.[51] The author expected that the annotated edition would appear in 1639.[52]

New edition (BG n° 950)

The new edition appeared in February or March 1640: *De veritate religionis christianae. Editio Nova, additis annotationibus in quibus testimonia. Parisiis. Sumptibus Seb. Cramoisy, Typographi Regii. MDXCL. Cum privilegio regis.*[53] It appears to have been a prestigious edition, produced by the royal printer and provided with a privilege from the Most Christian King (Louis XIII), much coveted by Grotius.

---

[49] *BW* III, n° 1325 (28 October 1628), p. 391: "Testimonia auctorum ut libris de Veritate religionis christianae addantur, non fert ratio occupationum mearum; quia nunc lego Hispanos, Italos, Belgas, qui de bello nostro scripserunt, ut cum iis quae ego olim scripsi conferam. Deinde sunt quaedam testimonia, quae explicatione, quaedam etiam, quae correctione quadam et argumentis ad id idoneis indigent, ne quid apud infirmos scrupuli haereat. Cum tempore tamen cogitabimus." Cf. *BW* III, n° 1347 (to W. de Groot, 8 December 1628), p. 428: "De testimoniis addendis ad libros de Veritate nunc cogitare non satis vacat. Tamen consilium tuum non sperno."

[50] *BW* X, n° 4132, pp. 360–1: "Feci notas cum multis novis ac veteribus testimoniis ad nostra de Iure belli ac pacis. Nunc omnia testimonia colligo ad firmanda quae nobis dicta de Veritate religionis christianae."

[51] *BW* X, n° 4270, p. 554: "Audies testes, vim testimoniorum expendes, iudicium feres. Ego iudicatum facio." Bignon's answer is not known.

[52] *BW* X, n° 4413 (to W. de Groot, 3 December 1639), p. 784: "Sub finem anni prodibit hic meus liber de Veritate religionis christianae cum notis."

[53] *BG* n° 950.

This was the first time Grotius had entrusted one of his works to the Paris publisher Sébastien Cramoisy,[54] who had already made repeated offers to print his writings.[55] Grotius had evidently had enough of Le Maire, but Cramoisy did not free him from the plague of printer's errors. When he sent the first copies to his friends the author pointed out the many printer's errors in the new edition.[56] At first he hoped that someone else would correct them, and thought of his brother Willem or his son Pieter,[57] but he had not the patience to wait for them, and soon drew up a list of corrections himself, which he sent to Willem. He wanted this list to be printed, if necessary at his own expense, and to be inserted at least in the copies intended for his friends. He had himself corrected the errors in the list of errata included at the end of Cramoisy's edition, and he proposed to add the new list of corrections after the list already printed.[58] A week later he asked his brother to cut the printed list out of the new edition and replace it by the new list of improvements.[59]

Grotius had earlier sent his brother a list of the persons to whom he wished presentation copies of his work to be given.[60] This list mentions his brother Willem, his father Jan de Groot and other 'relatives' (probably he meant Nicolaas, Dirk and Pieter van Reigersberch), as well as a number of friends and acquaintances in Holland: Heinsius, Saumaise, Beaumont, Wtenbogaert, Vossius and—if there were enough copies left—the sons of Vossius and Wicquefort.[61] Later

---

[54] Later Grotius would also have his work *De origine gentium americanorum dissertatio altera* [= *BG* n° 731] printed by Cramoisy.

[55] *BW* X, n° 4259, p. 531; n° 4288, p. 587.

[56] *BW* XI, n° 4543 (to M. Casaubonus, 5 March 1640), p. 120; n° 4547 (to C. Sarrau, [5 March 1640]), p. 124.

[57] *BW* XI, n° 4552 (to W. de Groot, 10 March 1640), p. 130.

[58] *BW* XI, n° 4561 (to W. de Groot, 17 March 1640), p. 144: "De erratis scripsi antehac. Nunc exactissimum tibi indiculum mitto, quem vel meis impendiis excudi, addique velim exemplis saltem iis, quae amicis dabuntur. Feci ego jam idem in erratis de Veritate religionis christianae. Nam quia nova in erratis errata erant, pagellae quaedam male indicatae, quaedam a me praetermissa, congeriem emendandorum alteram feci excudi, quam rogo addas iis exemplis, quae primo tempore ad te pervenient a Treselio."

[59] *BW* XI, n° 4568 (to W. de Groot, 24 March 1640), p. 158: "Pagella, quam misi erratorum in libris de Veritate religionis christianae excisa pagella, quae minus exacta est in libris, aut glutine jungi aut etiam cum modica plicatura affigi in locum illum poterit."

[60] *BW* XI, n° 4544 (to W. de Groot, [5 March] 1640), pp. 121–2.

[61] For this list and the persons named in it see H.J.M. Nellen, 'Le rôle de la correspondance de Grotius pendant son exil', in *The World of Hugo Grotius (1583–1645)*.

he was to ask his brother to deliver copies to De Courcelles and
Barlaeus as well.[62]

In March 1640 Grotius gave a bundle of copies for his family and
friends to the merchant Treselius.[63] Three months after they were sent
he learned that the bundle had been left in an inn somewhere en
route, and would be collected by an Amsterdam shipper.[64] The copies
did not reach Willem until July of that year.[65] The author reminded
his brother of his earlier request to insert the new list of corrections.[66]
He was satisfied that his apparatus of notes was favourably received in
both Holland and France.[67] Vossius expressed himself in very laudatory terms about the notes, and considered it an honour to be cited
in them.[68] Grotius tempered his friend's enthusiasm, and said that
he had written the notes for young readers, who could see at a
glance all kinds of agreements between profane authors on the one
hand and the history and doctrine of sacred Scripture on the other.[69]

Unauthorised editions (BG *nᵒs 951–3*)

On 6 August 1640 Willem de Groot wrote to his brother that Le
Maire was preparing a new edition of the notes to his apologetic
work. The Leiden publisher claimed to have more than a thousand

Proceedings of the International Colloquium organized by the Grotius Committee
of the Royal Netherlands Academy of Arts and Sciences, Rotterdam 6–9 April
1983, Amsterdam/Maarssen 1984, pp. 151–3.

[62] *BW* XI, nᵒ 4581 (to W. de Groot, 31 March 1640), p. 177.
[63] *BW* XI, nᵒ 4552 (to W. de Groot, 10 March 1640), p. 130.
[64] See *BW* XI, nᵒ 4693 (to W. de Groot, 15 June 1640), pp. 330–1; nᵒ 4706 (to W. de Groot, 23 June 1640), p. 351.
[65] *BW* XI, nᵒ 4731 (from W. de Groot, 9 July 1640), p. 383.
[66] *BW* XI, nᵒ 4743 (21 July 1640), p. 399.
[67] *BW* XI, nᵒ 4646 (to J. Wtenbogaert, 12 May 1640), p. 267; nᵒ 4805 (from W. de Groot, 27 August 1640), p. 481.
[68] *BW* XI, nᵒ 4854 (from G.J. Vossius, 17 September 1640), p. 539: "Accepi a fratre jurisconsultissimo de religione christiana opus aureum cum accessione notarum, quae plurimum illud illustrant multaque etiam doctissimos docent. Etiam in perhonorificam nostri mentionem incidi, quo nomine Excellentiae tuae debeo plurimum et maximas ago gratias, quod non desinas in loco tam sublimi persequi me affectu veteri vel etiam majori."
[69] *BW* XI, nᵒ 4923 (to G.J. Vossius, 10 November 1640), p. 611: "Laboris in colligendis disponendisque testimoniis ad libros de Veritate religionis christianae me non poenitet. Utile est iuventutem, cui ista scripsimus, habere in uno conspectu quaecunque apud profanos autores reperiuntur Sacrae Historiae aut dogmatibus consonantia. Quod tu addis de fructu etiam ad viros doctos inde perventurum, in ea tuam veterem agnosco benignitatem."

copies of the earlier edition left, which he hoped he would soon be able to sell with added matter, that is with the addition of Grotius' notes.[70] Le Maire evidently had a 'mixed edition' in view; he wanted to print Grotius' apparatus of notes and combine it with the already printed text of an earlier edition he had produced, in order to market the whole as a single volume. Grotius raised no objection to Le Maire's plan. It would not harm Cramoisy, because the latter had either already sold his copies or would soon sell them, albeit in France alone.[71] A few months later he again enquired about Le Maire's new edition.[72] His brother replied on 10 December that it had still not appeared.[73]

Le Maire's new edition came out before the end of the year 1640.[74] The apparatus of notes was provided with a separate title page.[75] The history of this edition is particularly complicated. We will not go into details, but merely remark that it was not a single 'mixed edition', but several mixed editions in a number of variants.[76] The printer's foreword makes it clear that Le Maire had acted entirely on his own initiative and responsibility, so that we cannot describe it as an authorised edition.[77] Grotius' judgement of this edition is not known, but his letters show at any rate that he had little interest in this latest edition of Le Maire.[78]

---

[70] *BW* XI, n° 4771 (from W. de Groot, 6 August 1640), p. 439: "Praeterita septimana fui Lugduni, ubi e Mairio intellexi parari a se novam editionem notarum ad commentarium de Veritate religionis christianae minore forma, qua ante librum excuderat, cujus exemplaria plus mille sibi superesse asseverabat, quae jam cum auctuario venditurus esset." By the new edition he must mean *BG* n° 952 or 953, and by the previous edition probably the pirate printing of 1639 (*BG* n° 949).

[71] *BW* XI, n° 4787 (to W. de Groot, 18 August 1640), p. 457: "Quod Mairius novam molitur editionem Annotatorum de Veritate religionis christianae, non improbo neque puto damnum inde sensurum Cramoisiacum, qui sua aut vendidit aut brevi venditurus est, vel in Gallia sola."

[72] *BW* XI, n° 4941 (to W. de Groot, 24 November 1640), p. 632.

[73] *BW* XI, n° 4964, p. 658.

[74] H. Grotius, *De veritate religionis christianae. Editio Nova, additis annotationibus, in quibus testimonia.* Leiden 1640 [= *BG*, n°ˢ 952–3].

[75] H. Grotius, *Annotationes ad libros de veritate religionis christianae*, Leiden 1640.

[76] On this see R. Breugelmans, 'Maire's editions of Grotius' *De veritate religionis christianae* from 1627 to 1640', *Quaerendo*, 22 (1992), 191–6. Breugelmans distinguished at least twelve different variants of this edition.

[77] Cf. S. Scheibe, 'Zu einigen Grundprinzipien einer historisch—kritischen Ausgabe', in G. Martens – H Zeller (eds), *Texte und Varianten, Probleme ihrer Edition und Interpretation*, Munich 1971, pp. 28–9.

[78] See *BG* n° 952, rem. 2.

Grotius did, however, make regular enquiries about a pirate edition that was published by Janssonius at Amsterdam in 1640.[79] This edition was virtually identical with Cramoisy's, as its title page announced.[80] On 10 December 1640 Willem de Groot informed his brother of the existence of this edition, which, he had learned, was being widely distributed.[81] Grotius replied that he wished to see this edition.[82] He repeated this request several times in the early months of 1641, above all because he wished to know if any changes had been made to the text.[83]

b. *Development of the text*

During Grotius' lifetime four authorised Latin editions of his apologetic work were published: *Sensus* (1627),[84] *De veritate* (1629),[85] *De veritate* (1633),[86] and *De veritate* (1640).[87] These editions reveal quite a number of textual changes, which cannot be dealt with in full in this chapter. We shall therefore confine ourselves to the most significant differences between the editions, and try to give a global picture of the development of the text on this basis.

Bewijs *(1622)*—Sensus *(1627)*

Grotius recast his Dutch poem as a Latin prose treatise in 1626. This was not a literal translation, but a paraphrase. The author felt free to formulate his arguments anew, but left the structure of his work unchanged in its main outlines. Smaller sections of the argu-

---

[79] H. Grotius, *De veritate religionis christianae. Editio Nova, additis annotationibus in quibus testimonia. Iuxta exemplar Parisiense. Sumptibus Seb. Cramoisy, Typographi Regii MDXCL* [= Amsterdam 1640: *BG* n° 951].

[80] The list of errata included at the end of the Paris edition is not found in this edition because the printer's errors mentioned are corrected in the text.

[81] *BW* XI, n° 4964, p. 658: "Addam igitur ad ea, quae ante octiduum scripsi, Mairium editionem de Veritate religionis christianae plus quam oportet differentem egregie a Jansonio Amstelodamensi delusum, cujus jam editio cum notis ubique prostat."

[82] *BW* XI, n° 4981 (to W. de Groot, 22 December 1640), p. 679.

[83] *BW* XII, n° 5029 (to W. de Groot, 26 January 1641), p. 57; n° 5061 (to W. de Groot, 16 February 1641), p. 105.

[84] *BG* n° 944.

[85] *BG* n° 946.

[86] *BG* n° 947.

[87] *BG* n° 950.

ment underwent the inevitable revisions, which were chiefly connected with the change from poetry to prose.

Grotius' *Bewijs* belongs to the genre of didactic verse,[88] which Aristotle had explicitly excluded from poetry.[89] Didactic verse was, however, held in high esteem by humanist scholars and poets.[90] A didactic poem has no formal characteristics that clearly demarcate it from other literary genres, but is distinguished solely by its didactic content.[91] For Grotius the nature of didactic verse made a seamless transition to prose possible. In the Latin treatise the alexandrines of the poem have disappeared, as well as a number of everyday examples and similes, which sometimes ornament the poem and sometimes weigh it down and make it long-winded. The text of the Latin prose treatise is considerably more concise and better documented; instead of allusions and descriptions the author now gives names and facts. The author brought out the structure of the work more clearly by adding clarifying transition passages at the crucial points of his argument. Grotius' exceptional mastery of Latin also enabled him to clothe his matter in a better style.

Most of the changes of content are found in the first book. The author eliminated, as we said, the address to the people of Holland with which the poem opened, and wrote a new introduction in the

[88] To my knowledge there is no good modern study of didactic verse. The only monograph is that of L.L. Albertsen, *Das Lehrgedicht. Eine Geschichte der antikisierenden Sachepik in der neueren deutschen Literatur mit einem unbekannten Gedicht Albr. von Hallers*, Aarhus 1967. This work is unfortunately highly unsatisfactory, as is convincingly shown by H.W. Jäger, 'Zur Poetik der Lehrdichtung in Deutschland', *Deutsche Vierteljahrschrift für Literaturwissenschaft und Geistesgeschichte*, 44 (1970), 544–76. There is a useful but unfortunately brief article by B. Fabian, 'Das Lehrgedicht als Problem der Poetik', in *Die nicht mehr schönen Künste. Grenzphänomene des ästhetischen* [Poetik und Hermeneutik, III: Herausgegeben von H.R. Jauss], Munich 1968, pp. 67–89. One can gain an agreeable impression of the history of this genre from *Europäische Lehrdichtung. Festschrift für Walter Naumann zum 70. Geburtstag*. Herausgegeben von H.G. Rötzer – H. Walz, Darmstadt 1981.
[89] See Fabian, 'Das Lehrgedicht', 68–70. Later Goethe was to call the didactic poem an intermediate form between poetry and rhetoric, and therefore not a poetic art in the full sense. J.W. von Goethe, *Werke* (Sophien-Ausgabe), Weimar 1903, vol. 41, 2, 'Über das Lehrgedicht', p. 225: "Das Lehrgedicht ist und bleibt ein Mittelgeschöpf zwischen Poesie und Rhetorik, eine Ab- und Nebenart, die in einer wahren Ästhetik zwischen Dicht- und Redekunst vorgetragen werden sollte."
[90] Didactic verse flourished especially in Neolatin literature, whose practitioners took the great classical masters (Aratus, Lucretius, Virgil and Ovid) as their models. See G. Roellenbleck, *Das epische Lehrgedicht Italiens im fünfzehnten und sechzehnten Jahrhundert: ein Beitrag zur Literaturgeschichte des Humanismus und der Renaissance* [Münchener romanistische Arbeiten, 43], Munich 1975.
[91] Cf. Jäger, 'Zur Poetik', 557–61.

form of a dedication to Bignon. Grotius also deleted many superfluous digressions. In §16 (the proof that biblical history is confirmed by external peoples), however, he added a long series of new testimonies.[92] The prayer to Christ with which the second book of *Bewijs* opens was replaced by a sentence explaining the intention of that book.[93] The third book underwent scarcely any changes, while the fourth shows noticeable variations only in the closing paragraph.[94] In the fifth book (a refutation of Judaism) Grotius went to work much more cautiously and scrupulously than he had in the Dutch original. On several points he cited new testimonies, which shows that he had incorporated new literature. In the last book the 'Address to the Hollanders' largely disappeared, though the author could not refrain, even in his Latin version, from a brief reminder of the circumstances in which the work had been written.[95]

Sensus *(1627)*—De veritate (*Leiden 1629*)

The second Latin edition, as its title page announces, was 'enlarged and improved' with respect to its predecessor. The changes consisted largely of corrections of printer's errors and expansions of the text. We shall pass over the printer's errors. More interesting are Grotius' additions of new evidence in the text. Most of this material is testimonies, that is historical facts and names that give additional confirmation of the argument. Grotius sporadically also added new arguments, which explained his thesis in more detail.

The first book has the greatest number of additions to the text. In §2 the testimony of Aristotle is added,[96] and in §7 that of Galen,

---

[92] Cf. *Bewijs*, pp. 21–3: 'Dat het joodse geloof ten dele is gesterkt bij het getuigenis der heidenen', and *Sensus*, pp. 24–9: 'Testimoniis extraneorum.'

[93] Cf. *Bewijs*, p. 30, and *Sensus*, p. 38: "Secundus igitur liber, fusis ad Christum in coelo iam regnantem precibus, ut ea nobis spiritus sui auxilia subministret, quae ad rem tantam nos idoneos reddant, consilium explicat, non hoc esse, ut omnia dogmata Christianismi tractentur, sed ut ostendatur, religionem ipsam Christianam verissimam esse atque certissimam, quod sic oritur."

[94] Cf. *Bewijs*, p. 112: "Beantwoording op 't geen gezegd wordt, dat enige deelen der christelijke leer zijn zwaar te geloven en bewijs dat dezelve of immers zo zware zaken gevonden worden in de Heidense schriften", and *Sensus*, p. 131: "Ostenditur praecipua Christianae religionis probari a sapientibus paganorum, et si quid in ea est difficile creditu paria apud paganos reperiri."

[95] *Sensus*, p. 202: "Postremo loco reversa, unde exierat, ad lectores populares oratio obsecrat eos, si quid hic boni est, de eo agant Deo gratias, si quid minus placeat, rationem ut habeant, tum communis naturae hominum ad multos errores pronae, tum et loci ac temporis, quo opus hoc effusum verius, quam elaboratum est."

[96] *VRC²*, p. 6: "Nam cum, quae ex hominum arbitratu veniunt, nec eadem sint

Strabo and the Stoics.[97] He provided §16, the portion that had also undergone heavy revision in the previous edition, with at least fifteen new testimonies.[98] Also noteworthy is the expansion of §22, in which the belief in life after death is defended. This paragraph was almost doubled in length, with a long series of new examples.[99] Here and there we find corrections that the author had applied even before the first edition appeared, but which were only included in this edition.[100] In §7 of the second book Grotius added some arguments to support his proof of the reliability of the reports of Jesus' resurrection.[101] In §20 he corrected a mistake about the place of burial of the Prophet Muhammad, changing 'Mecha' to 'Medina'.[102] We find an important new explanation of his method of proof in the closing paragraph of this book.[103] In §9 of the last book Grotius stated that Jesus may be called the Son of God, because according to the witness

---

apud omnes et saepe mutentur, haec autem notio nusquam non reperiatur, neque temporum vicissitudine mutetur, *quod ipsi etiam Aristoteli notatum, homini ad talia minime credulo*, [. . .] (The passage italicised by me was added in this edition.)

[97] *VRC*[2], pp. 13, 14, 16.

[98] See *VRC*[2], pp. 28–37.

[99] *VRC*[2], pp. 43–4.

[100] See *BW* III, n° 1093 (to W. de Groot, 17 August 1626), p. 66: " Libro primo in argumentis pro providentia bis posui 'canem'. Sed quia iactus infelix est, velim poni 'Venerium', et pro 'in alea' rectius erit 'in talis.'" Cf. *Sensus*, p. 20: "Nam in alea canem aliquoties jacere casus esse potest, at centies si quis canem jaciat, nemo erit qui non hoc ab arte aliqua dicat proficisci."; and *VRC*[2], p. 23: "Nam in alea Venerium aliquoties jacere casus esse potest, at centies si quis eundem jaciat, nemo erit qui non hoc ab arte aliqua dicat proficisci."

[101] *VRC*[2], pp. 57–8: "*Fama duntaxat inter suos tanti non erat, ut propterea homines simplices et quorum vita ac dogma ab fastu abhorrebat, tantam malorum vim subirent, neque vero sperare ullo modo poterant tantum progressum sui dogmatis, cui et intenta commodis suis natura, et ubique imperantium auctoritas repugnabant, nisi ex divino promisso. Accedat quod etiam hanc qualemcumque famam nullo modo durabilem sibi poterant promittere, cum Deo de industria suum in hoc consilium caelante, mundi totius exitium quasi de proximo imminens operirentur, quod et ipsorum et sequentium Christianorum scripta apertissimum faciunt.*"; *VRC*[2], p. 59: "Si non credidissent veram [. . .] *praesertim cum et facile praevidere possent et experimento statim discerent hanc professionem post se trahere mortem immensi agminis, cui sine justa causa causam dare a latrocinii scelere non abscedebat.*" (The passages italicised by me were added in this edition.)

[102] Cf. *Sensus*, p. 71 and *VRC*[2], p. 86. See also *BW* IV, n° 1386 (to W. de Groot, 14 April 1629), pp. 38–9: "Correxi in exemplari transmisso, quod de sepulchro Mahometis dixeram, et pro Mecha posui Medinam. Et tamen video esse qui de Mecha perseverent. Si quem nosti rerum Turcicarum gnarum, consule [. . .]".

[103] *VRC*[2], p. 97: "Si quis allatis hactenus argumentis pro christiana religione satis sibi factum non putet, sed magis urgentia desideret, scire debet, pro rerum diversitate, diversa quoque esse probandi genera, alia in mathematicis, alia de affectionibus corporum, alia circa deliberationes, alia ubi facti est quaestio: *in quo genere sane standum esse nulla suspicione laborantibus testimoniis, quod ni admitittur non modo omnis historiae usus periit, medicinae quoque pars magna, sed et omnis quae inter parentes liberosque est pietas, ut quos haut aliter noscamus.*" (The passage italicised by me was added in this edition.)

of the Muslims themselves, he was generated by God's paternal power
from the virgin Mary and recalled to life after his death (*in vitam
revocatus*).[104] On 10 July 1627 Grotius asked his brother Willem to
add these three words to the Latin text.[105] A week later he revoked
this instruction, because he had discovered that Muslims do not
acknowledge the return of Jesus to this life.[106] Nevertheless the words
concerned were included in the Latin edition, though they are not
found in the second edition.[107]

De veritate *(Leiden 1629)*—De veritate *(Leiden 1633)*

Grotius was dissatisfied with the second edition because of the large
number of printer's errors, and prepared a third edition, which like
the second was 'enlarged and improved'. He concentrated above all
on the correction of printer's errors. The number of additions in the
text is less in this edition than in the previous printing.

Once again the first book underwent the most changes. One striking correction concerns the spelling of Bignon's name in the dedication: Bignonus now became Bignonius.[108] Virtually all the additions
are new testimonies, and only very rarely did the author add supplementary arguments. In §16 of the first book he included six new
testimonies.[109] In §17 he referred to predictions of the future among
the Mexicans and Peruvians,[110] and named testimonies of apparitions

---

[104] *Sensus*, p. 195: "Nos vero cum Iesum Dei filium dicimus, hoc significamus,
quod ipse cum eum verbum Dei dicit, verbum enim ex mente suo quodam modo
gignitur, adde iam quod ex virgine, sola Dei opera vim paternam supplente, natus
est, in vitam revocatus [. . .]."

[105] See *BW* III, n° 1156, p. 143.

[106] See *BW* III, n° 1159, p. 148: "Quod nuper scripseram, de addendis voculis
aliquot ad disputationem adversus Mahumetistas ubi de appalatione filii Dei agitur,
re melius expensa revoco. Disputandum enim ex confessis et Mahumetistae ascen-
sum Iesu in coelum confitentur: reditum in vitam non agnoscant, qui nec ipsum
volunt in cruce mortuum, nisi φανταστικῶς. Itaque maneat ut fuit."

[107] See *VRC²*, p. 226.

[108] Cf. *VRC²*, p. 3: "Hugo Grotius De veritate religionis christianae, ad virum
amplissimum, *Hieronymum Bignonum*, Advocatum Regium in summo auditorio Parisiensi.
Quaerere identidem ex me soles, [. . .] *Hieronyme Bignone*, [. . .]"; and *VRC²*, p. 3:
"Hugo Grotius De veritate religionis christianae, ad virum amplissimum, *Hieronymum
Bignonium*, Advocatum Regium in summo auditorio Parisiensi. Quaerere identidem
ex me soles, [. . .] *Hieronyme Bignoni*, [. . .]" (my italics, JPH).

[109] *VRC³*, pp. 35–55.

[110] *VRC³*, pp. 56–7: "Addi his possunt oracula plurima et clarissima apud Mexicanos
et Peruanos, quae Hispanorum in eas terras adventum et secuturas inde calamitates praedixerunt."

in China, Mexico and other parts of America.[111] These additions show that Grotius was incorporating contemporary travel literature. In the last paragraph of the fourth book he made a few subtle changes of emphasis.[112] In the fifth book (§14 and §16) Grotius added a few supplementary arguments.[113]

De veritate *(Leiden 1633)*—De veritate *(Paris 1640)*

The Paris edition was not presented as the fourth but as a new edition. It included the substantial apparatus of notes, which in fact exceeded the text of the defence of the faith in bulk. The notes contain chiefly new testimonies, as the title of the edition proclaims.[114] In the sixth chapter of this study we shall deal with the notes separately, but we point out here that most of the annotations were added in the first book, more than three quarters of them being in §16.

The text of the new edition shows virtually no differences from the third edition. I have been able to find only two modest changes, apart from a few corrected printer's errors.[115]

---

[111] *VRC*³, pp. 57–8: "Referri hic possunt et somnia non pauca, [. . .] cuius generis illustria exempla ex probatissimis scriptoribus libro de anima Tertullianus congessit, et spectra, [. . .] et nostri quoque aevi testibus, qui in Sina, quique in Mexicana et aliis Americae partibus vixere."

[112] Cf. *Sensus*, p. 132: "Sic Plato a Chaldaeis edoctus divinam naturam distinguit in patrem; mentem paternam, quam et rationem et Dei germen vocat, mundi opificem, et animam sive spiritus quo cuncta contineantur"; and *VRC*³, pp. 216–17: "Sic Plato a Chaldaeis edoctus divinam naturam distinguit in patrem; mentem paternam, quam et Dei germen vocat, mundi opificem, et animam sive spiritus quo cuncta contineantur". Cf. also *Sensus*, p. 132: "A Deo assumi posse, naturam humanam, Iulianus tantus Christianorum hostis credidit,[. . .]; and *VRC*³, p. 217: "Cum humana natura divinam jungi posse, Iulianus tantus Christianorum hostis credidit, [. . .]".

[113] *VRC*³, pp. 263–4: "*Adde quod Hebraeorum magistri annotant, duas maximas dotes defuisse templo posteriori quae priori adfuerant, conspicuam quandam lucem divinae majestatis indicem et divinum afflatum*"; p. 268: "Atqui iam anni sunt mille et ultra quingentos, quod Iudaei patria carent, templo carent, et si quando novum aedificare voluerunt semper sunt impediti, *etiam flammarum globis ad fundamenta erumpentibus cum operarum pernicie, quod ab Ammiano Marcellino scriptore non Christiano proditum est.*" (The passages italicised by me were added in this edition.)

[114] H. Grotius, *De veritate religionis christianae. Editio Nova, additis annotationibus in quibus testimonia*, Paris 1640.

[115] Cf. *Sensus*, p. 110: "Quin et in Chaldaicum et in Hierosolymitanum, *id est semisyriacum*, translati sunt iidem libri, partim paulo ante, partim non multo post Christi tempora"; *VRC*ᴺ, p. 118. (The passages italicised by me disappeared in the edition of 1640.) Also *VRC*ᴺ, p. 141: "Crux Christi multos offendit, at quae de diis non narrant paganorum auctores? alios famulos, dissectos, *vulneratos*". (The last word was added in this edition.)

Conclusion

The development of the text of Grotius' apologetic work reveals three stages, which can be indicated as follows:

Translation: *Bewijs* (1622)—*Sensus* (1627)
Modification: *Sensus* (1627)—*De veritate* (1633)
Annotation: *De veritate* (1633)—*De veritate* (1640)

When his Dutch didactic poem was recast as a Latin prose treatise Grotius' apologetic work gained considerably in precision and conciseness. The author left the main lines of his argument largely unchanged, but modified the Latin text in the second and third editions, fighting a dogged and desperate struggle against printer's errors. He also made minor additions to his text. Most of the modifications and additions came in the first book. The last edition authorised by Grotius included a substantial apparatus of notes.

CHAPTER THREE

THE CONTENTS

Grotius' apologetic work consists of six books, the first three of which give a proof of the truth of the Christian faith and the last three a refutation of other religions. The division of the books is shown as follows in *Bewijs*:[1]

Book 1: On God and religion
Book 2: The truth and excellence of the Christian religion
Book 3: The credibility of the Bible
Book 4: Against paganism
Book 5: Against Judaism
Book 6: Against Islam

Our presentation of the contents is based on the last authorised edition of *De veritate* (Paris 1640).[2] For the moment we pass over the apparatus of notes, which will be dealt with later in a separate chapter (chapter 6). To bring out more clearly the structure of the work, which is not always equally evident, it seemed more sensible to make our own analysis of the contents of each book. In what follows we give first the analysis of each book and then a brief summary of its argument.

BOOK I: ON GOD AND RELIGION

Introduction
1 *The existence of God*
    1.1   God as first cause
    1.2   The agreement of all peoples

---

[1] *Bewijs* [BG n° 143], De verdeelinge der boecken: "I. Van Godt ende den godsdienst; II. Van de waerheyd ende treffelickheyd van den christelycken godsdienst; III. Van de gheloofwaerdigheyd der heylighe Schriften; IV. Tegen het heydendom; V. Tegen het jodendom; VI. Tegen de mahumetisterije." In the Latin editions the six books are not given titles.
[2] *BG* n° 950.

Argument

After the introduction the argument begins with a twofold proof of
God's existence. Reason teaches us, the first argument says, that the
long series of causes and consequences that prevails in the world

must necessarily have a first cause, to which one can give the name of God or divinity. The second proof of God's existence is based on the obvious agreement of all peoples (*consensus gentium*). It is a fact that the idea of the divine is found among all peoples on earth, primitive or civilised. The reason for this is either to be traced to divine revelation or to an uninterrupted human tradition. Every form of atheism is in conflict with right reason, and springs from a deplorable striving for novelty or from a corrupted brain.

The proof of God's existence leads naturally to an acknowledgement of his unity. For that which is necessary and entirely self-existent can only be single by nature. Since all perfection in the world must have a cause, God as first cause is the principle of unlimited perfection. From this it can be deduced that God is eternal, omnipotent, omniscient and perfectly good.

That God is the cause of all things appears from the purposeful structure of the entire cosmos. The miraculous composition of the human body shows that man must have been created by the most marvellous spirit. Animals, plants and trees, even the movements of the stars, are the expression of a purposeful intelligence, so that the assumption that the world came into being by chance must be dismissed as unreasonable. Evil does not exist of itself, but is the absence of good; the cause of evil therefore does not lie in God but in man, who makes an unjust use of the freedom of choice granted him by God. The doctrine of the two principles, which allots evil an origin of its own, must therefore be rejected.

That God also guides all his creation through his providence, is obvious from the purposeful form of nature. God's providence extends to both the earth and the stars. It is not restricted to the events of world history in general, but covers all particular things. The maintenance of the political order in the world in spite of all changes of governments and forms of government is a proof of God's providence, for it cannot be mere chance that world history has not resulted in chaos. But the best and most certain proof of divine providence is supplied by the testimonies of miracles that have occurred and prophecies that have been fulfilled. Above all the miracles that the Jewish faith has handed down through the ages must be regarded as credible.

The Jewish religion derives its credibility from the fact that it is still in existence at the present day. The most important miracles that this religion has preserved in its tradition are to be found in the 'books of Moses' (the first five books of the Old Testament), which derive their authority from their credibility and their antiquity. The credibility of these books is shown, among other things, by the faithful manner in which Moses describes his own faults. Furthermore it is clear that the books of Moses form the oldest literature in the world, because Greek letters and laws are unmistakeably of Hebrew origin. This is confirmed by the oldest testimonies of many other peoples, as an abundance of examples proves.

God's providence can also be proved from prophecies that have been fulfilled. Dreams and apparitions of spirits are as many indications of the existence of a divine providence. If miracles no longer occur and prophecies are no longer fulfilled, this is no argument to the contrary, for it is sufficient proof of the existence of providence that they once happened.

The existence of evil in the world does not disprove God's providence either. Even though evil may sometimes appear to go unpunished, that does not invalidate God's providence. On the contrary, the flourishing of the wicked can be interpreted as a sign that it is justified to expect a judgement after this life. A provident and just God cannot tolerate that evil should go unpunished and virtue unrewarded, and therefore there must be a judgement after this life. That is unthinkable if the human soul does not survive after the death of the body.

The last point is confirmed by the tradition of virtually all civilised peoples, and is by no means in conflict with natural reason. It follows that there can be no worthier goal for man than salvation after this life.

The nature of this salvation and the way in which it is to be won can only be guessed at by human reason. For certainty about these matters we are dependent on God's revelation. If one wishes to acquire this highest good, one must seek the true religion. The second book proves that Christianity is this true religion.

BOOK 2: THE TRUTH AND EXCELLENCE OF THE CHRISTIAN RELIGION

Introduction
1   *The factual truth of the Christian religion*
    1.1   Jesus of Nazareth actually lived
    1.2   His scandalous death on the cross
    1.3   After his death he was honoured by many wise men
    1.4   Thanks to the miracles he performed
        1.4.1   And these miracles could only have been performed by God

Argument

That Jesus of Nazareth actually lived is a fact witnessed not only by Christians but by many Jewish and pagan authors. In the same way it is firmly established that Jesus suffered a shameful death on the cross, but nevertheless was honoured very soon after his death by wise and far from ignorant people in many countries, even though many of them had to pay for their belief with their death. The only possible explanation of this is the miracles that Jesus performed. These miracles cannot possibly be ascribed to a natural force or an evil power, but only to God, who wished them to confirm the teaching of Jesus. The greatest miracle was undoubtedly Christ's resurrection from the dead. All Christians at all times have seen this event as the chief grounds of their faith. They could not possibly believe it to be true if the report did not go back to various utterly reliable witnesses. There is no reason whatever to doubt the reliability of their testimony. For why should they have lied, if they had nothing to gain by lying, but on the contrary only bitter suffering and sometimes certain death?

The resurrection is not an impossibility, as some assert. It would be logically impossible to state that someone is alive and dead at the same time, but it is certainly not a contradiction to say that someone lives again after his death, as various philosophers have shown. This assessment of Jesus' resurrection after death also confirms the truth of his doctrine, for it would be in conflict with God's justice and wisdom if a deceiver had been granted such honour and fame. Jesus himself predicted his death and resurrection, and declared that this would occur to prove the truth of his teaching.

Christianity is superior to all other religions. This is evident in the first place from the reward that this faith holds out in prospect to its adherents. For what can be more sublime than the salvation promised to Christians after this life? Man has received from Christ a certain knowledge of his destination: the immortality of the soul and the body. The objection that bodies once dissolved cannot be restored does not hold water, for why should God, who created man from nothing, be unable to restore what remains after death to form a body again?

The second reason why it can be stated that Christianity surpasses the other religions lies in the nature of its commandments. That is shown, for example, by its rules on the worship of God. The Christian cult is not coupled with all kinds of cruelties—such as the cultic practices of paganism—and does not have a superfluity of useless rules, like Judaism or Islam, but is distinguished as the most purely spiritual religion in existence. The duties of a Christian to his neighbours are of unequalled ethical content. Where other religions allow war and violence, and sometimes encourage them, Christianity alone believes that evil must not be requited with evil, but that a Christian must do only good. No better norms for the relations of man and woman can be found than those of Christianity. Whoredom and polygamy, which virtually all religions permit in one form or another, are forbidden by Christianity. Christ's law goes to the root of the evil and punishes even the hidden desire. The rules for the use of worldly goods are no less excellent. Christ's law admonishes us not to care for the things of this world, but to devote ourselves entirely to the spiritual and the eternal. Christians must always speak the truth, so that the swearing of oaths is only permitted in cases of extreme necessity. Christianity also encourages many other virtues, such as modesty, moderation, goodness, honesty and moral conduct.

The division that prevails among Christians cannot be deployed as an argument against the excellence of Christianity. In all arts and sciences there are differences of opinion to be seen, but they always remain within fixed bounds, because there is as a rule agreement on the main points. Thus the differences between Christians are also subordinate, while there is absolute clarity about the ethical rules that form the most important part of religion.

The superiority of Christianity is also evident from the perfection of its founder. The authors of Greek wisdom certainly did not lead irreproachable lives, Muhammad is universally known for his unchastity, and even Moses was not altogether free from sin. Christ, on the other hand, lived a life entirely without sin, while by his resurrection he also gave his followers a guarantee of the reward that awaited them after their death.

The Christian religion also excels all others by its miraculous expansion. It is in harmony with divine providence that the best religion should be the most widespread. And that is what happened with Christianity, which has penetrated to almost every corner of the world. This is all the more remarkable if one looks at the means by which this religion has been disseminated. It was not spread through the favour of kings and great philosophers, but through the support of the most humble and simple people. One should remember that the early Christians had to battle against the current, for there were no small obstacles to acceptance and confession of the Christian faith. Most people already adhered to a religion and were the less receptive to the new doctrine, which demanded sacrifices of persecution and death.

Those who are still not convinced by all these arguments should realise that there are several types of proof, depending on the nature of what is to be proved. The proof required in mathematics is different from that in questions of fact. In the latter case one is dependent on reliable testimonies. God has willed it that the evidence for the faith should not have been the kind that can be empirically established, but rather evidence sufficient to convince people of its truth: belief is an act of obedience to God.

BOOK 3: THE CREDIBILITY OF THE BIBLE

Introduction
1   *The New Testament*
    1.1   Authenticity
        1.1.1   The traditional attributions of the books to the authors named are reliable
        1.1.2   The books over which doubt exists
        1.1.3   The quality of the books
    1.2   Reliability
        1.2.1   The authors had knowledge of the truth
        1.2.2   They had no interest in lying
    1.3   Supernatural confirmation
        1.3.1   Miracles performed by the apostles
        1.3.2   Prophecies fulfilled
        1.3.3   God's care for the truth of the books
    1.4   Truth
        1.4.1   Not invalidated by the fact that certain books are rejected by some
        1.4.2   The New Testament does not contain absurdities
        1.4.3   Or unreasonable statements
        1.4.4   Or contradictions
        1.4.5   External testimonies confirm this
    1.5   Purity of the text
        1.5.1   The original texts have not been handed down in corrupt form

2   *The Old Testament*

Argument

It has been clear to everyone since the first centuries that most of the books of the New Testament are authentic, that is, they were written by the authors whose names appear above them. This is confirmed by early Christian and also by Jewish and pagan witnesses. Initially there was some uncertainty about certain books (2 Pet., Jude, 2 John, 3 John, Heb. and Rev.). That uncertainty derived, however, chiefly from ignorance, and soon disappeared in most cases. Only the author of a single book (Heb.) is wholly unknown, while some others (2 John, 3 John and Rev.) may have been written by authors who were not those named. In these cases one should pay more attention to the quality of the books than the names of the authors.

The books of the New Testament are not only authentic but also reliable, for their authors certainly wrote the truth. Those who deviate from the truth do so out of ignorance or in bad faith. Neither charge can be made against these authors, who without exception were familar with the things that they described and could not have lied, because they had nothing at all to gain by it.

Moreover, the truth of the New Testament books has been confirmed by supernatural means: the miracles that were performed by their authors, the miracles that took place for centuries on their graves, and the prophecies they made that were later fulfilled. In that way God himself gave no small witness of the good faith of these writers. Nor would it be in harmony with God's providence if such a large number of pious and good people had been misled by false books.

In spite of all the divisions that have disunited Christianity over the centuries, there are hardly any people to be found who do not acknowledge the books of the New Testament. Only a few (the Marcionites and Ebionites), have felt compelled to reject the books with which they did not agree, but they were condemned by all other Christians. The objection that the New Testament relates absurdities is unfounded. The prophecy of the resurrection of the dead and their return to life does not rest on an internal contradiction; and therefore it cannot be called impossible. There are no doctrines in these books that are in conflict with right reason, even though some of them are beyond human understanding. The books of the New Testament do not display great internal differences. There is the greatest imaginable agreement between them on the most important matters. If one were to attach too much weight to minor discrepancies in the description of events, one would not be left with a single reliable work of history. Finally there are no external testimonies worth mentioning that deny the truth of these books.

One might think that the text of the New Testament has not remained uncorrupted over time. But that idea is unfounded. True, some errors have crept in as manuscripts were transcribed, but that is not uncommon and even inevitable in such a long textual tradition. The claim that the text has suffered from deliberate alteration must be dismissed as wholly untenable. Even in apostolic times several manuscripts were in circulation, so that textual corruptions could speedily be detected. And the many translations and citations in early

Christian authors do not reveal any important differences from the
Greek text in the books of the New Testament.

The credibility of the documents of the Jewish faith is also firmly
established. The books of the Old Testament are authentic, for there
can be no doubt that they were written by the authors whose names
are attached to them (Moses and the prophets). Several ancient writings of other peoples confirm the truth of the Old Testament narratives. Christians certainly do not need to doubt the reliability of
the Jewish scriptures, because everywhere in the New Testament
there are citations that agree with the Old Testament. Although
Christ was not in the habit of sparing the Jewish scholars of the law
and the Pharisees, he never asserted that their sacred books had
been corrupted over time; while it is equally unlikely that such corruption should have taken place after Christ's time. The fact that
the Jews, in spite of their difference of opinion with Christians about
the Messiah, have made no changes to the texts that refer to the
Messiah and can be interpreted to their detriment, is no small argument for the credibility of these books.

BOOK 4: AGAINST PAGANISM

Introduction
1   *Polytheism*
    1.1   The unity of God
    1.2   The unworthy worship of evil spirits
    1.3   The worship of the dead
    1.4   Of the stars and natural elements
    1.5   Of dumb animals
    1.6   Of abstractions

2   *The unreliability of the pagan miracles and oracles*
    2.1   Not miracles of God
        2.2.2   Ambiguous oracles

3   *The fall of paganism*
    3.1   Paganism fell without human intervention
    3.2   This fall is not to be attributed to the stars

4   *The leading truths of Christianity were already to be found in the pagan philosophers*

Argument

Grotius opens with a general introduction to the section of his apologetic work devoted to refutation, in which he summons Christians to help those who do not share in the truth to find the right path. The first argument against paganism must be that there is not more than one God. If the pagans worshipped supernatural spirits, they must have known very well if they were dealing with good or evil spirits. Good spirits may only be worshipped if it is the will of the highest God. But the spirits that the pagans worshipped must have been evil, in view of the many wicked and scandalous excesses with which their worship was coupled.

The worship of the dead is pointless, for there is nothing to suggest that these souls can still bring anything to pass, and those so worshipped were often such thoroughly unvirtuous figures as Bacchus and Romulus. Another rather older error is the worship of the stars and the natural elements: fire, water, light and earth. These forms of worship are unreasonable, for they are not directed towards reasonable natures. But the lowest form of worship to which one can sink is to worship dumb animals, as the Egyptians did. Some pagans also worship things that in themselves have no existence but are qualities of something else. That means abstractions such as good fortune, health, love, joy, justice and moderation. But it is absurd and unreasonable to pay divine honours to these qualities, which in truth cannot be compared to independent things.

The miracles to which pagans appeal cannot be confirmed by credible testimonies. Some of the supernatural events that they relate must be ascribed to evil spirits. It is not miraculous that God should have allowed these events, since pagans, by deviating from the original natural truth, deserved to be misled. And if a true divine miracle really occurred among the pagans, this does not confirm paganism. The same applies to pagan oracles. If God's spirit had really revealed itself in them, then it must have given first a general rule of life and a certain guarantee of eternal reward, neither of which happened.

Pagan religion fell through its own weakness once human favour was withdrawn from it. Even at the time when it was still upheld by those in power it was already tottering to its collapse. Certain philosophers attributed the origin and fall of religions to the stars, but astronomy is practised in so many ways that very little certainty can be attached to it. Moreover it is unreasonable to assume that the stars influence the human mind, which is equipped with a free and sovereign will.

Pagans have the less reason to oppose Christianity because their own authors asserted many things that one can also find in Christianity. An even stronger argument is that the leading Christian truths had already been proved by the pagan philosophers, above all the Christian commandments. Even doctrines that can only be accepted from Christians with difficulty, such as the immortality of the soul and the future bodily resurrection of the dead, were already proclaimed by pagan authors. Plato had already developed an idea of the trinity in the divine nature and the necessity of the suffering of the righteous.

BOOK 5: AGAINST JUDAISM

Address to the Jews
1 *The miracles of Jesus*
        1.1.1   These were not the work of demons
    1.2   Nor were they achieved by verbal magic
    1.3   But they originated from God

2 *Jesus' teaching agrees with the Mosaic law*
    2.1   And holds out the prospect of a better law than the Mosaic
    2.2   Jesus only abolished certain commandments after his death
        2.2.1   Such as sacrifices
        2.2.2   Dietary laws
        2.2.3   The laws on festivals and the sabbath
        2.2.4   Circumcision
    2.3   The tolerance of the apostles on this point

3 *Jesus is the promised Messiah*
    3.1   The Jews believe that the Messiah is still to come
    3.2   But their own books show that he has already come
        3.2.1   His coming was not postponed because of the sins of the people
        3.2.2   The present state of Judaism is sinful
    3.3   The prophecies show that Jesus was the Messiah
        3.3.1   All the prophecies have been fulfilled
        3.3.2   The humble life and death of Jesus

4 *Jewish charges against Christianity are unfounded*
    4.1   Christians do not worship more than one God
    4.2   They do not pray to a human nature

A prayer for the Jews

Argument

Grotius opens with a friendly address to the Jews, in which he declares that the Jewish faith contains a part of the truth that has been fully brought to light in Christianity. The Jews ought to recognise the historicity of the miracles performed by Jesus, for they prove the miracles in which they themselves believe in the very same way that the Christians prove theirs, namely by appealing to reliable testimonies. Some Jews wrongly assert that the miracles of Jesus were brought about by demons, and that Jesus learned demonic arts in Egypt. One could say the same of Moses, who spent much longer in Egypt. It is an argument for Jesus' innocence that he was not accused of such arts either by the Roman or the Jewish authorities. The assumption that his miracles could have been performed by verbal magic is a Jewish fiction. Jesus' miracles found their justification in the law of Moses, which states that after Moses there would be other prophets whom the people would have to obey. Prophets are known in the first place by the miracles that they perform. The Jews are obliged to believe every prophet who performs miracles, provided that they are not led astray from the worship of the true God. They therefore have no reason whatever not to believe in Jesus, who performed only miracles that served the one true God.

The objection that the law of Christ does not agree entirely with the law of Moses is unfounded. The Jews themselves laid down the rule that on the instructions of a prophet every commandment, except the worship of the one God, can lose its force. And why should God no longer have the power to decree new laws after Moses? Because the Mosaic law was good, it does not follow that there can be no better law. The Mosaic law was certainly not perfect, but framed for the level of the ordinary people at the time. During his life on earth Jesus always observed the law of Moses, and only after his death did he abolish certain of its commandments. These concerned rules that were not good in themselves and had only a temporary and limited application to the Jews alone.

God had never been pleased by the commandments abolished by Jesus. Sacrifices had been instituted by him to restrain the Jews in Egypt from worshipping false gods, but they were later criticised by the prophets. The same applies to the prohibition of certain foods and the law on holy days. The law of the Sabbath included two elements: the commemoration of God's creation and the strict abstention from every form of work. The command to commemorate the creation is universal and retains its validity, while the ban on work was a specifically Jewish reminder of the exodus from Egypt, and as such had only a limited validity. Finally circumcision had been the sign of God's covenant with the Jewish people since the time of Abraham. But the promise to Abraham was completely fulfilled in Jesus, so that circumcision became superfluous. Even though Jesus freed the Jews from the heavy burden of the law, his apostles later permitted the Jews to maintain those commandments.

It is well known that the Jewish prophets foretold the coming of the Messiah. Christians assert that the Messiah has already come, while the Jews still await him. But the books of the Old Testament show that the Jews are in the wrong. The indications of time given in the book of Daniel show that the Messiah must have appeared long ago, that is in the time of Jesus. The objection that the coming of the Messiah has been postponed because of the sins of the people is unfounded, for the Messiah, according to Daniel, had to come precisely because of these sins. If the Jews take an honest look at their present state and compare it with what the law promised, they must conclude that the Messiah has already appeared. For the people is not living in the promised land, but dispersed over the whole earth and suffering great oppression. The Jewish teachers are suffering from a spiritual foolishness, shown by the scandalous fictions and ridiculous opinions that fill the Talmud. The Jews undoubtedly have to blame all this misery on a great sin, and that sin can be none other than the rejection of the Messiah.

Virtually everything that the Old Testament prophesied about the Messiah was fulfilled in Jesus. If some of these prophecies have not been fulfilled, that is chiefly the fault of the Jews themselves. Many of them have been offended by Jesus' humble way of life and death. Wrongly, for the Old Testament gives many examples of the exaltation of the humble and the humiliation of the proud. Furthermore, the suffering and death of the Messiah were announced in unambiguous terms by the prophet Isaiah. Many Jews allow themselves to be misled by their prejudice in favour of the pious life of their forefathers, and above all of the priests who condemned Jesus. But we cannot be surprised that these stubborn and corrupt Jews were greatly irritated by the pure and holy life of Jesus.

Two Jewish charges against Christianity deserve separate attention. The first is that Christians worship more than one God. This assumption rests on an inaccurate interpretation. Moreover, one may wonder why this accusation is not brought against the Jew Philo, who frequently referred to the triple nature of God, or the cabalists, who distinguished three 'lights' in God: Father, Son and Spirit. The second objection is that Christians worship a human nature instead of God. This charge too is unjust, for Christians do not honour the Messiah except as they are commanded to in the Psalms (Pss. 2 and 110).

Finally Grotius once again asks God to enlighten the understanding of the Jews and to forgive them.

BOOK 6: AGAINST ISLAM

An admonition to Christians

Argument

Grotius traces the origin of Islam back to the judgements of God against the early Christians. When Christianity was declared the official religion by the emperor Constantine and his successors, the true and simple piety that had flourished among Christians in the time of persecution began to weaken, and the world as it were entered the Church.

Christians began to quarrel among themselves and to wage war on others. Religion became a question of vain learning, and degenerated into all kinds of institutions. All manner of religious partisanship arose, and there were very few true Christians left. God punished these sins by allowing the Christian Roman Empire to be invaded by a deluge of foreign peoples. When this did not bring the desired result, God allowed Muhammad in Arabia to found a new religion, which is diametrically opposed to the Christian doctrine, but holds up a mirror to the way of life of the Christians of the time. In a short time Islam took possession by force of arms of a large part of the Christian world.

Islam does not permit the ordinary people to read the Koran, and does not allow freedom of examination. That alone is enough to unmask this religion in all its falsehood, for it is very unfair, and not at all in harmony with God's goodness, that the path to salvation may not be known to those who earnestly seek it. The Koran mentions various things that do not agree with the the biblical accounts. Muhammad explained this by asserting that the Bible was a forgery. In the original version of the gospel of John, he claimed, Muhammad as the consoler was foretold in a phrase that was later removed by the Christians. But the Christians had no reason to delete Muhammad's name before his coming, and after it they could no longer do so, because of the widespread dissemination of copies and translations of the New Testament.

A comparison of the life of Muhammad with that of Jesus clearly reveals who taught the better doctrine. As Muhammad himself admits, Jesus was the Messiah who was promised in the Jewish law and the prophets. Muhammad was born in the natural way, as even his followers admit. While Jesus led an irreproachable life Muhammad was for a long time a robber and obsessed with women all his life. Finally Jesus ascended to heaven, and Muhammad is still in his grave. If one compares their activities one forms the following picture. Jesus performed miracles, while Muhammad said of himself that he was not sent with miracles but with arms. The miracles ascribed to Muhammad can either have been easily performed by human trickery or they are not confirmed by a single reliable witness, or they are disproved by their own absurdity. The disciples of Jesus were pious and simple men, but the first Muslims should rather be called bandits, who lacked any form of humanity or piety. There is a world of difference between the ways in which the two religions were spread. Christianity owes its following to the miracles of Jesus and his apostles; Islam on the other hand was spread only by armed conquest. But wars waged for the sake of religion must be described as utterly irreligious. Christian ethics far surpass the Islamic rules. Christianity requires its followers to submit to their enemies rather than hate them, and demands unbreakable faith in marriage instead of polygamy. The Christian faith has, as it were, reached the adult level of an intellectual and internal ethical system, while Islam is a relapse into the infantilism of a system of rules and regulations.

The charge made by Muslims, that Christians speak of the son of a God who has no wife, is misplaced, for the word 'son' can also have a more exalted meaning. Jesus called himself the word of God. The son of God for Christians means no more than the word of God, because the word is born in one way or another from the reason. Jesus was born of a virgin by the intervention of God's spirit. And that is why Jesus can be called the son of God. The Koran, on the other hand, contains a mass of laughable and absurd things that one can only accept if one's reason is utterly confused.

The Christian humanist Grotius closes his defence of the faith, not with an all-embracing theoretical overview, but with an ethical call to his fellow Christians. He admonishes Christians of all denominations to lift up their hands to God, who has created all things and guides them with his providence, and to trust in Jesus, in whose name alone salvation can be achieved. He impresses on them the need to preserve the teaching of Christ as a priceless treasure, and to be assiduous readers of the holy scriptures. The scriptures are completely clear in themselves and not misleading, for they contain everything that is necessary to know for salvation. But let the scriptures be above all a stimulus to a genuinely obedient life. An admonition to mutual unity and peace follows. There may be no divisions or schisms among Christians. All Christians stand under the authority of a single teacher, Jesus Christ. One must use one's knowledge with moderation and caution, conscious of the weakness of all human understanding. It is better to devote one's talent to leading a better life, than to strive to excel in learning. Finally the author urges his readers to ascribe the good things in his work to God and the faults to the weakness of human nature and the circumstances in which the work was written.

CHAPTER FOUR

INTENTION AND METHOD

a) *Intention*

Background

Grotius wrote his apologetic work while imprisoned in the castle of Loevestein as the victim of a 'double monster trial'.[1] He regarded the charge against him, of disturbing the religious peace, as untrue and far-fetched.[2] In his eyes the outcome of the second trial was no less at variance with the truth. The canons of Dordt were at odds with the policy of tolerance he had defended for years. He was convinced that it was unlawful to forbid the defence of a given standpoint, and in matters of the truth he even regarded it as unjust in principle and impossible to condemn others.[3]

In a letter to the Antwerp philologist A. Schottus he related that he had been inspired during his captivity by a 'passionate striving for truth'. He spent most of his time and energy on the preparation of his apologetic work, in which his aim was to emphasise those things that distinguished Christians from the rest of humanity. At the same time, he said, he wanted to persuade Christians to refrain from controversies that scarcely concerned piety, in order to lead their spirits, irritated and embittered by these disputes, back to peace and unity.[4]

---

[1] The term is borrowed from W.J.M. van Eysinga, *Huigh de Groot, een schets*, Haarlem 1945, p. 73.

[2] See Fruin, *Verhooren*, 'Memorie', p. 72; cf. *Verantw.*, p. 170: "Wat mij belangt, deze beschuldiging tegen mij is strijdende niet alleen met de waarheid, maar ook met alle waarschijnlijkheid."

[3] Cf. *Verantwoordingh*, pp. 36–7.

[4] *BW* II, n° 662 (8 July 1621), p. 102: "Nam exemptus et negotiis publicis, quae vix ullam animo pacem indulgent, et turbae hominum plerumque per contagium noxiae, vitam egi quasi ἀσκητικὴν, maximamque partem temporis tum precibus, tum Sacrae Scripturae et veterum eius interpretum lectioni impendi, eo sane animo ut, quemadmodum in controversiis de gratia et libero arbitrio id, quod verum esse firme persuasus sum, magno potentium odio meoque periculo et professus eram libere, et pro eo, quo tum fungebar, munere tutatus, ita in caeteris partibus, seposito rerum temporalium respectu, veritatem aut iam cognitam, aut amplius—neque enim de profectu desperandum est—cognoscendam animose sequerer, in quo proposito et precatus sum hactenus, et nunc etiam precor, ut me conservet ac roboret.

The truth for which he searched so passionately in Loevestein had little to do with the questions of dogma that were the primary concern of the Synod of Dordt, but was much wider in its purpose. He chose to express his message in the form of an apology for the faith.

Apologetics

Christian apologetics were frequently practised in the first centuries of Christianity to win the new faith a place in ancient culture.[5] After Christianity had become the dominant religion, following the conversion of the emperor Constantine, the genre fell into disuse, a tendency that continued during the Middle Ages. The defence of the faith underwent a remarkable revival, however, at the time of the Renaissance.[6]

The Renaissance broke open the closed Christian world of the Middle Ages. Intellectual life was quickened by the spread of the printed book, the intensification of international trade, the flourishing of the arts and the increased intellectual intercourse between scholars in the various European countries. New horizons opened up, unknown worlds were discovered. Other religions and systems of thought made themselves felt, and gradually the position of Christianity as the only true religion became less self-evident. The truth of Christianity was up for discussion in wider and wider circles, so that there was a renewed interest in apologetics.[7] This interest was less lively among theologians, who since the Reformation had been preoccupied almost exclusively with their dogmatic disputes, than among Christian humanists, who were acutely aware of the dangers of external and internal attacks on Christianity's claim to possess the truth.[8]

Cum autem iis, quae praecipua sunt, praecipuam quoque curam deberi arbitrarer, primitias otii mei consecravi illis rebus, quae christianorum universitatem a reliquo humano genere segregant. [. . .] In eodem opere christianos omnes hortor, ut omissis ad pietatem minus facientibus controversiis, praecipue vero animos asperantibus rixis, ad pacem se concordiamque componant."

[5] For early Christian apologetics see *DTC*, I, pp. 1580–1602; *RGG*[3], I, pp. 480–5; *TRE*, III, pp. 371–411; and A. Dulles, *A History of Apologetics*, London 1971, pp. 22–71.

[6] Cf. Laplanche, *L'Évidence*, pp. 5–6.

[7] H.M. Barth, *Atheismus und Orthodoxie. Analysen und Modelle christlicher Apologetik im 17 Jahrhundert*, Göttingen 1971, pp. 20–8.

[8] P.O. Kristeller, *Renaissance Thought. The Classic, Scholastic and Humanist Strains*, [a revised and enlarged edition of *The Classics and Renaissance Thought*], New York etc. 1961, p. 86 "[. . .] It is probably preferable to limit the term Christian humanist to those scholars with a humanist classical and rhetorical training who explicitly discussed religious or theological problems in all or some of their writings."

As an apologist Grotius was less concerned with the growth of
atheism or other external threats to Christianity than with the internal division of Christianity, which he saw as the real menace to the
truth of the Christian faith.

The sickness of Christianity

Grotius had already voiced his concern over the internal division of
Christianity. In the foreword to his *Christus patiens* (1608) he pointed
with alarm to the apparently endless disunity to which Christianity
had fallen victim.[9] A year later he composed the following lines on
the death of Jacobus Arminius:

> Where are we [sc. Christians] going? We, a little flock that was cho-
> sen from the whole world, are so shamefully torn asunder! Again and
> again we are split by dissension, while the Turk laughs and the Jew
> does not grieve![10]

He saw the internal disunity of Christianity with despair. It was a
tragedy that in his eyes was all the more deplorable if one looked at
the *tertius gaudens*, the outsider. He regarded this division as a process
of schism that appeared to be never-ending. It was a sickness that
reminded him of cancer. Grotius made this comparison with a disease in the introduction to his earliest theological work, the *Meletius*.

> From the moment that Christianity spread far and wide, and the power
> of its enemies was broken, the way was open first for differences of
> opinion, then for differences of feeling. This sickness broke out long
> ago, but in the time of our fathers and our own time it has progressed
> so far that it has reached its climax [. . .] If we now look at the Indians,
> to whom we send our ships with such advantage, at the Turks, among
> whom you [sc. J. Boreel] have travelled, or at the Jews, who are now
> settling in our country, then, comparing ourselves with all these, we
> must recall our own almost forgotten need for one another. For are
> we not firmly joined together by that which divides us from others?[11]

---

[9] *Chr. Pat.*, in *Dichtwerken*, II 5a–b 55: "Haec eadem est quae sola christianorum
mentes adeo dissociatas atque divulsas, et tanto inter se odio certantes quanto amore
deberent, ferme invitas adhuc continet, neque in immensum a se invicem discedere
patitur."

[10] *Mort. J. Arm.* in *PC*, pp. 305–6: "Heu, quid paramus? Lectus orbe de toto/Grex
ille parvus lancinamur heu foede./Iterumque et iterum scindimurque discordes,/
Ridente Turca, nec dolente Judaeo!"

[11] *Mel.* 2.18–31: "Ex quo enim christianum nomen se latissime diffudit, et fracta
inimicorum vi inter se opinionibus primum, mox animis dissentire vacuum fuit, varia

Grotius saw the course of history as part of the Stoic scheme of origin and degeneration.[12] It pained him to admit that degeneration had reached a lamentable low point in his own time, or in other words that the sickness had reached its crisis. He invited his fellow Christians to seek a remedy by broadening their perspective and looking at outsiders, non-Christians. The effect of this, he felt, must be that Christians would realise their own unity: for the bonds that held them together must be much stronger than that which divided them from others.

Eirenism

Similar considerations must have induced Grotius to write his apologetic work. In a letter to his friend Georg Lingelsheim he relates that his intention in it had been to lead the sick and sorely tried souls of his own day away from everything that was alien to religion in general and to Christianity in particular.[13] He was undoubtedly referring to the dogmatic disputes of his own age. At the same time he drew the attention of the Paris magistrate Claude Sarrau to the part of his work that led people away from controversy and guided them back towards what all Christians had in common, or at least ought to have in common.[14]

Grotius probably hoped that his fellow Christians, like mutinous seamen—to use Willem de Groot's simile—would cease their internal

---

et nomina et studia nasci coepere, quae christianis christianos tam alienos facerent, quam non christiani christianis fuerant. Coepit jam olim ille morbus, sed patrum nostraque aetate eo excrevit, ut amplius quo procedat non habeat. Non enim frigus animorum nec simultates modo, sed odia iraeque implacabiles et, quod vix ante auditum, bella haud alio magis obtentu sumta, quam religionis eius, cuius propositum pax est. At si Indos illos, ad quos felicissime navigamus, aut quibuscum tu vixisti Turcas, aut qui nunc se nobis inserunt Iudaeos respicere liberet, deberemus vel illorum comparatione in animum revocare oblitam prope necessitudinem. Quomodo enim nos non coniungit, quod nos omnes ab illis aut omnibus aut singulis separat?"

[12] For the literature on this see Posthumus Meyjes, *Melet.*, commentary, p. 138.

[13] *BW* III, n° 1237, ([10 March 1628]) p. 262: "Mitto tibi, vir optime et inter amicos amicissime, Benoni, id est filium doloris mei, quem utinam Deus faciat Benjamin, i.e. filium dextrae, non meae, sed suae, quo omne, quod a religione universim sumta aut speciatim a christiana alienum est, educatur ex aegrotis et graviter periclitantibus animis, quibus inter alia mala foecundum est hoc seculum."

[14] *BW* III, n° 1238 (10 March 1628), p. 263: "Ego, qui ingenium tuum novi ab omni vitilitigatione alienum, studiosum pacis, non dubito, quin gratum tibi hoc opusculum futurum sit; vel hac parte, quod nos a controversiis avocans ad ea advertit, quae christianis communia sunt, certe esse debent."

quarrelling to join forces when they were attacked by a pirate ship or a common enemy.[15] Confrontation with outsiders must remind Christians of their unity and cure them of their unhealthy passion for controversy. Grotius wanted to open his contemporaries' eyes to the prospect of unity, a prospect that was a consolation and a relief for his own oppressed mind.[16] Clearly he expected that his work would have the same salutary effect on the minds of others.[17]

In the epilogue of his apologetic work he expresses his eirenic intentions unambiguously. This conclusion is an admonition to all Christians.[18] Entirely in tune with his Christian humanist ideals the author summons his fellow Christians to lead a pious and virtuous life (*praxis pietatis*). He adds an urgent call to mutual unity and peace. He invokes several passages from the Bible to emphasise that all partisanship and schism among Christians are utterly unlawful. Unfortunately they exist. To offer a remedy for them he points to the relativity of all human knowledge, reminding his readers that it is good to observe a certain degree of moderation in the quest for knowledge.[19] Differences of opinion are only very relative and must not be the occasion for mutual hate and enmity. One should devote one's talent to improving one's own life rather than to seeking to excel others in knowledge.[20] In short, Grotius believed that a certain scepticism could

---

[15] See *Bewijs*, pp. XXV–XXVI, 'Vermaningh tot vrede aen alle christenen'.

[16] Cf. *Mel.* 3, 39–44: "Itaque ego adversus nova quotidie dissidia et alios in fluctibus fluctus consolari me et recreare soleo eorum cogitatione, quae christianis hactenus Dei beneficio integra manserunt, quae cum sint et maxima et certissima et utilissima, facile apud me tantum valent ut, dum illa considero, minora alia et incertiora nec aeque utilia interim seponam. Saltem illa nos, ut ita dicam, privilegia cives unius esse civitatis evincant."

[17] See *BW* XII, n° 5393 (to J. Wtenbogaert, 28 September 1641), p. 545: "Ick hebbe alle mijn leven een grooten trecke tot de vereeniging van de christenheit ende, alzoo ick zie dat veelen zo in dit rijck [sc. France] als in andere rijcken daertoe arbeiden, hebbe ick niet connen naelaeten het mijne daerbij te brengen, zoo tot mijnes gemoeds gerustheid als om andere tot gelijcke ende betere gedachten op te wecken."

[18] Cf. *Bewijs*, p. 162: "Vermaning aan de Christenen om haar van allerlei hier voor wederlegd wangeloof te wachten en anderen tot het geloof te winnen", and *VRC* VI, 11, p. 239: "Peroratio ad christianos, qui ex occasione antedictorum officii sui admonentur."

[19] *VRC* VI, 11, pp. 243–4: "Sequitur post haec exhortatio ad mutuam concordiam, quam Christus suis abiens tam serio commendavit: non multos inter nos esse doctores debere, sed unum Jesum Christum; omnes christianos in idem nomen baptizatos, quare non debere inter ipsos sectas et scissuras, quibus ut remedium tandem adhibeatur aliquod, suggeruntur dicta illa Apostolica, sapiendum temperanter, pro modo cognitionis, quam cuique Deus admensus est."

[20] Cf. *Bewijs*, pp. 166–7.

be a salutary remedy against an unhealthy craving for doctrinal certainty, the product of arrogance, and the disunity that stems from it.

Necessary and unnecessary doctrines

The cause of the disease from which Christendom is suffering can be found in the excessive importance attached to doctrines, as Grotius had said in his *Meletius.* He himself is convinced that the most important part of religion consists of ethics, to which doctrine must be subordinated. Ethical rules are clear and simple, so that unity about them can be achieved rapidly. Many Christians, however, prefer to devote themselves to formulating doctrines, about which they can quarrel with others. If they paid more attention to ethics, they would have to struggle against their own natures instead. Grotius' conclusion is that the remedy for the disease must be found by limiting the number of necessary articles of faith.[21]

In Grotius' eyes the great number of Christian doctrines and the excessive importance attached to them were the chief obstacles to achieving a consensus that could serve as the basis for mutual unity and peace. He agreed with other Christian humanists that a distinction had to be made in the extensive corpus of Christian dogmatics between those articles of faith that were necessary for salvation and those that were not.

In his youthful work *Parallelon* he refers to Erasmus as the first who had purged human understanding of many superfluous and harmful doctrines, distinguishing them from the necessary truth that was imposed on us by the Holy Scriptures.[22] Although distinctions between the more and less necessary articles of faith had been drawn earlier in the middle ages,[23] Christian humanist authors generally regarded Erasmus as the *auctor intellectualis* of this distinction.[24]

[21] See *Mel.*, pp. 89–91.
[22] *Parall.* III, p. 34: "Tu [sc. Erasmus] sacrosanctam theologiam, Augiae stabulo inquinatiorem, spurcissimis cavillationum argutiis repurgasti, et liberali manu asseristi a crudeli sophistarum tyrannide. Tu primus humani ingenii instituta secrevisti ab ea necessitate, quae nobis divinis oraculis imponitur."
[23] Ockham was the first who had compiled a list of the necessary truths of the faith. He was followed in this by many others, among them Jean Gerson. For this see G.H. Tavard, *Holy Writ or Holy Church*, New York [1959] pp. 22–6, and G.H.M. Posthumus Meyjes, *Jean Gerson—Apostle of Unity. His Church Politics and Ecclesiology* [Studies in the History of Christian Thought, vol. 94] Leiden 1999, pp. 348–52.
[24] See J. Lecler, *Histoire de la tolérance au siècle de la réforme*, Paris 1955, pp. 142–6.

Grotius found another important source of inspiration in his teacher
Franciscus Junius Sr.[25] Even in the painful time of his trial he continued to call himself a follower of Junius.[26] In his *Eirenicon* of 1593
Junius had distinguished between necessary and unnecessary articles
of faith, and stated that only those doctrines about God that were
to be found in the Scriptures belonged to the fundamental articles
of faith.[27]

Like Erasmus and Junius Grotius was convinced that all the necessary doctrines had been declared in the Scriptures. In a speech to
the city council of Amsterdam (9 May 1616) he had distinguished
between fundamental and non-fundamental doctrines. The fundamental ones are those that are easily accepted by everyone, because
they are simple and all stated in the Scriptures. He regarded the
non-fundamental doctrines as a superstructure, on which differences
of opinion might be tolerated.[28] In the epilogue to his apologetic
work he asserts that the Scriptures contain everything that it is necessary to know for salvation:

> The writers of this word were all too faithful, and moreover guided
> by God's spirit, to have forgotten the slightest point of that which is
> necessary for you to know for your salvation.[29]

He nowhere indicated which doctrines he considered necessary and
which unnecessary. Like most eirenists Grotius used the distinction
between fundamental and non-fundamental, or necessary and unnec-

---

[25] For the relationship between Grotius and Junius see C. de Jonge, *De irenische
ecclesiologie van Franciscus Junius*, Nieuwkoop 1980, pp. 167–9, 302–4.

[26] Fruin, *Verhooren*, 'Deductie', pp. 257–8: "Van de theologie, soo veel mij noodich
was, hebbe ick mijne fundamenten genomen bij doctorem Junium saliger, wyens inten-
tie nopende de noodicheyt van de tolerantie van theologische questies tot heelinghe
van de verscheurde cristenheyt, ende insonderheyt van de evangelische kercken, uyt
zijn Irenico genoech is bekent.'

[27] Franciscus Junius, *Eirenicum de pace ecclesiae catholicae inter christianos, quamvis diversos
sententiis, religiose procuranda, colenda, atque continuanda* [= *Eirenicum*], in *Opuscula theologica
selecta*, [Recognovit et praefatus est Abr. Kuyperus], Amsterdam 1882, p. 440: "Fundamentum appellamus, sive (ut loquuntur vulgo) articulos fundamentales fidei, eos sine
quibus fides christiana constare non potest; cuiusmodi sunt articuli de Deo, qui fundamentum est salutis nostrae objectumque fidei immutabile. Qui ergo Scripturam et
fundamentum illud salutare tenent, quamvis in rebus singulis non aeque sit explicata
illorum fides, tamen ex forma externa quam impressit Deus, in Ecclesia Dei habendi
sunt." This sentence was cited by Grotius in *Ordin. Pietas*, in *OT* IV, 111 b, 43–51.

[28] *Orat.*, in *OT* IV, 178b, 30–62.

[29] *Bewijs*, p. 163: "De schrijvers dezes woord zijn al te trouw geweest,/ En daeren-
boven ook bestiert door Godes geest,/ Dan dat het minste punt bij haar zou zijn
vergeten/ Van 't geen U nodig is ter zaligheid te weten." Cf. *VRC* VI, 11, p. 240.

essary doctrines as a means of reaching a general consensus among Christians and thus promoting unity.[30] In this approach he differed from the professional theologians of the time, whom he regarded with a certain mistrust and disdain, for they were the men who kept pouring oil on the flames of controversy. He wrote to Casaubon that true community between Christians was not to be expected as long as theologians, who only fanned the flames, were in control.[31] Elsewhere he remarked that theologians would do well to follow the examples of lawyers, who as a rule were very well aware of the danger of too many definitions.[32]

Grotius had more confidence in an authority that would be strong enough to impose its will on the quarrelling parties. In his *Ordinum Pietas*, as advocate of Holland, he defended the government's policy of tolerance against the accusations of the theologian Sybrandus Lubbertus. It was not improper, he said, for the States of Holland to concern themselves with the religious quarrels, all the more so since they refrained from passing judgement on what was true or false, but paid attention only to what was necessary and what was not. For while theologians are often accustomed to lose themselves in such points of detail, which can barely be understood even by the most learned—let alone by themselves—truth has vanished into the depths, as that famous person said.[33]

---

[30] *BW* I, n° 229 (to I. Casaubon, 5 March 1612), p. 201: "Restat igitur ut separemus a non necessariis ea quae sine periculo deseri non possunt, et ut in his quidem planus monstretur consensus: de caeteris semoto paulisper opinionum dissensu, testata maneat animorum concordia."

[31] *BW* I, n° 239 (6 June 1612), p. 211: "Nec ulla, me judice, vera societas expectanda est, quamdiu theologorum hoc regnum erit, lites augere et accendere."

[32] *Imp.*, in *OT* IV, 231, b4–8: "Prima ut a definiendo abstineatur quantum fieri potest, hoc est salvis dogmatibus ad salutem necessariis, aut valde eo facientibus. Omnem in iure definitionem periculosam esse tradunt Iuris auctores. De theologicis idem quis merito dixerit, vetus enim est sententia, *de Deo etiam vera dicere periculosum est*."

[33] *Ord. Pietas*, 988, in Hugo Grotius, *Ordinum Hollandiae ac Westfrisiae Pietas* (1613) [Critical edition by Edwin Rabbie], Leiden 1995, p. 166: "Nihil ergo ab officio suo alienum, nihil apostolicis decretis contrarium fecerunt Hollandiae ordines cum de ecclesiasticis controversiis in conventu suo cognoverunt. Atque eo minus reprehendendi sunt, quod non inter verum falsumque judicium suum interposuerunt, sed inter necessarium et non necessarium; nam veritas, ut ille ajebat, interdum in profundo demersa est, solentque theologi tantas saepe minutias quaestionum sectari ut eas vix doctissimus quisque, vix ipsi intelligant." The famous person referred to is Democritus (Commentary—Rabbie, p. 327).

The vanished truth

Christian humanist scholars felt impelled by an exalted ideal of peace and order, and believed that their aristocratic self-image required them to stand aloof from the noisy quarrels of the populace and the preachers. The truth, Grotius stated, cannot be derived from the tumult of the people or the slanders of enemies.[34] For Grotius truth was indissolubly linked with peace: where there was no peace there could be no truth. In his poem on the death of Arminius he used the image of truth fleeing before proud, quarrelsome humanity with its sick eagerness for novelty, for holy truth is the friend of holy peace.[35]

Grotius evoked these dramatic images to emphasise the seriousness of the situation: truth had vanished into the depths and had then taken flight. The idea of disappearing truth must have occurred to him during his imprisonment, a time which, as he himself said, he spent in a passionate search for the truth.[36] Grotius was convinced that his contemporaries were dazzled by Christian doctrines, expecting to find their salvation in them, while they lost sight of truth and peace. He saw it as his task to open the eyes of the blind or, to use another image, to free the sick man from the grip of his disease. In this hope he held out a broad prospect of universal unity among all Christians. His truth was a reflection of the assumed golden age of primitive undivided Christendom.[37]

Grotius wanted to cure his contemporaries of their fixation with dogma. In stressing the relativity of Christian doctrines he was exceptional even by comparison with other Christian humanists. Later in life he left no doubt that he would rather abolish those doctrines that were harmful to social peace; in that respect, he said, it was more important to be a good citizen than a good Christian.[38] The only

---

[34] *Ann. ad Cass.* in *OT*, IV 542, a18–19: "Porro veritas ex vulgi rumoribus aut maledictis inimicorum colligi non potest."

[35] *Mort. J. Arm.* in *PC*, p. 305: "Ibi satur quiete, gaudii plenus,/ [. . .] Hinc tanta bella saeviunt magistratorum,/ Hinc odia plebis: interim fugit longe,/ Nec se videndam dimicantibus praebet/ Amica sanctae sancta veritas pacis."

[36] *BW* II, n° 662 (8 July 1621), p. 102.

[37] Cf. *Mel.*, 88.363–366: "Quod si ubique christiana vita nomini suo responderet, sine bellis, sine litibus, sine egestate, in summa pace atque concordia et rerum cuique sufficientium copia, aureum vere saeculum ageretur."

[38] See *Rivet. Apol. Disc.* in *OT*, IV 701, b32–36: "Paci christianorum studentis officium et hoc est, demoliri dogmata, quae pacem civilem perturbant. Prius est, bonum civem esse, quam bonum christianum." Cf. *Votum* in *OT* IV, 676 a30–5: "Hostis non sum, nisi eorum dogmatum quae credo noxia aut pietati aut societati humanae."

truth he accepted was that which served religious peace and social calm. Doctrines that gave occasion for unrest and conflict were inconsistent with the truth, which for Grotius was unimaginable without peace.

Apologetic strategy

In his apologetic work Grotius refrained from proving the truth of Christian doctrines, and thus disconnected apologetics from dogmatics. He did not consider it necessary to appeal to doctrines, at least in his apology for the Christian faith. In this he distinguished himself from virtually all the previous defenders of the Christian faith, but brought down on his head the criticism and reproaches of his contemporaries.

His brother Willem was quick to foresee this. As early as 1620 he predicted that many Christians would find the work lacking in essential things that, in their opinion, the author ought not to have omitted, such as the doctrines of the trinity and the divinity of Christ. It was obvious that they would draw from this the conclusion that Grotius himself doubted these doctrines, said Willem.[39]

Grotius felt that his brother had misunderstood him. He defended himself against the charge that he had passed over Christian doctrines in this work, and explained:

> It speaks for itself that I am not explaining the dogmas of the Christian faith, but my aim is that unbelievers, pagans, Jews and Mohammedans may know the Christian religion to be the true one, and take its dogmas from our sacred Scriptures.[40]

He was thus consciously addressing non-Christians, and allowed himself to be guided by the rhetorical rule that if one wishes to convince, one must base an argument not on one's own assumptions, but on those of one's audience. Grotius added that there could be

---

[39] ARA, 1911 XXIII, n° 32 (letter of W. de Groot to H. Grotius, 2 April 1620): "Non dubito etiam, quin aliqui institutum tuum calumniantes dicturi sint in scripto tuo non probari trinitatem neque divinitatem Christi, imo ne eius quidem, si bene memini, mentionem fieri: nec sufficiet malignis istis hominibus, si respondeamus id alienum a tuo proposito esse, neque enim perfectum a te christianum describi sed eius elementa adumbrari, nam omnia in peiorem sumere consueti, si quid tale a te praeteritum vident, id pro eo ac si de ipso dogmate dubites habituri sunt."

[40] *BW* II, n° 600 (to W. de Groot, 12 April 1620), pp. 30–1: "Res ipsa loquitur me non explicare dogmata christianae fidei christianis, sed hoc agere ut impii, ethnici, iudaei, mahometistae agnoscant veram esse religionem christianam, atque eius dogmata deinde petitum eant ex sacris nostris literis."

no place in his argument for the dogmas of the trinity and the divinity of Christ, because not a single outsider would be attracted to the
Christian faith by them. On the contrary, he stated, anyone who
attempted to prove these doctrines from any evidence but Scripture
was wasting his time.[41]

Many years later, when he was confronted with the accusation of
Socinianism, he again explained his apologetic strategy. Conscious
of what Junius had taught him, he offered no proof of the trinity
because he was in discussion with atheists, pagans, Jews and Muslims,
all of whom had to be led towards the Holy Scriptures, so that they
could derive such dogmas from them, for they would be unable to
understand them unless God revealed himself to them.[42]

In his *Eirenicum*, which we mentioned above, Junius had stated
that the authority of the Scriptures was the common principle of all
Christians, on the grounds of which everyone could come to the
truth of the Christian faith. The only thing that matters for a Christian,
according to Junius, is the acceptance of the Scriptures, in which
God himself reveals his truth.[43]

The conviction that outsiders cannot be convinced of the truth of
Christian doctrines by reasonable arguments, but only by the authority of Scripture, had found its classical statement in the theology of
Thomas Aquinas. In his *Summa contra gentiles* (1259–64) Thomas had
distinguished the natural from the supernatural knowledge of God:
natural theology is based on natural human reason, which can sup-
ply proof of the existence of God, his unity and so on. Supernatural
theology rests on revelation, and is beyond all human reason, as in

---

[41] *BW* II, n° 600, p. 31: "Dogmata περὶ τοῦ Τρίαδος, καὶ περὶ τῆς τοῦ Χριστοῦ
Θεότητος, inter argumenta locum habere non potuerunt. Neminem enim ista ad
christianam doctrinam allicient adhuc alienum: imo operam ludunt qui ista aliter
quam ex sacris paginis demonstrare conantur. Sacrarum autem paginarum bene
fundata auctoritate, debent et ista probata censeri."

[42] *BW* X, n° 3917 (to G.J. Vossius, 1 January 1639), p. 12: "Triados probationem
in eo libro directe aggressus non sum memor ejus, quod a viro magno socero tuo
[sc. Junio] audieram, peccasse Plessaeum et alios, quod rationibus a natura petitis
et Platonicis saepe non valde appositis testimoniis astruere voluissent rem, non ponendam in illa cum atheis, paganis, judaeis, mahumetistis disputatione, qui omnes ad
sacras literas ducendi sunt, ut inde talia hauriant, quae nisi Deo semet patefaciente
cognosci nequeunt." Cf. *BW*, VIII n° 3397, p. 814: "Dat ick de Deo niet en heb
bewesen dan generalia is waer, omdat ick houde, dat men ex naturalibus rationibus
niet verder en can gaen. Ende staet mij voor, dat doctor Junius in 't boeck van
Plessis quaed vond, dat hij meende trinitatem te bewijsen met natuirlijcke redenen,
quod ille putabat esse causam prodere, cum ea res probari nequeat, nisi ex revelatione."

[43] See Junius, *Eirenicum*, in *Opuscula*, pp. 436–9.

the knowledge of the trinity.[44] According to Thomas one cannot convince an opponent of Christianity of this supernatural truth by using rational arguments, but only by the authority of the Scriptures, confirmed by God's miracles, for no one will believe this truth unless God reveals himself.[45]

b) *Method*

Humanist dialectic

Laurentius Valla

Around 1440 Laurentius Valla completed his *Dialecticae Disputationes*, at least the first version of the work that later came to be known under that title.[46] As early as the fourteenth century Petrarch had complained of the sterile and diffuse dialectical systems of his time. Early humanist criticism of medieval dialectic reached its climax in Valla's work.[47]

Valla keenly criticised the use of language in such Aristotelian philosophers as Avicenna and Averroes, whom he described as barbarians in their use of Latin and Greek, and thus disqualified as

---

[44] Thomas, *ScG* I 3, 8: "Est autem in his quae de Deo confitemur duplex veritatis modus. Quaedam namque vera sunt de Deo quae omnem facultatem humanae rationis excedunt, ut Deum esse trinum et unum. Quaedam vero sunt ad quae etiam ratio naturalis pertingere potest, sicut est Deum esse, Deum esse unum, et alia huiusmodi; quae etiam philosophi demonstrative de Deo probaverunt, ducti naturalis lumine rationis."

[45] Thomas, *ScG* I 9, 28: "Sed quia tales rationes ad secundam veritatem haberi non possunt, non debet esse ad hoc intentio ut adversarius rationibus convincatur, sed ut eius rationes, quas contra veritatem habet, solvantur; cum veritati fidei ratio naturalis contraria esse non possit, ut ostensum est. Singularis vero modus convincendi adversarium contra huiusmodi veritatem est ex auctoritate Scripturae divinitus confirmata miraculis: quae enim supra rationem humanam sunt, non credimus nisi Deo revelante."

[46] A critical edition of the work appeared not long ago under the title *Laurentii Vallae Repastinatio dialectice et philosophie* (ed. G. Zippel), 2 vols, Padua 1982. According to Zippel the title corresponds to the original title of the first version, but the work became better known in its second version, which since the Cologne edition of 1530 has borne the title *Dialecticarum Disputationes libri tres*, or *Dialecticae Disputationes* for short. Zippel showed that there was also a third version, with the presumed title *Retractatio totius dialectice cum fundamentis universe philosophie*. We base our account on the second version, which has been known for centuries and is current, the *Dialecticae Disputationes*, and will cite it from the edition in Laurentius Valla, *Opera Omnia*, Scripta in editione Basilensi anno MDXL collecta, Turin 1962.

[47] For a good survey of early humanist criticism of scholastic dialectic see C. Vasoli, *La dialettica e la retorica dell'umanesimo. 'Invenzione' e 'metodo' nella cultura del XV e XVI secolo*, Milan 1968, pp. 28–40.

philosophers.[48] He despised scholastic jargon, which in his view concealed abstract and lifeless thought, and preferred the living current speech of the people, in which he saw a concrete reflection of human reality.[49] In his attempt to renew dialectic he sought to join hands with the classical rhetorical tradition of Quintilian and Cicero. In his opinion dialectic must be a succinct and simple matter, which was merely an auxiliary of rhetorical practice.[50]

Valla indicated the direction that a renewal must take, but he did not elaborate a new system of rhetoric himself.[51] This task was to be undertaken by Agricola.

Rudolph Agricola

The scholar Roelof Huusman of Groningen, better known as Rudolph Agricola, wrote his great work *De inventione dialectica* around 1480, though it was not published until 1515.[52]

Agricola did not wish to belittle the greatness of Aristotle, but he accused the Stagirite of failing to give a clear definition of dialectic.[53] Following in the footsteps of Cicero he defined dialectic as the science of explanation or argument.[54] This science consisted, as Cicero

---

[48] Valla, *DD* I, p. 644: "Nam Avicenna et Averrois plane barbari fuerunt, nostrae linguae prorsus ignari et graeca vix tincti. Quorum etiamsi magni viri fuerint, ubi de vi verborum agitur, quae plurima sunt in philosophia quaestiones: quantula debet esse autoritas?"

[49] Valla, *DD* I, p. 685: "Melius populus quam philosophus loquitur."

[50] Valla, *DD* II, p. 694: "Et vere possum adducere, quia nulla mihi doctrina brevior faciliorque quam dialectica videtur, quam aliis maioribus servit, [. . .]."

[51] Eloquently shown in D.R. Kelley, *Foundations of Modern Historical Scholarship. Language, Law and History in the French Renaissance*, New York/London 1970, pp. 28–39. See also S.I. Camporeale, 'Lorenzo Valla, Repastinatio, liber primus: retorica e linguaggio' in *Lorenzo valla e l'umanesimo italiano. Atti del convegno internazionale di studi umanistici (Parma, 18–19 ottobre 1984)*, Padua 1986, pp. 217–40; and H.B. Gerl, *Rhetorik als Philosophie: Lorenzo Valla* (Humanistische Bibliothek, I 13), Munich 1974, pp. 191–231.

[52] We cite from the standard edition: R. Agricola, *De inventione dialectica libri omnes et integri & recogniti, qui iam olim quidem in publicum prodierunt, sed trunci ac mutili nec minus item depravati, nunc demum ad autographi exemplaris fidem*, Cologne 1539.

[53] Agric. *DID* I, p. 15: "Ego Aristotelem summo ingenio, doctrina, eloquentia, rerum peritia, prudentiaque (et ut semel dicam) summum quidem hominem, sed hominem tamen fuisse puto, hoc est, quem et latere aliquid potuerit, quique ut non omnia primus invenerit, ita aliis post se invenienda aliqua reliquerit: qui etiam non omnia quae invenerat, crediderit in vulgus prodenda et nonnunquam fortasse contradicendi studio, quo maxima fere tentantur ingenia, non tam quid ipse sentiret, quam contra quod alius sensisset, dicendum putaret."

[54] Agric. *DID* II, p. 193; "Erit ergo nobis hoc pacto definita dialectice, ars probabiliter de qualibet re proposita disserendi, prout cuiusque natura capax esse fidei poterit." Cf. Cicero, *Topica*, II, 6.

had already stated, of two parts: 1) finding the arguments (*inventio*); and 2) judging or arranging the material found (*iudicium*).[55] Agricola regarded the first part of dialectic as the more important. Arguments could be found in 'topics' (*loci*), that is general views or sources of argument. These *loci* are general categories with common characteristics and form the reservoir from which arguments to support a convincing thesis can be drawn in every situation.[56] Agricola was unfortunately rather brief about the second part of dialectic, the ordering (*ordo*) or arrangement of arguments.[57]

Agricola's work broke new ground and became the standard work of sixteenth century humanist dialectic.

Petrus Ramus

In the twenties of the sixteenth century the Paris teacher Johannes Sturm introduced his pupils to the works of Agricola. One of them, Petrus Ramus (Pierre de la Ramée),[58] is said to have attracted attention in 1536 when he defended his thesis for the degree of master of arts, "Everything that Aristotle is supposed to have said is incorrect".[59]

Ramus developed into one of the most important philosophers of his day. He argued for a natural and practical dialectic, and simplified

---

[55] Agric. *DID* I, 178: "Cum sit enim solum istud propriumque dialectices munus, posse de qualibet re probabiliter, quantum ipsius natura patitur, argumentari: quod totum [. . .] duabus comprehensum est partibus; quarum una excogitandi argumenti viam docet, quam inveniendi vocant, cui parti omnis de locis destinatur disputatio: altera, cum inventum est argumentum formam quandam argumentandi, hoc est certam explorandi argumenti tradit regulam [. . .] ea dicitur iudicandi pars." Cf. Cicero, *Top.* II 6: "Cum omnis ratio diligens disserendi duas habeat partes, unam inveniendi alteram iudicandi, utriusque princeps, ut mihi quidem videtur, Aristoteles fuit."

[56] Agric. *DID* I, 9: "Haec igitur communia, quia perinde ut quicquid dici ulla de re potest, ita argumenta omnia inter se continent: idcirco locos vocaverunt, quod in eis velut receptu et thesauro quodam, omnia faciendae fidei instrumenta sint reposita. Non ergo aliud est locus, quam communis quaedam rei nota, cuius admonitu, quid in quaque re probabile sit, potest inveniri."

[57] Agric. *DID* III, p. 413; "Cum sit autem dispositio (ut Cicero inquit) ordo et distributio rerum quae demonstrat, quid quibus locis conveniat et collocandum sit, non abs re fuerit fortasse videre in primis, quotuplex sit ordo rerum quem in disponendo sequamur."

[58] The most important study of Ramus is still W.J. Ong, *Ramus. Method and the Decay of Dialogue. From the art of discourse to the art of reason*, Cambridge (Mass.) 1958. See also W. Risse, *Logik der Neuzeit*, Bad Cannstatt 1964, vol. 1, pp. 122–200, and N. Bruyère, *Méthode et dialectique dans l'oeuvre de La Ramée*, Paris 1984, pp. 41–84.

[59] *Quaecumque ab Aristotele dicta essent, commentitia esse.* For this thesis see Risse, *Logik*, p. 123. The historicity of the report that Ramus defended this thesis is not entirely beyond doubt.

the system of Agricola. He thought that dialectic could arrive at an absolutely certain knowledge of the truth.[60] Like Agricola he divided dialectic into the finding and the judging of arguments. He distinguished two sorts of arguments, which he described in classic Aristotelian terms as regular and irregular: regular arguments were elaborated in accordance with the rules of logic, and were convincing in themselves; irregular arguments consisted of data that eluded logic, and derived their conviction from external authority.[61] Divine and human testimonies belong among the latter class of arguments.[62]

Unlike Agricola, Ramus believed that the second division of dialectic (*iudicium*), which he also called 'method', was the more important. The essence of method is the ordering and arrangement of arguments into a coherent whole, a chain of arguments. He stated that a single method of proof ought to be adopted in every scientific discipline, according to which one advanced deductively from the generally known to the unknown.[63]

Ramus' system appeared attractive in its simplicity and pedagogic usefulness for the teaching of logic at the humanist schools and academies that were founded during or after the Reformation and were not permeated by scholastic tradition. This dialectic was applied not only by philosophers, but also by theologians,[64] jurists[65] and mathematicians.[66] Ramism found its most important following not so much in high culture, but in a variety of forms that were mixed with traditional Aristotelian logic.[67]

---

[60] Pierre de la Ramée, *Dialectique (1555)*. Édition critique avec introduction, notes et commentaires de Michel Dassonville, Geneva 1964, pp. 61–2.

[61] Ramus, *Dial.*, p. 64: "L'argument donques est artificiel ou inartificiel, comme Aristote le distribue au deuziesme de la *Rhétorique*." Cf. Aristot., *Rhet.* I [not II] 1355b 35.

[62] Ramus, *Dial.*, p. 98.

[63] Ramus, *Dial.*, pp. 144–5: "Méthode est un jugement discursif de divers axiomes homegenée [*sic!*], qui sont proposez pour estre du tout et absolument précédens de nature, plus évidens, plus clers et notoires, en telle sorte que l'on juge de la convenance qu'ils ont entre eux et sont plus facilement recues et retenus en la mémoire. [. . .] Et ainsi des axiomes homogenées, le premier de notice est disposé et mis au premier lieu et rang, le second au second, le troisiesme au troisiesme, et ainsi conséquemment. Et pource la méthode procède tousjours des choses génralles et universelles aux singulières. Car par ce ceul chemin l'on procède des antécédens qui nous sont du tout et absolument plus cogneus, à déclarer les conséquens incogneus. Ceste méthode est singulière et unique."

[64] Cf. J. Moltmann, 'Zur Bedeutung des Petrus Ramus für Philosophie und Theologie im Calvinismus', *Zeitschrift für Kirchengeschichte*, 68 (1957), 295–318.

[65] Risse, *Logik*, pp. 68–70.

[66] See J.J. Verdonk, *Petrus Ramus en de wiskunde*, Assen 1966.

[67] See Ong, *Ramus*, pp. 295–306.

Petrus Molinaeus and Rudolph Snellius

When Grotius matriculated as an undergraduate at the University of Leiden in 1594, humanistic scholarship there was at its zenith.[68] One of the obligatory subjects he had to study was logic. Teaching in that subject was dominated by the work of Aristotle,[69] but that did not mean a total rejection of the simpler and more practically oriented dialectic of such humanist authors as Ramus.[70] Grotius followed the lectures of Petrus Molinaeus, who was professor extraordinarius of logic at Leiden from 1593 to August 1595.[71] Molinaeus wrote a concise and clear work, which summarised his lectures, entitled *Elementa Logica* (1598).[72]

Molinaeus started from the logic of Aristotle, though here and there he differed from the Stagirite and followed later philosophers, including Ramus. He defined logic as the science that supplied the instruments with which to discover truth.[73] Like Agricola and Ramus he distinguished between the finding and the judging of arguments, but he added that judgement must not follow the finding but be simultaneous with it.[74] Like Ramus he divided all available arguments into regular and irregular.[75] Irregular arguments consist of divine and human testimonies, which derive their force not from reason but from the authority that emanates from them. He stated that in theology one is dependent on such divine testimonies as miracles and

---

[68] See W.J.M. van Eysinga, 'Iets over de Groots jongelingsjaren', *De Gids*, 105 (1941), 36–67, and better, J. Taal, 'Het geestelijk milieu van Grotius te Leiden', *Jaarboekje voor geschiedenis en oudheidkunde van Leiden en Rijnland* [= *Leids Jaarboekje*], 36 (1944), 124–42.

[69] See F. Sassen, 'Het oudste wijsgerig onderwijs te Leiden (1575–1619)', in *Mededeelingen der Nederlandsche Akademie van Wetenschappen*, New Series, 4, 1 (1941), 1–45; but better P. Dibon, *L'Enseignement philosophique dans les universités Néerlandaises à l'époque pré-cartésienne (1575–1650)*, Leiden 1954, pp. 1–79.

[70] See P. Dibon, 'L'influence de Ramus aux universités néerlandaises du 17e siècle', in *Actes du XIème congrès international de philosophie, Bruxelles, 20–26 août 1953*, 14 [Volume complémentaire et communications du colloque de logique] Amsterdam/Louvain 1953, pp. 307–11.

[71] On Petrus Molinaeus (1568–1658): J. Meursius, *Athenae Batavae*, Leiden 1625, pp. 173–4; *BWNG*, II, pp. 537–9; Haag, V, pp. 800–24, and G. Cohen, *Écrivains français en Hollande*, Paris 1920, pp. 176–9. For Molinaeus' influence on Grotius: F. Sassen, 'Grotius: philosophe aristotélicien', *Grotiana*, IX (1941–2), 38–53.

[72] P. Molinaeus, *Elementa logica*, Leiden 1598. In what follows we refer to the edition of Leiden 1607.

[73] Molinaeus, *Elementa*, p. 42: "Logica est ars effectiva instrumentorum ad inveniendum verum."

[74] *Ibid.*, pp. 107–8.

[75] *Ibid.*, pp. 117–19.

prophecies, which give the certainty that human testimony and reasoning can never offer.[76]

Grotius referred to this work by Molinaeus in a programme of study he drew up for B. Aubéry Dumaurier. In this he explicitly placed logic first in the order of the sciences. He advised the young Frenchman to begin with the subject, which is the instrument of both contemplative and practical philosophy. He did not think it necessary to read Aristotle himself, for a compendium such as that of Molinaeus or Crellius would be sufficient.[77]

During his Leiden years Grotius also immersed himself in mathematics and astronomy.[78] His teacher in this field was Rudolphus Snellius (Rudolph Snel van Royen).[79] Snellius had studied at several German universities, where he had fallen under the spell of Petrus Ramus' philosophy. He wrote a number of philosophical and mathematical handbooks, which offered introductions to or commentaries on several aspects of Ramus' logic.[80] Though he was first greeted with some reservations in Leiden as a Ramist, he was allowed the freedom to stand up for his ideas.[81]

Looking back on his academic career Snellius related that he tried

[76] *Ibid.*, pp. 179–80.

[77] *BW* I, n° 402 (15 December 1615), pp. 384–5: "Quare cum philosophia omnis divisa sit in contemplativum et activam, hanc praecipue curare debes, illam non ultra quam ut huic ancilletur. Commune utrique instrumentum est logica, a qua proinde initium fieri ratio imperat. Hanc nolim te petere ex ipso Aristotele–esset enim id prolixius et passim multa occurrunt nullius aut modicae frugis-sufficiet si compendium aliquid legeres, quale est Molinaei aut Crellii, [...]." By the latter Grotius was undoubtedly referring to F. Crellius, *Isagoge logica in duas partes distributa, in communem et propriam*, Neustadt 1581. This book was in Grotius' library: see Molhuysen, 'Bibliotheek', n° 157.

[78] Brandt-Cattenburgh, p. 8.

[79] Little is known of Rudolph Snellius (1546–1613): see J. Meursius, *Athenae Batavae*, Leiden 1625, pp. 117–22; *NNBW*, VII, cols 1152–5; J.A. Vollgraff, 'Pierre de la Ramée (1515–1572) et Willibrord Snel van Royen (1580–1620)' in *Janus. Archives internationales pour l'histoire de la médecine et la géographie médicinale*, Leiden 1913, pp. 596–625; and K. van Berkel, 'Universiteit en natuurwetenschap in de 17ᵉ eeuw, in het bijzonder in de Republiek' in *Natuurwetenschappen van Renaissance tot Darwin, Thema's uit de wetenschapsgeschiedenis*, ed. H.A.M. Snelders and K. van Berkel, The Hague 1981, pp. 116–20.

[80] For a summary of Snellius' works see Vollgraff, 'Pierre de la Ramée', 610.

[81] Snellius' appointment as professor extraordinarius of mathmatical sciences (1581) included a clause stipulating that it was to apply until someone more experienced in mathematics was found; see P.C. Molhuysen, *Bronnen tot de geschiedenis der Leidsche Universiteit: 1574–1610*, [RGP, 20] The Hague 1913, p. 26.

to teach his pupils the deductive method of proof, and impressed on them that this method was applicable not only to mathematics but to all the sciences.[82]

Legal dialectic

Since the beginning of the sixteenth century several jurists had been incorporating the achievements of humanist dialectic in their own field.[83] The Italian legal scholar Petrus Andreas Gammarus (Pietro Andrea Gambari), for example, published a legal dialectic in 1507, in which the topics (*loci*) of argumentation take centre stage.[84] Gammarus and his followers developed a rhetorical dialectic, which was strongly inspired by Cicero. So too was the Dutchman Nicolaus Everardius (Nicolas Everarts), who in his *Topicorum seu de locis legalibus liber* (1516) stated that the *loci* were the key to all the arguments that could prove or disprove the truth of a matter.[85]

Legal dialectic was an applied dialectic. The lawyers, who were eclectic and practically oriented, did not make a new contribution to the logical discussions of their time. In the second half of the sixteenth century such legal scholars as Freigius, Vulteius and Althusius turned to the method of Petrus Ramus. In its simplicity and practical application his deductive method also proved attractive to those who were not at all familiar with Ramus' philosophy.[86]

Grotius too appears to have been open to the influence of Ramism. At least, it seems to us that his first legal work *De iure praedae*, probably written between 1604 and 1606, bore its traces.[87] In the introduction

---

[82] R. Snellius, *Commentarius in Rhetoricam Audomari Talaei*, Leiden 1618, "Nicolao Zeistio Voerdenati Rudolphus Snellius", [fols 6–7].

[83] See D. Maffei, *Gli inizi dell'umanesimo giuridico*, Milan 1956, and Th. Viehweg, *Topik und Jurisprudenz*, Munich 1953. Good surveys can be found in H.E. Troje, 'Wissenschaftlichkeit und System in der Jurisprudenz des 16. Jahrhunderts', in *Philosophie und Rechtswissenschaft: zum Problem ihrer Beziehung im 19. Jahrhundert*, eds J. Blühdorn and J. Ritter, Frankfurt am Main 1969, pp. 63–88, and in Risse, *Logik*, I, pp. 67–72.

[84] P.A. Gammarus, *Legalis dialectica, in qua de modo argumentandi et locis argumentorum legaliter disputatur*, Bologna 1507.

[85] Nicolaus Everardus, *Topicorum seu de locis legalibus liber*, Louvain 1516, p. 1: "Loci appelantur sedes quaedam e quibus in rem quamvis confirmandam vel refellendam necessaria vel probabilia ducuntur argumenta, [...]. Arguendo et disputando veritas invenitur.' Grotius owned a copy of this work: see Molhuysen, "Bibliotheek", n° 225.

[86] See Risse, *Logik*, pp. 68–9 and Troje, 'Wissenschaftlichkeit', 77–8.

[87] *IPC* [= *BG* n° 684].

to this work he justifies his method, explaining that he has used two
kinds of proof.[88] The first method of argument is determined by natural reason, and is later described as 'regular proof' (*demonstratio arti-
ficialis*). The second sort is 'irregular' (*demonstratio inartificialis*), and consists
of an appeal to the authority of divine and human testimonies.[89]

In the following section Grotius explains to his readers the order
in which he will arrange his arguments. He starts from what is generally and entirely true, and advances gradually towards the specific
problem.[90] Then he states:

> But just as mathematicians, before they proceed to the proofs them-
> selves, usually begin by stating several general concepts with which
> everyone will easily agree, so that there is a fixed point to which the
> proof of what follows can return, so we too, in order to have a solid
> basis on which the rest can safely be erected, will indicate some rules
> and very general laws, by way of anticipations, which one must not
> so much learn as recall.[91]

Ramus' deductive arrangement is clearly at work here. The question
is: was Grotius himself aware of the Frenchman's work? We have been
unable to find any evidence that he was. Probably he had learned
this method of proof at second hand,[92] perhaps through a legal source
as intermediary.[93] His association of the deductive method with mathematics may suggest that he had the example of Snellius in mind.

In his *De iure belli* (1625) Grotius methodically embroidered the

---

[88] *IPC* I, pp. 5–7.

[89] For Grotius' method of proof in this work see P. Haggenmacher, *Grotius et la
doctrine de la guerre juste*, [Paris 1983], pp. 57–9.

[90] *IPC* I, p. 7: "Ordo autem instituto huic convenit, ut initio quid universim
atque in genere verum sit videamus, idque ipsum contrahamus paulatim ad proposi-
tam facti speciem."

[91] *IPC* I, 7: "Sed quemadmodum mathematici, priusquam ipsas demonstrationes
aggrediantur, communes quasdam solent notiones de quibus inter omnes facile constat praescribere, ut fixum aliquid sit, in retro desinat sequentium probatio, ita nos
quo fundamentum situm habeamus, cui tuto superstruantur caetera, regulas quasdam et leges maxime generales indicabimus, velut anticipationes, quas non tam discere aliquis, quam reminisci debeat."

[92] Grotius describes this system of dialectic arguement as *methodus*, while the concept of 'method' in Ramus referred exclusively to the deductive arrangement of the
arguments.

[93] I am, however, unable to point to a source. R. Feenstra remarked on the
influence of Ramus in Grotius' *Inleiding tot de Hollandsche Rechtsgeleerdheid*, and suggested the jurist Freigius as a possible intermediary. See R. Feenstra, 'La systématique du droit dans l'oeuvre de Grotius', in *La sistematica giuridica. Storia, teoria e
problemi attuali* [Biblioteca internazionale di cultura, 122] Rome 1991, p. 338.

framework of his youthful treatise.[94] In the foreword to his great work he stated that his first care had been to derive the proofs of natural law from several notions that were so certain that no one could deny them without doing violence to himself.[95] Thus he sought to build his system of law on an absolutely solid foundation.

Grotius' apologetic work

Order

In the introduction to his *De veritate* Grotius said that he had added a new work to existing apologetic literature because he wanted to use his own judgement (*iudicium*). To do so, he had selected what he found most convincing from books old and new, and set out the arguments with which he agreed in a certain order (*ordo*).[96]

The way in which he arranged the arguments in the first book of this work appears to be deductive, in conformity with the method of Ramus. He starts from what is absolutely certain and generally known, so that he has a firm foundation on which to build the rest of his case.[97] The foundation on which his argument rests is the rational belief, confirmed by all peoples, that a divine being exists.[98] From this absolutely certain knowledge of God's existence it is possible to deduce as self-evident his unity and other qualities: his perfection, eternity, omnipotence, omniscience and absolute goodness. Then follows the proof that God is the cause of all things, and that

---

[94] Cf. Haggenmacher, *Grotius*, pp. 447–56.

[95] *IBP* Prol. 39, p. 14: "Prium mihi cura hoc fuit, ut eorum quae ad ius naturae pertinent probationes referrem ad notiones quasdam tam certas ut eas nemo negare possit, nisi sibi vim inferat."

[96] *VRC* I 1, p. 102: "Quam ob causam videri potest magis ex usu fuisse alicuius illorum in sermonem popularem versio, quam inchoatio novi operis. Sed quid alii hac de re judicaturi sint, nescio: te quidem, tam benigno ac facili judice, facile spero me posse absolvi, si dicam, me lectis non illis tantum, sed et iudaeorum pro iudaica vetere, et christianorum pro christiana religione scriptis, *uti voluisse meo qualicunque judicio*, et animo dare negatam, cum id scriberem, corpori libertatem. [. . .] Itaque selegi ex veteribus ac novis, quae mihi se probabant maxime, omissis argumentis, quae parum mihi ponderis habere videbantur, et auctoritate eorum librorum, quos subdititios esse aut certo sciebam, aut merito suspicabar. Quibus autem ipse assentiebar, ea et *ordine certo* disposui, [. . .]". (Italics mine, JPH.)

[97] Cf. *IPC* I, p. 7.

[98] *VRC* I 2, p. 3: "Ac primo quidem libro, ut ostendam, non esse rem inanem religionem, ab eius fundamento ordior, quod est, numen esse aliquod."

his providence guides the cosmos. God's providence in turn evokes the expectation of a life after this life. On the grounds of the plausibility of this assumption, he states that human bliss must lie in the hereafter, and that those who would gain it must seek the true religion.

In the second book he proceeds to prove that Christianity is that true faith, and in the third he makes the case that one may rely entirely on the wholly accurate and authoritative testimony of the Bible for the content of Christianity. Thus the arguments of the first book hang together as links in a long chain, which is continued in the second and third books.

Reason and testimony
In the foreword to his edition of Stobaeus' *Dicta Poetarum* (1623) Grotius depicts the stages of historical development through which religious truth and certainty have passed: it began tentatively with the ancient poets, who although they had developed a few profound insights, still often sinned against the truth. Plutarch was right to consider that the statements of poets had to be tested against the judgement of stricter teachers, the philosophers. But philosophers too could err, for in religious matters the truth cannot be discovered by human reason alone. The ancient Hebrews were the first who added the certainty of divine revelation to their reason. And Christians ought to be all the more grateful to God, who has revealed to them everything that concerns the righteous life with such certainty that reasonable minds are left with no grounds to doubt it. For it is clear that what the prophets and the apostles handed down to us originated from God, and it is clear in the only way in which it can be: namely the wholly reliable testimony of the miracles performed by Christ and the apostles. That is why we are referred from the poets to the philosophers, and in turn to a third tribunal to which we must appeal, namely the prophets and apostles. Grotius concluded that we ought to accept as valid only those statements that can be upheld before this court.[99]

---

[99] Stob., *Dicta Poetarum*, Prol., pp. cij sqq., "Optime enim docet [sc. Plutarchus] poetarum dicta exigenda ad ea quae severiores professores, philosophi scilicet, dictant. Sed ne sic quidem vitatur periculum, nam et in his ipsis quae rationis dictu cognosci aliquatenus possunt, falli videmus philosophos, unde tanta inter ipsos placitorum discrepantia; et sunt quaedam res eius generis ut earum veritatem sola humana ratio per se indagare non possit. In quibus rebus cum alii philosophi saepe ab eo quod res est aberrant, tum ipse etiam in eo quem dixi libro Plutarchus, ut

Grotius was convinced that human reason alone did not offer a firm enough foothold to trace divine truth, and that full certainty was dependent on divine revelation. He saw a fluid transition from reason to revelation; reason is of divine origin,[100] while revelation in turn cannot be other than reasonable. Revelation supplies no more than a confirmation and assurance of what reason had already discovered.[101] Grotius puts the same argument in his apologetic work: reason can show only the truths of natural religion. To attempt to say any more than this about God's will or essence by appealing to reason alone was in his view a perilous undertaking because, as Plato had already admitted, nothing could be known about them without divine revelation.[102]

But in his presentation of the evidence Grotius does not invoke divine revelation, because his discussion is with non-Christians. His strategy, as we saw, is to lead them all to the books of the Old and New Testaments, so that they can learn from them for themselves what they could never understand without God's revelation.[103] In the

---

cum de providentia agit et de his quae post hanc vitam sunt exspectanda. Multum ergo Deo Optimo Maximo debuerunt Hebraei veteres, plus eidem christiani debemus, quibus omnia quae ad vitam recte instituendam momentum aliquod habent, ea certitudine sunt patefacta ut apud probos animos nullus dubitandi relinquatur locus. Nam a Deo profecta esse ea quae prophetae et apostoli nobis prodiderunt constant, quo unico modo constare id potest et quantum potest, editis prodigiis et ipsorum testimonio, cui fidem adstruit vitae innocentia, nullum ex mendacio lucrum, et multa mala, interdum mors quoque, ob id testimonium tolerata. [. . .] Sicut ergo a poetis ad philosophos, ita et a poetis est a philosophis ad tribunal tertium, hoc est ad prophetas et apostolos, nobis provocandum est; atque ea demum dicta rata habenda quae in hoc auditorio stare possunt." See also *Mel.*, App. I, pp. 167–8.

[100] Cf. *IPC* I, p. 2.

[101] For this see Posthumus Meyjes, *Mel.*, Introd., pp. 30–1.

[102] *VRC* III 12, pp. 131–2: "Tum vero quaecumque in primo libro ostensa sunt congruere rectae rationi, puta Deum esse et quidem unicum, [. . .] Ultra haec *pro comperto* aliquid affirmare aut de Dei natura aut de eius voluntate, solo ductu humanae rationis quam sit intutum ac fallax, docent tot dissonantia non scholarum modo inter se sed et singulorum philosophorum placita. [. . .] Quare optime Plato horum nihil sciri posse dicebat sine oraculo. Iam vero nullum proferri potest oraculum, quod tale revera esse majoribus testimoniis constet, quam ea sunt quae in libris Novi Foederis continentur." Cf. *Bewijs*, pp. 83–4: "Veel dieper in de wil of 't wesen Gods te treden/ Alleenelyk gestiert door 't roer van onser reden,/ is al te vol gevaers, het welk de saek bewijst,/ Alsoo den eene laekt het gunt den ander prijst,/ En soo strijd eeuwelyk het wanen met het wanen,/ Onseekerlyk gestelt op slibberige banen./[. . .] Daerom seyd Plato wel, niet kander sij *gewis*/ van deese saeken meer dan ons geopent is/ Door Goddelyke spraek. Nu van Gods Openbaringh/ En kan niet sijn bedaght een *seekerder* ervaringh,/ dan die ons is gegunt ten tyde van 't verbond/ Geleert door Christus self en syner kneghten mond.' (My italics, JPH.)

[103] Cf. *BW* II, n° 600 (to W. de Groot, 12 April 1620), pp. 30–1.

third book he demonstrates the reliability and credibility of the books of the Bible, but he does not argue from their testimony. He wishes to convince all unbelievers and believers in other faiths of the truth of the Christian religion, using the generally valid means of proof, that is rational arguments and human testimonies. Since he was convinced that reason fell lamentably short, he found himself dependent above all on human testimonies.

Certainty and probability

In the second book of *De veritate* Grotius remarks that there are different types of evidence, depending on the nature of the matter to be proved: in mathematics, the method of proof is different from that appropriate in questions of fact, where one is dependent on wholly reliable proofs and thoroughly worked out testimonies. They are not enough to provide observable or demonstrable evidence, but they can convince others.[104]

Grotius knew that if one appealed to testimonies one was dependent on human opinions, which could only offer probability and not certainty. This is a familiar tenet of Aristotelian philosophy, with which he was well acquainted. In *De iure belli* he invokes Aristotle when stating that it was impossible to reach the same degree of certainty in ethics as in mathematics.[105] He agreed with the Stagirite that opinions only have any force when there is a consensus, that is in so far as they are confirmed by all mankind, by most of them or by the wisest.[106] This description contains a variable quantitative element, which can be used to measure the probability of knowl-

---

[104] *VRC* II 23, p. 118: "Si quis allatis hactenus argumentis pro christiana religione satis sibi factum non putet, sed magis urgentia desideret, scire debet, pro rerum diversitate, diversa quoque esse probandi genera, alia in mathematicis, alia de affectionibus corporum, alia circa deliberationes, alia ubi facti est quaestio; in quo genere sane standum est nulla suspicione laborantibus testimoniis, quod ni admittitur non modo omnis historiae usus periit et medicinae quoque pars magna, sed et omnis quae inter parentes liberosque est pietas, ut quos haut aliter noscamus. Voluit autem Deus id, quod credi a nobis vellet, sic ut illud ipsum credere tamquam obedientiam a nobis acceptaret, non ita evidenter patere, ut quae sensu aut demonstratione percipiuntur, sed quantum satis esset ad fidem faciendam, remque persuadendam homini non pertinaci, [. . .]."
[105] Cf. *IBP* II xxiii, 1, p. 440: "Verissimum est quod scripsit Aristoteles, in moralibus non aeque ut in mathematicis disciplinis certitudinem inveniri, [. . .]."
[106] *IBP* II, xxiii, 4, p. 442: "Nam ἔνδοξα, sive probabilia sunt, Aristotele teste, quae omnibus videntur, aut plurimis, aut certe sapientibus; iisque rursum aut omnibus aut pluribus aut praestantioribus." Cf. Aristotle, *Top.*, 100a 25–100b 23.

edge: the greater the consensus, the greater the probability.[107] From
this it is a small step to the conclusion that if there is a universal
consensus, the probability becomes a certainty. Aristotle himself
appeared to have taken this step in his *Nicomachean Ethics*, in which
he states that what appears true to all mankind must indeed be
true.[108] Grotius too saw universal consensus as a criterion of objective
truth. In his legal work *De iure belli* he observed that he had incorporated as many different testimonies as possible, because he was
convinced that a universal consensus must have a universal cause.[109]

Grotius therefore could not offer the readers of his apologetic work
intrinsic certainty using rational arguments and historical testimonies. He
refused to appeal to a separate extrinsic certainty, to which Reformation
theologians had resorted.[110] Melanchthon, for example, had thought
that theology possessed a certainty of its own, distinct from that of
logic, that relied on divine revelation as contained in the Scriptures.
Man is confirmed in that certainty by the aid of the Holy Spirit.[111]
In the same way Calvin had argued that the truth of the Christian
faith is based on the divinity of the Scriptures, of which man has

---

[107] Cf. H. von Arnim, 'Das Ethische in Aristoteles' Topik', *Sitzungsberichte der Akademie
der Wissenschaften*, 205, 4 (1934), 335; "Bei einem streng logischem, d.h. nicht topisch-
dialektischen Beweisverfahren wäre es sinnlos, eine Sache dadurch besser begründen
zu wollen, dass man sie auf verschiedene Weise begründet. Anders beim topisch-
rhetorischem Beweis. Hier ist eine Sache umso besser begründet, je mehr Beweiszeichen
angeführt werden können, die für sie sprechen."

[108] Arist., *Eth. Nic.* 1172b 36–1173a1. For this see K. Oehler, 'Der consensus
omnium als Kriterium der Wahrheit in der antiken Philosophie und der Patristik'
Antike und Abendland, 10 (1961), 103–29.

[109] *IBP* Prol. 40, 15: "Usus sum etiam ad iuris huius probationem testimoniis
philosophorum, historicorum, poetarum, postremo et oratorum, non quod illis indis-
crete credendum sit, [. . .] sed quod ubi multi diversi temporibus ac locis idem pro
certo affirmant, id ad causam universalem referri debeat, quae in nostris quaestionibus alia esse non potest, quam aut recta illatio ex naturae principiis procedens,
aut communis aliquis consensus."

[110] See the excellent and still useful study of K. Heim, *Das Gewissheitsproblem in
der systematischen Theologie bis zu Schleiermacher*, Leipzig 1911, pp. 307–45. Cf. B.J.
Shapiro, *Probability and Certainty in Seventeenth Century England. A Study of the Relationships
between Natural Science, Religion, History, Law and Literature*, Princeton 1983.

[111] Ph. Melanchthon, *Loci communes* [Corpus Reformatorum, 21, 151]: "Sunt nor-
mae certitudinis juxta philosophiam tres: experientia universalis, noticiae principio-
rum et intellectus ordinis in syllogismo. In ecclesia habemus quartam normam
certitudinis patefactionem divinam, quae exstat in libris propheticis et apostolicis.
[. . .] Sed quia res sunt extra judicium humanae mentis positae, languidior est assen-
sio, quae fit, quia mens movetur illis testimoniis et miraculis, et juvatur a Spiritu
sancto ad assentiendum."

absolute certainty through the internal evidence of the Holy Spirit.[112]

Grotius absolutely refused to follow this path. He did not accept the supralogical standpoint of the Reformers, and declined to offer a different kind of certainty guaranteed by Christian revelation.[113] In this respect he followed the tradition of the Christian humanists, which was strongly influenced by Stoic philosophy.[114] In general Christian humanist authors distrusted every form of theological dogmatism, and preferred to observe a certain reticence.

A fine example of this attitude was given by the famous humanist Erasmus of Rotterdam, whose unmistakeable reticence in his discussion with Luther about the freedom of human will had irritated Luther intensely.[115] Erasmus deliberately refrained from appearing as a 'dogmaticus', and admitted that he would rather suspend judgement on this question, because ultimately it was one in which certainty was not attainable. He also frankly confessed that he could be wrong. To him Christian doctrines were no more than opinions, which could never be absolutely certain and free from doubt. He felt therefore that it was better to admit ignorance, for there were in theology things that were simply secret and hidden, and went beyond human understanding.[116] Since it was impossible to eliminate all uncertainty from human judgement, Erasmus was happy to rely on the authority of tradition, that is the teachings of the Church and the Scriptures.[117] A no less eloquent example of anti-dogmatism was given by Sebastian

---

[112] See Calvin, *Inst.* I 7, and cf. W. Krusche, *Das Wirken des heiligen Geistes nach Calvin*, Berlin 1957, pp. 202–12.

[113] Cf. *BW* II, n° 600, p. 31: "Non potest igitur sacrarum literarum veritas ex tali iudicio probari; ne idem sit se ipso prius atque posterius: sic et spiritus testimonium quo protestantes uti solent, a mea tractatione erat alienum, ubi cum extraneis disputatur."

[114] See G.H.M. Posthumus Meyjes 'Protestants irenisme in de 16de en eerste helft van de 17de eeuw', *NTT*, 36 (1982), 219–20.

[115] See R.H. Popkin, *The History of Scepticism from Erasmus to Descartes*, Assen 1964, pp. 1–16.

[116] D. Erasmus, *De libero arbitrio DIATRIBE sive collatio*, In *Opera omnia*, IX, Hildesheim 1962 (unchanged reprint of Leiden 1706), p. 1216: "Etiamsi visus sum mihi, quod illic Lutherus tractat, percepisse, attamen fieri potest, ut me mea fallat opinio, eoque disputatorem agam non iudicem, inquisitorem non dogmatisten, paratus a quocunque discere, si quid adferatur rectius aut compertius. [. . .] Sunt enim in divinis litteris adyta quaedam, in quae Deus noluit nos altius penetrare, et si penetrare conemur, quo fuerimus altius ingressi, hoc magis ac magis caligamus, quo vel sic agnosceremus et divinae sapientiae majestatem impervestigabilem, et humanae mentis imbecillitatem."

[117] Cf. Popkin, *Scepticism*, p. 16.

Castellio's famous work, *De arte dubitandi et confidendi ignorandi et sciendi libri II* (1563).[118] This doughty champion of Servetus and adversary of Calvin eloquently defended the frank admission of doubt in religious matters, as his title itself indicates.[119]

Grotius undoubtedly sympathised with the reticence of these Christian humanists. He certainly did not adopt an extreme form of scepticism, such as that of the ancient philosopher Carneades, who only recognised probable knowledge.[120] But at the close of his defence of the faith, as we saw, he referred to the relativity of all human knowledge as a remedy for the vainly arrogant and disputatious Christianity of his time. As he put it in the *Bewijs*:

> And so be sensible and unanimous for once; do not let your reason churn about in search of knowledge beyond what it is necessary to feel, but be wise accordingly: let each one know what is to be known, according to the measure of faith that God has granted him.[121]

Miracles

There was one category of testimony to which Grotius allowed decisive evidential force. In the passage cited above from his introduction to Stobaeus' *Dicta Poetarum* he remarked that Jews and Christians derived their certainty about religion from divine revelation handed down by the prophets and apostles in the Scriptures, and that the truth of this tradition could only be guaranteed by the wholly reliable testimony of miracles. In *De iure belli* he again emphasised the strength of the evidence drawn from the argument from miracles: the truth of the Christian faith cannot be made plausible by merely natural or rational arguments, but relies on the irrefutable testimonies of Christ's resurrection and the miracles performed by Christ and his apostles.[122]

---

[118] See S. Castellio, *De arte dubitandi et confidendi ignorandi et sciendi*, ed. E. Feist Hirsch [Studies in Medieval and Reformation Thought, 29] Leiden 1981.

[119] Cf. Popkin, *Scepticism*, pp. 9–13.

[120] *IBP* Prol. 16–18, pp. 8–9. For Carneades (ca. 213–129 B.C.) see L.M. de Rijk, *Middeleeuwse wijsbegeerte*, Assen 1977, pp. 268–70.

[121] *Bewijs*, p. 166: "Weest dogh, weest eens gezint; laat uw vernuft niet woelen/ Weetzughtigh boven 't gunt van nood is te gevoelen,/ Maer zijt van passen wijs: weet dat te weten staet,/ Elk nae 's geloofs aen hem by God gegunde maet."

[122] *IBP* II xx, 48, 1, p. 404: "Prius est veritatem christianae religionis, quatenus scilicet naturali ac primaevae religioni non pauca superaddit, argumentis mere naturalibus persuaderi non posse, sed niti historia tum resurrectionis Christi, tum miraculorum ab ipso et apostolis editorum: quae res est facti olim quidem irrefragabilibus testimoniis probata, sed olim ita ut haec quaestio facti sit et iam perantiqui."

Thomas Aquinas had called the argument from miracles the apologetic proof *par excellence* of the supernatural truth of the Christian religion.[123] In his *Summa contra Gentiles* Thomas had stated that an opponent of the Christian faith could only be convinced of its truth by an appeal to miracles, as visible signs of God's revelation.[124]

In Grotius' apologetic work the argument from miracles, or to be more precise the testimony of miracles, plays a special role. It is decisive at important points in the argument. In every book of his apologetic work the author invokes this testimony. In the first he calls the argument from miracles the most certain testimony of God's providence;[125] in the second he regards the miracles of Christ as the cause of the honours paid to him after his death;[126] in the third he states that the reliability of the authors of the New Testament is confirmed by the miracles they performed;[127] in the fourth he disqualifies the miracles of the pagans;[128] in the fifth the author places the miracles of Jesus in the foreground as the proof of the superiority of Christianity over Judaism;[129] and finally in the sixth book he states that the miracles of Muhammad pale in comparison with those of Jesus.[130]

Now this argument was by no means unusual in humanist apologetics. In the fifth chapter, however, we shall see that Grotius attached a noticeably higher value to miracles than had the predecessors from whom he borrowed the materials for his work. In his apologetic work he states that the value of the argument from miracles stands or falls by the reliability of the traditional testimonies to them.[131] If this reliability is guaranteed, the argument from miracles gains a special force in his thesis, as the surest proof of God's providence.[132]

---

[123] For Thomas' proof from miracles see A. van Hove, *La Doctrine du miracle chez Saint Thomas et son accord avec les principes de la recherche scientifique*, Paris 1927, pp. 229–52; and A. Lang, *Die Entfaltung des apologetischen Problems in der Scholastik des Mittelalters*, Freiburg 1962, pp. 110–19.

[124] See Thomas, *ScG* I 6 and I 9.

[125] *VRC* I 13.

[126] *VRC* II 4.

[127] *VRC* III 7.

[128] *VRC* IV 8.

[129] *VRC* V 2.

[130] *VRC* VI 5.

[131] *VRC* I 13, 15; "Referuntur quidem multa id genus fabulosa, sed quae testes sui temporis idoneos habuerunt, id est tales quorum nec judicium nec fides laboret, rejicienda non sunt, quasi omnino talia fieri non possint."

[132] *VRC* I 13, 15: "At certissimum divinae providentiae testimonium praebent miracula et praedictiones, quae in historiis exstant." Cf. *VRC* V 2, 180: "Neque enim potest Deus dogmati, per hominem promulgato, auctoritatem efficacius conciliare quam miraculis editis."

This is unmistakeably a weak spot in Grotius' chain of reasoning, where he was apparently betrayed by the ambiguity of miracles as both a divine and a human testimony. Miraculous events in themselves do not form divine testimonies, which according to humanist logic produce certain knowledge.[133] But traditional tales of miracles are human testimonies, which offer no more than probability or plausibility. In principle Grotius argues from human testimonies, but not infrequently he uses the divine testimony that lies behind these testimonies—clearly with the intention of being able to give his readers some certainty.

Summary

Eirenic motives impelled Grotius to write his apologetic work. He was deeply troubled by the internal division of Christianity, and regarded this division as a sickness, caused above all by the dogmatic rigidity of his contemporaries. To free them from their excessive fixation on doctrines he had pleaded in his earlier works for a reduction of Christian dogma to a small number of strictly necessary doctrines, all of which to be found in the Scriptures. He considered the truth of the Christian religion inextricably bound up with mutual peace and unity among believers. In his apologetic work he refrained from discussing Christian doctrines, well aware that that was not the way to attract a single non-Christian to Christianity. He wished to lead all non-Christians to the Bible, so that they could derive the contents of Christian doctrine from it for themselves. And so he had no need of dogmatics to defend the Christian religion.

Grotius made use of the principles of humanist dialectic, which had been developed in the fifteenth and sixteenth centuries by such scholars as Valla, Agricola and Ramus. He had learned these principles as a student at Leiden from his teachers Molinaeus and Snellius. In his first legal work, *De iure praedae*, he had deployed both 'regular' and 'irregular' arguments, that is reason and divine and human testimonies. He followed Ramus in his deductive arrangement of his material. This arrangement can also be observed in the first book of his apologetic work. His evidence in this work also rests on reason and testimony. Since he was in engaged in a discussion with non-Christians, he was unwilling to appeal to the divine testimony

---

[133] Cf. Molinaeus, *Elementa*, pp. 179–81.

of revelation. He felt reason could do no more than demonstrate the truths of natural religion. His most important evidence therefore consisted of human testimonies, even though he had to admit that they could not offer total certainty. In the tradition of the Christian humanists, however, he preferred a certain scepticism to a separate kind of theological certainty, and so he appealed to the testimony of miracles as a decisive historical-metaphysical proof of the truth of the Christian religion.

CHAPTER FIVE

SOURCES

Introduction

It is not easy to give a simple answer to the question of Grotius' sources. The author was a man of vast and many-sided erudition, as is well known, so that the number of eligible works appears enormous. The extensive apparatus of notes to his works, on closer inspection, offers little insight into his sources. Recent studies have revealed that Grotius did not base his legal works on the ancient literature that he cited so freely in his notes, but drew chiefly on sixteenth and seventeenth century sources, in particular the works of the Spanish neoscholastics.[1] And it has recently been shown that his theological work *De satisfactione* also relied largely on contemporary literature.[2]

The problem of the sources of his apologetic work has not yet been satisfactorily resolved, but the author himself gave us one pointer. In the introduction to *De veritate* Grotius states that he had used both Jewish and Christian apologetic literature in producing his work, and had selected his arguments from works old and new. But he does not say which works.[3] In the same introduction, however, he gives high praise to a number of humanist authors, namely Ramundus Sibiuda [= Sabundus], Juan-Luis Vives [= Vives] and Philippe Duplessis Mornay [Mornay].[4]

---

[1] See above all Haggenmacher, *Grotius*, *passim*; and R. Feenstra, 'Quelques remarques sur les sources utilisées par Grotius dans ses travaux de droit naturel', in *The World of Hugo Grotius (1583–1645)*, Amsterdam/Maarssen 1984, pp. 65–81.

[2] E. Rabbie, *Sat.* Introd., pp. 5–62.

[3] *VRC*, I 1, pp. 1–2: "Sed quid alii hac de re judicaturi sint, nescio; te quidem, tam benigno ac facili judice, facile spero me posse absolvi, si dicam me lectis non illis tantum, sed et judaeorum pro judaica vetere et christianorum pro christiana religione scriptis, uti voluisse meo qualicumque judicio, et animo dare negatam, cum id scriberem, corpori libertatem. [. . .] Itaque selegi ex veteribus ac novis, quae mihi se probabant maxime, omissis argumentis, quae parum mihi ponderis habere videbantur, [. . .]."

[4] *VRC*, I 1, p. 1: "Non enim ignoras, ut qui omnia legi digna et quidem tanto cum judicio legeris, quantum excoluerint istam materiam philosophica subtilitate

Apart from the work of Sabundus, the apologetic writings of these authors are certainly eligible candidates for the sources of Grotius' work. The rest of this chapter will show that Grotius' text displays important similarities in both its main lines and in detail to the apologetic works of Vives and Mornay.[5] This cannot be said for Sabundus' *Theologia naturalis seu liber creaturarum*. As its title indicates, this work, probably written between 1434 and 1436, is a proof of natural theology rather than a defence of the faith.[6] It enjoyed wide fame in the sixteenth century, chiefly thanks to the translation by Montaigne (1569); it was even praised by the extremely critical J.J. Scaliger.[7] Sabundus' work has little or nothing in common with Grotius' apology, and therefore cannot be identified as one of its sources. It seems that Grotius used the name of Sabundus as a cloak under which he wished to conceal another, that of Fausto Sozzini (Faustus Socinus). We shall attempt to demonstrate that Grotius must have borrowed a major part of his apology from an early work of Socinus, entitled *De auctoritate Sacrae Scripturae liber* (1588).[8] It is entirely understandable that Grotius should not have mentioned his name, for Socinus was regarded as one of the most dangerous heretics in the sixteenth and seventeenth centuries.

Each separate book of *De veritate* can be traced back, in our opinion, to a single chief source, schematically shown as follows:

De veritate: sources

Book 1: Mornay
Book 2: Socinus
Book 3: Socinus
Book 4: Mornay
Book 5: Mornay
Book 6: Vives

Raemundus Sebundus, dialogorum varietate Ludovicus Vives, maxima autem tum eruditione tum facundia vestras [sic] Mornaeus."

[5] J.L. Vives, *De veritate fidei christianae*, Basel 1543; and Ph. Duplessis-Mornay, *De la verité de la réligion chrestienne contre les athées, epicuriens, païens, juifs, mahumédistes et autres infidèles*, Antwerp 1581.

[6] The most recent edition is Raimundus Sabundus, *Theologia naturalis seu liber creaturarum*, [Faksimile-Neudruck der Ausgabe Sulzbach 1852, mit literargeschichtlicher Einführung und kritischer Edition des Prologs und des Titulus I von Friedrich Stegmüller], Stuttgart-Bad Cannstatt 1966.

[7] See Posthumus Meyjes, *Mel.*, Introd., p. 70 (n. 197).

[8] Dominicus Lopez S.J. [= Faustus Socinus], *De auctoritate Sacrae Scripturae liber*, Hispales [= Amsterdam?] 1588.

Anyone who compares Grotius' text with the apologetic works of
these authors will be struck by the agreements, not only between
the arguments, but between the patterns of argument. This finding
leads to the conclusion that, besides the components, Grotius also
took the structure of his argument from others. This procedure of
imitatio was not uncommon in his time and can be described as classicist.[9] Grotius found in the works of his predecessors the patterns
on which he embroidered his own argument. He made very free
use of this material, stamping his own character on it by reformu-
lating it and modifying it.[10] He had a strong preference for conciseness and therefore frequently condensed the arguments of his
predecessors. This reduction is the most striking feature. Here and
there he also added arguments and examples. At least once in each
book he broke with the previous pattern of his model text by insert-
ing an excursus of his own.

Grotius displayed the greatest independence in the first book, which
we shall therefore deal with at greater length than the others.

Book I—Mornay

In this book Grotius unfolded a deductive pattern of argument that
led him from the existence of God to the essence of true religion.[11]
The main lines of his argument agreed with the classical scheme of
natural theology, as it can be found, for example, in the *Summa contra Gentiles* of Thomas Aquinas.[12] Grotius had no need, however, to
go back to the work of the *doctor angelicus*, for this scheme was a
commonplace in his time.[13] His most important source for this book
was probably the apologetic work of Mornay.[14] Grotius' argument

---

[9] Cf. C.S. Baldwin, *Renaissance Literary Theory and Practice. Classicism in the Rhetoric
and Poetic of Italy, France and England 1400–1600*, New York 1939; E.R. Curtius,
Europäische Literatur und Lateinisches Mittelalter, 6th ed., Bern/Munich 1967, pp. 253–76;
B. Völker-Hetzel, 'Klassizismus', in *Handlexikon zur Literaturwissenschaft*, 2nd ed., Munich
1974, pp. 226–30.

[10] Cf. *VRC*, I 1, p. 2: "Itaque selegi ex veteribus ac novis, quae mihi se probabant maxime, omissis argumentis, quae parum mihi ponderis habere videbantur,
[. . .]."

[11] See chapter IV, pp. 000–000.

[12] Thomas, *ScG*, I c. 9.

[13] See H.M. Barth, *Atheismus und Orthodoxie. Analysen und Modelle christlicher Apologetik
im 17. Jahrhundert*, Göttingen 1971, pp. 172–216.

[14] Mornay, *Ver*. The work was later translated into Latin by the author himself.
The contents of the Latin version hardly differ from the French original. For

not only corresponds with that of the Frenchman in its main lines, but displays striking parallels in its details.

Their common pattern of argument, overall, is as follows: both Mornay and Grotius begin with a proof of God's existence and go on to deal with his unity and qualities.[15] They proceed to show that God was the creator or cause of all things,[16] and that his providence governs all things.[17] They then prove that the human soul is immortal,[18] and finally state that the highest good of man is salvation after this earthly life, which can only be achieved by following a path revealed by divine revelation. This revelation, in turn, is only accessible through the true religion.[19]

Grotius broke with the pattern of his French predecessor on one point to give an explanation of his own (§13–§18). He gave additional proof of God's providence in the form of testimonies of miracles and prophecies that had occurred in history. The argument from miracles led him into a lengthy historical excursus on the long life of the Jewish faith, the reliability and antiquity of the books of Moses, and their confirmation by external testimonies.

The first thing that strikes us in Grotius' use of Mornay's argument is the enormous reduction of the material. Grotius' text contains no more than one ninth of the corresponding matter in Mornay. Grotius turned his forerunner's diffuse and discursive volume into a tightly reasoned deductive argument. This revealed an unmistakeable difference in character: while Mornay fell easily into long philosophical reflections, Grotius was wary of all forms of speculation. This was the result of a difference in philosophical outlook: the Frenchman was strongly attracted by Platonism, while the Dutchman was imbued with the philosophy of the stoics. Moreover, Grotius deliberately passed over all specific notions of Christian dogmatics, such as the trinity, the creation and sin, which allowed him to omit whole sections, even whole chapters, of Mornay's text. In his letter

---

bibliographical data see A. Cioranesco, *Bibliographie de la littérature française du XVIᵉ siècle*, Paris etc. 1959, nᵒs 16237–16285. Grotius must have been very familiar with Mornay's work, for he had probably used it already in producing his *Meletius*. See Posthumus Meyjes, *Mel.*, Introd., p. 70.

[15] Cf. *VRC*, I 1–6 and Mornay, *Ver.* I–IV.
[16] Cf. *VRC*, I 7–9 and Mornay, *Ver.* VII–X.
[17] Cf. *VRC*, I 10–21 and Mornay, *Ver.* XI–XIII.
[18] Cf. *VRC*, I 21–24 and Mornay, *Ver.* XIV–XV.
[19] Cf. *VRC*, I 25–26 and Mornay, *Ver.* XVIII–XX.

to his brother Willem, mentioned above, Grotius declared that not a single outsider would ever be converted to Christianity by Christian doctrines.[20]

We shall see that, apart from the use he made of Mornay's work, Grotius must also have drawn sporadically on other sources. These included classical authors such as Aristotle[21] and Cicero, as well as such heretics as Socinus and Vanini.[22] Both the first and the second books of Grotius' *De veritate* show notable similarities to his own *Meletius*, allowing the suspicion that the author had the unpublished manuscript close at hand while composing his apologetic work.[23]

§2 *Proofs of God*

After his introduction (§1) Grotius begins, like Mornay, with the traditional proofs of God's existence. The Frenchman had divided his first chapter into two parts: the first proved that God existed, the second that all men shared this belief.[24] This twofold approach can be recognised in the first section of Grotius' work. Mornay had developed in great detail the 'teleological' or 'physico-theological' proof of God, which was borrowed from Aristotelian philosophy: the contemplation of the world in all its variety leads irrevocably to the conclusion that there must be a first cause or prime mover that set everything in motion.[25] Grotius, however, preferred the 'cosmological' proof of God's existence, according to which the series of causes

[20] See *BW* II, n° 600, p. 31: "Neminem enim ista ad christianam doctrinam allicient adhuc alienum; imo operam ludunt qui ista aliter quam ex Sacris paginis demonstrare conantur. Sacrarum autem paginarum bene fundata auctoritate, debent et ista probata censeri."

[21] See Molhuysen, 'Bibliotheek', 'Boecken die de huysvrouwe van de voors. de Groot . . . sijn laten volgen, om opt Huys te Louvesteijn te mogen gebruycken', n° 36: 'een boeck van Aristoteles.'

[22] J.C. Vanini, *Amphitheatrum aeternae providentiae, divino-magicum, christiano-physicum, nec non astrologo-catholicum. Adversus veteres philosophos, atheos, epicureos, peripateticos et stoicos*, Lugduni [= Lyons] 1615 [= Van. *Amph.*]. Grotius apparently saw this book in Loevestein, according to a letter from Willem de Groot to Vossius of 23 March 1620; see Rademaker, 'Books', App. 8, 22.

[23] See Molhuysen, 'Bibliotheek', 'Boecken die de huysvrouwe van de voors. de Groot . . . sijn laten volgen, om opt Huys te Louvesteijn te mogen gebruycken,' n° 337: 'Twee boecken met de handt geschreven, in folio'. One of these books may have been the manuscript of his *Meletius*.

[24] Mornay, *Ver.* I, pp. 1–20: 'Qu'il ya un Dieu et que chacun consent en une Divinité'.

[25] Mornay, *Ver.* I, pp. 1–13. Cf. Aristotle, *Phys.* VII 242 a[16]–b[19].

and consequences that the world reveals is traced back to a first cause, which is called God.[26]

This proof of God's existence also goes back to Aristotle, who in his *Metaphysics* stated that since one cannot endlessly trace the series of causes and consequences revealed in the world back to prior causes, one must necessarily assume the existence of a first cause.[27] The Stagirite's reasoning was annexed by Christian theologians in the middle ages, and found its classical expression in the *Summa Theologica* of Thomas Aquinas.[28] Thomas developed five variants of this proof, also called the five ways.[29] Grotius' argument in this section appears to be a combination of Thomas's second way (the first cause) and third way (the first necessity). The pure Aristotelian argument of the prime mover had fallen into discredit in the sixteenth century.[30] In its place the simpler and less speculative proof of the first cause had become the most common variant of the cosmological argument.[31]

Grotius paid significantly more attention to the so-called historical proof of God, in which the existence of a supreme being is derived from the consensus of all peoples (*consensus gentium*).[32] Mornay had stated that a belief in the existence of God was found all over the world, among all peoples, at all times and at every level of development.[33] Grotius invited his readers to take a similar *tour d'horizon*, and came to the same conclusion.[34] While Mornay had invoked a whole series of ancient philosophers and poets in support of this argument, Grotius, after the second Latin edition, named only Aristotle.[35]

---

[26] Cf. *Mel.* 6 5–7: "Esse Deum non modo consensus hominum latissime patens sed et ordo ex se dependentium causarum rerumque gradus clarissime testantur."

[27] See Aristotle, *Metaphys.* II 994 a; XII 1072 b$^{4-14}$.

[28] See H.A. Davidson, *Proofs for Eternity, Creation and the Existence of God in Medieval Islamic and Jewish Philosophy*, New York/London 1987.

[29] See Thomas, *STh* I^a 2, art. 3, Resp.

[30] Cf. Van. *Amph.*, pp. 1–7.

[31] See Barth, *Atheismus*, pp. 218–24.

[32] *Mel.* 6.5–7.

[33] Mornay, *Ver.* I, p. 13: "Qu'on coure de l'Orient en Occident et du Midi au Septentrion, qu'on recherche tous les siècles l'un après l'autre; partout où il s'est trouvé des hommes, il s'y trouvera aussi une espèce de religion, un service de Dieu, des prières, des sacrifices. La diversité y est bien grande, mais en ce point, il y a a un consentement: qu'il y a un Dieu."

[34] *VRC* I, 2, pp. 3–4: "Accedit quod, sive olim cogitas, sive nuper repertas orbis partes spectemus, ubi modo, ut diximus, aliquid est humanitatis, exserit se haec notitia, [. . .]." Cf. Mornay, *Ver.* I, pp. 14–15.

[35] *VRC* I 2, 3; cf. Mornay, *Ver.* I, p. 15.

But that was a commonplace of humanistic apologetics rather than a statement of a source.[36] Aristotle was not regarded as the *auctor intellectualis* of this argument, which was developed in the philosophy of the stoics and had received its classic formulation in the work of Cicero.[37] It was thanks to Calvin above all that the appeal to the *consensus gentium* had become the most important proof of God in Protestant apologetics.[38] The Reformer had stressed this argument in his *Institutio*, to make it clear that every one possessed an innate natural knowledge of God. This gave him a suitable platform from which to attack atheism, for this universal notion leaves no room for ignorance or denial of God's existence.[39]

Grotius follows Calvin and Mornay in linking this proof of God's existence to a refutation of atheism.[40] Mornay had not entered into discussion with atheists, but simply silenced them.[41] So too did Grotius, who coupled the universal consensus of all peoples with certain notions from natural law, such as right reason and virtue. From the observation that atheism differed from the *consensus gentium* he drew the conclusion that this way of thinking was unnatural and therefore unreasonable and immoral. His rejection of atheism therefore involves an intellectual and moral condemnation of it.[42] He does not mention the names of any atheists or atheistic schools of thought, but it is clear that like Mornay he had Epicureans and atomists chiefly in mind.[43] He follows the tradition of humanist apologetics by not even alluding to contemporary atheistic tendencies, because they can offer no more than variations on old familiar themes.[44] The only charge he brings against his unnamed opponents is that their assumptions about the succession of generations without a beginning (the Epicureans) and the chance combination of indivisible particles (the atomists) are just as difficult to conceive as they are incredible.[45]

---

[36] See Laplanche, *L'Évidence*, pp. 79–80.
[37] See Cic. *ND* I 16, 43–17, 44; *Tusc.* I 30, 2.
[38] See Laplanche, *L'Évidence*, p. 79, and Barth, *Atheismus*, pp. 183–96.
[39] Calv. *Inst.* I 3, 102.
[40] Mornay *Ver.* I, pp. 15–20; Cf. *Mel.* 6.5–10.
[41] For this see Laplanche, *L'Évidence*, pp. 53–68.
[42] Cf. *Mel.* 6.7–9.
[43] Mornay, *Ver.* I, pp. 15–17, and see Laplanche, *L'Évidence*, pp. 57–9.
[44] Cf. Van. *Amph.*, [fol. 8v–8r]: "Quare primum hunc librum de Dei providentia tanquam aciem quandam composuimus, et adversus veteres philosophos direximus, ut qui illorum praesidio innituntur moderni athei, eorum impetu perfracti et labefacti concidant."
[45] Cf. Mel. 29.121 (where the Epicureans are named).

Finally he answers some objections that Mornay had attributed to
the sceptics: firstly, that God cannot be seen; secondly, that he is
beyond the grasp of human understanding.[46]

Mornay had regarded the universal consensus of peoples on the
existence of God as a natural datum, that is a generally known fact
that was naturally implanted in the human mind.[47] Grotius, however, was not satisfied with this, and sought a deeper cause for this
phenomenon. He offers two possibilities: either this consensus goes
back to a divine revelation, or to an uninterrupted tradition since
the first people on earth.[48] Although these possibilities are not mutu-
ally exclusive, one has to say that Grotius leaned towards the idea
of a universal ancient tradition.[49]

He also raised the idea in other works. In *De iure belli*, for example, he unambiguously traced the universal consensus of all peoples
back to a tradition dating from the earliest humans.[50] In another
work he recognised that there had been breaks in the tradition, and
that the pure primeval religion of the first humans had been frag-
mented and corrupted, but he maintained that the tradition had
never been totally lost.[51] Grotius' ideas evoke reminiscences of the

---

[46] Mornay, *Ver.* I, pp. 16–18.

[47] See Mornay, *Ver.* I, pp. 13–14.

[48] *VRC*, I 2, p. 3: "Nam cum, quae ex hominum arbitratu veniunt, nec eadem
sint apud omnes, et saepe mutentur; haec autem notio nusquam non reperiatur,
neque temporum vicissitudine mutetur, quod ipsi etiam Aristoteli notatum, homini
ad talia minime credulo; omnino causam ejus aliquam dari convenit, quae se ad
omne genus humanum extendat: quae alia esse non potest, quam aut oraculum Dei
ipsius, aut traditio, quae a primis humani generis parentibus manarit; [. . .]".

[49] *VRC*, I 22, p. 69: "Quae antiquissima traditio a primis (unde enim alioqui?)
parentibus ad populos moratiores paene omnes manavit, [. . .]". Cf. *Mel.* 30.145–6.

[50] IBP II xx, 45, 3, pp. 400–01: "Sed quia hanc rationem et similes alias non
omnes capiunt, sufficit quod ab omni aevo per omnes terras, paucissimis exceptis,
in has notiones consenserunt et hi qui crassiores erant quam ut vellent fallere, et
alii sapientiores quam ut fallerentur, quae consensio in tanta et legum et opinionum
aliarum varietate, satis ostendit traditionem a primis hominibus ad nos propagatam,
ac nunquam solide refutatam, quod vel solum ad fidem faciendam satis est." Cf.
Sat. X 16, 256. "Quamquam autem haec sufficere poterant, libet tamen ex com-
muni gentium notitia, aut potius ex vetustissima traditione per omnes terras diffusa,
sacri expiatori naturam paulo uberius explicare. Quin ante legem Mosis sub statu
legis naturalis qui dicitur sacrificia fuerint, dubitari non potest, quorum ritus a Deo
traditos hi qui diluvio superfuere per terras omnes dispersi ad posteros trasmiserunt,
mansitque aliquamdiu [. . .] incorrupta religio, donec plurium ideoque falsorum deorum cultus in eius locum succresceret." See also *Annot. in NT* (ad Matt. 5:17), in
OT II 34 b45–9.

[51] Cf. *Excerpta*, "Benigno Lectori", a iij: "Ita factum ut sensim illa a communibus
humani generis parentibus tradita religio velut evanesceret, paucis hic et illic se
monstrantibus tabulis quasi naufragae veritatis, [. . .]."

stoic theory of the 'Logos spermatikos', according to which divine reason had revealed itself at the beginning of time and left only 'seeds' in creation.[52]

§3 God's unity

Unlike Mornay Grotius made a fluid deductive transition from God's existence to his unity.[53] He had already argued in *Meletius* that the proof of God's unity rested on the same arguments as the proof of his existence.[54] In his apologetic work he proceeds from the pattern of causality that had brought him in the previous section to acknowledge God as the first necessary cause. Here he argues that God as a wholly self-sufficient being is a natural principle, which in actuality can necessarily only be one. In this he closely follows Aristotle, who in his *Metaphysics* had discussed the actuality and unity of the prime mover.[55]

§4–§6 God's qualities

Grotius then proceeds to prove that God has certain qualities, namely complete perfection, eternity, omnipotence, omniscience and absolute goodness. We find the same summary in Mornay, who however had first argued at length that God's qualities can only be deduced by establishing what God is not.[56] Grotius avoids this lengthy detour, and concludes that God's perfection follows directly from his unity.[57] In this connection he used the Greek word τελειότης.[58] This appears

---

[52] See H. Meijer, *Geschichte der Lehre von den Keimkräften von der Stoa biz zum Ausgang der Patristik nach den Quellen dargestellt*, Bonn 1914; C.J. de Vogel, *Greek Philosophy. A Collection of Texts with Notes and Explanations*, vol. III, Leiden 1973, pp. 64–6. The theory of the 'Logos spermatikos' won a place in Christian apologetics through the Greek apologete Justin Martyr (ca. 100–67). Justin Martyr, *II Apol.* VIII, 1–5. On this see R. Holten, 'Logos spermatikos, Christianity and ancient philosophy according to St Justin's Apologies', *Studia theologica*, 12 (1958), 109–68; and J. Daniélou, *Message évangelique et culture hellénistique aux IIᵉ et IIIᵉ siècles*, Paris 1961, pp. 42–50.

[53] See Mornay, *Ver.* II, pp. 20–38: 'Qu'il y a un seul Dieu'. Cf. H. Heppe/ E. Bizer, *Die Dogmatik der evangelisch reformierten Kirche*, Neukirchen 1958, pp. 41–2.

[54] Cf. *Mel.* 20.13–16.

[55] Cf. Aristot. *Metaphys.* XII, 1071 b¹⁵⁻²³; 1072 a²⁵–b¹⁵; 1074 a³⁸⁻³⁹.

[56] Mornay, *Ver.* IV, pp. 61–74: 'Que c'est que nous pouvons comprendre de Dieu'.

[57] *Mel.* 21.19–20: "Praeterea quicquid praestantissimum omnino aut dici aut cogitari potest, id christiana religio Deo tribuit, caetera removens."

[58] *VRC* I 4, 5.

to be an allusion to Aristotle, who had stated that the prime mover
was also perfection (τὸ τέλειον) itself.[59]

Grotius then needs only a few sentences to establish God's other
qualities. Aristotle had regarded the prime mover as eternal and
absolutely good.[60] Grotius only needed to add omnipotence and omniscience, two qualities that do not suit an immoveable prime mover
that stands outside the world, but do belong to a personal God who
intervenes in the world. This is an essential difference from the philosophy of the Stagirite.

While Mornay had followed his explanation of God's qualities with
a proof of the trinity, Grotius passes over this Christian dogma
entirely.[61] In this he also differed from his own *Meletius*, in which he
had included the trinity in the doctrine of God.[62]

§7 God as the cause of all things

Grotius concludes from his previous explanation that God is the
cause of all things, but does not specifically speak of him as the creator, as he had in *Meletius*.[63] Behind the fitness of all created things
for their purpose he sees the work of an ordering and creative principle.[64] The acknowledgement of a fitness for purpose in nature, or
the teleological explanation of nature, can already be found in
Aristotle, but he had not drawn from it the conclusion that a creative principle existed. The Stagirite was inclined to believe that the
world had existed from eternity and had never had a beginning.[65]
The teleological view of nature was later adopted by the stoics, who
attributed the fitness for purpose of nature to a demiurge or master craftsman.[66]

---

[59] Aristot. *Metaphys.* XII 7, 1072 b[31]–1073 a[3]; cf. *Metaphys.* c II 2, 994 b7–9. Cf.
Thomas, *S. Th.* I[a] 4, 1 Resp.: "Deus autem ponitur primum principium, non mate-
riale, sed in genere causae efficientis: et hoc oportet esse perfectissimum."

[60] Cf Aristot. *Metaphys.* XII 7, 1072 b[27–32]; *Phys.* VIII 259 a[8–20].

[61] Mornay, *Ver.* V: 'Qu'en l'unique essence de Dieu subsistent trois personnes,
ce que nous appellons trinité.'

[62] *Mel.* 22.

[63] Cf. *Mel.* 26.90–92: "Factorem esse iisdem liquet argumentis quibus Deus esse
convincitur, causarum nimirum serie, quae nisi in una prima quiescere non potest;
[. . .]."

[64] Cf. *Mel.* 28.109–11.

[65] Aristotle, *Phys.* II 198 b[10]–199 b[33]. The teleological explanation of nature had
been developed earlier by Diogenes of Apollonia; see De Vogel, *Greek Philosophy*, I,
n° 163a.

[66] See De Vogel, *Greek Philosophy*, III, pp. 51–5.

Mornay and Grotius took up stoic philosophy as a way of fighting Aristotle with his own weapons. Grotius carefully followed the line of Mornay's argument: the contemplation of nature in all its parts led irrevocably to the finding that it was underlain by a certain purposeful intelligence. The world cannot have come into being by chance, but must have been created by the highest of all intelligences. The human race had not existed from eternity, as Aristotle asserted, but had its origin at a certain point in time.[67]

Grotius confines himself to this general philosophical argument, and unlike Mornay he does not add a detailed proof of the Christian doctrine of creation.[68]

§8–§9 Evil in the world

Grotius answers two traditional objections about the existence of evil in the world, in the same way in which they had been dealt with by Mornay.[69] He begins by stating that the origin of evil cannot be attributed to God, but must be sought in man, who can misuse for evil purposes the free will given him by God.[70] He attacks the doctrine of the two principles, one good and one evil, using the well known Augustinian idea that evil has no independent existence, but is merely the absence of good (*privatio boni*). He does not say who his opponents are here, but he was undoubtedly alluding to the Manichaeans.[71]

§10–§11 God's providence

Grotius deduces God's providence from elements of his previous argument, namely God's goodness, omniscience and omnipotence, and finally the general fitness of things for their purpose.[72] Like Mornay he sees the care shown by all creatures for their offspring as a form of goodness, which can hardly be denied to God as the

---

[67] Cf. *VRC*, I 7, p. 6; and Mornay, *Ver.* VII, pp. 130–42: "Que le monde a eu commencement".
[68] See Mornay, *Ver.* IX, pp. 176–229: "Que la sagesse humaine a recognu la création du monde"; and X: "Que Dieu a crée le monde de rien; c'est à dire sans matière".
[69] See Mornay, *Ver.* III, pp. 31–8.
[70] Cf. *Mel.* 29.124–31.
[71] Cf. *Mel.* 29.129–34 and Mornay, *Ver.* III, pp. 31–2.
[72] Cf. *Mel.* 8.25–35.

father of all things.[73] After this concise proof of God's providence he proceeds to tackle a number of classic errors.[74] First he disproves the view that providence is confined to the heavenly sphere and does not intervene in sublunary affairs. In a corresponding passage of *Meletius* he had attacked the Epicureans.[75] Here he answers them with the argument that the stars in their courses are at man's service, so that man, like the stars, is necessarily under God's providence. This was an argument that Vanini had already used against the Epicureans.[76] Against the second error, which claimed that providence only cared for things in general and not for every particular event, Grotius appealed to the omnipotence and omniscience of God. Like Mornay, he does not identify whom he is attacking here.[77]

§12 The maintenance of the political order

Grotius sees another proof of God's providence in the durability of some states as well as in the great political changes brought about by such great historical figures as Cyrus, Caesar and Alexander. One can see this argument as a variation on a theme of Mornay, who had stated that God's providence steered a middle course between what the ancient philosophers called destiny or fate (*fatum*) and chance (*fortuna*).[78] Grotius however sees providence as closer to destiny than to chance.[79] Perhaps he was opposing Machiavelli, who had asserted that the stability and instability of forms of government was not based on divine providence, but was entirely dependent on earthly laws. Machiavelli had allowed chance (*fortuna*) a large role in explaining successful *coups d'état* by several great men.[80]

---

[73] Mornay, *Ver.* XI, pp. 231–2: "Et animaux aussi que l'un membre fait pour l'autre et chacun pour le Tout; un désir d'engendrer des tetins pour allaicter, un soin industrieux pour nourrir et conserver leurs petits."

[74] Cf. Mornay, *Ver.* XI, pp. 235–51.

[75] *Mel.* 8.25–8.

[76] Cf. Van. *Amph.*, pp. 197–202.

[77] Cf. Van. *Amph.*, pp. 238–43 (Vanini refers to the Averroists in this connection).

[78] Mornay, *Ver.*, XIII, pp. 283–301: "Que la sagesse humaine a recognu la providence, et comme la chemine entre le destin et la fortune."

[79] Grotius' interest in this subject is also apparent from a collection of sentences that appeared posthumously under the title *Philosophorum sententiae de fato et de eo quod in nostra est potestate*, in *OT* IV, pp. 377–453.

[80] See F. Deppe, *Niccolò Machiavelli. Zur Kritik der reinen Politik* [Kleine Bibliothek, Wissenschaft, 445] Cologne 1987, pp. 199–263; A. Buck, *Machiavelli* [Erträge der

Grotius made precisely the opposite assertion, invoking 'philosophers and historians' whom he did not name.[81] Presumably he was thinking of the stoic philosophers, who had linked God's providence with destiny, and of historians influenced by stoicism, who included Posidonius, Tacitus and Ammianus Marcellinus.

§13 Miracles

Grotius described miracles and prophecies as the most certain proofs of God's providence.[82] On this point he departed from Mornay's pattern of argument, for Mornay had not made any such claim. The argument from miracles is also absent from Grotius' youthful *Meletius*, but receives all the more emphasis in his apologetic work. In the previous chapter we saw that Thomas Aquinas, above all, had identified the argument from miracles as the proof of God's providence *par excellence*.[83]

In late scholasticism doubt came to be felt about the epistemological trustworthiness of the argument from miracles.[84] For the Reformers miracles had no importance, or virtually none.[85] At the end of the sixteenth century Catholic theology brought miracles back into prominence, so that the counter-reaction in Protestant apologetics led to a revaluation of miracles.[86]

Grotius claimed that the value of a miracle stood or fell by the reliability of the testimonies in which it was recorded.[87] He had no

---

Forschung, 226], Darmstadt 1985, pp. 58–96; P. Mesnard, *L'Essor de la philosophie politique au XVI*[e] *siècle*, 3rd ed. Paris 1969, pp. 17–77; M. Stolleis, *Arcana imperii und ratio status*. Bemerkungen zur politischen Theorie des frühen 17. Jahrhunderts, Göttingen 1980, pp. 7–9.

[81] *VRC*, I 12, p. 14: "Providentiae divinae circa res hominum non leve argumentum et philosophi et historici agnoscunt in conservatione rerumpublicarum, [. . .]."

[82] *VRC*, I 13, p. 15: "At certissimum divinae providentiae testimonium praebent miracula et praedictiones, quae in historiis exstant."

[83] Thomas, *ScG*, III 98–110; cf. *STh*, I[a] 105 art. 7.

[84] See A. Lang, *Die Entfaltung des apologetischen Problems in der Scholastik des Mittelalters*, Freiburg 1962, pp. 119–28.

[85] Calvin did admit the biblical miracles but found them unimportant, because they belonged to a closed phase in history. He emphatically rejected post-biblical miracles, which could only generate a pernicious superstition; see Calvin, *Inst.* IV 19, 6. On this topic: U. Mann, *Das Wunderbare. Wunder-segen und Engel*, [Handbuch systematischer Theologie, 167] Gütersloh 1979, pp. 19–47.

[86] See Laplanche, *L'Évidence*, pp. 189–92.

[87] Cf. *VRC*, I 13, p. 15; and *Bewijs*, p. 17.

doubt that miracles were possible, because God was omniscient and omnipotent, and consequently must be able to suspend the natural order he himself had created. He leaves some room in his explanation of miracles: they may be the work of spirits subordinate to God (angels or demons), but in that case one may just as well ascribe them to God himself, who either worked through these spirits or in his wisdom permitted them to work miracles.[88]

§14 The Jewish religion reliable because of its antiquity

Grotius' argument now takes a curious turning. He uses the argument from miracles to switch from a rational argument to an historical proof. After he had cited miracles as a proof of God's providence in the previous section, one might expect that he would proceed to show that genuine miracles had in fact occurred. But instead he takes the opportunity to insert a long historical explanation of the reliability of the Jewish religion. To achieve this transition he employs a remarkably idiosyncratic reasoning, taking the miracles that underlay the foundation of the Jewish faith as his historical yardstick for the reality of all miracles. He based this reasoning on the assumption that the credibility of the Jewish faith was beyond all doubt. To prove this assumption he employs three historical arguments: firstly the long life of the Jewish religion (§14), secondly the truth of Moses and the antiquity of his books (§15), and thirdly the testimonies of pagan historians that agree with the books of Moses (§16).

The argument from the long life of the Jewish faith is well known from hellenistic-Jewish apologetics, which used it to disarm the objection that this religion was a mere novelty.[89] Although it was therefore a traditional argument, it cannot be ruled out that Grotius borrowed it from Faustus Socinus' *De auctoritate Sacrae Scripturae liber*, a work of which, as we shall see, he probably made intensive use when composing the second and third books of his apologetic work.[90] Socinus had stated that the extreme antiquity and the survival of Judaism were proofs of its truth, and that the long life of this faith

---

[88] Cf. Aug. *Civ.* XXI 6–7.
[89] See for example Philo, *Vit. Mos.* II, 12–17.
[90] In what follows we shall cite from the best known edition of the work in Faustus Socinus, *Opera omnia in duos tomos distincta. Tomus primus continens eius opera exegetica et didactica [. . .]*, in *Bibliotheca fratrum Polonorum quos unitarios vocant*, vol. I. Irenopoli [= Amsterdam] 1656, pp. 265–80 [= Soc. *ASS*].

must have its origin in the unshakeable basis on which it stood and the miraculous events that had marked its foundation.[91] Grotius finds the cause of the durability of the Jewish religion in the miracles that underlay the foundation of the Jewish faith by Moses, the accounts of which were handed down by a long tradition. He traces this tradition back to the Hebrews, who were themselves the witnesses of these miracles.

The word 'Hebrews' was used in Jewish and early Christian apologetics to designate the ancestors of the Jews who lived before and during the Mosaic legislation and who were considered the earliest representatives of true religion.[92] In his *Bewijs* Grotius refers to them variously as 'the Hebrews', 'the descendants of Abraham' and 'the forefathers of the Jews'.[93] The reasoning that the long duration of the Jewish faith originated in the miracles handed down by the Hebrews also fits in with a tendency in Jewish apologetics, which laid great emphasis on the miracles that underlay the Jewish faith.[94] The belief in miracles was so popular and generally accepted in the Graeco-Roman world at the beginning of our era that every religion sought legitimacy by appealing to them.[95]

---

[91] Soc. *ASS* IV, p. 279: "Vidimus, alias omnes antiquas religiones, quamvis minus multo ad colendum difficiles paulatim evanuisse, adeo ut illarum vix extet memoria. Haec [sc. judaica religio] tamen antiquissima conservatur adhuc in hunc usque diem. Cuius rei causa alia nulla esse potest, quam ipsam initia habuisse gravissima firmaque fundamenta post quae consecutae fuerint confirmationes et corroborationes apertae ac manifestae, prout in ipsa ista historia legitur, quibus rebus cum caeterae antiquae religiones modo non prorsus caruerint, necesse fuit, quemadmodum aliis omnibus humanis rebus contingit, ut tandem corruerint, et ad nihilum venerint."

[92] For the 'Hebrews' in Eusebius see G. Schröder, Introduction, in Eus. *PE* VII (SC n° 215, pp. 50–2, 56).

[93] See *Bewijs*, pp. 18, 19, 23, Cf. *VRC* I 16, n. 88, where he explains that the Hebrews descended from the Assyrians. He would later derive the name Hebrews from the fact that Abraham and his followers crossed over the river Euphrates according to Joshua 24: 2–3; *Annot. in VT* (ad Gen. 11:1) in *OT* I 10b 29–30.

[94] Cf. Ios. *Ant. Iud.* II.272–80; and Philo, *Vit. Mos.* I.156–8. On this see O. Betz, 'Miracles in the writings of Flavius Josephus', in *Josephus, Judaism and Christianity*, ed. L.H. Feldman – G. Hata, Leiden 1987, pp. 212–35.

[95] E. Schüssler Fiorenza, 'Miracles, Mission and Apologetics: an Introduction' in *Aspects of Religious Propaganda in Judaism and Early Christianity*, ed. E. Schüssler Fiorenza, London 1976, p. 10: "For the propaganda of religion it was especially inportant to show that its founder or leading figure had such miraculous, divine capacities. For instance, the literature of Jewish apologetics and propaganda therefore expanded the miracles of the Exodus in order to prove that Moses was a divine miracle worker and charismatic figure." Cf. R.M. Grant, *Miracles and Natural Law in Graeco-Roman and Early Christian Thought*, Amsterdam 1952, pp. 104–27.

Grotius saw another proof of the divine origin of the Jewish religion in the readiness of the Jewish people—who were known for their stubbornness—to bow beneath the yoke of a very strict law, with particularly painful rules such as circumcision. We find this historic-psychological argument in Socinus also.[96]

§15 *The reliability and antiquity of the books of Moses*

Grotius considered the reliability of Moses, in whose books these miracles are recorded, to be proven by the fact that according to Jewish tradition God himself had instructed Moses and appointed him to lead the Jewish people. There is no reason whatever to assume that Moses spoke falsehoods in his own interest, for he was not at all concerned for his own honour and advantage. This argument too is traditional. It was used by the Jewish authors Philo and Josephus, whose apologetic works allotted an exceptionally important place to Moses.[97] But Socinus too had used this argument to demonstrate the reliability of Moses as a biblical author.[98]

The unexcelled antiquity of Moses' writings is a no less powerful proof of their reliability.[99] This thesis had already been developed in hellenistic-Jewish apologetics, again to refute the charge of novelty,[100] and was later to be enthusiastically adopted by early Christian apologetes.[101] Grotius was probably following Mornay, who had characterised the Bible as older than all other literature.[102] The Frenchman had appealed to the Jewish apologete Eupolemus, stating that the Jews had learned their writing from Moses, had in turn handed it

---

[96] Soc. *ASS* IV, p. 279: "Etenim, nisi verum esset, eos antiquitus legem illam accepisse, quam adhuc, ut sanctissimam, retinent idque ea ratione, qua in historia legitur, id est ita, ut apparuerit eam a Deo proficisci, fieri vix potuisset, ut se tot ceremonialium (quae vocant) praeceptorurm jugo subdidissent; praesertim a plurimis cibis abstinendi, quibus alii omnes communiter vescuntur, et inter quos non pauci sunt suavissimi palatoque gratissimi, potissimum vero seipsos circumcidendi, quod ceremoniale praeceptum, vel ipsum per se, videtur fidem facere posse, legem illam humanum inventum non fuisse."

[97] Ios. *Ap.* II, 158 and Philo, *Vit. Mos.* I.150–3. On this see W.A. Meeks, 'The Divine Agent and his Counterfeit in Philo and the Fourth Gospel' in *Aspects of Religious Propaganda*, London 1976, pp. 43–50.

[98] Soc. *ASS.* I, pp. 270–1.

[99] Cf. *Mel.* 53.395–7.

[100] See for example Ios. *Ap.* II, 154–6; *Ant. Iud.* I.16.

[101] See Laplanche, *L'Évidence*, pp. 71, 161–9.

[102] Mornay, *Ver.* XXIV, p. 552; "La Bible est plus ancienne que toutes autres écritures."

on to the Phoenicians, and that the Phoenician Cadmus had in turn handed it on to the Greeks.[103] In his *Bewijs* Grotius also mentioned Cadmus and made a direct connection between the Greek and Hebrew letters.[104] In the Latin version he states that the Greek alphabet was of Syrian or Hebrew origin.[105]

The hellenistic Jewish thesis that Hebrew was the original tongue of humanity found powerful advocates among the humanists. The orientalist and theologian Guillaume Postel, for example, attempted in 1538 to prove that Hebrew was the mother of all other languages and that the Hebrews had, as it were, colonised the whole world by giving it their letters, laws and arts.[106] J.J. Scaliger, a pupil of Postel, devoted a long excursus to the origins of the Greek letters in his great chronological work *Thesaurus Temporum* (1606).[107] Here he stated that evident agreements in the form and sequence of the alphabets showed that the Greek letters must be of Phoenician origin. The Phoenician letters were used earlier by all the Canaanites and Hebrews, he explained, simply because no other alphabet was in use from the time of Moses to the destruction of the Temple.[108]

---

[103] Mornay, *Ver.* XXIV, p. 558: "Eupolemus, au livre des Roys de Iudée, dit que Moise enseigna les lettres aux juifs, les juifs aux Phoeniciens, les Phoeniciens aux Grecs par Cadmus." Cf. Eus. *PE* X 5.1–2.

[104] *Bewijs*, p. 21.

[105] *VRC*, I 15, pp. 17–18: "Accedit indubitata scriptorum Mosis antiquitas, cui nullum aliud scriptum possit contendere, cuius argumentum et hoc est, quod Graeci, unde omnis ad gentes fluxit eruditio, literas se aliunde accepisse fatentur, quae apud ipsos literae et ordinem et nomen et ductum quoque veterem non alium habent quam Syriacae sive Hebraicae, [. . .]." Cf. *Mel.* 53.403–8: "Scriptorum in hoc volumine primus Moses, Diodoro vetustissimus legislatorum, ante cuius aetatem scripta nulla possunt proferri; nec mirum, cum Graeci, unde omnis literatura in alias gentes emanavit, literas ipsas a Phoenicibus se accepisse fateantur, quae quidem Phoenicum literae eaedem sunt quae Hebraeorum, unde et nomina literarum apud Graecos Phoenicia sive Hebraica." The idea that Greek or Athenian culture was the source of all civilisation was developed by the pagan rhetorician Aristides (2nd century). See J.H. Oliver, 'The Civilizing Power. A Study of the Panathenaic Discourse of Aelius Aristides', in *Transactions of the America Philosophical Society*, NS, 57 (1968), 5–36.

[106] G. Postel, *De originibus seu de Hebraicae linguae et gentis antiquitate deque variarum linguarum affinitate liber. In quo ab Hebraeorum Chaldaeorumve gente traductas in toto orbe colonias vocabuli Hebraeci argumento, humanitatisque authorum testimonio videbis*, Paris 1538. On this see A. Borst, *Der Turmbau von Babel. Geschichte der Meinungen über Ursprung und Vielfalt der Sprachen und Völker*, vol. III, 1, Stuttgart 1960, pp. 1128–9; and G. Dubois, *Mythe et langage au seizième siècle*, Bordeaux 1970, pp. 69–71.

[107] Scal., *Thes. temp.*, Animadversiones in Chronologia Eusebii, pp. 102–13: "Digressio de literarum Ionicarum origine ad locum Eusebiani numeri MDCXVII illustrandum."

[108] Scal. *Thes temp.* p. 103: "Habes exemplum literarum Phoeniciarum una cum figuris diversis Graecarum, ex quarum comparatione per te ipsum colligere potes

In the Annotations on the Old Testament published shortly before his death Grotius remarks that both the Jews and the Syrians claimed to possess the most ancient language. He states that Hebrew was the tongue of those who came from Chaldea and later settled in Canaan. That language had gradually adapted to the situation in Canaan, but did not differ in essentials from Phoenician, apart from a few dialectal peculiarities. The primeval language of humanity, according to Grotius, no longer existed in its pure form, though remnants of it could be found in existing languages.[109]

Grotius ends this section with the argument that the oldest Greek laws, from which Roman laws were later derived, originated in the laws of Moses. Mornay had put the same argument, invoking Diodorus Siculus to prove that Moses was the earliest legislator.[110]

§16 Confirmation by external testimonies

As his third proof of the credibility of the Jewish religion Grotius names the confirmation of the Mosaic books (the Pentateuch) by external testimonies. In his *Bewijs* he shows this schematically and in narrative form; in the Latin version he gives a long list of testimonies, which he later completed with a gigantic apparatus of notes. The basic pattern of this section, which remained the same through the various versions, must have been borrowed from the work of his predecessor Mornay.

This argument was first developed in hellenistic Jewish apologetics, but found its classical form in the work of Eusebius of Caesarea. In the ninth book of his *Praeparatio Evangelica* Eusebius cited a series of historical testimonies he believed to confirm the Old Testament

---

id, quod secundo loco proposuimus, Graecas literas e Phoeniciis natas, quum idem ordo sit eademque forma earum quae Phoeniciarum, quibus omnes olim et Chananaei et Hebraei usi sunt, adhucque Samaritani utuntur; neque aliae in usus fuerunt a temporibus Mosis, ad excidium templi." Scaliger probably took the view that the Hebrew alphabet was the same as the Samaritan and that both languages were ultimately derived from Phoenician, from the work of his first teacher in oriental languages, Guillaume Postel. Cf. G. Postel, *Linguarum duodecim characteribus differentium alphabetum introductio ac legendi modus longe facilimus*, Paris 1538, cii^v–civ^v.

[109] *Annot. in VT* (ad Gen. 11:1) in *OT* I 10b 26–40.

[110] Mornay, *Ver.* XXIV, p. 558: "Aussi dit Diodore Sicilien, qui'il a appris des égyptiens (ennemies toutefois de Moise et de sa race), qu'il avait été le premier legislateur de tous [. . .]." Cf. *Mel.* 53.403–5: "Scriptorum in hoc volumine primus Moses, Diodoro vetustissimus legislatorum, ante cuius aetatem scripta nulla possunt proferrri, [. . .]. For the inaccuracy of the citation see Posthumus Meyjes, *Mel.* Comment., p. 152.

narrative from the Flood up to and including the Babylonian captivity.[111] These were for the most part very ancient and enigmatic pagan authors such as the Chaldean Berosus, the Egyptian Manetho and the Babylonian Abydenus. The works of all these authors had already been lost, but extensive fragments were preserved in such Jewish apologetes as Alexander Polyhistor and Josephus, on whom Eusebius drew.[112] In the next chapter we shall see that these mysterious and unreliable testimonies fascinated humanist authors.[113]

Josephus and Eusebius had both begun their comparative historical accounts with the Flood.[114] Mornay and Grotius, however, began with the creation of the world. The French apologete opened with an account of the pagan fables about the creation, tacitly alluding to the Phoenician cosmogony ascribed to Sanchuniathon.[115] Grotius too began with the testimony of this obscure Phoenician, which had been handed down by Eusebius, who cited it in the translation of Philo of Byblos.[116] Grotius followed the pattern of his French model but here and there he altered the emphasis. Mornay had dealt with the Flood after the creation of humanity,[117] but Grotius passed over this topic completely, to contemplate the pure and simple life of the earliest humans on earth.[118] In *De iure belli* he remarks that among certain American tribes something of the original purity and simplicity of life was still to be seen.[119]

---

[111] Cf. Eus. *PE* IX 11–40.

[112] On the doubtful character of these ancient testimonies, clearly cited at second hand by these Jewish apologetes, see Th. Reinach, 'Introduction', in Ios. *Ap.* (Texte établi et annoté par Th. Reinach, et traduit par L. Blum), Paris 1972, XXVIII.

[113] See chapter VI, pp. 000–000.

[114] Cf. Ios. *Ant. Iud.* I, 3 sqq. and Eus. *PE* IX 11.

[115] Mornay, *Ver.* XXVI, p. 620: "Sur cette vérité les Phoeniciens et les Egyptiens ont façonné leurs fables. Qu'au commencement il y avait des ténèbres, et un air spirituel, et un chaos infini, que cet esprit convoita ce chaos, que de leurs embrassements naquit un certain Moth, c'est à dire Limon, dont furent produits tous les animaux. Nul ne peut nier, que cela ne soit une copie mal prise, du vif et du naturel de Moise." Cf. Eus. *PE* I 10, 1–2.

[116] *VRC*, I 16, pp. 18–21: "Nam quae ille de mundi origine scripta reliquit, eadem ferme erant et in antiquissimis Phoenicum historiis, quas a Sanchuniathone collectas vertit Philo Byblius; [. . .]."

[117] Mornay, *Ver.* XXVI, pp. 620–1.

[118] *VRC*, I 16, pp. 35–6: "Primam hominis vitam cum simplicitate fuisse, et nudo corpore, docebant et Aegyptii, unde aurea poetarum aetas, etiam Indis celebrata, ut apud Strabonem est."

[119] Cf. *IBP*, II ii, 1, pp. 140–1.

Mornay and Grotius confirmed the biblical report of the long lives of the earliest people from the 'ancient' testimonies of Berosus, Manetho, Hiromus, Hestiaeus, Hecataeus, Hellanicos and Hesiod.[120] They were convinced that virtually all the peoples of the earth had handed down the tale of a Flood. They also believed the accounts of the tower of Babel and the burning of Sodom to be universally accepted. Grotius gave an evocative description of the latter event in his *Bewijs*, apparently borrowed from Mornay, who in turn had taken it from Strabo.[121] The history of Abraham and his sons finds its confirmation in the ancient testimonies of Berosus and others, borrowed from Josephus and Eusebius.[122] While Mornay continued with the history of Moses, Joshua, Saul, David and so on until the miraculous tale of Jonah, Grotius interrupted the series at the appearance of Moses.[123] He would continue the presentation of this evidence in the third book of his apologetic work.[124]

§17 Prophecies

This long excursus is followed by a concise summary of the proof from prophecies. Grotius considered it a strong proof of the providence of God that certain Old Testament prophecies had been realised. All the examples he cites could have been borrowed from Mornay.[125] In the Dutch version he confined himself to those Old Testament prophecies, but in *De veritate* he also cites oracles of the Mexicans and Peruvians, which are alleged to have predicted the coming of the Spaniards and the ensuing calamities.[126] In these prophetic dreams and apparitions he sees further proofs of God's providence.[127]

---

[120] Cf. Mornay, *Ver.*, XXVI, pp. 620–1; and *VRC*, I 16, p. 37.
[121] Cf. *Bewijs*, p. 22, and Mornay, *Ver.* XXVI, p. 627.
[122] Mornay, *Ver.* XXVI, pp. 627–30; and *VRC*, I 16, pp. 53–5.
[123] Cf. Mornay, *Ver.* XXVI, pp. 636–42; and *Bewijs*, p. 23. In his Latin version Grotius added a brief confirmation of the miracles of Elijah, Elisha and Jonah; see *VRC*, I 16, pp. 55–63.
[124] See *VRC*, III 16, pp. 139–44.
[125] Mornay, *Ver.* XV, pp. 593–602.
[126] *VRC*, I 17, p. 65: "Addi his possunt oracula plurima et clarissima, apud Mexicanos et Peruanos, quae Hispanorum in eas terras adventum, et secuturas inde calamitates praedixerunt." Grotius cites his sources for this information in his note.
[127] *Ibid.*, pp. 65–6. Here he followed the example of Roman Catholic theologians and Protestant apologetes of his time, who catered for a widespread interest in everything that savoured of the mysterious and the supernatural; see Laplanche, *L'Évidence*, pp. 189–91.

§18–§19 Objections

Grotius deals briefly with the objection that miracles no longer occurred and that prophecies were no longer made in his own day. Mornay had also met this objection with the rhetorical remark that the pagans would not have invented false miracles, or even the word 'miracle', if there had been no true miracles.[128] Grotius observes that it is sufficient proof of God's providence that miracles had ever happened. He adds that it would be illogical if the laws of nature could be arbitrarily suspended. This argument fits the stoic idea that supernatural intervention is an exception to the rules and laws of nature, which in itself are sufficient proof of God's providence.[129]

Grotius dismisses the thorny objection that the existence of evil in the world is in conflict with God's goodness as easy to answer; this expression is typical of his theological style.[130] He feels that it is sufficient to give a brief summary of the usual apologetic arguments, to which he had already partly referred in §8 and in all probability had taken over from Mornay.[131]

§20–§21 Judgement after this life

Two brief sections about the judgement after this life in fact comprise a single reasoning, which allows a fluid transition in Grotius' argument. Even though evil in the world sometimes appears to go unpunished, this does not mean that divine providence simply ignores human actions. On the contrary, since God cares for all things and is just, but wrong nevertheless happens, one must conclude that a judgement is to be expected after this life, if evil is not to go unpunished and virtue unrewarded.[132] This argument does not appear in Mornay. Grotius had used it earlier in his *Meletius*, invoking Seneca.[133] The argument was developed by the stoics and later became current in Christian apologetics.[134]

---

[128] Mornay, *Ver.* XXVI, pp. 642–3.
[129] See Laplanche, *L'Évidence*, pp. 147–9.
[130] Cf. Posthumus Meyjes, *Mel.* Introd., pp. 30–1.
[131] Mornay, *Ver.* XII, pp. 27–9. Cf. *Mel.* 29.125–9.
[132] *VRC*, I 20, p. 68.
[133] *Mel.* 15.26–9.
[134] See for example Calv. *Inst.* I 5, 10.

§22 The survival of the soul confirmed by tradition

Mornay's defence of God's providence had been followed directly
by a proof of the immortality of the soul. He had cited first the
rational arguments and then the historical testimonies.[135] Grotius
inverted this order, appealing first to tradition and then to reason
to prove that the soul survived the death of the body.[136] He carefully avoided speaking of 'the immortality of the human soul', which
may indicate that he preferred the stoic tradition to the Platonic.[137]
Mornay had stated that the belief in the immortality of the soul was
found in all times and places.[138] Grotius explained this general consensus by assuming a common original tradition from the earliest
humans.[139] He then cited a long series of historical testimonies from
various ages and cultures, most of which he must have borrowed
from Mornay.[140]

§23–§24 Confirmation by reason

Grotius then attempts to make the case for the survival of the soul
plausible using rational arguments. While Mornay had supplied cir-
cumstantial philosophical and speculative proofs of this thesis, Grotius
simply concludes that the natural causes through which material
things are corrupted do not apply to the soul. He finds positive indications of the independence of the soul from the body in the mastery that man has been given over his actions, in human yearning
for immortality and above all in the undeniable working of the
conscience.[141]

---

[135] Mornay, *Ver.* XIV, pp. 301–45: "Que l'âme de l'homme est immortelle"; XV,
pp. 345–85: "Que l'immortalité de l'âme est enseigné par les anciens philosophes
et cru de tous peuples et nations".
[136] Cf. *Mel.* 18.66–71; "Animum vero non interire cum philosophis plerisque—
[. . .]—sentit christiana religio, adstipulante non modo vetustissima omnium prope
gentium fide, sed ipsa etiam ratione qua discimus in animo mentem esse, Dei ima-
ginem, perpessionis expertem."
[137] See De Vogel, *Greek Philosophy*, III, n° 957, pp. 95–6.
[138] Mornay, *Ver.* XV, p. 345.
[139] *VRC*, I 22, p. 69; "Quae antiquissima traditio a primis (unde enim alioqui?)
parentibus ad populos moratiores paene omnes manavit, [. . .]."
[140] See Mornay, *Ver.* XV, pp. 345–85.
[141] Cf. Mornay, *Ver.* XIV, p. 327; see also *Mel.* 10.47–50; 28.113–15.

§25 The destiny of man is bliss after this life

In two sentences he works towards the conclusion of his argument, that man is destined for bliss after this life. Mornay had needed five lengthy chapters to reach this conclusion.[142] Grotius was able to be so concise because he did not linger over the fixed point of every Christian apology: the corruption of human nature, or sin,[143] which had loomed very large in Mornay's argument.[144] One cannot say that Grotius was blind to the reality of sin and ignored a pattern of salvation in which sin was overcome by grace.[145] In his apologetic work, however, he was unwilling to invoke specifically Christian concepts. In this section he simply infers from the previous argument that, once it is established that the soul can survive the death of the body, man can have no worthier fate than bliss after this life. The essence of this salvation is that man should become as like God as possible—a notion already developed by Plato and the Pythagoreans.[146]

Mornay had arrived at the same conclusion, though only after first giving it a broad philosophical underpinning and confirming it by a long procession of historical testimonies.[147] Unlike his French predecessor Grotius refrained from a more detailed philosophical and historical explanation, and chose only to cite the testimonies of Plato and the Pythagoreans.[148]

The second sentence of this section in Grotius' works reads: 'what this bliss is like, and what it can be compared with, men may conjecture but if something has been revealed by God, it must be considered

[142] See Mornay, *Ver.* XVI–XX, pp. 385–493.

[143] He dealt with this theme at much greater length in his *Meletius* by linking various notions from Christian thought (Augustine) and ancient philosophy (Plato, Aristotle, Cicero); see *Mel.* 13–18.

[144] Cf. Mornay, *Ver.* XVI, pp. 385–413: "Que la nature de l'homme est corrompue et l'homme déchue de sa première origine, et comment"; XVII, pp. 413–33: "Que les anciens sont d'accord avec nous de la corruption de l'homme et cause de celle".

[145] Cf. *Mel.* 34–40.

[146] *VRC*, I 25, p. 74: "Quod si animus et eius est naturae, quae nullas habeat in se intereundi causas, et Deus multa nobis signa dedit, quibus intelligi debeat, velle ipsum ut animus superstes sit corpori, non potest finis homini ullus proponi ipso dignior, quam ejus status felicitatis; et hoc est, quod Plato et Pythagorici dixerunt, bonum esse homini Deo quam simillimum reddi."

[147] Mornay, *Ver.* XVIII, pp. 433–55: "Que Dieue est le souverain bien de l'homme et pourtant que le principal but de l'homme doit estre de retourner à Dieue"; XIX, pp. 455–69: "Que les plus sages sont d'accord de tous temps, que Dieu est le but et bien principal de l'homme".

[148] Mornay, *Ver.* XIX, pp. 459–60.

the truest and most certain'.[149] Mornay too had stated that the true
religion is the only way to the highest good, but had added that
man had gone astray from God through sin, for which he required
forgiveness, which was promised by the true religion.[150] Mornay saw
a deep gulf between death, which man deserved as a sinner, and
eternal life, which was promised him; and he regarded the true religion as the bridge that must lead him back across that gulf to God.[151]
Grotius does not mention this gulf, and instead refers only to the
uncertainty of human reason, which can only be eliminated by the
certainty of divine revelation.[152]

§26 To gain this bliss, one must seek the true religion

Grotius closes this book with the remark that eternal bliss is promised
by Christianity above all other religions, and that is why his next
book will investigate whether it is indeed the true religion.[153] This
allows him to round off his argument much more rapidly than
Mornay, who had first given a definition of the concept of religion,
and then a detailed list of the hallmarks of the true religion.[154] For
Grotius it was enough to prove that knowledge of man's eternal bliss
was offered by the true religion.[155] Grotius confined himself in this
work to proving that Christianity was this true religion. He tacitly
assumed that whoever is convinced of this can learn the path to salvation from that religion and can achieve salvation by choosing to
follow it. But he mentions only the first and last steps on that path,
and leaves it to his readers to imagine the path itself.

Book 2—Socinus

In the introduction to this book Grotius declares that it is not his
intention to deal with all the doctrines of the Christian faith, but to

---

[149] *VRC*, I 25, p. 74; "Qualis autem ea sit felicitas et quomodo comparetur, possunt quidem homines conjecturis indagare; sed si quid eius rei a Deo patefactum
est, id pro verissimo et certissimo haberi debet."
[150] Mornay, *Ver.* XX, pp. 469–93: "Que la vraie religion est le chemin pour par-
venir à ce but et souverain bien, et quelles en sont les marques".
[151] Mornay, *Ver.* XX, p. 471.
[152] Cf. *VRC*, III 12, pp. 131–3.
[153] *VRC*, I 26, p. 74: "Quod cum christiana religio supra alias se nobis adferre
polliceatur, sitne ei fides habenda, secunda huius operis parte examinabitur."
[154] Mornay, *Ver.* XX, pp. 471–93.
[155] Cf. *Mel.* 12.66–7.

show that the Christian religion is true.[156] This is a noticeable difference between his approach and the usual pattern of apologetics.[157] Instead of a dogmatic treatment he seeks to prove the superiority of Christianity as a factual matter. But it is wrong to assume, as some have, that this proof originated with Grotius.[158] One can find a line of argument that matches his almost exactly in the *De auctoritate Sacrae Scripturae liber* [= *De auctoritate*] of Faustus Socinus.[159] Socinus wrote this work around 1580, when he was employed as a lawyer at the court of Isabella de' Medici in Florence and was stimulated to make an intensive study of the Bible by his uncle Lelio Sozini. It was the outcome of humanistic biblical research in the vein of Lorenzo Valla. The work first appeared in 1588, under the pseudonym Dominic Lopez S.J.[160] At first it was much appreciated by both Roman Catholics and Protestants, but this enthusiasm melted away like snow before the sun once the true author became known.[161]

Grotius' argument in the second book of his apologetic work agrees in its main lines with the second chapter of Socinus' *De auctoritate*. The Italian's proof had consisted of two parts: in the first he demonstrated that the Christian religion excelled all others; and in the second that this religion must be true on factual grounds. Christianity excels all other religions in three respects: in the promise it holds

---

[156] *VRC*, II 1, p. 75.

[157] In his *Meletius* Grotius had given a traditional explanation of the leading Christian dogmas; see *Mel.* 34–58.

[158] Cf. Laplanche, *L'Évidence*, p. 36.

[159] On this work see, amongst others, C.C. Sandius, *Bibliotheca anti-trinitariorum . . .*, Freistadt [= Amsterdam] 1684, pp. 66–7 [reprinted in the series 'Bibliotheka Pisarzy Reformacyjnyck' n° 6 [Warsaw 1967]; E.M. Wilbur, *A History of Unitarianism, Socinianism and its Antecedents*, Cambridge (Mass.) 1945, pp. 390–1; D. Cantimori, *Italienische Haeretiker der Spätrenaissance*, Basel 1949, pp. 336–40; G. Pioli, *Fausto Socino, Vita—Opere—Fortuna. Contributo alla storia del liberalismo religioso*, Modena 1952, pp. 98–106; Z. Ogonowksi, 'Faustus Socinus, 1539–1604' in *Shapers of Religious Traditions in Germany, Switzerland and Poland, 1560–1600*, ed. J. Raitt, New Haven/London 1981, pp. 195–209; and G.H. Williams, *The Radical Reformation*, Kirksville Missouri 1992, pp. 1162–9.

[160] Dominicus Lopez S.J. [= Faustus Socinus], *De auctoritate Sacrae Scripturae liber*, Hispali 1588. Copies of the Latin edition of 1588 are to be found in Paris and Tilburg. Socinus had originally written the work in Italian, and later made his own translation imto Latin. The first Latin edition appeared, according to the title page, from the press of Lazarus Ferrerius in Hispali [= Seville]; see Sandius, *Bibliotheca*, p. 66. But it is assumed that this imprint is fictitious and that the work was really printed in Amsterdam. A copy of this edition is extant in the Biblioteca Nacional in Madrid; see Wilbur, *History*, p. 390 (n. 24).

[161] See Wilbur, *History*, p. 390.

out, in the rules it prescribes, and in the way in which it has managed to spread. The truth of the Christian religion is apparent from
the fact that Jesus lived and suffered a shameful death, but was later
honoured, that he performed miracles and rose from the dead.[162]

Grotius inverts the order of these two parts, beginning with the
proof of the factual truth before proceeding to prove the superiority of Christianity. He argues that Jesus lived and suffered a shameful death but was still worshipped after his death, that he performed
miracles and rose from the dead. He then goes on to show that
Christianity excels all other religions in the reward that it offers, the
rules that it prescribes, and in its miraculous expansion.[163]

The assumption that Grotius could have developed the same argument entirely independently of Socinus is hardly plausible. The points
of resemblance are so striking in both their main lines and in detail
that one must assume that Grotius had Socinus' book close at hand
when he was preparing his own apologetic work. This hypothesis is
confirmed by the finding that the agreements with *De auctoritate* extend
beyond the second book into the third. We are not, of course, the
first to notice the resemblance between the two books. As early as
1644 André Rivet remarked on Grotius' indebtedness to Socinus in
his apologetic work.[164]

We have no tangible proofs of the assumption that Grotius used
the work of Socinus. His correspondence offers nothing to suggest
this, but this says little, for the letters of these years do not mention
the works of Vives or Mornay either. Nothing is known with certainty of how Grotius obtained a copy, or if he owned a copy himself. It is not improbable that Gerard Vossius, who nearly every
month sent a chest of books to Loevestein, let the prisoner have his
copy. Vossius owned an anonymous edition of *De auctoritate* published

---

[162] Soc. *ASS* II, pp. 271–5.

[163] *VRC*, II, pp. 75–120.

[164] See H. Bots/P. Leroy, *Correspondance intégrale d'André Rivet et de Claude Sarrau*,
II, Amsterdam 1980, n° 273 (Rivet to Sarrau, 5 September 1644), p. 370: "Vous
voyéz Monsieur, qu'il [sc. Th. Morton] ne loüe pas en ce qu'il a escrit pour accorder
les Religions, mais en ce qu'il [= Grotius] a escrit de *verit[ate] Relig[ionis] Christianae*,
qui est un livre bien suivi, mais qui doibt beaucoup a celuy de Socin de *auctor[itate]
S[acrae] Script[urae]*, et qui a des maximes qui portent au meme but que Socin." Cf.
Wilbur, *History*, pp. 390–1: "His little treatise [sc. Socinus' *De auctoritate*] was much
esteemed by both Catholics and Protestants until its true authorship was discovered; and its argument was adopted in 1639 by Grotius in his famous work *De veritate religionis christianae*, and by the Catholic bishop Huet in his *Demonstratio evangelica*."

at Steinfurt in 1611, with a foreword by Conrad Vorstius.[165] In this Vorstius emphatically denied Socinus' authorship.[166] It is therefore possible that Grotius used this work without knowing that Socinus was the author. That would explain why he was later to deny any influence of Socinus on his work.

We recall that Grotius originally shared the general distaste for Socinianism. In 1611, for example, he told the Calvinist preacher Antonius Walaeus that he did not regard Socinians as Christians, or even as heretics; their views deviated so far from general Christian faith that they could barely be distinguished from Muslims.[167] In the following years, as a defender of the remonstrants, he was repeatedly tarred with the brush of Socinianism, with which the contra-remonstrants tried to blacken their adversaries. Grotius felt it useful to compose a polemic against Socinus' best known work, *De Iesu Christo servatore*, in which he sought to clear himself and the remonstrants from the suspicion of Socinianism.[168] This resulted in his work *De satisfactione Christi adversus Faustum Socinum Senensem*, which was published in 1618 with a foreword by Gerard Vossius.[169] This work failed to achieve the desired effect, and ironically only aroused even stronger suspicions of Socinianism.

In itself, it is not implausible to assume that Grotius felt attracted to this work by the Italian jurist and amateur theologian. Socinus' book is the fruit of humanist study of the Bible, as initiated by Lorenzo Valla, and shows no signs of the anti-trinitarian ideas for which he later became notorious. Its aproach might be characterised as rational and liberal, with arguments mainly based on historical grounds. Socinus' legal and historical argumentation and his rational

---

[165] See *Catalogus librorum Gerardi Vossii* [= Ms. of the University Library Amsterdam], fol. 244ʳ: "Socinus De auctoritate Sacrae Scripturae (in praef. Vorstii) Steinfurt 1611".

[166] The title page of this edition states: *De auctoritate S. Scripturae. Opusculum his temporibus nostris utilissimum, quemadmodum intelligi potest ex praecipuis rerum quae in ipso tractantur, capitibus. Ea vero proxime seqq pagellis notata sunt. In praefatione ad lectorem ratio huius editionis exponitur. Steinfurti excudit Theoph. Caesar 1611* [= Petit n° 19]. Petit mentions another edition, which appeared earlier that year without the preface by Vorstius.

[167] *BW* I, n° 215, p. 186: "Samosatenianos autem et si qui sunt similes, non modo universali omnium christianorum sed nec haereticorum nomine dignor: quae enim ipsi docent cum universali omnium aetatum atque gentium fide pugnant et christianitatem, quantum ego intelligo, nomine retinent, re destruunt; itaque hos a mahumetistis non longe separo, qui ne ipsi Iesu maledicunt."

[168] See E. Rabbie, *Sat.* Introd., pp. 10–19.

[169] *BG* n° 922.

undogmatic approach were very similar to those of Grotius, who certainly during his imprisonment bitterly deplored the dogmatic quarrels that tormented his age.[170]

In the second chapter of *De auctoritate* Socinus had presented a factual proof of the truth of the Christian religion instead of a natural theology. Religion, he argued, rested on divine revelation and was by no means a universal natural thing, for there were peoples who were entirely without religion.[171] In other words he denied the *consensus gentium* on that point, to which Grotius attached so much importance. A few paragraphs later Socinus says that he would have no trouble in giving a rational proof of God, but that he refrained from it, because it would take up too much space and was moreover unnecessary.[172] Although he was rather ambiguous about the possibility of a natural knowledge of God, he leaves us in no doubt that he regarded such a proof as completely superfluous.[173] This was a very profound difference from Grotius, who in the first book of his apologetic work took so much trouble to construct a solidly based natural theology. But Grotius' method was to accumulate arguments: he retained a natural theology and supplemented it by a factual proof, the model for which he found in Socinus.

It seems plausible that in building up his argument Grotius followed the model of Socinus, even though he inverted the order of the main components. He supplemented his predecessor's argument with additional facts, explanations and testimonies. This supplementary material appears to have been borrowed for the most part from the apologetic work of Mornay. Grotius broke with the pattern of Socinus' argument on one point, a digression on the superiority of Christian ethics (§12–§17). This excursus appears to have been made up of material from his own *Meletius*.

---

[170] One can find confirmation of his interest in Socinianism in an excerpt he made from the Catechism of Rakow of 1609; see Ms. Rotterdam, RK 416, fols. 163–4: "Ex Catechismo Samosateniano."

[171] Soc. *ASS* II, p. 273: "Nam cum religio res naturalis nequaquam sit, (alioqui non invenirentur nationes omni prorsus religione carentes; quales in nostra aetate quibusdam in locis inventae sunt, ac nominatim in regione Brasiliae; [. . .] cum, inquam, religio nequaquam res naturalis sit, sed si vera est, patefactio sit quaedam divina, non modo non verisimile est, sed prorsus fieri non potest, ut religio illa quam Deus velit aeternam esse atque omnibus gentibus communem, ipsius certissimo ac singulari jussu et opera passim in orbe terrarum cuiuscunque generis hominibus praedicata non fuerit."

[172] Soc. *ASS* II, pp. 273–4.

[173] For this see Pioli, *Fausto Socino*, pp. 102–4.

§1–§4 Life, death and posthumous worship of Jesus of Nazareth

Socinus had begun the second part of his argument by stating that
Jesus had lived and had been put to a shameful death.[174] Grotius
begins with the same unshakeable biographical facts about Jesus.[175]
The Italian proceeded to state that despite his death Jesus was worshipped by many wise people, thanks to the miracles he had performed.[176] Grotius sees a strict cause and effect relationship in this,
and declares that there can be no other reason for the posthumous
worship of Jesus than the miracles he performed.[177]

§5–§6 Jesus' miracles and resurrection

The miracles of Jesus cannot be ascribed to natural powers, said
Socinus, but show that he was a divine man (*homo divinus*).[178] Grotius
takes over this idea but does not refer to Jesus as a divine man.
Moreover he adds to Socinus' argument the remark that Jesus' miracles could not have been performed by sorcery or evil spirits, or
even by good spirits under God.[179] This digression appears to have
been taken from Mornay's apology.[180]

---

[174] Cf. Soc. *ASS* II, p. 274: "Quod si isti mihi concedunt, fuisse quendam Jesum
Nazaraenum, qui professus fuerit, se praecepta dare cuiusdam religionis, ut quidem
concedere sunt coacti, tum eos interrogo, an credant hunc Jesum, id curantibus
eiusdem nationis hominibus, turpi morti fuisse traditum tanquam hominem sedi-
tiosum quique Deum blasphemaret, et populo imponeret."

[175] *VRC*, II 1–2, pp. 75–7.

[176] Soc. *ASS* II, p. 274: "Iam si ita res habet undenam fieri potuit, ut tam magnus hominum numerus, inter quos multi fuerunt cordatissimi atque eruditissimi,
antiquis suis religionibus sua sponte abjuratis, aliisve opinionibus depositis, in quibus
consenuerant, et de quibus penitus persuasi erant, seque ipsos interim ludibrio
milleque vexationibus periculisque evidentibus, immo certae, atroci, turpique morti
exponentes, religionem amplexi fuerint, cuius eiusmodi homo auctor erat, quia suis
ipsis scelestissimos ac prorsus infamis existimatus fuerat? Est sane omnino necessarium, probabilia argumenta maxima, eaque talia, quae vim animis facerent, exsti-
tisse, istum vera dixisse. [. . .] Non negant hodie, nec unquam negarunt ipsi Jesu
Nazaraeni interfectores, eum mirabilia quaedam magna ac multa fecisse ad ea
confirmanda, quae dicebat, quae fatentur vi ordinari et naturali fieri non posse."

[177] *VRC*, II 3–4, pp. 78–80.

[178] Soc. *ASS* II, p. 274: "Non negant hodie, nec unquam negarunt ipsi Jesu
Nazaraeni interfectores, eum mirabilia quaedam magna ac multa fecisse ad ea
confirmanda, quae dicebat, quae fatentur vi ordinari et naturali fieri non posse.
[. . .] Itaque secundum ipsam eorum legem ac disciplinaam necesse est confiteri,
Jesum Nazaraenum fuisse revera hominem divinum."

[179] *VRC*, II 5, pp. 78–80.

[180] See Mornay, *Ver.* XXX, pp. 733–9.

Socinus believed that the decisive proof was Jesus' resurrection from the dead. He even called this 'the most important foundation' of the Christian faith.[181] In this connection Grotius speaks of the 'leading foundation' of the faith.[182] Socinus had substantiated the historical probability of the resurrection by demonstrating the credibility of the eye witnesses in a broad legal and rhetorical plea.[183] We find the same proof from witnesses in Grotius, who adds a few remarks of his own. Besides the first direct eye witnesses he cites Paul, because he claimed to have seen Christ in heaven on his own conversion.[184]

§7–§8 The resurrection not impossible, but a sign of truth

Grotius' answer to the objection that the resurrection was impossible is to be found almost complete in Socinus.[185] The same applies to the conclusion to this series of arguments: once Christ's resurrection is established, the truth of his doctrine is in fact sufficiently proven.[186]

§9 Christianity excels all other religions

This section forms a transition to Grotius' second series of arguments, which corresponds to Socinus' first. In the title of his second book the Italian had distinguished between those who were willing

---

[181] Soc. *ASS* II, p. 274: "Verum ulterius progrediamur, ipsosque interrogemus, an credant illos, qui primi omnium post turpem in orbis terrarum conspectu Jesu Nazaraeni mortem, ausi sunt ipsi amplecti, aliisque publice suadere ipsius Jesu disciplinam, credidisse, aliisque confirmasse, Jesum Nazaraenum revixisse? Respondebunt sine dubio veritate coacti, se id credere. Quandoquidem disciplina ista illud in se continet, immo, ut potissimo sui ipsius fundamento, eo utitur, sine quo manifeste apparet, eam universam corruere."

[182] *VRC*, II 6, pp. 80–1: "Miraculis a Christo editis par argumentum praebet Christi ipsius post crucem, mortem, sepulturam, admirabilis reditus in vitam. Id enim non modo ut verum, sed ut praecipuum suae fidei fundamentum, adferunt omnium locorum et temporum christiani, [. . .]."

[183] Soc. *ASS* II, pp. 274–5.

[184] See *VRC*, II 6, pp. 83–4.

[185] *VRC*, II 7, pp. 84–5; Cf. Soc. *ASS* II, p. 275: "Nam si quis dixerit, priori isti rei similiter rationem repugnare simulque naturam ipsam; respondebo, aliud esse alicui rei repugnare, aliud vero eam non assequi nec percipere."

[186] *VRC*, II 8, pp. 85–6. Cf. Soc. *ASS* II, p. 275: "Ex iis, quae hactenus disputata sunt, facile intelligi potest, verum esse, Jesum Nazaraenum a morte in vitam rediisse, et ob eam rem, non solum unum aliquem Deum esse, eumque homines singulatim curare, sed etiam ipsius Jesu religionem esse veram."

to assume that there can be a true religion but were not yet convinced that it was Christianity, and those who denied that any religion could be true.[187] Grotius seems to allude to this distinction by stating that one must choose between the alternatives: either reject every religion, or accept Christianity as true.[188] Like Socinus he states that Christianity shows its superiority in the heavenly reward it offers, the rules it prescribes and its successful expansion. Grotius' proofs are noticeably fuller than his predecessor's. Though he follows Socinus' argument, he adds to it explanations and testimonies of his own.

§10 The excellence of the reward that the Christian religion offers

Here Grotius does not speak of the 'promises' of Christ, as Socinus had, but uses the word 'reward' (*praemium*), which implies the fulfilment of that promise.[189] The Italian author had argued that Christ's promises were much more exalted and divine than those of Moses, who never promised anything more than earthly things, or of Muhammad, who merely dreamed of physical pleasures.[190] Grotius also drew a comparison with ancient philosophy. He could have taken these additional points from his *Meletius*.[191]

§11 Bodies dissolved can be restored

In this connection Grotius departs from Socinus' model to answer the objection that bodies once dissolved cannot be restored. He gives a detailed natural philosophical refutation, which shows that an omnipotent God must be allowed the power to recombine after its dissolution the matter he has himself composed from its elements. This argument had not been used by Socinus but it was found in Mornay. Grotius not only used the same argument as the French apologete but also appealed to the same testimonies.[192]

---

[187] Soc. *ASS* II, p. 271: "In quo hoc idem demonstratur iis, qui nondum credunt christianam religionem esse veram. Primum iis, qui credunt aliquam esse, aut esse posse veram religionem. Deinde iis, qui existimant, nullam veram religionem esse posse."

[188] *VRC*, II, 9, p. 86: "Sane aut omnis omnino Dei cultus repudiandus est, [...] aut haec admittenda religio, non tantum ob factorum testimonia, de quibus iam egimus, verum etiam ob ea quae religioni sunt intrinseca. [...]."

[189] *VRC*, II 10, p. 86: "Praemii propositi excellentia."

[190] See Soc. *ASS* II, p. 272.

[191] Cf. *Mel.* 13.4–5; 14.14–16; 15.17–23; 16.33–9; 18.62–5.

[192] In this connection both name Zoroaster, the stoics and the Aristotelian philosopher Theopompus: cf. *VRC*, II 11, pp. 90–2 and Mornay, *Ver.* XXXIV, pp. 847–9.

§12–§17 Christian ethics

Socinus had merely remarked that the commandments of other religions paled by comparison with those of Christianity like feeble lamps before the sun.[193] Grotius for his part offered an explanation of the finesses of Christian ethics, which appears to have been drawn almost entirely from his youthful work *Meletius*.[194]

He discusses six aspects of Christian ethics: 1) service to God; 2) duties to one's fellow men; 3) the rules on the relations of men and women; 4) the use of temporal goods; 5) the swearing of oaths; 6) some other matters. The only difference from *Meletius* is in his arrangement of his material.[195] In the apologetic work his argument is determined by a comparison between pagan, Jewish and Islamic ethics on the one hand, and the Christian commandments on the other. Such a comparison is not found in *Meletius*.

§18 The internal division of Christianity

The internal division of Christianity is not an argument against the excellence of its doctrine. Grotius' argument in this section again agrees strikingly with that of Socinus.[196] For all the differences of opinion that unavoidably prevail among Christians, they are all agreed on the main points: and these concern Christian ethics.[197]

§19 The excellence of Jesus as a teacher

Socinus had emphasised that Jesus was the first to practise the commandments he imposed on others and the first to fulfil the promises he made to his disciples. Moses had admittedly given laws to the

---

[193] Soc. *ASS* II, p. 272: "Quin potius, quaenam alia religio est cuius praecepta, si cum praeceptis christianae religionis comparentur, non videantur tanquam exiguum et obscurum aliquod lumen soli oppositum atque collatum?"

[194] Cf. *Mel.* 60–87.

[195] See *Mel.* Comment., pp. 154–60, where all the parallels between *Mel.* 60–87 and *VRC*, II, pp. 12–17 are given.

[196] Soc. *ASS* II, p. 272: "Sed dicet quispiam: quanam ratione vis, me quidquam de christiana religione judicare posse, cum nesciam, qualisnam sit ista christiana religio propter tot tamque diversas immo contrarias opiniones, quae antiquitus fuerunt, hodieque sunt, de rebus ad eam pertinentibus? Respondeo, istas tot tamque diversas aut etiam contrarias opiniones, nihil impedire, quo minus de summa quadam constare possit eius religionis, quae summa sine dubio id est, in quo omnes qui eam religionem profitentur videntur convenire, [. . .]."

[197] *VRC*, II 18, pp. 106–7.

Jews and promised them earthly happiness, but he had not been allowed to share in it himself; and Muhammad had promised his followers all kinds of joys, but had not given them a single guarantee that these promises would be fulfilled.[198] One finds the same argument in Grotius, albeit in a different order and with an additional brief excursus on the uncertain knowledge and unvirtuous life of the Greek philosophers.[199]

§20–§22 The marvellous expansion of Christianity

The excellence of the Christian religion is also apparent from its enormous expansion (§20). This expansion is marvellous, in view of the weakness and simplicity of those who first proclaimed Christianity (§21) and the great impediments that stood in the way of conversion to this religion (§22). This historical argument can also be found, in concise form, in Socinus.[200] Grotius remarks that it is in harmony with divine providence that the best religion should be the most widespread.[201]

§23 For those who demand still more proof

The final section of Grotius' second book appears to be a summary of the fifth chapter of Socinus' *De auctoritate*.[202] The Italian author had attacked the error of those who demand an utterly irrefutable proof, remarking that such people overlook the specific nature of the Christian religion: faith, which is a touchstone for human virtue.[203]

---

[198] Soc. *ASS.* II, p. 272.

[199] *VRC,* II 19, pp. 107–11.

[200] Soc. *ASS* II, pp. 272–3.

[201] See *VRC* II 20, 111: "Conveniebat divinae providentiae id efficere, ut quod optimum esset pateret quam latissime. Id autem contigit religioni christianae, [. . .]."

[202] Soc. *ASS* V, p. 279: "In quo detegitur error illorum, qui fidei libris istis adjungendae eiusmodi argumenta postulant, quibus nemo sese ulla ratione opponere queat."

[203] Soc. *ASS* V, pp. 279–80: "Iam tametsi quae hucusque scripsimus, satis fortasse esse debeat ad id efficiendum, quod ab initio proposueramus: tamen visum est nobis, antequam huic nostrae scriptioni finem imponamus, monere lectorem eos, qui ut iis fidem adjungant, quae scripta sunt in Vetere Novoque Testamento, ejusmodi arguementa et rationes postulant, quibus neme sese opponere aut repugnare queat, quaeque unicuique eius rei certam et indubitatam fidem faciant, hos, inquam, ostendere, se religionis naturam parum attente considerasse; quae ea est, ut quemadmodum multi loquuntur, fidei meritum requirat, sitque hominum probitatis tanquam lapis quidam lydius, praesertim vero eius religionis, quae a Novo Testamento continetur, de qua una ob eam causam, quae saepius dicta est, satis est nos loqui."

He illustrated this statement with a fine rhetorical passage: it is not
God's will that the truths of Scripture should be so obvious that the
reward of immortality should be within everyone's grasp. God has
offered the virtuous sufficient clarity for them to be rewarded for
their virtue; but he has left the unvirtuous in uncertainty so that
they shall not escape their punishment.[204]

We find a similar argument in Grotius:

> God willed that what he required us to believe, in such a way that
> he could accept this belief from us as an act of obedience, should not
> be so clear that it could be apprehended immediately by the senses
> or on the grounds of a demonstration, but just clear enough to be
> credible and to convince one who is not a pertinacious unbeliever, so
> that the word of the gospel should serve as a touchstone to bring light
> to those who were eligible for it.[205]

Like Socinus he sees the cause of unbelief not in a lack of available
evidence, but in human ill will.[206] Grotius concludes by observing
that the long duration and great expansion of Christianity must be
attributed to miracles; and if these are still denied, then a religion
that has had such a powerful effect without miracles must be regarded
as even greater than any miracle.[207] This reasoning is a variation on
the passage from Dante that Socinus had cited at the close of his
De auctoritate.[208]

---

[204] Soc. *ASS* V, p. 280: "Sapientissime igitur noluit Deus ut praemium immor-
talitatis, id est rei cunctis desideratissime, a se omnibus propositum, quicumque Jesu
Christo obedierint, humano generi paucis quibusdam exceptis, qui nimirum fidem
facere aliis possent eorum, quae ipsi viderant, certum indubitatumque illa ratione
apparet, et idcirco nequaquam fecit, ut Novi Testamenti scripta, in quibus eius
praemii apertissima fit mentio, quaeque de eo constanter affirmant, eiusmodi essent,
ut nullo odio quisquam sese eis opponere posset. Sed satis esse voluit, si et haec
scripta et alia quae sunt eius praemii argumenta, eiusmodi forent, quibus iure et
possit et debeat fides adhiberi, talia demum, ut ei qui probus est aut ita compara-
tus, ut probus facile evadere queat, sint satis; ei vero qui improbus est, et prae
malitia sua probus fieri nequit, non sint satis, ut hac ratione illorum probitate detecta,
horumque malitia, justissimam causam habeat hos quidem puniendi, illos vero
praemio afficiendi, [. . .]."
[205] *VRC*, II 23, p. 119: "Voluit autem Deus id quod credi a nobis vellet, sic ut
illud ipsum credere tanquam obedientiam a nobis accepteret, non ita evidenter
patere, ut quae sensu, aut demonstratione percipiuntur, sed quantum satis esset ad
fidem faciendam, remque persuadendam homini non pertinaci, ut ita sermo Evangelii
tanquam lapis lydius, ad quem ingenia sanabilia explorarentur."
[206] *VRC*, II 23, p. 119.
[207] *VRC*, II 23, pp. 119–20.
[208] Soc. *ASS* VI, p. 280: "Is [sc. Dante Alighieri] igitur in sua poemate, quod
comoediam ipse vocavit, Cantico 24 Paradisi, inducit Petrum Apostolum interro-

Book 3—Socinus

The third book of *De veritate* is no less unconventional in its contents than the previous book. In a letter to his brother Willem, written immediately after he had completed his apologetic work, Grotius wrote that he had not wished to prove the truth of the Holy Scriptures by invoking the infallible judgement of the Church, as Roman Catholics did, or the testimony of the Spirit, as many Protestants had, because he was engaged in a discussion with non-Christians.[209]

It is remarkable that Grotius passed over the 'internal testimony' of the Holy Spirit.[210] In Reformation theology this concept was the foundation of *sola scriptura*, a central principle of the Reformers, who had used it to free themselves at a stroke from the authority of the Church and tradition. The Reformers had insisted that the Scriptures, as the revelation of God's word, were entirely self-evident and did not derive their authority from external human institutions. The doctrine of the internal testimony of the Holy Spirit found its definitive statement in Calvin's *Institutio*.[211] The Genevan Reformer stated that the authority of the Holy Scriptures could not be founded on anything but God's revelation itself, of which man could only be fully assured by the internal testimony of the Holy Spirit, which speaks in the Scriptures.[212] This testimony of the spirit cannot be replaced, Calvin claimed, by human reasoning and testimonies, which, as auxiliary and subordinate arguments, can do no more than confirm a truth already discovered.[213] Calvin stated that those who believed they were able to prove the credibility of the Scriptures by exclusively human reasoning and testimony were on the wrong path.[214]

But despite Calvin's prohibition, Grotius deliberately chose this

---

gantem ipsum, undenam proficisceretur ea fides, qua se praeditum esse dixerat, hoc est persuasio de rebus divinis, se vero ipsum respondentem ad eum, qui sequitur modum. [. . .] *Quod debet probari? Haud quisquam id tibi jurejurando, si orbis terrae sese convertit ad christianismum, inquam ego, sine miraculis, hoc unum est tale, ut reliqua non sint centesima pars,* [. . .]."

[209] *BW* II, n° 600, p. 31: "Non potest igitur Sacrarum literarum veritas ex tali iudicio [sc. the infallible judgement of the Roman Catholic Church] probari; ne idem sit se ipso prius atque posterius: sic et Spiritus testimonium quo protestantes uti solent, a mea tractatione erat alienum, ubi cum extraneis disputatur."

[210] Cf. Laplanche, *L'Évidence*, pp. 101–8, 117–28.

[211] For this doctrine see W. Krusche, *Das Wirken des Heiligen Geistes nach Calvin*, Berlin 1957, pp. 202–12.

[212] Calv. *Inst.*, I 7.

[213] *Ibid.*, I 8, 13.

[214] *Ibid.* I 7, 4.

wrong path. He was not original in this either. Humanist biblical scholarship since Valla and Erasmus had subjected the Scriptures to the same criteria as profane texts, and to that extent had already desacralised them.[215] The young humanist Faustus Socinus in his *De auctoritate* tried to confirm the credibility of all the books of the Bible using purely human testimonies, that is without appealing to super-human institutions such as divine inspiration or the internal testi-mony of the Holy Spirit.[216]

In his first chapter Socinus had addressed those who were already convinced of the truth of the Christian religion.[217] In so doing he separated the question of truth from that of the credibility of the Scriptures, so that he could treat the Bible as if it were any other historical work. Grotius employed the same manoeuvre at the begin-ning of his third book, when he turned to those who were already convinced that Christianity was the true religion.[218] His argument agreed in its main lines with the proofs that Socinus had developed in the first chapter of his youthful work.

Socinus presented his method of proof as follows: he wished to investigate four possible reasons for doubting the credibility of the Bible: 1) if the author of one of the books is unreliable because there are grounds to doubt his good faith or knowledge of events (relia-bility); 2) if the authorship is unknown (authenticity); 3) if there is reason to suspect that the books had been altered or forged (textual purity); 4) if there are convincing historical testimonies that cast doubt on the truth of the book (veracity). He considered the credibility of the books of the Old and New Testaments proven if none of these grounds for doubt applied to them.[219]

---

[215] See W.G. Kümmel, *Das Neue Testament. Geschichte der Erforschung seiner Probleme*, Freiburg 1970, p. 11.

[216] See Cantimori, *Italienische Haeretiker*, p. 336. For the contribution of Socinianism to the development of historical-critical biblical scholarship, see K. Scholder, *Ursprünge und Probleme der Bibelkritik im 17. Jahrhundert. Ein Beitrag zur Entstehung der historisch-kritischen Theologie* [Forschungen zur Geschichte und Lehre des Protestantismus, 33], Munich 1966, pp. 34–55.

[217] Soc. *ASS* I, p. 265: "In quo demonstratur iis, qui iam credunt Christianam religionem esse veram, non posse eos jure dubitare de auctoritate librorum Veteris & Novi Testamenti."

[218] *VRC*, III, p. 121: "Qui iam his quae allata sunt argumentis, aut si quae praeter hanc sunt alia, persuasus eam quam christiani profitentur religionem veram opti-mamque crediderit, ut partes eius omnes ediscat, mittendus est ad libros antiquis-simos eam religionem continentes, quos Novi Testamenti aut Foederis potius libros dicimus."

[219] Soc. *ASS*, p. 265: "Quatuor sunt, ut videtur, causae, cur jure dubitari possit

Grotius used the same argument, that is, he adopted the same four criteria used by Socinus to judge the credibility of the Bible. He employed a different order, dealing first with the authenticity, then the reliability, then the veracity and finally the textual purity of the New Testament. Finally he briefly applied these criteria to the books of the Old Testament.

Grotius appears not only to have followed Socinus' method of proof, but to have taken over many of his separate arguments. In addition he gives his own explanation of the miracles and prophecies of the New Testament authors (§7–§8). These arguments, however, are not easy to reconcile with the proofs given by his predecessor. While Socinus had confined himself strictly to human testimonies, Grotius appealed to divine testimonies to prove the reliability of the New Testament authors. In itself that was not an unusual argument. In Reformation theology the miracles and prophecies of the prophets and apostles belonged to the external or secondary arguments that confirmed the authority of the Scriptures.[220]

In his *Bewijs* Grotius remarked that the miracles performed by the authors of the New Testament point to divine inspiration.[221] This remark is not found in the Latin version.[222] One may infer from this that the appeal to inspiration was not of primary importance in Grotius' proof. That does not mean that he doubted that the authors of the books of the New Testament were inspired. He refers incidentally to the inspiration of some of these authors in his apologetic

---

de auctoritate libri cuiuspiam. Prima est, si scriptor parum sit fide dignus, aut non eiusmodi, de cuius fide et scientia dubitari nequeat. Altera est, si revera scriptor ignoretur. Tertia, si constet aut justa suspicio sit, librum depravatum fuisse aut aliquo modo immutatum. Quarta vero et postrema, si non rejicienda testimonia adsint, quod libro isti nequaquam sit adhibenda fides. Si igitur demonstratum fuerit, nullam ex praedictis quatuor caussis locum habere in eo libro, qui Novum Testamentum appellatur, demonstratum utique etiam fuerit, injuria de eius auctoritate dubitari."

[220] On this see E. Schnabel, *Inspiration und Offenbarung. Die Lehre vom Ursprung und Wesen der Bibel*, Wuppertal 1986, pp. 24–31.

[221] *Bewijs*, p. 82: "Nadien tot hier toe zeer krachtelijk is gebleken/Dat deze schrijvers al 't geen daar zij van spreken/Wel wisten, dat haar ook geen ontrouw heeft vervoerd,/Waar bij komt dat Gods geest heeft haar gemoed beroerd,/gelijk God zelve heeft betuigd door menig wonder,/[. . .]." Grotius stated elsewhere that miracles are a sign of the working of the Holy Spirit: see *Onderwysinge der gedoopte kinderen* [*BG* n° 151], p. 178: "Hoe kon de Heil'ge Geest de waarheit Christi stercken? Doordien hy in hem wroght, door wonderlijcke werken."

[222] Cf. *VRC*, III 10, pp. 128–31.

work, but does not draw far-reaching conclusions from this.[223] In general he regards the credibility of the authors of the New Testament as sufficiently guaranteed by their reliability as historical testimonies. In fact he does not need the theologoumenon of inspiration for his proof.

Grotius showed that he was not an adherent of the orthodox Reformation doctrine of verbal inspiration, which maintained that the whole of the Scriptures had been dictated by God to the authors of the Bible, who were no more than helpful amanuenses.[224] On the contrary, he emphasised the autonomy and freedom of the authors of the books of the Bible, but without wholly eliminating the factor of inspiration. Compared with Reformation views he restricted this factor to a secondary argument.[225] In later theological works he was roundly to declare his opinion that not all of the Scriptures were inspired. He did not deny that the prophets and apostles could have been lent wings by God's spirit, but for many historical parts of the Bible the most that could be said is that they were written in a spirit of piety. Thus for Grotius the Gospel and Acts of Luke were not the product of divine inspiration, but simply a reliable eye-witness account.[226] Elsewhere he states that the Holy Spirit had indeed confirmed the apostles and evangelists in what they had to say about the evangelical doctrine, but that their work, in everything else, remained human work.[227]

---

[223] *Bewijs*, p. 73: "De schrijvers dragen zich voor lui met Godes geest/Uitnemelijk begaafd, voorgangers van de leer." *VRC* III 5, p. 125: "Neque falli potuit Apocalypseos scriptor in iis visis, quae sibi divinitus immissa dicit; aut ille ad Hebraeos, in iis, quae profitetur se aut a Dei spiritu aut ab apostolis ipsis didicisse." See also *VRC* VI 11, p. 240: "Nam et fideliores fuisse eorum scriptores et afflatus divini pleniores, quam ut necessaria veritate nos fraudare vellent, eamve nube aliqua obtegere. [. . .]."

[224] See Schnabel, *Inspiration*, pp. 33–6.

[225] For Grotius' attitude to inspiration and canonicity see J. Leipoldt, *Geschichte des neutestamentlichen Kanons*, II, Leipzig 1908, pp. 153–7. See also H.J. de Jonge, 'Hugo Grotius exégète du Nouveau Testament', in *The World of Hugo Grotius (1583–1645)*, Amsterdam/Maarssen 1984, pp. 97–115.

[226] Cf. *Votum* in *OT* IV 672b 49–673a 10; and *Discussio*, in *OT* IV 722a 58–723a 20.

[227] *Annot. in NT* (ad Act. 7:3), in *OT* III 594a 22–24: "Spiritus Sanctus Apostolos et Evangelistas confirmavit in doctrina evangelica: in caeteris rebus, ut hominibus, reliquit quae sunt hominum." Grotius' views remind us of Melanchthon's doctrine of inspiration. The *Praeceptor Germaniae* confined inspiration to the doctrinal parts of the Scriptures, excluding the historical sections of the Bible, and regarded only the prophets and apostles as divinely inspired authors. See J.N. Bakhuizen van den Brink/W.F. Dankbaar, *Handboek der Kerkgeschiedenis*, III, Leeuwarden 1980, pp. 89–90.

Grotius' appeal to the miracles and prophecies of the authors of the New Testament here serves only as a secondary argument to prove the reliability of these accounts, which for him remained first and foremost human testimonies. Grotius deals capably with the proof from testimonies, and like his fellow-jurist Socinus he often gives his arguments a juridical turn. He avoids the weak points and unnecessary repetitions in the Italian's argument, and here and there adds arguments of his own, which as we shall see were largely borrowed from the apologetic work of Mornay.

The rhetorical-legal proof that both Socinus and Grotius employed did not add any new scholarly insights to existing knowledge of the Bible. Socinus cannot be denied the merit of a certain methodical consistency.[228] Grotius rather drew back from this radicalism, and steered a middle course between the Italian's completely historical treatment and the Reformation doctrine of inspiration.[229]

§1 The credibility of the New Testament

In the introduction to this book Grotius, like Socinus, addresses those who are already convinced of the truth of the Christian religion. The content of that religion is found in the books of the New Testament. He justifies this assertion with the aid of an idea that is also found in Socinus: it is no more than fair to take at their word the adherents of any belief who appeal to certain books for the contents of their doctrine.[230]

Following Socinus' example Grotius formulates his method of proof in rhetorical terms: whoever seeks to impugn a book that has been respected for centuries is obliged to produce convincing counterproofs; as long as he fails to do so, one must assume the credibility of that book.[231]

§2–§4 Authenticity

Grotius deals with Socinus' second criterion in the same way as his first. Most of the books of the New Testament, he states, were written

---

[228] See Cantimori, *Italienische Haeretiker*, p. 336.
[229] Cf. A.H. Haentjens, *Hugo de Groot als godsdienstig denker*, Amsterdam 1946, p. 29.
[230] Soc. *ASS* II, p. 273.
[231] Cf. Soc. *ASS* I, p. 265: "Si igitur demonstratum fuerit, nullam ex praedictis quatuor caussis locum habere in eo libro, qui Novum Testamentum appellatur, demonstratum utique etiam fuerit, injuria de eius auctoritate dubitari."

by the authors whose names are given in their titles. Socinus had
made the same assertion and pointed out that certainty about the
historical identity of an author depends entirely on the testimonies
of his contemporaries or those who lived soon after him.[232] In the
first Christian communities the identity of most of the authors of the
New Testament books was not in doubt, and this is confirmed by
such early Christian authors as Justin Martyr, Irenaeus and Clement
of Alexandria.[233] Grotius added only the name of Tertullian.[234]

Like Socinus, Grotius readily admits that there was some initial
uncertainty about the authorship of some of the books of the New
Testament, i.e. 2 Peter, James, Jude, 2 John, 3 John, Hebrews and
Rev. But these doubts had very soon disappeared.[235] Socinus was
only unsure of the authorship of the epistle to the Hebrews (Hebr.).[236]
Grotius states flatly that the author of this epistle is unknown. As
for 2 John, 3 John and Rev. he cautiously observes that there are
some who doubt if these were in fact written by the apostle John
or by another of the same name.[237]

Clearly he does not think it appropriate to go into this question
in a defence of the faith. He would later do so in his Annotations
on the New Testament. In that book he showed himself less cautious, and ascribed Hebrews to the evangelist Luke,[238] James not to
the apostle but to the bishop of Jerusalem of the same name,[239] 2
Pet. to his successor in the bishopric of Jerusalem, Simeon,[240] Jude
to Jude the successor of bishop Simeon,[241] 2 and 3 John to the elder
John,[242] and finally Rev. to the apostle John.[243]

---

[232] Soc. *ASS* I, p. 267.

[233] Soc. *ASS* I, p. 238: "Id quod nos hodie quoque magna ex parte videmus, ex
scriptis quae ad nostram aetatem pervenerunt Justini, Irenaei, et Clemens Alexandrini,
qui omnes tres tempori illi proximi fuerunt, praesertim vero Justinus."

[234] *VRC*, II 2, p. 122.

[235] Cf. Soc. *ASS* I, pp. 268–9.

[236] Soc. *ASS* I, p. 269: "Quod attinet ad Epistolam ad Hebraeos scriptam, non
dubium est quin ad hunc usque diem immo hodie multo magis quam pluribus retro
actis seculis, dubitatum fuerit ac dubitetur, quisnam eam scripserit."

[237] He seems to have forgotten that in the previous section he had already ascribed
2 and 3 John to the 'elder John': *VRC*, III 3, p. 123.

[238] *Annot. in NT*, in *OT* III 1010 a1–40.

[239] *OT* III 1073; 1113a 27–30.

[240] *OT* III 1113a 27–30.

[241] *OT* III 1151 a 7–11.

[242] *OT* III 1147 a 1–21.

[243] *OT* III 1159 a 1–44. Grotius' teacher Scaliger was even more critical, and
doubted the authenticity of 1 John. See H.J. de Jonge, 'The Study of the New

Like Socinus Grotius remarks that the credibility of a book is not dependent so much on the knowledge of its authorship as on its authority. For Socinus this criterion was adequate.[244] Grotius adds that the authors of the New Testament, compared with other writers, gained greatly in credibility from their status as apostles.[245]

§5–§6 Reliability

Socinus found another reason to doubt the credibility of a book in the unreliability of the author, either because he had no certain knowledge of the things that he described, or because he lied. He first observed that the authors of the New Testament were familiar with the events they related.[246] Matthew, John, Peter and Jude were disciples of Jesus and thus very familiar with what they wrote about. He also included James among the apostles.[247] A similar argument is to be found in Grotius, who offers the further possibility that James was a close relative of Jesus.[248] Both agree in the opinion that Paul cannot be accused of ignorance, because Christ revealed himself to him. Luke and Mark, as colleagues of Paul and Peter, also knew very well what they wrote about. The author of Revelation could not have been mistaken, because his visions were inspired by God himself.[249] This last argument is certainly not the strongest. Socinus had passed over the unknown author of Hebrews, while Grotius was content to remark rhetorically that this author must have derived

---

Testament' in *Leiden University in the Seventeenth Century. An Exchange of Learning*, ed. Th.H. Lunsingh Scheurleer and G.H.M. Posthumus Meyjes, Leiden 1975, p. 84.

[244] See Soc. *ASS* I, pp. 268–9.

[245] *Bewijs*, p. 73: "De schrijvers dragen zich voor lui met Godes geest/Uitnemelijk begaafd, voorgangers van de leer." Cf. *VRC* III 4, p. 123: "Sic etiam cum, qui libros scripserunt, de quibus nunc agimus, et prima aetate se vixisse testentur, et donis apostolicis fuisse praeditos, sufficere id nobis debet."

[246] Soc. *ASS* I, pp. 265–6.

[247] Soc. *ASS* I, p. 266: "Exstant similiter Epistolae quaedam Jacobi, Petri, Johannis, et Judae, qui omnes Christi apostoli fuerunt, [. . .]."

[248] *VRC*, III 5, p. 124: "Idem de Jacobi dici potest, qui aut apostolus fuit aut, ut alii volunt, proximus consanguineus Jesu, et ab apostolis constitutus Hierosolymorum episcopus."

[249] *VRC*, III 5, p. 125: "Neque falli potuit Apocalypseos scriptor in iis visis, quae sibi divinitus immissa dicit [. . .]". Cf. Soc. *ASS* I, p. 266: "Habetur praeterea liber Apocalypsis dictus, qui admirabilem quandam visionem continet, in qua satis obscure multa praedicuntur futura, quae omnia ad Christi ecclesiam spectant. Cuius visionis veritatem, id est, an et qualis fuisset, optime is noverat, qui eam scripsit; cum ipse affirmet sibi eam contigisse, seque illam vidisse."

his knowledge either directly from God's Spirit or from the apostles.[250]

Both Socinus and Grotius believed that it was clear that the authors of the New Testament did not wish to lie. Those who accused the testimonies of bad faith must give reasons why they should have lied. Liars in general are out to win an advantage or avoid a danger. Both jurists had little difficulty in defending the authors of the New Testament against such an accusation.[251]

§7–§9 Supernatural confirmation

Grotius develops an independent argument here, which, as we said, deviates from that of Socinus. He invokes the testimonies that God himself has given to confirm the reliability of the authors of the New Testament.[252] These testimonies consist of the miracles they performed and the prophecies in their books that have since been fulfilled. Grotius refers to the apostolic miracles, and for convenience he identifies the apostles with the authors of the New Testament. His conception of the apostolic miracles is very broad, for besides the miracles mentioned in the New Testament, he also refers to the miraculous deeds of Peter that were supposedly described by the Greek historian Phlegon, as well as the miracles said to have been witnessed for many years around the graves of the apostles and related in the apocryphal Acts of the Apostles.[253] These had been well known proofs in early Christian literature, but later came to be considered entirely unreliable.[254] Grotius also counts the prophecies in the New Testament as testimonies from God and further confirmation of the reliability of the authors of these books.[255]

Grotius proceeds to use a semi-metaphysical, semi-rhetorical argument that can also be found in Socinus: it would be in conflict with God's providence if so many pious and virtuous people had been deceived by false books.[256]

---

[250] *VRC*, II 5, p. 125: "Neque falli potuit Apocalypseos scriptor in iis visis, quae sibi divinitus immissa dicit; aut ille ad Hebraeos, in iis, quae profitetur se aut a Dei Spiritu, aut ab apostolis ipsis didicisse."

[251] Cf. *VRC*, III 6, pp. 125–6 and Soc. *ASS* I, pp. 266–7.

[252] *VRC*, II 7, p. 126: "Contra vero bonae ipsorum [sc. the authors of the New Testament] fidei Deus ipse testimonia illustria reddidit, editis prodigiis, quae cum magna fiducia ipsi ipsorumve discipuli, publice asseverarunt, additis personarum locorumque nominibus et circumstantiis caeteris."

[253] *VRC*, III 7, p. 127.

[254] For these references see Bergman, 'Suppl. Annot.', p. 264.

[255] *VRC*, III 8, pp. 127–8.

[256] Cf. *VRC* II 9, 128, and Soc. *ASS* I, p. 270.

§10–§14 Veracity

Grotius raises three objections, which had also been dealt with by
his Italian predecessor, albeit in different places. First he discusses
the objection that certain Christians have rejected a number of the
books of the New Testament. Socinus had only touched on this problem in passing, and had confined himself to a few remarks on the
Ebionites, who rejected all the epistles of Paul.[257] Grotius adds the
Marcionites, who only recognised the Gospel of Mark and about ten
of Paul's epistles.

The objection that the New Testament contains inconsistencies
had been discussed by Socinus in a separate chapter of *De auctoritate*.[258] Grotius merely refers to an earlier section of his apology, in
which he had defended the possibility of Jesus' resurrection from the
dead.[259] He deals at greater length with the objection that the New
Testament contains unreasonable doctrines. In the fourth chapter of
his work Socinus had shown in detail that Christian doctrines were
reasonable, but that some truths have been made known only by
divine revelation.[260] Grotius is more concise on this point, and offers
a brief explanation of the relationship of reason and revelation.[261]

This enquiry into the inconsistencies between the books of the
New Testament brings Grotius back to the first chapter of Socinus'
work.[262] The Italian had stated that the New Testament did not contain inconsistencies either in doctrine or in the most important historical passages. He admitted that there were differences in the less
important historical portions, but these by no means undermined the
credibility of the New Testament as a whole. Moreover writers who
were not faithful to the truth would have avoided every sign of contradiction.[263] Grotius uses the same arguments. He recognises minor
inconsistencies in the books of the New Testament, in the description

---

[257] See Soc. *ASS* I, p. 268.
[258] Soc. *ASS* III, pp. 275–6: "In quo probatur breviter cunctis in universum, neminem posse causam ullam justam afferre, cur libris istis fidem non adhibeat."
[259] Cf. *VRC*, III 11, p. 131 and II 7, pp. 84–5.
[260] Soc. *ASS* IV, pp. 276–9: "In quo ostenditur istis libris majorem debere fidem
adjungi quam aliis communiter adjungatur doctrinam historiamve aliquam conti-
nentibus."
[261] *VRC*, III 12, pp. 131–3.
[262] Soc. *ASS* I, p. 267: "Dico igitur, quod attinet ad repugnantias aut diversitates,
quae in Novi Testamenti scriptis inveniantur, nulla esse, quae aut non videatur quidem vera, sed tamen non sit, aut non in re sit parvi, sed potius nulli momenti."
[263] Soc. *ASS* I, p. 267.

of circumstances, and admits that they are not always easily recon-
ciled. But this does not impair the general credibility of the authors
of the New Testament.[264]

Finally there is the objection that doubt must be cast on the truth
of a book because of unfavourable external testimonies. Socinus was
particularly brief on this point, and stated that he knew of no testimonies that would make it impossible to believe the books of the
New Testament.[265] Grotius put it even more emphatically: "I declare
with confidence that such testimonies will not be found . . .".[266]
Although he really felt this was sufficient, he added that there were
in fact many external testimonies that confirmed the truth of the
New Testament.

§15 Purity of the text

Grotius follows Socinus entirely in his discussion of the textual corruptions of the New Testament. He states that though there are such
small textual differences in the many manuscripts handed down, they
owe their existence to negligence or misplaced care in transcription.
They are no more than slips of the pen, inevitable in books that
had been so frequently copied over so many centuries.[267] Like Socinus
he maintains that major textual changes could not have been introduced, because they would have led unavoidably to glaring inconsistencies in the New Testament and the textual tradition in manuscripts
and old translations; but there is no question of these.[268]

§16 Credibility of the Old Testament

Socinus did not think it necessary to devote much attention to the
credibility of the books of the Old Testament, because the New

---

[264] *VRC*, III 13, pp. 133–4.
[265] Soc. *ASS* I, p. 270: "Quandoquidem nulla (quod sciam) testimonia extant hominum hac in re fide dignorum, quod Novi Testamenti scriptis, si modo christiana religio vera est, fides non sit adhibenda."
[266] *VRC*, III 14, p. 135: "At ego cum fiducia affirmo, talia [sc. testimonia] repertum non iri, [. . .]."
[267] Cf. *VRC*, III 15, pp. 136–7, and Soc. *ASS* I, pp. 269–70.
[268] Cf. Soc. *ASS* I, p. 270: "Ea est, quod plusquam verisimile censeri debet, Deum, cuius bonitas et providentia infinita est, non permisisse, ut illa scripta, quibus continebatur potissima, quam sui ipsius suaeque voluntatis simulque salutis nostrae, humano generi, tot hoc ab orbe condito tempore, largitus est notitia, quaeque ut talia, quae eam continerent, a vere piis in ipsum Deum hominibus semper recepta fuerunt, ulla ratione depravata ac corrupta fuerint."

Testament was itself a manifest confirmation of it.[269] Grotius was more aware than Socinus of the autonomous value of the Old Testament, and noticeably more careful in his treatment of it.[270] Socinus had, however, gone into some detail on the credibility of Moses as an author.[271] Grotius was content to refer to the first book of his apologetic work.[272] He adds that the Old Testament narrative after Moses was confirmed by pagan testimonies,[273] and substantiates this claim by summarising a number of them (Berosus and others); this appears to continue the list in §16 of his first book. We assume that Grotius took these testimonies, like those in his first book, from Mornay.[274] He goes on to give a proof of the textual purity of the Old Testament, as Socinus had done.[275] In addition to Socinus' arguments Grotius cites the extent of the Jewish diaspora, which made changes in the text almost impossible, as well as the old translations of the Old Testament and citations in the works of Josephus and Philo, which taken together show no important differences from the traditional Hebrew text. His last argument in this book is again very similar to those of Socinus: the Jews have shown their integrity by refusing to alter the texts from which Christians conclude that Jesus was the long promised Messiah.[276]

Book 4—Mornay

Like medieval apologetes, humanist defenders of Christianity felt a natural superiority over non-Christian religions. To attack paganism was for them no more than an obligatory part of an apology for

---

[269] Soc. *ASS* I, p. 270: "Hactenus nobis videmur satis aperte demonstrasse, si concedatur, christianam religionem esse veram, nullam esse causam, cur dubitari debeat de auctoritate eius libri, qui Novum Testamentum appellatur. Ex quo, ut ab initio diximus, necessario sequitur, non esse similiter, cur dubitetur de auctoritate eius libri, qui appellatur Vetus Testamentum, cum is a Novo Testamento manifeste confirmetur."

[270] *VRC*, III 16, p. 138: "Nunc cum Deo visum fuerit etiam judaicae religionis, quae vera olim fuit, et christianae non exigua testimonia praebet, instrumenta nobis relinquere, non abs re erit his quoque fidem suam adstruere."

[271] Soc. *ASS* I, pp. 270-1.

[272] *VRC* I 15.

[273] *VRC*, III 16, p. 139: "Non repetam hic, quae in Mosis commendationem dicta sunt supra. Neque vero pars tantum illa prima a Mose tradita, ut primo libro ostendimus, sed et recentior historia multos paganorum habet adstipulatores."

[274] See Mornay, *Ver.* XXVI, pp. 636-42.

[275] Soc. *ASS* I, p. 271.

[276] Cf. Soc. *ASS* I, p. 271.

the faith. But they were attacking an enemy that had been dead for centuries, that is the ancient paganism of Greek and Roman antiquity. Many of the early Christian apologetes and fathers of the Church had amassed an enormous arsenal of arguments against it, on which the humanists could draw freely.[277]

Entirely in tune with other humanist apologetes Grotius in this book addresses himself chiefly to ancient paganism, though he makes a few references to contemporary paganism in Africa and America.[278] Almost the whole of his argument can be traced back to early Christian and patristic literature. All of that material had been prepared for him by Mornay, and everything suggests that the Frenchman was Grotius' primary source for this part of his argument. It is noticeable that Grotius' argument was much more condensed than Mornay's. He omitted most of the many names, examples and digressions with which the French apologete had larded his argument. But on two points in this book (§4–§7, §12), he develops an argument of his own.

§1—Introduction

Grotius opens this book with an introduction to the whole refutatory part of his apologetic work, in which he urges his readers to feel a certain pity for those in error. A similar tone of patronising sympathy can be detected in Mornay.[279]

§2–§3 Against polytheism

Grotius continues his attack on paganism, like Mornay, with a brief refutation of polytheism.[280] He does not deny the existence of supernatural good and evil spirits. He avoids the traditional terms 'angels' and 'devils', which Mornay had used, but for the rest he presents the same arguments as the Frenchman: the spirits that the pagans worshipped can only have been evil, in view of the pernicious customs that accreted around their cults.[281]

---

[277] See Laplanche, *L'Évidence*, pp. 74–5, 172–3.
[278] *Bewijs*, pp. 99, 101, 103.
[279] Cf. Mornay, *Ver.* XXI, pp. 509, 527.
[280] Mornay, *Ver.* XXI, pp. 509–10.
[281] Cf. Mornay, *Ver.* XXI, pp. 526–7.

§4–§7 Forms of idolatry

Grotius' treatment of idolatry differs slightly from Mornay's. The Frenchman had devoted an entire chapter to the classical argument that the pagan gods were originally men to whom divine honours were paid after their death.[282] This explanation was developed by the Greek thinker Euhemerus in the fourth century B.C. and later adopted by early Christian apologetes and fathers of the Church under the influence of the stoics and Cicero.[283] Grotius applied it in a very broad sense. He states that the pagans worshipped not only men who had died (§4) but also the stars and earthly elements (§5), animals (§6) and abstract concepts (§7).

Mornay had given so many examples and descriptions of pagan idolatry in order to arouse ethical indignation.[284] Grotius, on the other hand, emphasised the unreasonableness of such practices. His argument on this point is a variation on the typically stoic theme of the hierarchical and purposeful ordering of nature, in which humanity occupies the highest place.[285] Given this fixed ordering of the cosmos, it is unreasonable for the higher (man) to worship the lower (lifeless matter, stars, elements, animals and abstractions).[286]

§8–§9 Pagan miracles and oracles

In this section Grotius again closely follows Mornay's argument: the miracles that the pagans invoked are mostly to be ascribed to natural causes, concealed by deceit or ignorance.[287] The pseudo-miracles of Simon Magus and Apollonius of Tyana can serve as examples of deceit. The pagan miracles that truly occurred must not be attributed to God, but to evil spirits.[288] The only point that Grotius adds to his predecessor's argument is the remark that it is not surprising that God should have permitted evil spirits to work a few miracles,

---

[282] Mornay, *Ver.* XXII, pp. 509–25: "Que les dieux adorez par les gentils estoient hommes consacrez à la posterité."

[283] Laplanche, *L'Évidence*, p. 75.

[284] Mornay, *Ver.* XXII, pp. 509–25.

[285] Grotius also developed this line of reasoning in the first book; see *VRC*, I 7, p. 12.

[286] Cf. Cic. *ND* II 21–25, 62–63.

[287] Cf. Mornay, *Ver.* XXIII, pp. 540–5.

[288] Mornay, *Ver.* XXIII, pp. 542–3.

since the pagans deserved to be deceived, for they had early strayed
from the true religion.[289]

Grotius applies the same remarkable historical-psychological explanation to the pronouncements of oracles: the pagans were rightly
deceived by them, because they had scorned the notions that reason and the most ancient tradition had implanted in every human
being.[290] This remark evokes reminiscences of the idea he had already
put forward of a universal natural knowledge of God and a pure
primeval religion.[291]

He follows his French predecessor in pointing out the ambiguous
and therefore hardly credible character of the pagan oracles. In most
cases they can be explained in a natural way.[292] A few oracles, however, are acknowledged by both apologetes, such as the oracle of
Apollo that, according to Porphyry, summoned the pagans to worship only the God of the Jews,[293] and the famous Sibylline oracles
that an ancient Christian interpretation believed to announce the
coming of Christ.[294]

§10–§11 The downfall of paganism

Grotius then puts forward two historical arguments, both of which
he could have found in many passages of Mornay's work.[295] The
first argument says that the pagan religion cannot have been founded
on truth, because it collapsed as soon as human support was withdrawn from it. He agrees with Mornay that the downfall of paganism went hand in hand with the rise of Christianity, which also put
an end to the power of demons.[296] The second argument deals with

---

[289] *VRC*, IV 8, p. 164: "Neque est, quod miretur quisquam, passum esse summum Deum, ut mira quaedam a pravis spiritibus ederentur, cum deludi talibus
praestigiis meriti essent, qui a veri Dei cultu pridem defecerant."

[290] *VRC*, IV 9, p. 165: "Eadem ferme omnia aptari possunt et ad id solvendum,
quod de oraculis opponunt, praecipue quod diximus, meritos eos homines, ut sibi
illuderetur, contemtis illis notitiis, quas cuique ratio aut vetustissima traditio sug-
gerit." The first Latin edition uses the word 'natura' instead of the words 'ratio aut
vetustissima traditio'; see *Sensus*, p. 125.

[291] Cf. *VRC* I 1, and I 22.

[292] Mornay, *Ver.* XXIII, pp. 534–40.

[293] Mornay, *Ver.* XXIII, p. 805.

[294] Mornay, *Ver.* XXXII, p. 787.

[295] All these arguments can be found in Eusebius and Augustine; see Laplanche,
L'Évidence, pp. 156–7, 173.

[296] Mornay, *Ver.* XXXII, pp. 799–802.

the objection that the rise and fall of religions must be attributed to the effect of the stars. Mornay had mentioned the Arab astronomer Abu Masar (9th century) and the Christian philosopher Roger Bacon (ca. 1220–92) as the *auctores intellectuales* of this objection.[297] Grotius as usual does not overburden his readers with names, and merely speaks of 'philosophers'.[298]

§12—The leading truths of Christianity are already found in the ancient philosophers

In the last section of this book Grotius offers an account that is not to be found in Mornay. He seeks to demonstrate two points: first, that the leading truths of the Christian religion already occur in the pagans; and second, that certain Christian doctrines that are difficult to believe are found in ancient philosophers.[299] He includes only ethics among the most important points of Christianity. His rejection of paganism as a whole is linked to a positive evaluation of certain pagan philosophers who had already pointed out important fragments of the Christian truth. This apologetic strategy had already been adopted by early Christian authors.[300] Grotius expresses himself cautiously: "if something is difficult to believe in the Christian religion, one will also find such things in the wisest pagans".[301] He illustrates this statement by reference to well known agreements between the philosophy of Plato and Christian doctrine.

In Christian apologetics there had long been a strong tendency to point to the real or supposed agreements between Christianity and Platonic philosophy. Justin Martyr, one of the first defenders of the faith, had noticed this parallel and had inferred from it that Plato owed much of his wisdom to the Jewish prophets, especially Moses.[302] This assumption had already been put forward in hellenistic

[297] Mornay, *Ver.* XXXIII, p. 820. The Frenchman was clearly drawing on Pico della Mirandola here; see Laplanche, *L'évidence*, p. 314, n. 240.
[298] *VRC*, IV 11, p. 169: "Fuere philosophi, qui ut ortum ita interitum religionis cuiusque astris adscriberent."
[299] Cf. *VRC*, IV 12, p. 171: "Ostenditur praecipua Christianae religionis probari a sapientibus paganorum, et si quid in ea est difficile creditu, paria apud paganos reperiri."
[300] See Laplanche, *L'Évidence*, p. 175.
[301] *VRC*, IV 12, p. 173; "Quod si quid est in christiana religione creditu difficile, apud sapientissimos paganorum paria inveniuntur, [. . .]."
[302] Iust. M. *Apol.* LIX–LX. Cf. Tert. *Apol.* XLVII.

Jewish apologetics, and was attached to the chronological idea, mentioned above, that the books of Moses were the most ancient books in the world.[303] Grotius, who subscribed to this idea in the first book of his apologetic work, does not go so far as to state that Plato had borrowed his wisdom from Moses, but he does remark that "Plato had been taught by the Chaldeans".[304]

Humanist apologetes such as Ficino, Steuco, Vives and Mornay were attached to the theory that Plato had drawn on the so-called *prisca theologia* (ancient theology), that is Chaldean and Egyptian sources, which in turn were assumed to go back to Moses.[305] They appealed to texts that were ascribed to such mythical figures as the Egyptian Hermes Trismegistus, the Greek Orpheus and the Roman Sibyls, and were thus assumed to be very ancient, though in reality they were produced in the first centuries A.D.[306] Early Christian authors very readily appealed to these texts. At the end of the 15th century Marsilio Ficino again drew attention to this ancient theology by publishing a translation of the text ascribed to Hermes Trismegistus.[307]

Many humanists fell under the spell of these and other mysterious texts, believing them to contain traces of the most ancient theology in the world, which in many respects agreed wonderfully well with both Christian doctrine and Platonic philosophy. This gave the apologetes a magnificent historical proof of the fundamental unity of Christianity and Platonism. But in 1614 the great scholar Isaac Casaubon shattered this dream by unmasking the *Corpus Hermeticus* as a forgery of the first centuries A.D.[308]

Grotius corresponded with Casaubon and was aware of his friend's work very soon after its publication.[309] In his apologetic work he

[303] See Daniélou, *Message évangelique*, pp. 42–3.
[304] *Bewijs*, p. 113; "Ziet hoe Aristons zoon bij de chaldeen geleid, [. . .]." Cf. *VRC*, IV 12, p. 175: "Sic Plato a chaldaeis edoctus . . .".
[305] See Laplanche, *L'Évidence*, pp. 77–82.
[306] D.P. Walker, *The Ancient Theology. Studies in Christian Platonism from the Fifteenth to the Eighteenth Century*, London 1972, pp. 1–22.
[307] Hermes Trismegistus, *Pimander seu de potestate et sapientia Dei*. In latinum traductus a Marsilio Ficino, Florence 1470.
[308] I. Casaubonus, *De rebus sacris et ecclesiasticis exercitationes xvi ad Baronii Annales*, London 1614. For this see A. Grafton, 'Protestant versus Prophet: Isaac Casaubon on Hermes Trismegistus', *Journal of the Warburg and Courtauld Institutes*, 46 (1983), 78–93; later included in A. Grafton, *Defenders of the Text. The Traditions of Scholarship in an Age of Science, 1450–1800*, London/Cambridge, Mass. 1991, pp. 145–61.
[309] See *BW* I, n° 334 (to I. Casaubon), 4 May 1614): "Avidissime exspectatas tuas in Baronium Animadversiones Erpennii ex manu accepi."

makes no appeals to Hermes Trismegistus, though they had been frequent in Mornay.[310] Later he was to criticise his French predecessor on this point, citing Casaubon.[311] That does not mean, however, that he radically rejected all the texts of the ancient theology. In the first book of his apologetic work, as we saw, he had repeatedly cited the *Orphica*, though he was forced to admit that these texts could not be attributed to Orpheus.[312] In this chapter he appealed to the *Sibylla carmina*,[313] although Casaubon had cast doubt on the authenticity of these texts too.[314] Moreover, in his notes he cites Zoroaster, who was assumed to be the author of the the *Oracula Chaldaica*,[315] and Pythagoras, to whom the *Carmen Aureum* was wrongly ascribed.[316]

The most striking agreement between ancient theology and Christianity, in the eyes of the humanists, concerned the doctrine of the trinity. Mornay, who had devoted an entire chapter of his apology to the confirmation of trinitarian doctrine by pagans and Jews, found traces of it in Zoroaster, Hermes Trismegistus and Orpheus, and later in Plato and the neoplatonists.[317] But Grotius appealed exclusively to Plato.[318] Like Mornay he saw other agreements between pagan philosophy and Christian doctrine in Julian the Apostate's acknowledgement of the possibility of God's becoming man, and in the suffering of the righteous.[319] For the latter he again referred to Plato.[320]

---

[310] See J. Harrie, 'Du Plessis Mornay, Foix-Candale and the Hermetic Religion of the World', *Renaissance Quarterly*, 31 (1978), 495–514.

[311] *Riv. Apol. Disc.* in *OT* IV 687 b18–33.

[312] *VRC*, I 16, pp. 29–30: "[. . .] et ante eos scriptori antiquissimo, non illorum hymnorum, quos nos sub eo nomine habemus, sed eorum carminum, quae vetustas Orphica appelavit, non quod Orphei essent, sed quod ab eo tradita continerent."

[313] *VRC*, IV 9, pp. 166–7.

[314] See A. Grafton, 'Protestant versus Prophet: Isaac Casaubon on Hermes Trismegistus', *Journal of the Warburg and Courtauld Institutes*, 46 (1983), 88.

[315] *VRC* IV 11, n. 6.

[316] *VRC* IV 12, n. 8.

[317] Mornay, *Ver.* VI, pp. 96–106.

[318] Cf. *Mel.* 22.33–6, where Grotius cites a parallel passage from Aristotle.

[319] Mornay, *Ver.* XXXIII, p. 832.

[320] This reference was a commonplace in patristic literature: see E. des Places, 'Un thème platonicien dans la tradition patristique: le juste crucifié (Platon, *République*, 361 e4—362 a2)', *Studia patristica*, 9 (1966), 30–40.

Book 5—Mornay

Grotius' refutation of Judaism is significantly more detailed than his
attack on paganism. In itself this is not remarkable, for the Jewish
religion—unlike ancient paganism, a religion that still tenaciously
survived—had long posed greater problems for Christian apologetics. They could not treat Judaism as a negligeable quantity. Since
Christianity had grown out of Judaism, Christian polemicists had to
be careful not to cut the roots of their own faith. The apostle Paul
had been one of the first to find it necessary to give an account of
the special relationship between Judaism and Christianity.[321] Justin
Martyr, Tertullian and other early Christian apologetes laid down
the main lines of Christian polemics with Judaism, on which the
middle ages and the Renaissance continued to embroider.[322]

Knowledge of the Jewish religion outside Judaism itself was confined
to a few in the middle ages, but in the Renaissance more and more
Christians came to be better informed about Jewish theological literature. The Talmud and other important Jewish works appeared
in print, and such Christian scholars as J. Reuchlin and C. Pellicanus
acquired a more thorough knowledge of the Hebrew language and
its literature. The humanist watchword, *ad fontes*, applied equally in
the field of judaica. These developments led to chairs of Hebrew
being founded at Christian universities, so that a new kind of spe-
cialist emerged, the Christian hebraist.[323] The first important representatives of this field were Sebastian Munster, Paul Fagius, Johannes
Buxdorf senior and Gilbert Gennebrard. In the sixteenth and seventeenth centuries hebraists were also appointed to universities in
the Dutch Republic, among them Thomas Erpenius and Constantijn
L'Empereur at Leiden; both men were friends of Grotius.[324] These
learned hebraists, by their translations and commentaries, opened
the eyes of the Christian world to the wealth of Jewish tradition.

---

[321] Above all Rom. 9–11.
[322] See among others A.L. Williams, *Adversus Judaeos. A Bird's Eye View of Christian
Apologiae until the Renaissance*, Cambridge 1935; B. Blumenkranz, 'Vie et survie de la
polémique antijuive', *Studia patristica*, 1 (1957), 460–76; and Laplanche, *L'Évidence*,
p. 76.
[323] See R. Loewe, 'Christian hebraists' in *EJ*, 8 (1971), pp. 16–17.
[324] On Erpenius: W.M.C. Juynboll, *Zeventiende eeuwse beoefenaars van het Arabisch in
Nederland*, Utrecht 1931, pp. 86–7, 196–8; on L'Empereur: P.T. van Rooden, *Theology,
Biblical Scholarship and Rabbinical Studies in the Seventeenth Century. Constantijn L'Empereur
(1591–1648), Professor of Hebrew and Theology at Leiden*, [Studies in the History of
Leiden University, vol. 6], Leiden etc. 1989.

Humanist apologetes borrowed a great deal of material from their works, so that they could attack the Jews with their own weapons. This is clearly seen in the apologetic work of Mornay, who through the medium of Gennebrard and other hebraists was able to cite the Jerusalem and Babylonian Talmud, the Targumim, several Midrashim and cabbalistic literature.[325]

Grotius appears to have borrowed most of the material for this book from Mornay's apologetic work. One difference from the Frenchman's arguments is immediately obvious: Grotius refrains from all parade of learning in the text of his apology. On the points in his argument where it is essential to refer to the works of his Jewish opponents, he is content to use such vague terms as 'your side' or 'your teachers'. In a few cases he is more specific, and speaks of 'your Talmudists' or 'your cabbalists'.[326] In the Dutch version of his apologetic work he refers only once to the Targum and the Talmud,[327] and names a single rabbi.[328]

It is as if Grotius felt it was dangerous even to mention Jewish names, apart from the hellenistic Jewish authors Josephus and Philo. His attitude to rabbinical literature in general and the Talmud in particular is ambivalent. He finds in the Talmud repeated confirmation of his own arguments, even though he refuses to admit this fully, but at the same time he leaves us in no doubt that he has a low opinion of the religious and moral contents of this book of the Jewish law.[329] In his regulations for the Jews of 1617 Grotius pleaded for a restriction on the freedom of the press for the Jewish community in the Republic, and proposed a ban on the printing, ownership or use of blasphemous books, offensive to the Christian religion.[330] In his accompanying commentary he remarked that as far as he was

---

[325] See Laplanche, *L'Évidence*, pp. 178–9.

[326] *Bewijs*, pp. 136 and 148.

[327] *Ibid.*, p. 149.

[328] *Ibid.*, pp. 148–9: "De zoon van Neheman houdt t' eenemael gewis,/Dat dit de hoogste bood en d'eersten Engel is." Grotius is undoubtedly referring to the medieval rabbi Moses ben Nachman Gerondi, also known as Nachmanides (1194–1270).

[329] *Bewijs*, p. 136; "Maar eene zwindelgeest, als met een duistere mist,/Heeft het verstand verdwelmd van uwen talmudist./Want in dat grote boek, 't welk zij de mondwet noemen,/(Waarop zij hoger dan op Mozes' schriften roemen)/Veel kluchten staan, die niet en kunnen zijn geloofd,/Dan bij de luiden die van oordeel zijn beroofd."

[330] *Remonst.*, pp. 117–18.

concerned, the Talmud too might be forbidden.[331] Later in his his
life he stated that he had nothing to do with Jewish traditions after
the time of Christ, because God's spirit had deserted the synagogues
since that time.[332] Grotius' correspondence to 1620 and the inventory of his library made in 1619 appear to suggest that his knowledge of Jewish literature when he wrote his apologetic work was not
particularly deep.

Though Grotius appears to have taken most of his arguments
against Judaism from the apologetic work of Mornay, he deviates
very noticeably from the path taken by his predecessor on one point:
he gives a detailed account of the abolition of certain commandments of the Mosaic law by Jesus (§6–§12). As we shall see, he must
have gone back to earlier apologetic literature for this. He may have
borrowed the introduction and conclusion of this book from another
minor work of Mornay's.[333]

§1 Address to the Jews

Grotius' introductory section is an address to the Jews. It has a
remarkable parallel in the opening of Mornay's *L'Advertissement aux
juifs* (1607). Here Mornay had addressed the Jews directly, in the
second person, to show his sympathy for them, but also to admonish them urgently to acknowledge Jesus as the Messiah.[334] Grotius'
address is in the same tone, and is a sign of his comparatively mild
philosemitic attitude. A few motifs in this introduction evoke reminiscences of his earlier regulations for the Jews, such as the natural
connection of Jews and Christians, and their common recognition
of the Old Testament as a source of God's revelation.[335]

§2–§5 Miracles of Jesus

His first arguments against Judaism refer to the Jewish refusal to
recognise the miracles of Jesus. In his apologetic work Mornay had

---

[331] *Ibid.*, p. 124.
[332] *Animadv. in animadv. Riv.*, in *OT* IV 648a: "Traditiones post Christum iudaicas
nihili facio: eo enim tempore Spiritus Dei deseruit synagogam ut praedictum fuerat."
[333] Mornay, *L'Advertissement aux juifs sur le venue du messie*, Saumur 1607. On this
see Laplanche, *L'Évidence*, pp. 20–1. We have found nothing to suggest that Grotius
used this work in Loevestein.
[334] See the passage cited in Laplanche, *L'Évidence*, pp. 20–1.
[335] See *Remonst.*, p. 111.

followed tradition and begun with the theme of the expectation of the Messiah.[336] It is not surprising that Grotius should have placed the miracles of Jesus first, given the exceptional importance he attaches to miracles throughout his apology.[337] He argues that the Jews must consider the miracles conclusively proven by reliable testimonies; that those miracles were not the product of sorcery or a magical name, as some Jews allege; and finally that they must have been of divine origin, because Jesus taught only the service of the one true God. The whole of this proof is to be found in Mornay's great apologetic work.[338]

Neither of the apologetes names the target of his argument: the suggestions that Jesus made use of arts of sorcery learned in Egypt, and that he had read on a stone in the temple of Solomon a secret name of God that emanated magical power, are offered in the so-called *Toledoth Yeshu*.[339] This collection of popular Jewish tales forms a parody of the Gospels, and its oldest parts probably date from as early as the first centuries of the Christian era. These tales mock Jesus mercilessly, disqualifying him as the Messiah and dismissing his miracles as fraudulent.[340]

§6–§12 *Jesus' teaching agrees with the Mosaic law*

The second series of arguments concerns the relationship of the Mosaic law to the law of Christ, an old and constantly recurring point of discussion between Jews and Christians. Mornay had dealt with this problem very briefly.[341] Grotius is much more detailed than his French predecessor. Evidently as a jurist he was much more interested in this subject, to which he was to recur in several later works.[342] I have the impression that he bases his argument in this

---

[336] Mornay, *Ver.* XXVIII–XXIX.

[337] He underlines one of the strengths of the argument from miracles in this connection, see *VRC* V 2, p. 180: "Neque enim potest Deus dogmati per hominem promulgato auctoritatem efficacius conciliare quam miracula editis."

[338] See Mornay, *Ver.* XXX, pp. 733–9.

[339] On this see S. Krauss, *Das Leben Jesu nach jüdischen Quellen*, Berlin 1902; B. Blumenkranz, *Juifs et chrétiens dans le monde occidental 430–1096*, Paris/The Hague 1960, pp. 169–70; and Laplanche, *L'Évidence*, pp. 315–16 (n. 278 and the literature cited there).

[340] See Laplanche, *L'Évidence*, p. 178.

[341] Mornay, *Ver.* XXXI, pp. 773–83.

[342] Cf. *Annot. In NT* (ad Matt. 5:17) in *OT* II 34b 16—36a 41; and *IBP* I 1 16, pp. 31–3.

section chiefly on Justin Martyr and to a lesser extent on Tertullian.[343] He probably had the works of both these early Christian authors at hand in his prison cell.[344] He may also have used some Jewish texts by Josephus Albo and David Kimchi, which had been translated by the hebraist Gilbert Gennebrard and collected in an edition that Thomas Erpenius sent to Grotius in Loevestein.[345]

The most important questions that the Jews put to Christians about the abolition of the Mosaic law were: is it possible that Jesus could have changed the sacred and inviolable law of Moses? And if so, how did he do so? Up to a point Grotius' answer to the first question (§6) is the same as Mornay's: if God changed the Mosaic law through Jesus, that does not mean that God's essence itself is liable to change. God merely adapted his laws to the development of humanity, just as a father's rules for older children are different from those he lays down for a small child.[346] Mornay and Grotius agree thus far. The Frenchman had stated that Jesus did not bring a new law, but the Gospel.[347] Grotius, however, is not impressed by the Reformation's opposition of the law and the Gospel, and he agrees with Justin Martyr and Tertullian that Jesus brought a better law than Moses.[348] As one of the reasons why the law of Jesus was better than that of Moses, he says that Moses offered rewards only in this world, while Jesus promised eternal life.[349] Grotius had already used this argument earlier in his apology, and it is also found in Socinus.[350]

---

[343] See Iust. M. *Dial. Tryph.* and Tert. *Adv. Iud.* For the passages in question see below.

[344] He had read Tertullian 'right through' in his cell at The Hague. See Fruin, *Verhooren*, p. 70. He had his own copy of Justin Martyr and had it sent to him in Loevestein by his wife: see Molhuysen, 'Bibliotheek', 'Boecken die de huysvrouwe van voors. De Groot . . . sijn laten volgen, om . . . opt Huys te Louvesteijn te mogen gebruycken', n° 330.

[345] *BW* II, n° 596 (to G.J. Vossius, 15 December 1619), p. 27: "Misit mihi Erpennius Gennebrardi excerpta ex Albone Iudaeo. Liber ipse Albonis, ut audio, magnus est, exstatque eiusdem alter scriptus a patre Davidis Kimchii, quos non transferri miror.' Gennebrard's book is *R. Iosephi Albonis, R. Davidis Kimhi et alius cuiusdam Hebraei anonymi argumenta, quibus nonnullos fidei christianae articulos oppugnant, G. Genebrardo interprete,* Paris 1566 [= Gennebr. *Albonis argumenta*].

[346] Cf. Mornay, *Ver.* XXXI, pp. 781–2.

[347] Mornay, *Ver.* XXXI, p. 783.

[348] Cf. Iust. M. *Dial. Tryph.* I 11; and Tert. *Adv. Iud.* 2.

[349] *Bewijs*, p. 120.

[350] Soc. *ASS* II, p. 273; cf. *VRC* II, 11.

Grotius' treatment of the question of the relationship of Jesus' law to that of Moses is quite independent of Mornay's. He states that Jesus in his earthly life complied with the rituals prescribed by the Mosaic law and only abolished them after his death. God took no particular pleasure in that part of the law, which was specially adapted to the circumstances of the Jewish people. This argument can be traced back in its entirety to Justin Martyr.[351] This conclusion is confirmed by a virtually identical argument in *Annot. in NT*, in which Grotius cites Justin Martyr four times in a short space.[352]

In a similar passage of *De iure belli* he also appeals to this early Christian author.[353] Justin Martyr had distinguished between a generally valid, permanent part of the law of Moses and a part specifically adapted to the circumstances of the Jewish people, which included the prescribed rituals. He regarded the value of these rituals as indifferent to Christians, because of their specific and temporary nature.[354] Grotius also states that Moses' ritual prescriptions in themselves had no value and were neither good nor bad. Elsewhere he refers to them by the Greek term *adiaphora*, the Latin equivalent of which was *indifferentia*, originally a stoic term but later annexed by Christian theologians.[355] To illustrate the temporal nature of these rules he points out that many Old Testament figures who lived before Moses, such as Abel, Enoch, Noah and Melchizedek, led lives acceptable to God without any inkling of these laws.[356]

In the following section Grotius goes on to consider several separate institutions of that ritual law. He begins with sacrifices (§8), and states that God had instituted them to restrain the Jews from the worship of false gods. In a letter to Vossius, clearly in reply to a question, he claims that his discussion of sacrifices had not been inspired by reading Socinus, but agreed with Justin Martyr and the Jewish authors Moses Maimonides and Josephus Albo.[357] Grotius may

---

[351] Iust. M. *Dial. Tryph.* I 11–13, 44–47.

[352] *Annot. in NT* (ad Matt. 5:17); in *OT* II 34b 16–36a 41.

[353] *IBP* I i 16, pp. 31–3.

[354] Iust. M. *Dial. Tryph.* I 44–47. On this see Theodore Stylianopoulos, *Justin Martyr and the Mosaic Law*, Missoula Montana 1975, pp. 127–30.

[355] Cf. *Annot in NT* (ad Matt. 5:17), in *OT* II 35b 60–61; and *Annot. in VT* (ad Exod. 20:4), in *OT* I 40a 52–60.

[356] Iust. M. *Dial. Tryph.* I 19 3–5.

[357] *BW* II, n° 608, p. 37: "De sacrificiis non memini apud Socinum legere; sed videtur mihi ea esse sententia Iustini Martyris, quem et alii sequuntur, tum vere et inter Hebraeos Maimonidae et Albonis."

indeed have based his argument on those authors. Justin Martyr had
asserted that God instituted sacrifices to restrain the Jews from the
worship of false gods.[358] Grotius could have become acquainted with
the two Jewish authors in the collection made by Gilbert Gennebrard.
That contains, among others, a translation of an apologetic text by
Albo, who cites Maimonides to support his claim that the sacrifices
had been imposed on the Israelites to keep them from worshipping
false gods.[359] In this section, following a regular practice of Christian
apologetes, Grotius confronts the Jews with a series of citations from
the Psalms and prophets of the Old Testament.[360]

He also relates the dietary rules of the Mosaic law to the idolatry into which the Jewish people had fallen during their captivity in
Egypt (§9). Once again this explanation appears to be borrowed from
Justin Martyr.[361] To bring out the temporary nature of this law he
follows Justin Martyr in referring to several pre-Mosaic Old Testament
figures, who were free to eat all living creatures.[362] Finally he mentions a pronouncement of Jewish 'teachers' that God would abolish
the prohibition on certain foods and the distinction between clean
and unclean animals at the coming of the Messiah.[363] He must have
owed this information to Mornay, who named a 'rabbi Hadarsan'
in this context.[364]

Grotius attributed a twofold significance to the rule for the sabbath (§10). Originally this prohibition had been imposed to commemorate the creation of the world. Biblical history teaches that this
remembrance did not require rest; only later did it come to involve
a complete avoidance of all work. But that restriction had been
imposed on the Jewish people later, when they were released from
Egypt, and it served to remind them of their former slavery.[365] Like

---

[358] Iust. M. *Dial. Tryph.* 19.6 and 22.1.
[359] Gennebr. *Albonis argumenta*, p. 16: "Cur sacrificia in veteri lege instituta, [. . .].
Respondeamus oblationes non fuisse Israelitis imperatas nisi secundario, ne scilicet
idolis sacrificarent, sicuti placet R. Mosi Maimonis filio, istiusmodi objectio prorsus
corruet."
[360] Cf. Mornay, *Ver.* XXXI, pp. 775–6 and Iust. M. *Dial. Tryph.* I 22.7–10.
[361] Iust. M. *Dial. Tryph.* I 20.1–4.
[362] Cf. Iust. M. *Dial. Tryph.* I 20.1.
[363] *Bewijs*, pp. 119–20.
[364] Mornay, *Ver.* XXXI, p. 777: [In margine] Rabbi Hadarsan in Gen. 41". On
the French exegete Moses Ha-Darshan (11th century) see *JE*, IX, pp. 64–5.
[365] It did not escape Vossius that Grotius' view differed from the normal one.
For Grotius' reply see *BW* II, n° 608, p. 37: "De sabbato ita sentio: pios ante
Mosem sabbatis memoriam coluisse creationis per preces et convivia familiaria.

Justin Martyr he considers that Christians are not bound by the sabbath, which was clearly instituted as a specific mark of the Jewish
people.[366] His reference to the rabbinical rule that one who brings
a message from God may break the sabbath law, was probably again
borrowed from Mornay.[367]

His argument on circumcision (§11) agrees entirely with the views
of Justin Martyr and Tertullian: circumcision was a specific sign of
the covenant between God and the Jewish people, which Jesus made
superfluous through the new covenant.[368] This sign did not exist
before Abraham; indeed God had been well pleased with Abraham
before he was circumcised, so that it cannot be said that God's grace
is dependent on this sign.[369] Grotius concludes his excursus with the
remark that Jews who converted to Christianity were made welcome
by the apostles and allowed to retain their old customs, provided
that they did not attempt to persuade others to adopt them (§12).
This argument must have been borrowed from Justin Martyr, and
once again emphasises the indifference of the Jewish ritual law.[370]

§13–§20 The expectation of the Messiah

The third series of arguments concerns the Jewish and Christian
expectation of the Messiah. We can deal with this briefly, because
Grotius in fact offers no more than a summary of Mornay's argument, Mornay in turn had followed the patterns of patristic and
medieval apologetics.[371]

The starting point of the discussion is a belief in the coming of
a Messiah (§13). The Jews believed that God's Anointed had yet to
come, and Christians believed that he had already appeared: that

---

Rigidum autem illud otium peculiariter indictum Hebraeis, tum ut notum dis-
creticum, tum solatium adversus dominorum in servos saevitiam." We are probably dealing here with Grotius' own interpretation, which only partly agreed with
the authors named in the note to §10 (n. 2), Moses Gerundensis (= Moses ben
Nachman Geroni) and Isaac Arama. They distinguish between two views of the
sabbath law, as Grotius does, but include the ban on work in both. The reference
to these authors appears to be borrowed from Menasseh, *Concil.* 150–1. Grotius
explained his view further in *Annot. in VT* (ad Exod. 20:8) in *OT* I 44 B40–45 B 38.

[366] Iust. M. *Dial. Tryph.* I 23.1. Cf. *Annot. in VT* (ad Exod. 20:8) in *OT* I 45
a10–16, where Grotius explicitly cites Justin Martyr and Tertullian.

[367] Mornay, *Ver.* XXXI, p. 776 (Midrash Num. 13).

[368] Cf. Iust. M. *Dial. Tryph.* I 16, 19; and Tert. *Adv. Jud.* 3.

[369] Iust. M. *Dial. Tryph.* I 23.4.

[370] Iust. M. *Dial. Tryph.* I 46.7–47.2.

[371] Laplanche, *L'Évidence*, p. 179; and Blumenkranz, *Juifs et chrétiens*, pp. 243–56.

was the fundamental point of difference on which the whole discussion turned.[372] Grotius, following Mornay, confronts his Jewish
adversaries with a number of passages from the Old Testament, from
which it can be calculated that the Messiah must have come in the
time of Jesus (§14). He uses the same biblical texts as the French
apologete but in a different order.[373] He expressly gives first place
to the prophecy in Daniel 9:21–6, a passage that since the time of
Tertullian had been the leading proof text for the Christian calculation of the coming of the Messiah.[374] Both Mornay and Grotius
considered this calculation proven by the fact that some Jews in the
time of Jesus believed others, such as Herod and Judas Gaulonita,
to be the Messiah.[375]

Grotius states that a learned Jew who lived fifty years before Christ
had concluded from the prophecy of Daniel that the coming of the
Messiah could not be more than half a century away.[376] He says
that he took this reference from a commentary by the English biblical scholar Hugh Broughton, a work supplied to him in Loevestein
by Thomas Erpenius. In 1626 he asked his brother Willem to send
him this commentary, so that he could find the name of the Jewish
scholar mentioned in his *Bewijs*.[377] The name proved to be *Nehumia*
[= Nehemia], as the author discovered a year later.[378]

---

[372] Mornay, *Ver.* XXIX, pp. 700–01.
[373] Mornay, *Ver.* XXIX, pp. 705–12.
[374] Tert. *Adv. Jud.* 8.
[375] Cf. Mornay, *Ver.* XXIX, p. 716.
[376] *Bewijs*, p. 133: "Waer uit [sc. Dan. 9:2–5] een kloek Hebre, die leefd' een
jubeltijd/Voor onse Nasareen, heel opentlick belijd,/Dat meer dan vijftigh jaer niet
soude staen te beyden,/Of hy en sou daer sijn daer Daniel van seyde."
[377] *BW* III, n° 1091 (to W. de Groot, 4 August 1626), pp. 63–4: "Rogo ex eodem
Vossio et aliis, si opus est, exquiras, an reperiri possit liber Hugonis Brochtoni in
Danielem, latine versus a nostro Johanne Borelio. Usus sum eo libro in carcere
beneficio Erpenii. Et puto in eo me reperisse nomen et locum rabbini, qui L circiter
annos vixerit ante Domini nostri adventum quique ex Daniele intra illos L annos
messiam venturum praedixerat." This concerns H. Broughton, *Commentarius in Danielem.*
Primum Anglice scriptus ab Hughone Broughtono, nunc Latinitate donatus per
Ioannem Boreel, Basel 1599.
[378] *BW* III, n° 1145 (to W. de Groot, 1 May 1627), p. 127: "Libro quinto [sc.
in *VRC*], qui est adversum Iudaeos, in paragrapho, qui ostendit Messiam venisse
ex praesignificatione temporis, designavi sine nomine magistrum hebraeum, qui annis
quinquaginta Dominum nostrum praecessit, negavitque ultra quinquaginta annos
protrahi posse tempus adventus. Nomen tunc non succurrebat. Post reperi esse
Nehumiam. Itaque scribe in eo loco: In Iesum tam bene convenit, ut magister
hebraeus Nehumias, qui annis quinquaginta eum praecessit, aperte iam tum dixerit,

As for the objection that the coming of the Messiah was delayed because of the sins of the Jewish people (§15), Grotius deals with it in the same way as Mornay, who had attributed this assertion to 'rabbi Hillel'.[379] And he agrees with his French predecessor in seeing the miserable state of the Jews as further proof that the Messiah must already have come, for their condition is a sharp contrast with what the Mosaic law had promised them (§16). Both apologetes conclude that the Jews must blame their diaspora and their spiritual blindness on their rejection of the Messiah who had already appeared.[380] All the prophecies about the Messiah in the Old Testament had been realised in Jesus Christ (§17). Here Grotius appeals to the same traditional historical proofs and biblical passages as Mornay.[381]

The Christian conviction that the Messiah had already appeared could not fail to provoke a reply from the Jews. In the middle ages this topic was fiercely argued. The discussion centred on two points: 1) the signs in the Old Testament prophecies that were or were not fulfilled; and 2) the person of Jesus as the Messiah.[382] Grotius deals first with the objection that certain prophecies about the Messiah had not been realised in Jesus (§18). His answer appears to be taken in its entirety from Mornay's argument.[383] The same applies to his treatment of two well known Jewish objections to the person of Jesus. The first concerns Jesus' humble birth (§19).[384] The second deals with his unfavourable reputation among the Jews, and is based on the assumption that the Jews who rejected Jesus in his lifetime led a pious life (§20).[385]

§21–§22 Jewish objections

The Christian doctrines of the trinity and incarnation had long provoked sharp criticism from Jewish opponents, but they did not play

---

non posse etc." Cf. *VRC*, V 14, p. 203. For the passage in Broughton see *BW* II, n° 1091, p. 64 n. 1.

[379] Mornay, *Ver.* XXIX, p. 718 (he probably means Hillel ben Berechiah, see *JE*, VI, pp. 400–01).

[380] Mornay, *Ver.* XXIX, pp. 720–3.

[381] Mornay, *Ver.* XXX, pp. 723–30.

[382] Blumenkranz, *Juifs et chrétiens*, pp. 251–5. See also W.J. de Wilde, *De messiaansche opvattingen der middeleeuwse exegeten Rasji, Aben Esra en Kimchi vooral volgens hun commentaren op Jesaja*, Wageningen 1929.

[383] Cf. Mornay, *Ver.* XXXI, pp. 769–72.

[384] Cf. Mornay, *Ver.* XXXI, pp. 767–9.

[385] Cf. Mornay, *Ver.* XXXI, pp. 762–7.

a role in the polemics between Jews and Christians until the middle
ages, so that the humanists could not fall back on the patristic
authors.[386] Grotius' answers to these objections agree with those of
Mornay. He begins with the Jewish charge of polytheism made against
the Christians because of their dogma of the trinity. In his sixth
chapter Mornay had given a whole series of Jewish parallels to the
Christian view of the trinity.[387] Grotius selects two examples from
this series. He first refers to 'your cabbalist', who is said to have
spoken of three lights and three numbers in God's being.[388] Mornay
had attributed this view to rabbi Simon ben Jochia, who was assumed
to be the author of the well known cabbalistic work *Sohar*.[389] The
second reference borrowed by Grotius is to Philo Judaeus. Mornay
had been frank enough to acknowledge that Philo in fact distinguished God from God's word but did not speak of the third person, the Holy Ghost.[390] Grotius does not mention this, but appears
to be aware of Philo's omission, for he inserts here a brief digression on the Jewish 'Shekina', which he saw as a counterpart of the
Holy Ghost. The Shekina, according to Grotius, had been referred
to by 'the son of Neheman' [rabbi Moses ben Nachman Geroni] as
the messenger or angel of God, who guides the world.[391] He may
have taken this digression from the work by Gennebrard referred to
above.[392] Grotius adds a few remarks, which once again he must
have borrowed from Mornay: the Messiah is called God's word in
the Targum,[393] while according to the Talmud in the time of the
Messiah everyone would be able to point to God.[394] Mornay, however, had given the Midrash and not the Talmud as his source for
the latter statement. It seems that Grotius later realised his mistake,
for this passage does not occur in the Latin version.[395]

---

[386] Blumenkranz, pp. 256–65.
[387] Mornay, *Ver.* VI, pp. 106–12.
[388] *Bewijs*, p. 148. In the Latin version he speaks of *cabbalistae* in the plural; see
VRC V 21, pp. 221–2.
[389] Mornay, *Ver.* VI, p. 107. The real author of the Aramaic book *Sohar* is presumed to be Moses de Léon (1250–1305): see *BW* VII, n° 2554, p. 92 n. 1.
[390] Mornay, *Ver.* VI, p. 112.
[391] See *Bewijs*, pp. 148–9.
[392] Gennebr., *Albonis argumenta*, p. 37.
[393] Mornay, *Ver.* XXVIII, p. 685.
[394] *Bewijs*, p. 149.
[395] See *VRC*, V 21, p. 222.

Turning to the Jewish accusation that Christians worship a human nature, Grotius answers it with several scriptural passages, which can also be found in his French predecessor. He first declares that the contents of Psalm 110, which deals with the priest-king, can be applied to Jesus Christ and not to David or Abraham.[396] Psalm 2, according to both apologetes, also applies to Jesus.[397] Finally, he follows Mornay by saying that the cabbala speaks of a mediator who is called the son of Enoch.[398]

§23 Prayer

Grotius closes this book with a short prayer for the Jews, which in the Dutch poem is addressed to Christ and in the Latin version to God.[399] We find a similar conclusion in Mornay's *L'Advertissement aux juifs*.[400]

Book 6—Vives

Until well into the seventeenth century the Christian polemic with Islam was chiefly determined by two factors: 1) a fixed negative picture of this religion; and 2) a very limited knowledge of Islamic sources.[401] The main lines of this picture of Islam, as stereotyped as it was negative, had been sketched as early as the Byzantine theologians John of Damascus (ca. 675–ca. 750) and Niketas of Byzantium (ninth to early tenth century). These theologians lived under the threat of the growing political power of Islam, and in their fear and hatred they created a picture of their enemy that was roughly as follows: Muhammad was not a prophet but a bandit and debauchee, his doctrines absurd, his commandments scandalous, the Koran full of absurdities, Islam as a whole was a heresy, even a precursor of

---

[396] Cf. Mornay, *Ver.* XXVIII, p. 683; and *Bewijs*, p. 149. In the Latin version he adds that David Kimchi was also inclined to the opinion that this Psalm could refer only to the Messiah: *VRC*, V 22, p. 223. See Kimchi on this in Gennebr. *Albonis argumenta*, p. 60.

[397] Mornay, *Ver.* XXVIII, pp. 683–4.

[398] Cf. *Bewijs*, pp. 150–1; and Mornay, *Ver.* XXVIII, p. 688.

[399] Cf. *Bewijs*, p. 151; and *VRC*, V 23, p. 225.

[400] Mornay, *L'Advertissement aux juifs*, Saumur 1607, p. 229.

[401] For a good survey of the genre: H. Bobzin, 'Islam und Christentum (7.–19. Jahrhundert)' in *TRE*, XVI (1987), pp. 336–49.

the Antichrist.[402] This portrayal was adopted by western Christians in the middle ages.[403]

The maintenance of this negative picture as a rule went hand in hand with a basic ignorance of Islam. The first person to attempt to change this was Peter the Venerable (1092–1156), abbot of Cluny.[404] During a journey in Spain the abbot asked several scholars who knew Arabic to translate the Koran and some other Islamic writings. These translations were produced between 1141 and 1143 in Toledo, and are therefore known as the *Corpus Toletanum*.[405] The project of Peter the Venerable, the initiator of Christian study of Islam, however, found few imitators. His open and serious approach to this religion soon gave way to an attitude of rejection and indifference.[406] In the following centuries it was Dominicans and Franciscans above all who concerned themselves with the study of Islam. In the early fourteenth century the Florentine monk and pilgrim Ricoldo Pennini da Montecroce, O.P. [= Ricoldo] wrote one of the most important works against Islam, the *Confutatio Alcorani*.[407] This work was translated into many languages, including Greek, French, English and German, and until well into the sixteenth century it continued to exert a decisive influence on both western and Byzantine polemics with Islam.

When the threat from Turkish power made itself felt at the gates of Vienna in the sixteenth century the old Christian image of hostile Islam gained a new timeliness. Like John of Damascus, Luther believed that the advance of the Islamic Turks foreshadowed the imminent coming of the Antichrist. As such, in his eyes Islam had

---

[402] See above all A.Th. Khoury, *La Controverse byzantine avec l'islam*, Paris 1969, pp. 8–15, and Idem, *Polémique byzantine contre l'islam* (VIIIᵉ–XIIIᵉ siècle, Leiden 1972, pp. 11–18. Older literature is also still useful: C. Güterbock, *Der Islam im Lichte der byzantinischen Polemik*, Berlin 1912, and H.G. Beck, *Kirche und theologische Literatur im byzantinischen Reich*, Munich 1959.

[403] N.A. Daniel, *Islam and the West. The Making of an Image*, Edinburgh 1960, pp. 1–7, and R.W. Southern, *Western Views of Islam in the Middle Ages*, Cambridge Mass. 1962, pp. 29–33.

[404] See J. Kritzeck, *Peter the Venerable and Islam*, Princeton 1964, pp. 3–37.

[405] Kritzeck, *Peter the Venerable*, pp. 51–69. See also P. Venerabilis, *Schriften zum Islam*. Ediert, ins Deutsche übersetzt und kommentiert von R. Glei [Corpus Islamo = Christianum, series latina 1], Altenberge 1985, pp. xi–xxvii.

[406] See Southern, *Western Views*, pp. 42–66.

[407] For this see U. Monneret de Villard, 'La vita, le opere e i viaggi di fratre Ricoldo da Montecroce O.P.', *Orientalia Christiana Periodica*, 10 (1944), 227–74 (esp. 266–74).

a close relationship with the Roman Catholic Church, which was ruled by the Antichrist.[408] The German Reformer therefore saw great value in an intellectual assault on the religion of Muhammad, which would also imply an attack on the papacy. But he went back to a medieval work. In 1542 Luther published a German translation of Ricoldo's *Confutatio Alcorani*.[409] A year later the Swiss Protestant humanist Theodorus Bibliander published an impressive collection, which contained, besides some contemporary works on the history of the Turks, exclusively medieval literature on Islam.[410]

The attack on Islam in the sixteenth century appears to have gained no new features, or hardly any. Many Christians were wholly absorbed in their own internal divisions, and their self-evident feeling of superiority led them to dismiss the study of the faith of Muhammad as not worth the effort. Islam was not a serious intellectual problem for Christendom at that time.[411] Moreover only a handful of scholars knew the Arabic language.[412] Virtually all Christian authors were therefore dependent on secondary works for their knowledge of Islam. This applied to the humanist apologetes as well.[413] They regarded an attack on Islam as a more or less obligatory part of the defence of the faith, and went back to the old arguments.[414] Their treatment was conservative and characterised by the same shortcomings as medieval polemics: the retention of a fictitious image of the enemy and ignorance of the Islamic sources.

Grotius, however, had some interest in and knowledge of Arabic, and was a friend of the Leiden Arabist Thomas Erpenius.[415] But his

[408] H. Bobzin, 'Martin Luthers Beiträge zur Kenntnis und Kritik des Islam', *Neue Zeitschrift für systematische Theologie und Religionsphilosophie*, 27 (1985), 262–89.

[409] M. Luther, *Verlegung des Alcoran, Bruder Richardi Prediger Ordens, verdeutscht durch D. Martin Luther*, Wittenberg 1542.

[410] Th. Bibliander, *Machumetis Saracenorum principis, eiusque successorum vitae, doctrina, ac ipse Alcoran. [. . .] His adiunctae sunt confutationes multorum et quidem probatiss. authorum, Arabum, Graecorum, et Latinorum, [. . .]. Adiuncti sunt etiam de Turcarum sive Saracenorum [. . .] origine et rebus gestis, [. . .]. Haec omnia in unam volumen redacta sunt, opera et studio Theodori Bibliandri*, [Basel] 1543.

[411] See Southern, *Western Views*, p. 12.

[412] J. Fück, *Die arabischen Studien in Europa vom 12. bis in den Anfang des 19. Jahrhunderts* [Beiträge zur Arabistik, Semitistik und Islamwissenschaft], Leipzig 1944, pp. 85–253.

[413] See K.H. Dannenfeldt, *The Renaissance Humanists and the Knowledge of Arabic*, New York 1955.

[414] Laplanche, *L'Évidence*, pp. 176–7.

[415] A. Eekhof, 'Heeft Hugo de Groot Arabisch gekend?', *NAK*, n.s. 17 (1924), 231–4. On Erpenius, see Juynboll, *Zeventiende eeuwse beoefenaars*, pp. 85–7, 196–8.

writings and correspondence reveal virtually no interest in Islam. On one occasion he expressed the hope that Islam would not profit too much from the division of Christianity.[416] This was his chief concern, and the religion of Muhammad, in itself, left him fairly indifferent. His attack on Islam in this book consists entirely of traditional Christian arguments,[417] but he does not dispose of the task as quickly as Mornay, who had needed only a few pages to refute Islam.[418]

Grotius must have taken his material largely from the apologetic work of Juan-Luis Vives.[419] This Spanish humanist had devoted a whole book of his work *De veritate fidei christianae* (1543) to an attack on Islam.[420] This refutation is in turn largely based on Ricoldo's *Confutatio Alcorani*.[421] Grotius is noticeably more concise than the Spaniard. He deviates from his predecessor's argument on one point, in the first section of this book, to put forward an explanation of his own.

§1 Origin of Islam

Grotius opens with an historical explanation, in which he traces the origin of Islam back to God's judgement on Christians. This raises a topic that had troubled many minds, chiefly in the sixteenth century.[422]

---

[416] *BW* IX, n° 3890 (to L. Camerarius, 18 December 1638), p. 759: "Deum tamen orare pergo, ne nostrae discordiae mahumetismo pridem praepotenti novas aperiant vias."

[417] See J.W. Spaans, 'Het bewijs van de waarheid der christelijke religie. Hugo de Groot "teghen de Mahumetisterije"', [unpublished *doctoraal* thesis, University of Leiden Faculty of Theology, 1982].

[418] See Mornay, *Ver.* XXXIII, pp. 829–31.

[419] For the life and works of J.L. Vives see C.G. Noreña, *Juan-Luis Vives* [Archives internationales d'histoire des idées, 34], The Hague 1970; Alain Guy, *Vivès ou l'Humanisme engagé* [Philosophes de tous les temps], Paris 1972; and *Erasmus in Hispania, Vives in Belgio*, Acta Colloquii Brugensis, 23–26.IX.1985, ed. J. IJsewijn and A. Losada [Colloquia Europalia], Louvain 1986.

[420] I refer to J.L. Vives, *De veritate fidei christianae*, 'Liber quartus contra sectam Mahumetis', in *Opera*, Basel 1555, II, pp. 455–82 [= Vives, *Ver.*]. On Vives an an apologete see Paul Graf, *Ludwig Vives als Apologet*, Freiburg 1932. I consulted the Spanish translation of this study, which appeared under the title *Luis Vives como apologeta. Contribución a la historia de la apologetica por el Dr Pablo Graf.* [Traducción directa del alemán por José M. Millas Vallicrosa], Madrid 1943.

[421] See Graf, *Luis Vives*, pp. 99–114.

[422] See C. Göllner, *Turcica. III. Band: Die Türkerfrage in der öffentlichen Meinung Europas im 16. Jahrhundert*, Bucharest/Baden-Baden 1978, pp. 171–226.

As early as the end of the fourteenth century the English theologian John Wyclif had seen an analogy between Islam and the decadent Christianity of his own time. In his eyes both religions were dominated by pride, lust for possessions and power, and violence. Wyclif saw the origin of Islam in the faults of Christianity.[423] The idea that the expansion of Islam could be blamed on the crisis in Christianity became a commonplace in the sixteenth century, largely through the influence of Luther. Like Wyclif, the German Reformer wished to use this idea to shift attention from the external enemy of Christianity to the internal.[424] In the sixteenth century many works on the history of the Turks (*Turcica*) were published, and their interest centred on the question of the origin of the Turkish empire.[425] The French humanist Guillaume Postel wrote that God had allowed Islam to emerge in order to hold up a mirror to Christians in which they could see their own sins.[426] A century earlier the Byzantine historian Laonikos Chalkokondyles, who was to be named in Grotius' notes, had demonstrated a concrete historical connection between the divisions of early Christianity and the rise of Turkish power.[427]

It is possible that Grotius used one of these works on Turkish history in the composition of his first section, but he may also have made use of ideas that were generally known. Some parts of his argument, however, may go back to older sources. His depiction of the decay and degeneration of primitive Christianity could have been borrowed from Ammianus Marcellinus, whom he was to cite extensively in the notes to this section.[428]

Grotius states that Islam arose with God's permission as a punishment for the corruption of Christianity. The religion of Muhammad is at odds with Christian doctrine, but it offers a mirror of the decay

---

[423] For this see Southern, *Western Views*, pp. 77–82.

[424] Bobzin, 'Martin Luthers Beiträge', 267–8.

[425] See Göllner, *Turcica*, pp. 229–51.

[426] G. Postel, *Des histoires orientales et principalement des Turcs*, Paris 1575, pp. 60–9. On this see G. Atkinson, *Les Nouveaux Horizons de la renaissance française*, Paris 1935, pp. 244–52.

[427] L. Chalkokondyles Atheniensis, *De origine et rebus gestis Turcarum libri X*, Basel 1556, pp. 5–8. On this see Göllner, *Turcica*, pp. 247–8.

[428] He probably read the works of this historian in Loevestein. See *BW* II, n° 598 (to N. van Reigersberch, 14 June 1619), p. 15: "Ick wilde oock wel over een tijd te leen gebruycken Senecam philosophum, de leste editie, ende Ammianum Marcellinum, als oock Ariani Epictetum."

of Christianity at the time.[429] In this way, like Wyclif and Luther,
Grotius suggests an analogy between the external and internal foes
of Christianity.[430]

§2–§3 The Koran

Vives' refutation of Islam, which takes the form of a fictitious dialogue between a Christian (*christianus*) and a Muslim (*alfaquinus*), opens
with a reconnaissance of the terrain.[431] The Muslim says right away
that he is not permitted to discuss the law of Muhammad or to
investigate it.[432] The Christian replies that indeed it is not without
danger to explain the secrets of salvation to the rude and ignorant
populace, but that reasonable people must be free to investigate
them, for otherwise they are defenceless against all kinds of deceit.[433]
Grotius adds to Vives' arguments only the remark that Islam for-
bids the common people to read the Koran.[434] This inaccurate charge
is also found in Mornay.[435] A traditional reproach against Roman
Catholics is here turned against another enemy: Islam.[436]

Grotius deals in some detail with the Muslim accusation that
Christians had falsified the Bible.[437] Like Vives he takes the example of the passage of the Gospel of John in which Jesus foretells the
coming of the Paraclete to his disciples (Joh. 14:16). Some Muslims
alleged that the original text of the gospel had contained a passage

---

[429] *Bewijs*, p. 154: "Also daar is ontstaen een trotse wreede wet/Omtrent de roode
zee door d'hand van Mahumet,/Seer vreemd van Christus leer, een spiegel dogh
van 't leven/Waer toe het Christendom sigh hadde toen begeven."

[430] Cf. *Annot. in NT* (ad Matt. 24:27), in *OT* II 232 b37–38: "Quorum commenta
cum Ebionis aliorumque erroribus commiscens Mahumetes novum dogma producit,
quod nihil aliud quam ingens depravatio Christianismi."

[431] Vives, *Ver.* IV, pp. 456–8.

[432] Vives, *Ver.* IV, p. 456: "AL. Ille vero Mahumeticam probabat, et vetabat nos
ex iussis Mahumetis ipsius quicquam de illa disputare aut inquirere, sed tenere
firmiter traditiones patrum, nec ab illis vel latum unguem esse deflectendum."

[433] Vives, *Ver.* IV, p. 456: "CH. Non est profecto quod negem periculosum esse,
rudes atque ignaros homines de mysteriis religionis disserere, sed id eruditi et pru-
dentiores et cordatiores in populo sine periculo tum possunt facere, tum etiam
debent. [...] Attentio igitur et inquisitio ad inveniendam veritatem valet, men-
dacium vero in segnitie ac negligentia subrepit."

[434] *VRC*, VI 2, pp. 130–1: "Haec religio plane ad fundendum sanguinem facta,
multum ritibus gaudet, credique sibi vult nulla inquirendi libertate: unde et librorum, quos sanctos habet lectio plebi interdicta est."

[435] See Mornay, *Ver.* XXXIII, p. 830.

[436] Cf. *VRC* (Koecher 1740), p. 546.

[437] Vives, *Ver.* IV, pp. 462–4.

about Muhammad, which was later suppressed by the Christians. Vives and Grotius refute this assertion using similar arguments: Christians before the coming of Muhammad had no reason whatever to remove his name, because of course they could not have known who Muhammad was; while after his death they were no longer in a position to do so, because of the many copies and translations of the Bible that were in circulation by that time.[438]

§4–§8 Christianity and Islam

These sections offer a comparison between Christianity and Islam, with reference to their respective founders (§4),[439] the miracles they performed (§5),[440] their first followers (§6),[441] the way in which the two religions spread (§7),[442] and finally the commandments they lay down (§8).[443] Grotius brings a new and tighter arrangement to material that was found spread through Vives' text. He adds to Vives' summary of Islamic pseudo-miracles the example of the dove that flew to Muhammad's ear.[444] The English scholar Edward Pocock, who translated Grotius' apologetic work into Arabic, related that the author had told him he had borrowed this example from Christian sources, in particular from Scaliger.[445]

---

[438] Vives, *Ver.* IV, p. 461: "CH. Venio ad id quod dicis, promissum fuisse a Christo Mahumetem, id vero erasum a nostris. Nam illo loco, quo dicitur, et mitto vobis spiritum consolationis, Mahumetem erat adscriptum, deletum autem a nobis, odio vestri. Quaero ante omnia, quinam eraserunt? Priores Mahumete, an posteriores? Prioribus nulla est causa, nesciebant enim quis aut qualis Mahumetes erat futurus, [. . .]. Posteriores non fecerunt, nam Mahumetes ipse iam de eo conqueritur"; p. 463: "Quod si ante Mahumetem corruptum est utrunque testamentum, cur ad testimonium suorum dictorum remittit vos ipse ad legem et Evangelium, cur non certiores reddebat suos, [. . .]. Post Mahumetem autem non potuerunt corrumpi, nam omnia quae ante Mahumetem a nobis sunt scriptoribus prodita, conformia sunt huic Evangelio, quod nunc habemus; nec tanta librorum multitudo, tot locis dispersa, potuit uno consensu vitiari."

[439] Cf. Vives, *Ver.* IV, p. 461.

[440] Cf. Vives, *Ver.* IV, p. 462.

[441] Cf. Vives, *Ver.* IV, pp. 470–1.

[442] Cf. Vives, *Ver.* IV, pp. 458–60.

[443] Cf. Vives, *Ver.* IV, pp. 471–6.

[444] *VRC*, VI 5, p. 234: "Nempe, quae aut arte humana facile possunt effecta reddi, ut de columba ad aurem advolante, [. . .]."

[445] E. Pocock, *Specimen historiae Arabum*, Oxford 1806 [first edition: Oxford 1650–1], pp. 191–2: "His autem quae ab authore nostro adducuntur, addunt alii eiusdem farinae multa, de quibus quid censendum sit docet nobilissimus et doctissimus Hugo Grotius in 6. De veritate religionis christianae libro, ubi et ipse eorum nonnulla

§9–§10 Islamic accusations

Grotius rejects the Islamic objections to the Christian idea of Jesus as the son of God in the same way as Vives, retorting that Muhammad ascribed many things to God that could rightly be dismissed as unworthy, e.g. that God's hand was cold.[446] He disarms the counter-objection that God could not have had a son without a wife, by offering a spiritual explanation of this Christian concept.[447] Finally he lists several absurdities in Muslim doctrine, all of which without exception he could have found in the work of the Spanish humanist.[448]

§11 Epilogue

In his last book Vives had offered a recapitulation of the most important themes of the whole work.[449] This example may have suggested to Grotius the idea of rounding off his own apology with a summary epilogue. But he goes entirely his own way by closing with an admonition, which is undoubtedly the most personal part of his whole apologetic work.

---

recensens, columbae ad Mohammedis aurem advolare solitae meminit; cuius cum nullam apud eos mentionem reperim ac clarissimum virum ea de re consulerem, se in hoc narrando non Mohammedistarum, sed nostrorum hominum fide nixum dixit, ac praecipue Scaligeri, in cuius ad Manilium notis idem narratur." Pocock probably referred to a passage of Scaliger's commentary on Manilius, but that speaks only of carrier pigeons and not of the miraculous dove that flew to Muhammad's ear: J.J. Scaliger, *Castigationes et notae in Manilii Astronomicon*, Leiden 1600, pp. 437–8. Perhaps Grotius borrowed this well known example of Christian apologetics from a verbal communication from his teacher.

[446] Vives, *Ver.* IV, p. 464: "Videamus iam qualem facit Mahumetes Deum, quam absurdum, quam non solum alienum ab eo qui ipse est, sed omnino diversum et contrarium. [. . .]. Manu ait se a Deo tactum, quae erat frigidissima."

[447] Cf. Vives, *Ver.* IV, pp. 465–6.

[448] Vives, *Ver.* IV, pp. 471–6.

[449] Cf. Vives, *Ver.* V, pp. 482–524: "De praestantia doctrinae christianae."

CHAPTER SIX

THE NOTES

Many years after Grotius had produced his apologetic work he added
an extensive apparatus of notes to the text. It was not until 1639,
almost twenty years after the Dutch version of the text had been
written, that he set to work on this. The edition of *De veritate* published in 1640 was the first to include the apparatus of notes. The
notes form a heterogeneous body of citations, references to literature and arguments. They vary greatly in nature and extent: some
offer no more than brief references to the literature, others cite passages illustrating the train of thought in the text, and yet others form
arguments in themselves by linking citation and reasoning.

The connection between the notes and the text is throughout
rather arbitrary. Sometimes there is even a tension between the content of the note and the corresponding text, because the latter is
based on sources other than the literature to which the notes refer.
Contrary to what the reader might expect, the notes offer little insight
into the sources that Grotius used to compile his text. For example,
we do not find a single reference to the works of Mornay, Socinus
or Vives. In the title of this new edition Grotius indicates that his
chief aim in the notes was to produce additional testimonies.[1] The
apparatus of notes should therefore be regarded, not as a statement
of his sources but as a supplement containing additional evidence.

We have seen that the function of the testimonies for Grotius was
to lend external authority to his argument.[2] He did not rank them
in significantly different categories of authority. Reformation theologians granted the Bible absolute authority as a divine testimony and
only allowed human testimonies a relative value by comparison, albeit
in various degrees.[3] Grotius' notes follow a typically humanist pattern,
being primarily intended to assemble the broadest possible consensus

---

[1] *De veritate religionis christiana. Editio Nova, additis annotationibus in quibus testimonia.*
[2] See chap. IV, pp. 00, 00.
[3] Cf. P. Fraenkel, *Testimonia Patrum. The Function of the Patristic Argument in the
Theology of Philip Melanchthon*, Geneva 1961, pp. 187 sqq.

of historical testimonies. In a letter to Vossius Grotius remarked that
young readers would be able to see at a glance in his notes all kinds
of agreements between sacred history and profane authorities.[4]

The way in which Grotius used classical antiquity and Christianity
to create a harmoniously connected whole, which spoke with one
voice on the most important parts of doctrine and ethics, is strongly
reminiscent of the harmonising view of antiquity taken by Erasmus.
In the *Paraclesis*, for example, Erasmus had explained that much of
Christ's teaching had also been revealed by Socrates, Aristotle,
Diogenes, Epictetus and the stoics.[5] Besides representing pagan thought
as homogeneous, he also found agreements between pagan and
Christian ideas.

Grotius derived his material from many literary traditions. These
various textual traditions formed, as it were, a reservoir of evidence
on which he drew freely for his testimonies, without paying much
attention to the historical and literary contexts in which they had
functioned. Often his notes give a deluge of names without further
text or explanation. The lawyer knows that merely naming a testimony in itself has some value as evidence. The testimonies serve to
reinforce what he has already stated.

Grotius' notes are intended to maximise the evidential force of his
testimonies in two ways. In the first place he stresses the multiplicity
of testimonies as often as he can. One of the assumptions of dialectical-
rhetorical argument was: the more testimonies the better the proof.[6]
Grotius was convinced that if reports from various testimonies agreed
with one another they indicated a universal consensus, which is a
sign of universal truth. In the foreword to *De iure belli* he states that
he has incorporated the widest possible range of authorities, because
a universal consensus must be underlain by a universal cause.[7]

---

[4] Cf. *BW* XI, n° 4923 (to G.J. Vossius, 10 November 1640), p. 611: "Laboris in
colligendis disponendisque testimoniis ad libros de Veritate religionis christianae me
non poenitet. Utile est iuventutem, cui ista scripsimus, habere in uno conspectu
quaecunque apud profanos autores reperiuntur Sacrae Historiae aut dogmatibus
consonantia. Quid tu addis de fructu etiam ad viros doctos inde perventuro, in ea
[sic. *BW*, read: eo?] tuam veterem agnosco benignitatem."
[5] See D. Erasmus, *Paraclesis*, in *Ausgewählte Werke*, ed. H. Holborn – A. Holborn,
Munich 1933, p. 145.
[6] See chap. IV, pp. 000, 000.
[7] *IBP*, Prol. 40, p. 15: "Usus sum etiam ad iuris huius probationem testimoniis
philosophorum, historicorum, poetarum, postremo et oratorum, non quod illis indis-
crete credendum sit, [. . .] sed quod ubi multi diversis temporibus ac locis idem pro

Apart from this consensus Grotius also stressed the antiquity of the testimonies as an important indicator of their truth. He shared the logical assumptions of his time in believing that the older the testimony, the greater its authority.[8] Grotius refers to many sorts of literature, but in his citations he shows a clear preference for the classical authors of Greek and Roman antiquity. He explains this preference in *De iure belli* on these grounds: the better the times and the peoples from whom the examples are borrowed, the greater their authority.[9] Apart from Latin citations he also gives Greek references, which he always provides with a Latin translation. Grotius' references are not always equally precise, for now and then he merely refers to an author's name, sometimes mentions both author and work, and rarely indicates the precise passages he has in mind.

It is remarkable that he makes not a single reference to contemporary theological dogmatic literature, though he refers sporadically to the historical works of such contemporaries as J.J. Scaliger and G.J. Vossius. Instead he offers an abundance of references to early Christian and patristic literature. It was his strategy to present the authors of the early Church as the testimonies *par excellence* of the truth of the Christian religion. He was convinced that the Christianity of that time had possessed precisely those hallmarks of truth that later ages lacked: peace and consensus.

In what follows I shall confine myself to an overall treatment of the apparatus of notes. More than 90 per cent of the notes consist of testimonies in the form of references to literature and citations. I have sought to understand this reference system by distinguishing the types of literature that the author used: I) classical literature of Greek and Roman antiquity; II) early Christian and patristic works; III) the Bible; IV) legal literature; V) contemporary travel literature; VI) humanist works; VII) Jewish literature; and VIII) literature of and about Islam. Thanks to his famous erudition Grotius was able

---

certo affirmant, id ad causam universalem referri debeat, quae in nostris quaestionibus alia esse non potest, quam aut recta illatio ex naturae principiis procedens, aut communis aliquis consensus."

[8] See Molinaeus, *Elementa logica*, pp. 179–80.

[9] Cf. *IBP*, Prol. 46, p. 17: "Historiae duplicem habent usum, qui nostri sit argumenti: nam et exempla suppeditant, et iudicia. Exempla quo meliorum sunt temporum ac populorum, eo plus habent auctoritatis; ideo Graeca et Romana vetera caeteris praetulimus. Nec spernenda iudicia, praesertim consentientia: ius enim naturae, ut diximus, aliquo modo inde probatur, ius vero gentium non est ut aliter probetur."

to draw widely on many sources. Only his references to Jewish and Islamic literature were cited, as we saw, at second hand.

To form an impression of Grotius' method of work we shall look in more detail at the content of several of the fuller notes, which form arguments in themselves. The enormous number of notes to §16 of the first book, which probably go back to an unpublished juvenile work of Grotius, and the large number of Jewish testimonies in the notes to the fifth book deserve separate attention.

Book 1

The apparatus of notes to the first book is three times as long as the corresponding text. That is exceptional; the notes to the other books take up roughly the same space as the texts concerned. Moreover the notes are very unequally spread over the various sections of the first book. Fifteen of the twenty six sections have no notes at all, while a single section (§16) has no fewer than 110, a number that justifies separate treatment (ad VII).

The testimonies that Grotius offers in the notes to this book can be classed in seven distinct literary traditions: I) classical literature; II) early Christian and patristic works; III) the Bible, IV) Jewish literature; V) contemporary travel literature; VI) humanist works; and a special feature of the first book: VII) very ancient testimonies from Egyptian, Phoenician, Orphic and Pythagorean theology (*Philarchaeus*).

I) Grotius' most frequent references in these notes are to authors of Greek and Roman antiquity. Though he drew support for his argument in the main text variously from Aristotelian, Platonic and stoic philosophy, he gave pride of place in the notes to authors influenced by the stoics, such as Plutarch, Cicero, Seneca, Tacitus and Chrysippus.[10] The first part of his argument (§§1–6), largely based on the philosophy of Aristotle, is entirely without notes. In general Grotius prefers to cite ancient poets such as Virgil, Lucretius, Horace and Ovid, rather than philosophers.[11] He repeatedly appeals to historians and geographers, including Herodotus, Pliny, Suetonius, Tacitus and Strabo.[12]

---

[10] *VRC*, I 7.5 [= n. 5]; 15.1; 17.10, 11; 22.2, 6, 9, 12.
[11] *Ibid.*, 7.5; 17.12; 22.2, 3, 10, 11, 12.
[12] *Ibid.*, 7.1, 5; 17.10, 12; 22.4, 5, 6, 7, 8; 24.3.

II) Grotius frequently refers to early Christian and patristic literature, for preference the works of Justin Martyr, Tertullian, Origen, Chrysostom, Clement of Alexandria and Eusebius of Caesarea.[13] From the work of the last two authors he also drew many ancient testimonies for the notes to §16 (ad VII).

III) Unlike the notes to the other books, he makes only a few references here to the Bible.[14]

IV) He makes frequent references to the hellenistic Jewish historian and apologete Josephus, who as we shall see plays a particularly important role in the notes to §16.[15] Grotius also gives a few citations from the other hellenistic Jewish author, Philo.[16] He refers occasionally to the Talmud and to medieval Jewish works by various other authors, including Maimonides, Abenesdra, Juda Levita and Benjamin of Tudela.[17]

V) A separate group of testimonies is formed by more or less contemporary travel literature by such Spanish and Portuguese authors as José de Acosta, Antonio de Herrera y Tordesillas, the Inca Garcilaso de la Vega, and Fernao Mendes Pinto.[18] This literature was also incorporated in the notes to *De iure belli*. Grotius is extremely summary in his references to these works, being content merely to name the authors, not always accurately.[19] This carelessness suggests that he considered these testimonies less important.

VI) Grotius attached much more weight to the authority of humanist scholars such as Lipsius, Scaliger, Drusius and Vossius. In his notes to this book he makes five references to Scaliger,[20] two each to Vossius[21] and Lipsius,[22] and one to Drusius.[23] He calls Drusius 'the most meritorious in the study of Holy Scripture',[24] and describes

---

[13] *Ibid.*, 7.1, 5; 15.1; 16 passim; 17.3, 7, 8, 10, 11; 19.1; 22.1, 3, 9, 14; 23.2; 25.1.

[14] *Ibid.*, I 17.1, 3, 4; 22.2

[15] *Ibid.*, 14.1, 2; 16 passim; 17.2, 7.

[16] *Ibid.*, 14.3 and 4.

[17] *Ibid.*, 7.1 (Juda Levita, Abenesdra); 7.3, 5 (Maimonides); 16.59 (Benjamin of Tudela); 16.98, 112, 113 (Talmud). In our discussion of the notes of book 5 we shall see that Grotius gave most of his Jewish references at second hand.

[18] *Ibid.*, 16.39, 56; 17.9; 22.13.

[19] See Bergman, 'Suppl. Annot.' pp. 253–4, 257.

[20] *VRC*, I 15.1; 16.1, 32, 78, 86.

[21] *Ibid.*, 15.1; 16.87.

[22] *Ibid.*, 17.10, 11.

[23] *Ibid.*, 16.70.

[24] *Ibid.*, 16.70.

his teacher Scaliger and his friend Vossius in one of the notes as 'great men'.[25] Elsewhere he refers to Scaliger as *maximus*.[26] Finally Grotius twice cites from his own translation of Aratus' *Phaenomena*,[27] and three times refers to his own legal treatise *De iure belli*.[28]

As we saw, Grotius' notes reveal his preference for the harmonisation of many testimonies from various traditions. In the same breath he refers to authors from classical, Jewish and Christian literature. Great differences between certain traditions or within a field of scholarship do not appear to disturb him: in one note he refers to both Ptolemy and Copernicus.[29]

The very first note of this book offers a good example of his method of work. In the text of §7 Grotius refers to the Greek geographer Strabo, who had pointed out the appropriateness of the differences in height and the consequent division of the world into land and water. The note not only cites the relevant passage from Strabo, but also mentions that the same observation had been made by the Jewish authors Judas Levita and Abenesdra, and by the Christian Chrysostom.[30] In one brief passage Grotius thus brings out a broad consensus between ancient, Jewish and Christian thought.

The fifth note of the same section, apart from testimonies, also contains reasonings that make it into an argument in itself.[31] Here Grotius begins his assault on Aristotle, who is not even named in the text. To disprove the Stagirite's view that the world was not created and that the human race had had no beginning, he cites a series of very disparate authors, among them Tertullian, Tatian, Lucretius, Virgil, Horace, Pliny, Seneca, Tacitus and Maimonides, all of whom he believes to contradict the Stagirite's opinion. He then turns Aristotle against himself, confronting him with his own pronouncements, before concluding the note:

> Learn this from Plato, that the world had a certain origin, and this from Aristotle, that it was not born, and you will have the same opinion as the Jews and the Christians.[32]

---

[25] *Ibid.*, 15.1.
[26] *Ibid.*, 16.86.
[27] *Ibid.*, 16.11; and 18.
[28] *Ibid.*, 15.2; 16.23, 33.
[29] *Ibid.*, 22.14.
[30] *Ibid.*, 7.1.
[31] *Ibid.*, 7.5.
[32] *Ibid.*, 7.5: "Sume de Platone mundi originem fuisse aliquam, ab Aristotele non esse genitum, et habebis ipsam judaeorum christianorumque sententiam."

We find the same remark, almost word for word, in his youthful work *Meletius*.[33]

In the notes to §23 he invokes Aristotle twice, both times to support his argument.[34] But he says nothing to show that the Stagirite in fact held a very different opinion on the main thesis of the text, the immortality of the human soul. In the notes to the following section, which deals with the same theme, he gives two citations from Plato.[35] Probably he wished to give the impression that the two great philosophers were in agreement on this point. In §19 he ascribes the evil in the world to human free will, a sore point for his contemporaries.[36] In the note, therefore, he does not appeal to his fellow remonstrants, but prefers the early Christian authors Tertullian and Origen, who were above all suspicion.[37]

Grotius' notes, as we said earlier, are not free from inaccuracies. He felt free to deviate from his main text in them. For example, in §25 he refers to Plato and the Pythagoreans, who are supposed to have asserted that the highest human good is to be as like God as possible.[38] This is correct, for the expression 'as like God as possible' derives from Plato and is found in a slightly different form in several of the Pythagoreans.[39] But in the relevant note he does not refer to the works of the ancient philosophers themselves, but to the Christian author Clement of Alexandria, who, according to Grotius, had remarked that the stoics had taken this opinion from Plato.[40]

VII) *Philarchaeus*. In the foreword to his early work *Sacra* (1601) Grotius mentions a work on which he was engaged, entitled *Philarchaeus*. He announces that it will confirm the history of Moses from many

---

[33] *Mel.* 26.93–95: "Cum igitur Plato genitum vult mundum, Aristoteles aeternum, errant sane, at ipsorum argumenta hoc ipsum probant, quod Christiani credimus. Nam et Plato recte colligit coepisse aliquando mundum, nec minus recte Aristoteles non esse genitum. Sequitur ergo ut factus sit."

[34] *VRC*, I 23.1, 2.

[35] *Ibid.*, 24.2, 3.

[36] *Ibid.*, 19, pp. 67–8.

[37] *Ibid.*, 19.1.

[38] *Ibid.*, 25, 74.

[39] For the passages in Plato see Ragnar Holte, *Béatitude et sagesse. Saint Augustin et le problème de la fin de l'homme dans la philosophie ancienne*, Paris 1962, p. 46.

[40] *VRC*, I 25.1. Grotius refers here to Clem. Al. *Strom.* V 15, 95, 1–2 [= GCS, II: ed. O. Stählin, Berlin 1960, p. 338]. Cf. Clem. Al. *Opera Graece et Latine*, ed. D. Heinsius, Leiden 1616, *Strom.* 433 C1–5: "Stoici dixerunt esse finem philosophiae, secundum naturam vivere: Plato autem Deo assimilari, ut ostendimus in secundo Stromate, et Zeno Stoicus qui id accepit a Platone."

ancient pagan testimonies, which contained not unimportant details from Egyptian, Phoenician, Orphic and Pythagorean theology.[41] He appears to refer to the same work in the autobiographical sketch he composed for Meursius' *Illustris Academia* (1613), in which he mentions an unpublished 'Illustratio Historiae Mosaicae ex scriptis Ethnicorum'.[42] Remarkably enough, this work is not named in the reissue of Meursius' work of 1625.[43] After that date no more was ever heard of this mysterious work of Grotius.

The bibliographers Ter Meulen and Diermanse put forward the theory that Grotius incorporated this youthful work in the notes to this section of *De veritate*.[44] This does not appear implausible. In the notes to the apologetic work we find, among others, the promised testimonies from Egyptian, Phoenician, Orphic and Pythagorean theology, which confirm the Mosaic history. In the foreword to his *Sacra* Grotius had spoken of 'very many testimonies' (*plurima testimonia*), and the number of notes to this section is disproportionately large. In total the notes contain ten times as much matter as the text of the section to which they refer.[45] By far the greater part of the material for these notes may indeed have formed part of the corpus of testimonies he had collected in his youth. He would not have needed to add much afterwards, and only a few notes contain references to literature published since 1613. If we bear in mind that he compiled the entire apparatus of notes to *De veritate* within a few months, we are almost forced to assume that he already had them largely at hand in completed form. It is not unlikely that Grotius decided not to publish his *Philarchaeus* once Scaliger's great *Thesaurus Temporum* appeared in 1606.[46]

Grotius' interest in this material was probably aroused by Scaliger himself, his teacher at the university. In his *De emendatione temporum*

[41] *Sacra*, 'Lectori', in *Dichtwerken*, I 1a, p. 295: "Primum in sacris dialogus, cui Philarchaeo nomen, iam in manibus est, in quo Mosis sacra historia plurimis ethnicorum confirmatur testimoniis, si tamen ita loquendum de re quae per se firma externo ad fidem auxilio non eget. In eo multa ex Aegyptia, Phoenicia, Orphica, Pythagorica theologia non contemnenda promerentur."
[42] [J. Meursius], *Illustris Academia Lugd.-Batava: id est virorum clarissimorum icones, elogia ac vitae, qui eam scriptis suis illustrarunt*, Leiden 1613, [Piiij'].
[43] J. Meursius, *Athenae Batavae, sive de urbe Leidensi et academia, virisque claris qui utramque ingenio suo atque scriptis illustrarunt*, Leiden 1625, pp. 207–8.
[44] See *BG*, Addenda, n° 944: Rem. 3, 650.
[45] In one of the editions of 1640 (*BG* n° 941), the main text of this section takes up 7 pages (pp. 17–23), the notes no less than 74 pages (pp. 149–223).
[46] See Posthumus Meyjes, *Mel.* Comment., p. 152.

(1583) Scaliger had presented a powerful and eloquent plea for a comparison of biblical history with data from profane history. In fact he acknowledged no essential distinction, for chronology, between profane literature and the Holy Scriptures, since all literature ought to be subjected to the same source criticism. It was true that he regarded the Bible as the only basis for a sure chronology, but those who neglected the traditional historical narratives of neighbouring cultures would deprive themselves of historical knowledge, for then there is no fixed point by which the biblical details can be dated.[47] In the second edition of this work (1598) Scaliger added an appendix containing a number of textual fragments from Berosus, Manetho and other ancient historians, which he had found scattered through Josephus and Eusebius.[48] Scaliger considered these texts indispensable for a right understanding of Old Testament history.[49] If minor discrepancies between sacred history and the work of the ancient writers should appear, one had to realise that these men had lacked the true instruments with which to find the truth, for in these histories too God had wished to bear testimony to his truth, so the Leiden scholar assures us.[50] In his second great chronological work, *Thesaurus temporum* (1606), Scaliger again stressed the apologetic value of the most ancient historical testimonies.[51]

---

[47] See Scal., *Emend. temp.*, p. 2: "Soli sacri libri supersunt, ex quorum fontibus certa temporum ratio hauriri possit. Sed omnis temporum cognitio inutilis est, nisi certa epocha in illis deprehendatur, ad quam omnium temporum contextus, tam antecedentium, quam consequentium referri possit."

[48] Scal. *Emend. temp.* Veterum Graecorum fragmenta selecta, quibus loci aliquot obscurissimi Chronologiae Sacrae et Bibliorum illustrantur [= Fragm.]. On this see A. Grafton, 'Joseph Scaliger and Historical Chronology: the Rise and Fall of a discipline', *History and Theory*, 14 (1975), 156–85 (esp. 168–70).

[49] Scal. *Emend. temp.*, Fragm. IX: "Hae veterum scriptorum reliquiae, tanquam ex naufragia tabellae in unum libellum a nobis coniectae sunt, ne iterum naufragium facerent, quod quidem hactenus illis contegit, dum apud Josephum et Eusebium disiectae et neglectae nemini fidem utilitatis suae faciebant, praesertim iis, qui in tractatione historiae Biblicae omne externorum scriptorum auxilium negligunt. Horum sinistra iudicia satis confutantur istarum reliquiarum fide, ut constare potest ei, qui tam accurate eas cum istis notis leget, quam putide ipsi eas aspernati sunt. Tantum abest, ut eas historiae sacraae inutiles dixerit, ut sine illis nullam certam Epocham temporis in sacra chronologia apprehendi posse iudicaturus sit."

[50] Scal. *Emend. temp.*, Fragm. XL: "Quod non omnia 'pros akribian' cum sacra historia conveniunt, condonanda potius sint hominibus veris instrumentis veritatis destitutis, quam propter illos naevolos ea reiicienda, in quibus etiam veritatem suam testatus esse Deus voluit."

[51] See Scal. *Thes. temp.*, Prol. [fols. 1–2].

Earlier the Dominican Giovanni Nanni (ca. 1432–1502), better known as Joannes Annius of Viterbo, had drawn attention to Berosus and the other ancient authors in his work *Berosi sacerdotis chaldaici antiquitatum libri quinque cum commentariis* (1498).[52] Annius claimed to have discovered new texts of Berosus and the other very early historians, which were not to be found in the Jewish and early Christian authors and which would shed a completely new light on the course of world history. Annius alleged that the material discovered was more ancient and more trustworthy than all the existing literature, and that it proved that biblical history would have to be rewritten on many points. This plausibly written work, which at first sight appeared staggering, fired the imagination of many humanists. Although suspicions of forgery had been raised earlier, Annius was not definitively unmasked until Joseph Scaliger's rigorous source criticism put an end to the bold speculations of Annius and his followers.[53] Scaliger's distaste for this deceit had not destroyed his interest in the genuine works of the ancient historians Berosus and Manetho, but forced him to limit himself strictly to the well know hellenistic Jewish and early Christian works of Josephus and Eusebius of Caesarea in particular. Eusebius, for Scaliger, at least had the merit of having shown that Moses had lived before the earliest date to which the mythical history of the pagans went back.[54]

Grotius, like his teacher, derived his ancient testimonies exclusively from hellenistic Jewish and early Christian literature. He appealed to such well known names as Berosus, Manetho and Abydenus, but also to the less familiar authors, among them Sanchuniathon, Megasthenes, Menander, Alexander Polyhistor, Aristobulus, Artapanus and Hecataeus.

What was he seeking to prove from all these testimonies? In the main text of this section he expresses a wish to demonstrate the agreement between the books of Moses and the external testimonies. He takes it as axiomatic that the Mosaic books were the oldest in the

---

[52] See A. Grafton, 'Traditions of Invention and Inventions of Tradition in Renaissance Italy: Annius of Viterbo', in *Defenders of the Text. The Traditions of Scholarship in an Age of Science, 1450–1800*, Cambridge, Mass./London 1991, pp. 76–103.

[53] See Grafton, 'Joseph Scaliger and Historical Chronology', 164–70.

[54] Scal. *Thes. temp.*, Prol. [fol. 3]: "Sed quemadmodum [sc. Julianus Africanus] propter excellentiam operis imitatorem nactus est Eusebium, ita eundem propter errores castigatorem habuit, qui primus omnium ostendit majorem quidem vetustatem Mosis esse, quam omnem fere memoriam intervalli gentium mythici, [...]".

world. In the notes he also appears to wish to give further proof of
the theory that ancient culture originated with the Hebrews. According
to this theory there must have been a process of cultural transfer
from the Hebrews to the Phoenicians and Egyptians, from them to
the Greeks and finally from the Greeks to the Romans.[55] This version
of events originated in hellenistic Jewish literature and must originally
have been intended to refute the charge of 'novelty' brought against
the Jewish religion by hellenistic writers. Humanist authors were again
fascinated by the underlying idea that the whole of western civilisation
had a single genesis, and that its deepest roots were Jewish.[56]

At the beginning of §16 Grotius points out parallels between the
biblical account of creation on the one hand and the Phoenician,
Indian, Egyptian and Greek cosmogonies on the other. In his notes
he illustrates this by indicating the many agreements between the
texts of these various traditions. Here and there he also gives an historical explanation of the parallels observed. For example, he repeatedly states that the Greek cosmology was of Phoenician origin. He
tries to make this plausible by pointing out that the ancient Greeks
traded with the Phoenicians, that Linus was of Phoenician origin,
Orpheus drew on Phoenician sources, and Hesiod lived near Thebes,
a city founded by the Phoenician Cadmus.[57] He does not say in so
many words that the Phoenicians in turn had derived their culture
from the Hebrews, but he appears to suggest this by citing com-
pelling textual agreements. The logic he applies to these agreements
is based above all on supposed etymological links.[58]

The first note of this section offers a fine example of this logic.
Grotius wished to prove that

> what Moses has handed down about the origin of the world is virtually
> the same as what is found in the most ancient histories of the Phoenicians,
> collected by Sanchuniathon and later translated by Philo of Byblos.[59]

---

[55] See Laplanche, *L'Évidence*, p. 162.

[56] It was not until the middle of the seventeenth century that this idea of a single genesis of culture and religion began to be abandoned. See C.G. Dubois, *Mythe
et langage au seizième siècle*, Bordeaux 1970, pp. 32–3.

[57] These statements are found in *VRC*, I 16.1 and 5.

[58] Laplanche, *L'Évidence*, pp. 165–6.

[59] *VRC*, I 16, pp. 18–20: "Nam quae ille [sc. Moses] de mundi origine scripta
reliquit, eadem ferme erant et in antiquissimis Phoenicum historiis, quas a
Sanchuniathone collectas vertit Philo Byblius, [...]."

Not one of the works of Sanchuniathon has survived, and almost nothing is known about him even today, but Grotius regarded him as the most ancient historian after Moses. The hellenistic author Philo of Byblos (first and second centuries A.D.) wrote a history of Phoenicia, in which he claimed to have incorporated fragments of Sanchuniathon in translation. The work of this Philo of Byblos is also lost, but several fragments, including passages translated from Sanchuniathon, were preserved in the *Praeparatio evangelica* of Eusebius.[60] Scaliger had noted the importance of these fragments and investigated them.[61] He believed that these texts reflected what the Phoenicians had taken over from Moses.[62] No wonder that Grotius revealed a clear preference for Sanchuniathon over the other ancient testimonies in his notes.[63] Recent research has clearly demonstrated the hellenistic colouring of these fragments of Sanchuniathon, casting serious doubt on their authenticity.[64]

How does Grotius set to work in this note? Clearly his object is to show the agreement between the biblical account of creation (Gen. 1) and the cosmogony ascribed to the Phoenician Sanchuniathon. That was not a simple task, for in Gen. 1 the creation was the act of a God who stood outside creation and called the world and all its phenomena into being by his word; while the Phoenician cosmogony is an example of a sexual creation myth, in which the elements combine to generate life. Grotius opens his note with a verbatim citation of the Greek text of Philo of Byblos, as found in the *Praeparatio* of Eusebius.[65] Then follows his exegesis. Philo had referred to the love of the spirit for its own principles. Grotius finds an allusion to this love in the Hebrew word *merachepet* of Gen. 1:2, which says that God's spirit 'floated' or 'brooded' above the waters. *Merachepet* is a rare form in the Old Testament, and can mean both 'float' and 'brood'. Grotius chooses the latter meaning and explains that this word in the text of Gen. 1:2 actually means 'a dove sitting on an egg', the spirit being interpreted as the symbol of the dove. Sanchuniathon's

---

[60] See Eus. *PE* I 10.
[61] A.I. Baumgarten, *The Phoenician History of Philo of Byblos*. A Commentary, Leiden 1981, p. 1.
[62] Scal. *Emend. temp.*, Fragm. XXXVI–XXXVIII.
[63] See *VRC*, I 16.1, 36, 51, 63, 73, 75, 77, 78, 82.
[64] Baumgarten, *Phoenician History*, pp. 128–9.
[65] Cf. *VRC*, I 16.1; and Eus. *PE* I 10, 1–2.

words 'the love of the spirit for its own principles' also alluded to brooding over an egg, according to Grotius.[66]

This is, however, a tortuous explanation that does violence to both texts. The Phoenician cosmogony clearly speaks of an erotic-incestuous desire of the spirit for its own principles, and not of a mother bird brooding over her eggs; nor is the latter meaning to be found in the text of Genesis. Philo goes on to relate that the love of the spirit for its own principles produced 'Mot', which some interpret as 'mud', others as a corrupted watery substance.[67] Grotius associates this Phoenician word Mot with the Greek word *motos* (turbulence), which must be the same as the Hebrew word *tehom* (flood, primeval waters) of Gen. 1:2. In his opinion this is the same as the Greek concept *abyssos*, the unstable abyss, which ultimately means no more than the heap of mud referred to in Philo. This arbitrary and improbable etymology brings Grotius to his desired goal. To support his argument he makes passing reference in this note to a whole series of authors, among them Plutarch, Apollonius, Virgil, Numenius, Tertullian, 'Rabbi Salomo' (= Salomo ben Isaac, or Rashi), Josephus, Macrobius, Arnobius, Calcidius, Anaxagoras, Orpheus (= pseudo-Orpheus), and finally his teacher Scaliger.[68]

Grotius regularly names such ancient Phoenician and Babylonian authors as Sanchuniathon, Berosus and Abydenus, but by comparison cites far fewer of the testimonies of Egyptian, Pythagorean and Orphic theology he had promised in his youthful work. He took his Egyptian references from the well-known compilations of Diogenes Laertius and Diodorus Siculus.[69] He devotes only one note to the Pythagoreans, whom he also appears to have known only from secondary literature.[70] In six notes he refers to the so-called 'Orphic theology', that is to the texts that were rightly or wrongly ascribed to the mythical figure of Orpheus.[71]

Several groups of verses have been handed down under the name of Orpheus: 1) the 'Orphic Hymns', which probably date from the

---

[66] *VRC*, I 16.1.

[67] Recent research has drawn parallels with the Ugaritic god Mot, whose domain also consisted of mud; see Baumgarten, *Phoenician History*, pp. 112–13.

[68] *VRC*, I 16.1 (p. 20).

[69] *Ibid.*, 16.3, 34.

[70] *Ibid.*, 16.102.

[71] *Ibid.*, 16.1, 5, 9, 32, 83, 86.

second or third centuries after Christ; 2) the *Argonautica*, which was only composed in the fourth century A.D., and 3) the 'Orphica', parts of which may be of very early date (sixth century B.C.).[72] Scaliger acknowledged that some parts of these 'Orphica' were of great value for confirming the antiquity of sacred history.[73] Grotius appeals to the 'Orphic Hymns', the *Argonautica* and the 'Orphica'. In the first note he states that Orpheus drew on Phoenician sources.[74] He thereby suggests that the mythological figure was the author of at least one group of the works attributed to him. Later he speaks of a very ancient author, not of the hymns known under that name, but of the verses that the ancients called 'Orphica', not because they were by Orpheus himself but because they contained things handed down from him.[75] He draws his Orphic citations from the works of Athenagoras, pseudo-Justin, Clement of Alexandria and Eusebius of Caesarea.[76] In one note he simply refers to Scaliger.[77] Elsewhere he adopts his teacher's proposed emendation of a single letter in the fragment of the 'Orphica' preserved by Eusebius, so that the text appears to contain an allusion to Moses.[78] However, Scaliger's proposed emendation has not stood the test of modern textual criticism.[79]

Besides these alleged very ancient testimonies, which had probably already been incorporated in his *Philarchaeus*, Grotius also cites many classical authors, among them Homer, Virgil, Plutarch, Pliny, Ovid, Maximus Tyrius and Strabo. From the last of these he also takes several Indian references.[80] He makes frequent use of the well-known compilations of Diodorus Siculus and Diogenes Laertius.[81] Early Christian and patristic literature is also widely represented in these notes, especially the great works of Clement of Alexandria and Eusebius of Caesarea, which were reservoirs of ancient testimonies.

---

[72] See Walker, *The Ancient Theology*, pp. 14–16.
[73] Scal. *Emend. temp.*, Fragm. XLIII.
[74] *VRC*, I 16: "Sic et Orpheus sua a Phoenicibus hausit, [. . .]."
[75] *VRC*, I 16, pp. 29–30: "[. . .] et ante eos scriptori antiquissimo, non illorum hymnorum, quos nos sub eo nomine habemus, sed eorum carminum, quae vetustas Orphica appelavit, non quod Orphei essent, sed quod ab eo tradita continerent."
[76] *Ibid.*, 16.1, 9, 83.
[77] *Ibid.*, 16.32.
[78] Cf. *VRC*, I 16.86, and Scal. *Emend. temp.*, Fragm. LVIII.
[79] See Eus. *PE* XIII 12.
[80] *VRC*, I 16.2, 35.
[81] *Ibid.*, 16.3, 10, 13, 34, 51, 65, 71, 93, 113.

Finally Grotius makes sporadic references to other types of literature, namely Jewish works,[82] contemporary travel literature[83] and
works of humanist scholarship.[84]

Book 2

The apparatus of notes in this book takes up about as much space
as the text. The notes are evenly distributed across the relevant sections and contain almost exclusively testimonies in the form of references to literature and citations. Grotius adds occasional arguments
and explanations. He takes his testimonies from the following types
of literature: I) early Christian and patristic works; II) classical literature; III) the Bible; IV) Jewish literature, and V) legal sources.

I) While the notes in the first book had been predominantly classical testimonies, in this second book early Christian and patristic
testimonies are to the fore. Grotius found many points of contact
with his argument in these authors, because they too had defended
Christianity on external grounds.[85] The authors of the early Church,
however, had not altogether refrained from discussing dogmas, as
Socinus and Grotius did.

Tertullian was the most frequently cited author in this book, as
he was in the whole work. Clearly the work of this jurist and amateur theologian appealed strongly to Grotius, who claimed to have read
him 'right through' in his cell in The Hague.[86] But there is little
sign of this in his apologetic work. All the notes that refer to or cite
Tertullian concern secondary points of Grotius' argument. Other early
Christian authors to whom he refers frequently include Justin Martyr,
Lactantius, Clement of Alexandria, Augustine and Chrysostom.

II) Testimonies from ancient literature take up an important share
of these notes. In most cases Grotius mentions this literature in combination with early Christian testimonies, a clear sign of his conviction

---

[82] *Ibid.*, 16.98, 112, 113 (Talmud).
[83] *Ibid.*, 16.39 (Fernao Mendes Pinto), 6 (Fernao Mendes Pinto, Jose de Acosta
and Antonio de Herrera y Tordesillas).
[84] *Ibid.*, 16.1. (Scaliger), 32 (Scaliger), 70 (Drusius), 78 (Scaliger), 86 (Scaliger), 87
(Vossius).
[85] Cf. Laplanche, *L'Évidence*, p. 72.
[86] Fruin, *Verhooren*, 'Memorie', p. 70.

that ancient and early Christian culture could be harmonised. In the notes to the first part of his argument (§1–8) he refers chiefly to historians such as Tacitus, Suetonius and Pliny the Younger, while in the second part (§10–23) he gives preference to Cicero, Seneca and Plutarch.

III) Grotius makes a few dozen references to the text of the Bible, and in one place to the apocryphal 'Acts of Pilate' (*Acta Pilati*), for which he refers in the accompanying note to the early Christian author Epiphanius.[87]

IV) A few notes contain references to Jewish literature. Grotius refers, as he had in the previous book, to the account of the travels of Benjamin of Tudela.[88] Other medieval Jewish authors named include Maimonides, Josephus Albo and Levi ben Gerson.[89] Rabbinical literature is represented by several references to the tractates of the Talmud and to one Midrash.[90] He also refers to the hellenistic Jewish author Flavius Josephus.[91]

V) Grotius refers sporadically to legal literature. To confirm his assertion that the human body always remains the same in spite of great material changes, he cites the Roman jurist Alfenus Varus.[92] He owes to Lactantius a reference to the other great Roman jurist Domitius Ulpianus.[93] Finally he makes one reference to the Portuguese canonist Seraphinus de Freitas.[94]

It is striking that the notes of this book are in general much shorter than those in the first book. Although Grotius is happy to pile up references and citations, the result is generally not much more than a list of testimonies. Only a few notes offer rather longer excursuses, forming arguments in themselves.

In the first section, for example, he refers to the Roman historians Suetonius, Tacitus and Pliny the Younger to prove that Jesus had really lived. He adds three notes. That on Tacitus opens with a brief citation from the historian, followed by the statement, taken from

---

[87] *VRC*, II 2.2. Grotius had a copy of Epiphanius' work in Loevestein. See Rademaker, 'Books,' p. 26.

[88] *VRC*, II 2.1. See Bergman, 'Suppl. Annot.', pp. 258–9.

[89] *Ibid.*, 7.1; 12.7; 13.11, 12.

[90] *Ibid.*, 4.12; 13.12.

[91] *Ibid.*, 7.1; 14.7.

[92] *Ibid.*, 11.1. In *De iure belli* Grotius referred to precisely the same passage, also in connection with the unity of the human body: *IBP* II ix, 3, 1–2, p. 239.

[93] *Ibid.*, 22.1.

[94] *Ibid.*, 20.8.

Augustine, that the accusations of scandalous deeds and hatred of humanity made against the Christians (and Jews) were due to their neglect of the cult of idols. Grotius appeals to Varro and Seneca to support his claim that the Romans themselves for the most part regarded the official theology less as a religion that appealed to their minds, than as the performance of an outward duty prescribed by law, which deserved to be kept up more for good morality than for its own sake.[95] Grotius' interpretation does violence to the traditional accounts, because Seneca, in the passage cited by Augustine, had in mind only the attitude of the wise man and not the customs of the people.[96]

The argument is continued in the eighth note of §19, which refers to the remark that the criterion of value in a pagan religion is what is publicly accepted. In this note he refers first to a passage in Xenophon and recalls the remark of Seneca, which he had paraphrased in the note we have discussed. He adds a citation from Augustine about Seneca: 'he honoured what he despised, he did what he himself attacked, he prayed to what he scorned'.[97] Certainly, Grotius adds, agreeing with Plato and Porphyry, it is not without danger to explain the truth about religion to the people.[98] But in his view it was a sufficient condemnation of ancient philosophical systems, that the fear of this danger had had more influence on Greek, Roman and barbarian philosophers than an honest search for the truth.[99] In the third note of §1 Grotius refers to a passage in Pliny the Younger, which he also cites in another connection.[100] He is honest enough to add that Pliny had not had a particularly favourable opinion of the steadfastness of the Christians, which he mentions, but saw it as a sign of stubborn inflexibility.[101]

---

[95] *Ibid.*, 1.2.

[96] Cf. Aug. *Civ.* VI 10.

[97] *VRC*, II 19.8: "Repete hic Senecae verba, quae ex Augustino supra citavimus; post quae sic Augustinus: 'colebat quod reprehendebat, agebat quod arguebat, quod culpabat adorabat.'" [= Aug. *Civ.* VI 10].

[98] Cf. *Imp.* in *OT* IV 231, b6–8: "De theologicis idem quis merito dixerit, vetus enim est sententia, 'de Deo etiam vera dicere periculosum est.'"

[99] *VRC*, II 19.8: "Eius autem periculi metum Graeca et Latina et barbara philosophia pluris fecit, quam veri sinceram professionem, quod vel unum sufficit, ne quis tales sibi per omnia sequendos putet."

[100] *Mel.* 59.9–14; *IBP* II xx, 49, 1, pp. 405–6; and *Annot. in NT* (ad Matt. 5:34), in *OT* II 59a 38–41.

[101] *VRC*, II 1.3.

Book 3

The notes to this book are relatively few and rather unevenly distributed over the sections. About three quarters of the whole apparatus of notes refer to the last section (§16). The other sections are sparsely annotated, chiefly with references to literature and hardly any citations. Grotius refers to the following types of literature: I) the Bible; II) early Christian and patristic literature; III) Jewish literature; IV) ancient classical literature; and V) legal sources.

I) By far the great majority of references are to biblical passages, which is easily explained by the subject matter of this book. Grotius refers chiefly to the New Testament; only the notes to the last section contain a few references to the Old Testament.

II) Once again Grotius refers frequently to early Christian apologetes and fathers of the Church. The author most frequently cited and named is again Tertullian.[102] He makes several references to Irenaeus, Clement of Alexandria, Eusebius of Caesarea and Origen, and one reference each to Chrysostom, Augustine, Epiphanius and Jerome.

III) Grotius refers twice to the hellenistic Jewish author Philo.[103] In two notes he mentions several Targumim.[104] He also refers to the Talmud,[105] and to 'the very learned Menasseh ben Israel', a Jewish scholar of his own time whom he was to mention repeatedly in the notes to the fifth book.[106] Finally in the notes to §16 he frequently refers to the work of Josephus, as we shall see.

IV) His references to classical literature are significantly less frequent than in the previous books. He cites Herodotus, Plutarch, Phlegon and Horace, and merely refers to Plato, Aristotle, Strabo and Quintilian.

V) The large number of references to legal literature is most striking. They chiefly concern the testimonies that play such an important role as evidence in Grotius' argument. He refers to the medieval jurists Speculator [= Guilelmus Durandus][107] and Baldus de Ubaldis.[108] He also refers to the humanist jurist Andreas Gail, whose work he

---

[102] *VRC*, III 2.1; 10.1; 10.3–4; 10.6; 12.5; 14.2.
[103] *Ibid.*, 10.3; 16.19.
[104] *Ibid.*, 16.21 (Targum Onkelos and Targum [Pseudo-] Jonathan), 16.22 (Targum Hierosolymitanum).
[105] *Ibid.*, 16.25 (Shebuoth).
[106] *Ibid.*, 13.1.
[107] *Ibid.*, 13.7.
[108] *Ibid.*, 1.1.

had had by him in Loevestein.[109] Where possible he combines legal references with references to other types of literature, perhaps to broaden his argument. References to legal literature are coupled, for example, with references to the Roman historians Valerius Maximus and Julius Capitolinus,[110] with citations from Tertullian and Plutarch,[111] and elsewhere with biblical references.[112] Besides such classical Roman jurists as Julius Paulus and Herennius Modestinus,[113] he also cites the text of the *Corpus Juris Civilis*.[114]

The notes to §16 are particularly copious. Our discussion of this text has already shown that part of the last section of this book can be regarded as a continuation of §16 of the first book,[115] namely the portion that confirms the Old Testament history of Moses from pagan historians. The seven notes added here agree in content and fullness with the notes to the relevant section in the first book, and therefore may originally have formed part of Grotius' youthful work *Philarchaeus*. They contain very lengthy citations, almost all of them taken from Josephus and Eusebius.[116] From Josephus Grotius takes the testimonies of the 'ancient' historians Berosus, Menander of Ephesus, Megasthenes and Hecataeus; while from Eusebius he takes chiefly the citations from Abydenus. He shows a clear preference for the Babylonian priest Berosus and the Assyrian writer Abydenus.[117] As in the notes to the first book on several occasions he appeals in this connection to his teacher Scaliger.[118] Grotius harmonises these alleged ancient testimonies, just as he had in the first book, with references to classical authors, who include Herodotus, Diodorus Siculus, Diogenes Laertius, Plutarch and Aeschylus, and with the early Christian apologetes Tertullian, Justin, Tatian and Clement of Alexandria.

---

[109] *Ibid.*, 1.1. Cf. Rademaker, 'Books', p. 27.

[110] *VRC*, III 4.1.

[111] *Ibid.*, 12.5.

[112] *Ibid.*, 13.7.

[113] *Ibid.*, 4.1; 12.5.

[114] *Ibid.*, 4.1; 13.7; 15.1.

[115] *Ibid.*, 16, p. 139: "Neque vero pars tantum illa prima a Mose tradita, ut primo libro ostendimus, sed et recentior historia multos paganorum habet adstipulatores."

[116] *Ibid.*, 16.1–7.

[117] *Ibid.*, 16.2: "Berosus ex quo haec et alia supra protulimus, Beli sacerdos fuit post Alexandri Magni tempora, [. . .] Nabuchodonosori mentionem alteram ex Abydeno Assyriorum scriptore nobis tradidit Eusebius tum in Chronico, tum in fine noni de Praeparatione."

[118] *Ibid.*, 16.2: "Uxor illa Nabuchodonosori est Nitocris Herodoto, libro eius primo, ut docuit magnus Scaliger in praeclara Temporum Emendatorum Appendice"; *Ibid.*, 16.3: "De caeteris vide Scaligerum."

Book 4

The notes to this book are few in number and generally not very full. Grotius takes his testimonies from four types of literature: I) classical literature; II) early Christian and patristic literature; III) the Bible; and IV) Jewish literature.

I) The great majority of the testimonies are taken from the literature of classical antiquity. Grotius presents them with the intention, as far as possible, of turning the pagans' own weapons against them, the same strategy he employed in the refutation of Judaism and Islam. Early Christian apologetes had already annexed pagan authors as testimonies for Christianity and against paganism, appealing to such undisputed authorities as Plato and Cicero as well as to the fervent enemies of Christianity, above all Celsus, Porphyry and Julian the Apostate. Humanist apologetes continued this practice. In these notes, as in the previous books, Grotius wishes to appeal to a broad consensus of ancient opinion, which even includes the opponents of Christianity.

He passes over Celsus altogether and refers only once to the emperor Julian the Apostate.[119] The most frequently cited author in the notes of this book is the Greek neo-Platonist philosopher Porphyry (234–304). This pupil of Plotinus had written a great work in fifteen books against Christianity, which was lost but of which some fragments are preserved in Christian authors. Eusebius of Caesarea transformed this great adversary of Christianity into a testimony for Christian truth.[120] Grotius copies this tactic and enlists Porphyry to confirm his own argument. He gives at least twelve citations from him, eight of them from his philosophical work *De abstinentia*.[121] Eusebius and Augustine had frequently cited the oracular pronouncements of mythical figures such as Hecate and Apollo from Porphyry's collection *De philosophia ex oraculis haurienda*.[122] Grotius also readily cites the oracles collected by Porphyry, as he found them in Eusebius and Augustine, though he does not always mention these sources.[123] He has five citations from these oracles,[124] yet in some

---

[119] *VRC*, IV 12.11.

[120] Odile Zink, 'Introduction' in Eus. *PE* IV–V, 1–17 (*SC* n° 206, pp. 19–28).

[121] *VRC*, IV 2.1; 6.3; 12.1; 12.11. These citations largely refer to deception by evil spirits. As early as Eusebius, Porphyry was regarded as an authority on demons.

[122] This work was later consigned to the flames by the Christian emperors and lost, so that we are dependent on the citations in Eusebius and Augustine.

[123] See for example *VRC*, IV 8.3. He refers only to 'Oraculum Hecates apud Porphyrium'. The oracles cited are in this case taken from Eus. *PE* V 8.

[124] *VRC*, IV 8.3; 9.7.

passages the absence of a citation is noticeable. In the text of §9, for example, Grotius mentions an oracle of Apollo named by Porphyry that was said to have proclaimed that only the one God of the Hebrews ought to be worshipped and that the other gods were spirits of the air;[125] yet in the relevant note he does not cite the text of Porphyry, but is content to indicate where it can be found in Augustine and Eusebius.[126] The same section also mentions the Sibylline oracle that had supposedly unwittingly foretold the coming of Christ. Here too the relevant note lacks a citation.[127] Clearly it was enough for Grotius that the fourth Eclogue of Virgil had alluded to the Sibylline oracle, and he accepted the current Christian interpretation of this oracle as an allusion to Christ.

Plato was another of Grotius' star witnesses. Here too he was happy to follow Eusebius, who had regarded Plato as the philosopher *par excellence*, whose wisdom—derived from Moses—in many respects prefigured Christian doctrine.[128] Grotius' notes, however, give the impression that he was less familiar with Plato's philosophy. He gives only three citations from the *Republic*,[129] another at second hand from Origen,[130] and a few references.[131] To one of the citations he added a translation by the later neo-Platonist Calcidius and the suggestive remark that, according to Justin Martyr, the statement of Plato agreed with the opinion of Moses.[132]

In the text of §12 Grotius asserted that Plato had distinguished a trinity in the divine nature: 1) the father; 2) the father's spirit, which is also called the seed of the father or the creator of the world; and 3) the soul, in which all things are contained.[133] As usual in Christian apologetics, this credited Plato with a theory held by the neo-Platonists. In the note, added later, it is remarkable that he does not cite Plato but refers to two letters (to Dionysius and Hermias, and to Erastos

---

[125] *Ibid.*, 9, p. 167.
[126] *Ibid.*, 9.7. In this note he cites other oracles, but they are less relevant.
[127] *Ibid.*, 9.4; 5.6.
[128] For this see G. Favrelle, 'Commentaire', in Eus. *PE* XI (*SC* n° 292, pp. 239–393).
[129] *VRC*, IV 11.5; 12.12.
[130] *Ibid.*, 2.2.
[131] *Ibid.*, 12.3; 12.10.
[132] *Ibid.*, 11.5. But this is an understatement, for the early Christian apologete had claimed that Plato had 'taken' this from Moses, because Moses antedated all the Greek authors. See Just. M. *1 Apol.* 44.8.
[133] *VRC*, IV 12, p. 175.

and Koroskos), which were wrongly ascribed to the great Greek philosopher.[134] This reference is weak even if one assumes the authenticity of the letters, for although the first letter speaks of three cosmic principles, it is far from clear if it means three gods or essences of one god; and while the second letter admits a distinction between a divine father as Lord of the universe on the one hand, and the cause or creator of all things on the other, it does not mention a third god or principle.[135] But such Christian apologetes as Clement of Alexandria, Eusebius and Cyril had remarked that these enigmatic fragments had been interpreted by later Platonists in such a way as to suggest striking agreements with the Christian doctrine of the Trinity.[136] Grotius takes over from Eusebius and Cyril the references to the neo-Platonists Plotinus, Numenius and Amelius, and also appeals to the later Platonists Proclus and Calcidius.[137] He cites Calcidius' commentary on Plato's *Timaeus* five times in the notes to this book.[138] His familiarity with this work is easily explained, since his friend Johannes Meursius had dedicated his new edition of Calcidius' commentary to him in 1617.[139]

Cicero also deserves separate attention. It is well known that Grotius was attracted to Cicero's eclectic philosophy, which was strongly oriented towards practical ethics.[140] We have already shown that certain parts of Grotius' argument appear to be inspired by this writer. In the notes to this book Grotius cites five passages from the works of Cicero.[141]

Grotius also refers to a wide range of ancient authors, among them the Greek dramatists Euripides, Menander and Sophocles, the Roman historians Livy, Tacitus, Suetonius and Pliny the Elder, and the Latin poets Virgil, Ovid, Horace and Juvenal.

---

[134] *Ibid.*, 12.10.
[135] See the paraphrase of the relevant frgaments of the letters in Eus. *PE* XI 16.
[136] See H.D. Saffrey and L.G. Westerink, 'Histoire des exégèses de la *Lettre II* de Platon dans la tradition platonicienne', in Proclus: *Théologie platonicienne*, II, Paris 1974, pp. xx–lx.
[137] *VRC* IV 12.10.
[138] *Ibid.*, 4.1; 9.2; 11.5; 12.10.
[139] *Chalcidii V.C. Timaeus de Platonis translatus. Item Eiusdem in eundem Commentarius*, ed. Meursius, Leiden 1617. Grotius thanked Meursius for this in a letter of 10 September 1617, *BW* I, n° 531, pp. 583–4. See also Molhuysen, 'Bibliotheek', n° 223. On Meursius' edition and the use that Grotius made of it see J.H. Waszink, 'De editionibus', in Plato, *Timaeus a Calcidio translatus*, ed. J.H. Waszink, [Corpus Platonicum Medii Aevi, IV] 2nd ed., London/Leiden 1975, pp. CLXXII–CLXXIII.
[140] See Posthumus Meyjes, *Mel.* Introd., p. 67.
[141] *VRC*, IV 9.1; 9.3; 12.1; 12.12.

II) Grotius makes frequent references to early Christian apologetes and other ancient Christian authors. Eusebius of Caesarea takes pride of place, not only because of the citations and references to his work, but also because of the way in which he served, as we saw, as a channel for such important pagan testimonies as Porphyry and Plato. Grotius also refers regularly to his favourite authors Justin Martyr, Tatian, Tertullian, Clement of Alexandria, Arnobius, Lactantius, Augustine and Cyril of Alexandria.

III–IV) It should be mentioned that Grotius makes no more than six references to the Bible in the notes to this book,[142] and three to the hellenistic Jewish authors Josephus and Philo.[143]

Book 5

The apparatus of notes to this book is the most extensive in the whole work, after that to the first book. Five classes of testimony can be distinguished, derived from I) the Bible; II) early Christian and patristic literature; III) classical works; IV) legal sources; and V) Jewish literature.

I) Since about half of Grotius' references are to biblical passages, he obviously attached a decisive importance to this evidence. He makes a single reference to apocryphal literature (2 Macc.) and cites one apostolic father (the Letter of Barnabas).[144]

II) The number of references to early Christian literature is small. Even Justin Martyr and Tertullian, whom he had used intensively in the main text, are only referred to a few times.[145] He refers sporadically, without showing any clear preference, to Origen, Eusebius of Caesarea, Chrysostom, Tatian, Irenaeus, Theodoretus and Epiphanius.

III) The number of references to ancient Greek and Roman classical authors is even smaller. Grotius appeals almost exclusively to such historians as Livy, Tacitus, Suetonius, Ammianus Marcellinus and Pliny the Younger.

IV) Two notes contain references to legal sources.[146]

---

[142] *Ibid.*, 2.1; 3.3; 6.2; 8.6; 10.1; 12.1.
[143] *Ibid.*, 3.1; 8.7 (both to Josephus); 6.1 (Philo).
[144] *VRC*, V 9.3; 19.10 (Grotius here cites Barnabas from Clement of Alexandria).
[145] *Ibid.*, 8.1; 10.4; 11.4; 14.11; 17.2.
[146] *Ibid.*, 7.14; 14.10.

V) The large number of references to various Jewish sources is very noticeable. There are about a hundred, but a clear discrepancy between the body of the text and the testimonies named in the notes can also be detected. Grotius was in the habit of alluding to his Jewish adversaries in the text as 'your side', 'some' or 'some Jews'. This would lead the reader to expect references, but it is precisely here that explanatory notes are missing, so that the reader is left uncertain whom Grotius had in mind in the main body of his text. Instead the author gives a mass of references on subordinate points of his argument, many of which appear to have hardly any connection with the main text.[147]

Grotius' knowledge of Jewish literature grew considerably in his Paris years, that is after the text of his apologetic work had been written. This is made clear by the notes to this work and also by those to his *De iure belli*, written at roughly the same time, and by his Annotations on the Old and New Testaments.[148] His correspondence for these years gives an impression of the way in which he acquired this knowledge.

It is clear that Grotius made grateful use of the flowering of Jewish studies that was taking place at the time. As a leading member of the Republic of Letters he was well informed about developments in the field, and corresponded easily with the important hebraists of his time, such as Wilhelm Schickard, Joseph de Voisin and Constantijn L'Empereur.[149] Before and during his imprisonment he received help and advice from the arabist and hebraist Thomas Erpenius, who supplied him with information on Jewish history.[150] Grotius also built up a useful relationship with Constantijn L'Empereur, Erpenius' successor in the chair of Hebrew at Leiden University from 1627. Between 1630 and 1640 the Leiden scholar published a series of translations from and commentaries on medieval Jewish literature, which Grotius studied eagerly. It was in the same years that Grotius became ac-

---

[147] See Meijer, *Remonst.*, Intr., pp. 63–4.

[148] Phyllis S. Lachs, 'Hugo Grotius' use of Jewish Sources in On the Law of War and Peace', *Renaissance Quarterly*, 30 (1977), 181–200; and A.W. Rosenberg, 'Hugo Grotius as Hebraist', *Studia Rosenthaliana*, 12 (1978), 62–90.

[149] See for example *BW* IV, n° 1371; and V, n° 1945 (to Schickard); VII, n°s 2495, 2554, 2644 (from and to De Voisin); VIII, n° 3262; IX, n° 3708 (from and to L'Empereur).

[150] *BW* I, n° 493 (to G.J. Vossius, 31 December 1616), p. 543: "Simul Meursium oravi ut Balsamonis usum mihi redderet, Erpennium vero ut in quibusdam hebraicae historiae quaestiunculis me iuvaret." See also *BW* I, n°s 496, 545.

quainted with the work of Menasseh ben Israel. This rabbi of Spanish descent, who lived in Amsterdam, had a great reputation as a scholar, and kept up friendly contacts with such liberal Christian humanists as Barlaeus and the Vossius family. It was thanks to Vossius' mediation that Grotius began his correspondence with Menasseh ben Israel.[151] But he also corresponded with such interested 'laymen' as Martin Ruarus and Samuel Johnson about Jewish literature.[152] Grotius therefore had several channels of information at his disposal.

His correspondence reveals that he was interested above all in the many translations of Jewish literature that were being produced at this time. He asked the translators and commentators with whom he corresponded (among them Schickard, De Voisin and L'Empereur), to send him their works, even when they had not yet appeared. When he received them he expressed his gratitude for this literature, but rarely omitted to urge the authors to undertake even more works.[153]

The eagerness and impatience that Grotius displayed in his letters give the impression that his knowledge of Jewish literature was dependent on the translations and commentaries of his contemporaries. Probably he had a working knowledge of classical Hebrew but not of the much more difficult rabbinical language.[154] He would therefore probably have had no direct access to the rabbinical and medieval Jewish literature, but would have been dependent on secondary works.

Which contemporary works does Grotius name in his notes? He twice refers to Menasseh ben Israel's well known work the *Conciliator*, but all the evidence suggests that he made much more intensive use of it than he admits.[155] In a note to the third book he mentions Menasseh as a great scholar in Jewish literature.[156] He makes a single reference to Christian Gerson's book against the Jews.[157] Closer

---

[151] *BW* IX, n° 3900: bijl. n° 7 (from Menasseh); and *BW* X, n° 4326 (to Menasseh).

[152] *BW* V, n°ˢ 1871, 1873 and 1904 (from and to Ruarus); and *BW* IX, n° 3781 (to Johnson).

[153] *BW* IV, n° 1371 (to Schickard); *BW* VII, n° 2554 (to De Voisin); *BW* IX, n° 3708 (to L'Empereur).

[154] See Meijer, *Remonst.*, Intr. pp. 58–9.

[155] *VRC*, V 5.2; and 21.6. Menasseh ben Israel's work was written in Spanish, but soon appeared in a Latin translation entitled *Conciliator, sive de convenientia locorum Sacrae Scripturae, quae pugnare inter se videntur*, Francofurti [= Amsterdam] 1633.

[156] *VRC*, III 13.1: "Sive judaeos sumas. Quorum diversissimas sententias tum alibi videas, tum apud illarum literarum doctissimum Manassem Israelis filium, libris de Creatione et Resurrectione."

[157] *VRC*, V 16.13. The Jewish scholar Christian ben Meir von Bibberbach Gershon

acquaintance with this book reveals that Grotius must have been indebted to it for many of his references to the Talmud and medieval Jewish literature.[158] He may also have used Gerson's translations from the last chapter of the Talmud tractate Sanhedrin, 'Chelec'.[159] Possibly he consulted other secondary works that he does not name at all, among them several by Constantijn L'Empereur.[160] It must have been through L'Empereur that he became familiar with the Bible commentaries of Isaac ben Judah Abarbanel, Moses Alshech and Joseph ibn Yahya,[161] authors whom he names several times in these notes and who would have remained inaccessible to him without the mediation of the Leiden professor.[162]

In the notes to the previous books he makes several references to the narrative of the travels of the twelfth century Spanish rabbi Benjamin of Tudela.[163] Undoubtedly he knew this only in the Latin translation (*Itinerario*), published by Constantijn L'Empereur in 1633.[164]

Grotius' references to Jewish literature in the notes to this book cover a wide field of judaica, in which six different types can be distinguished: 1) medieval Jewish commentaries on the Bible; 2) rabbinical literature of the Talmud and Midrashim; 3) the works of Maimonides; 4) Targumim; 5) cabbalistic literature; and 6) hellenistic Jewish works. He cites only from the last class, which he could consult himself; for the others he was probably dependent on interpretative works.

(1569–1627) converted to Christianity in the year 1600, after which he called himself Christian Gerson. The work to which Grotius refers is *Des jüdischen Thalmuds fürnehmster Inhalt und Widerlegung*, Goslar 1607. This work went into six editions in the seventeenth century alone. M. Ruarus referred to it once in a letter to Grotius; see *BW* V, n° 1904 (30 December 1633), pp. 218–19.

[158] We consulted Christian Gerson, *Des jüdischen Thalmuds Auslegung und Widerlegung*. Neu bearbeitet von J. Deckert, Vienna 1895 (copy in UB Utrecht, H. oct. 2617).

[159] *Chelec oder thalmudischer Jüdenschatz, ist ein Capittel des jüdischen Thalmuds dessen fürnehmster Inhalt in der Vorrede an den Leser und im letzten Register zu finden ist. Der werthen Christen zu einer Prob fürgestellet und frewlich verdeutschet durch Christianum Gerson*, Helmstadt 1610.

[160] L'Empereur's copy of Grotius' *VRC* contains the note: 'donum pro opera praestita', from which one can infer that L'Empereur actually assisted Grotius. See Van Rooden, *L'Empereur*, p. 178.

[161] C. L'Empereur, *D. Isaaci Abrabanielis et R. Mosis Alschechi Comment. in Esaiae prophetiam, cum additamento eorum quae R. Simeon e veterum dictis collegit. Subjuncta [. . .] refutatione et textus nova versione ac paraphrasi*, Leiden 1631. [= *ComJes.*]; and *Paraphrasis Josephi Iachiadae in Danielem, cum versione et annotationibus*, Amsterdam 1633 [= *ParaDan.*].

[162] Cf. *BW* IX, n° 3708 (to C. L'Empereur, 7 August 1638), p. 506: "Sum enim inquisitor satis diligens in talia, quae nisi abs te tuique similibus dari non possunt."

[163] *VRC*, I 16.59; and II 4.1.

[164] For this see Van Rooden, *L'Empereur*, p. 164.

His references to the various types of Jewish literature are much more careless than usual. They are throughout extremely summary, often incomplete. As a rule Grotius is content to give the author's name without naming his works. He consistently omits the precise references, which his intermediaries always quote. And even these summary references to names are not free from inconsistencies, which can be explained on the assumption that he was dependent on secondary literature. All the signs suggest that he merely transcribed the references he found without further modification, so that he copied the different styles of reference from the different secondary works.

1) The majority of references in these notes are to medieval Jewish Bible commentaries. This is not surprising, since it was these works above all that had been translated and provided with commentaries by Menasseh, L'Empereur, Gerson and other contemporaries of Grotius. The most important exegetes and commentators whom he names are Solomon ben Isaac (Rashi), Abraham ben Meir ibn Ezra, David Kimchi, Isaac ben Judah Abrabanel, Moses Alshech, Joseph ibn Yahya, and Levi ben Gerson. Most of these references can be traced back to L'Empereur (especially those to Abrabanel, Alshech and ibn Yahya), and to Gerson (especially those to Rashi, Kimchi, Saadia, Levi ben Gerson and Bechai). We find several inconsistencies in these references, which point to a defective knowledge of the sources.

For example, he refers in one place to Rashi as 'Solomon Jarchi'[165] and elsewhere as 'Rabbi Salomo'.[166] The identification of Rashi with Solomon Jarchi is due to a Christian misunderstanding, a mistake made by Raymundus Martini and later copied by such hebraists as Münster, Buxtorf junior and L'Empereur.[167] The explanation of Grotius' ambiguity is that he must have taken the references to 'Solomon Jarchi' from L'Empereur,[168] and those to 'Rabbi Salomo' from the converted Jew Gerson.[169] It is not clear if Grotius knew to whom he was referring. His references to the Spanish rabbi Moses ben Nachman Geroni offer another example of lack of clarity. In the main text he calls him 'Moses Nehemanni filius',[170] and in the

---

[165] *VRC*, V 14.2 and 19.13.
[166] *Ibid.*, 14.3.; 14.7; 17.16; 19.19; 20.17; and 21.9.
[167] See Lachs, 'Hugo Grotius' use of Jewish Sources', 185; *BW* V, n° 1871, p. 173 n. 5 (Meulenbroek).
[168] Cf. *VRC*, V 19.13 and Emp. *ComJes.*, p. 17.
[169] Cf. *VRC*, V 14.3 and Gerson, *Thal.*, p. 167.
[170] *VRC*, V 21, p. 221.

note 'Moses Gerundensis'.[171] Did he realise that he was referring to one and the same person? For Grotius the mere naming of names is often sufficient indication of his testimonies.

2) Grotius' references to the rabbinical literature of Talmud and Midrashim contain many errors and obscurities. Once again the inconsistency in the references is striking. Grotius speaks in one place of the Talmud, elsewhere of the 'Gemara Babylonica', or the 'Gemara Hierosolymitana', sometimes refers to Talmud tractates without referring to the corpus as a whole, and at other times exclusively to parts of the tractates. Thus we find next to one another such references as 'Pereck Cheleck',[172] and 'in Talmud capite ultimo de Synedrio'.[173] References to the 'Gemara Babylonica' and 'Gemara Hierosolymitana' appear to have been taken from L'Empereur,[174] and the bare mentions of Talmud tractates such as 'Taanit' and 'Aboda Zara' from Gerson.[175] When he merely names the 'Perec Chelec' in his notes, he could have been thinking of Gerson's translation of the chapter of the same name in the Talmud tractate Sanhedrin.[176]

Grotius took over the details given by his intermediaries indiscriminately and often carelessly. In the notes to §19 he borrows a whole string of references from L'Empereur, among them a reference to the tractate 'Sota' in the Babylonian Gemara.[177] Grotius gives the title of the tractate in Hebrew letters, certainly following the example of the Leiden hebraist, but makes a mistake in one of the letters, so that he refers to a non-existent Talmud tractate.[178]

Presumably he took most of his Talmud references from Gerson. The same applies to his references to the Midrashim. In a few cases he refers to the old exegetic Midrash 'Bereshit Rabbah',[179] and the Midrash 'Ekah Rabbati',[180] but also to the homiletic Midrashim 'Shemot Rabbah' and 'Debarim Rabbah'.[181] A reference such as

---

[171] *Ibid.*, 10.2 This reference must have been taken from Menasseh, *Concil.* pp. 150–1.
[172] *Ibid.*, 7.19 and 18.10.
[173] *Ibid.*, 14.9.
[174] Cf. *VRC*, V 14.6; 19.17; and Emp. *ComJes.*, pp. 21–2, 44–5.
[175] Cf. *VRC*, 16.11 and Gerson, *Thal.*, pp. 46–7.
[176] *VRC*, V 7.19 and 18.10. See Bergman, 'Suppl. Annot.', p. 270.
[177] Emp. *ComJes.*, p. 45.
[178] *VRC*, V 19.17. See Bergman. 'Suppl. Annot.', p. 273. The possibility that this was a printer's error cannot be entirely excluded.
[179] *Ibid.*, 15.4; 17.2; 17.16.
[180] *Ibid.*, 16.10; 21.8, 11.
[181] *Ibid.*, 15.1 and 16.10.

'Rabboth explicat'[182] compels one to wonder if Grotius really understood this material.[183]

3) A special problem that presents itself concerns several references to the Talmud for which corresponding passages cannot be found. In the text of §3 he states that the members of the great Sanhedrin were familiar with magical arts.[184] He adds a note with the following content: 'Thalmud titulo de Synedrio, et titulo de Sabbato'.[185] But one will search these tractates in vain for a passage that confirms Grotius' statement. A corresponding passage can, however, be found in a work that is described as a 'Compendium of the Talmud'. This is the *Mishneh Torah* of Maimonides, and the relevant passage is found in the chapter Sanhedrin ('Hilkot Sanhedrin'), where Maimonides states that the members of the Sanhedrin had to be acquainted with several arts and sciences, among them the arts of magic.[186]

Grotius' attention had been drawn to this passage in 1638 in a letter from Menasseh ben Israel to Vossius, actually addressed to Grotius.[187] Would it have escaped him that Menasseh referred to Maimonides and not to the Talmud? The possibility appears to be ruled out, because Grotius told Vossius that his opinion agreed well with that of Maimonides.[188] Would he have assumed that his readers would understand that the reference was not to the Talmud but to the work of Maimonides?[189] But this cannot have been the case, because for example the second part of the same note certainly does refer to a Talmud tractate and not to Maimonides.[190] Such references

---

[182] *Ibid.*, 19.13; cf. Emp. *ComJes.*, p. 53.

[183] See Meyer, *Remonstr.*, p. 64.

[184] *VRC*, V 3, p. 181: "Et si verum est, quod tradunt Judaei, senatores magni Synedrii gnaros fuisse magicarum artium, ut reos possent convincere, [...]."

[185] *Ibid.*, 3.8.

[186] Maimonides, *Mishneh Torah*, 'Hilkot Sanhedrin', II 1. See Maimonides, *The Code of Maimonides*, Book XIV: the Book of Judges. Translated from the Hebrew by Abraham M. Hershman, London/Oxford 1949, p. 7.

[187] *BW* IX, n° 3900, Bijl. n° 7 (Menasseh ben Israel to G.J. Vossius, 4 June 1638), p. 802. Menasseh wrote this letter in reply to a question that Grotius had put to him through Vossius (see *BW* IX, n° 3554, p. 248); it was therefore really intended for Grotius.

[188] *BW* IX, n° 3716 (to G.J. Vossius, 7 August 1638): "Video eum [sc. Menasseh] in illo loco explicando consentire cum magni judicii doctore Maimonide."

[189] This view is defended in Rosenberg, 'Hugo Grotius as hebraist', 81–3.

[190] The second part of the reference relies on a mistake and according to Koecher does not concern the Talmud treatise 'Sabbat' nor the 'Hilkot Sabbat' of book 3 of Maimonides' *Mishneh Torah*, but the Talmud tractate 'Menachoth'. See Bergman, 'Suppl. Annot.', pp. 268–9.

as 'in Talmude titulo de Synedrio' 'Thalmudico titulo de Synedrio'
and 'Thalmud de Synedrio' appear to agree at times with the *Mishneh
Torah* ('Hilkot Sanhedrin'), and at other times with the treatise of
the same name in the Talmud.[191] The only plausible explanation
seems to be that Grotius regularly worked backwards from Maimonides'
Compendium of the Talmud to the Talmud itself—a working method
that was not uncommon at this time.[192] This makes it clear how he
could refer to such non-existent tractates as 'de rege', a reference
that must have been derived from the *Mishneh Torah* 'Hilkot melakim'
(laws of the kings).[193]

   Grotius' correspondence between 1630 and 1640 reveals a special
interest in Maimonides' *Mishneh Torah*, a vast synthesis of the entire
system of Jewish law. This work in fourteen books offers a clear and
businesslike survey of Jewish legislation, omitting all the dialectic and
mysticism that characterised the Talmud. It was for that reason that
seventeenth century Christian humanists like Cunaeus, Selden and
Grotius felt such an attraction for this compendium.[194] But the acces-
sibility of the work was no small problem, for it was written in a
difficult Hebrew. There were Arabic translations of the whole and
Latin translations of small parts of this great work. In a letter to
Ruarus Grotius wrote that he did not consider the Hebrew and Latin
versions of Maimonides' work accurate, and was therefore dependent
on the Arabic (did he assume that this was the original?)[195] At any
rate he showed himself particularly delighted when Joseph de Voisin
presented him with some Latin translations of the *Mishneh Torah* in
1636.[196] He assured the French hebraist that his translations were
very worthwhile and had aroused in him a desire for more.[197] De

---

[191] Rosenberg assumes that in references of this type in the notes to *De iure belli*
Grotius was thinking exclusively of Maimonides' work; see Rosenberg, 'Hugo Grotius
as hebraist', 81–2.
   [192] It was followed, for example, by John Selden: see I. Herzog, 'John Selden
and Jewish Law', *Journal of Comparative Legislation and International Law*, XIII (1931),
236–45 (esp. 242–4).
   [193] Cf. *VRC*, V 7.12, 9.4; and Maimonides, *Mishneh Torah*, 'Hilkot Melakim', VIII,
11.
   [194] See Aaron L. Katchen, *Christian Hebraists and Dutch Rabbis. Seventeenth Century
apologetics and the Study of Maimonides' Mishneh Torah*, Cambridge, Mass./London 1984,
pp. 4–14.
   [195] *BW* V, n° 1873 (to M. Ruarus, 2 August 1633), p. 177: "Maimonidae quae
sententia fuerit, scire non possumus nisi consulto Arabico codice. Nam hebraea versio, ut iam de latina nihil dicam, alicubi parecaraKcqh."
   [196] See *BW* VII, n° 2495 (to J. de Voisin), p. 1.
   [197] *BW* VII, n° 2554, p. 92: "Maimonidae quae vertisti, dignissima sunt lectu
incenduntque in me multa videndi talia desiderium, audaciam etiam id a te postulandi."

Voisin replied that he would be glad to comply with Grotius' request, and planned to make further translations from Maimonides.[198] It is not known if De Voisin ever carried out this plan.

In all there are ten covert references to Maimonides' *Mishneh Torah* in these notes.[199] It is difficult to establish which parts of the *Mishneh Torah* were accessible to Grotius in translations, commentaries and other works by his contemporaries.[200] Once he probably refers to a translation of 'Hilkot Yesodei ha Torah' made by W.H. Vorstius.[201] And we can infer from his correspondence with Vossius and Menasseh ben Israel that he was also familiar with 'Hilkot Sanhedrin'.[202]

Grotius makes a further three references in these notes to another work by Maimonides, *More Nebukim* ('Doctor Dubitantium').[203] Taking all the explicit and implicit references together, Maimonides is by far the most important Jewish testimony in this book. Grotius told Vossius that he regarded Maimonides as almost the only Jew of sound judgement.[204]

4) Grotius appeals in seven notes to various Targumim, the Aramaic paraphrases of the Hebrew Bible. Here too a certain inconsistency can be detected in his method of annotation. He speaks of 'Chaldaeus interpres', 'paraphrastes Chaldaeus' or 'Chaldaeum targum'.[205] On one occasion he is more specific, referring to two Targumim of the Pentateuch.[206] He probably borrowed these references too from various intermediary works.[207] His excerpts show that in any case he used a Targum translation by the sixteenth century Christian hebraist Paul Fagius.[208]

---

[198] *BW* VII, n° 2644, pp. 223–4.
[199] *VRC*, V 3.8; 7.12; 9.4; 17.1, 2, 16; 20.17; 21.1; 22.10.
[200] For a survey of the available Latin translations see Jacob I. Dienstag, 'Christian Translators of Maimonides' Mishneh Torah into Latin', in *Salo Wittmayer Baron Jubilee Volume on the Occasion of his Eightieth Birthday*. English section, vol. 1, Jerusalem 1974, pp. 287–310.
[201] *VRC*, V 21.1. He probably had in mind Maimonides, *Constitutiones de fundamentis legis Rabbi Mosis fil. Maiiemon, Latine redditae per Guilielmum Vorstium*, Amsterdam 1638.
[202] *BW* IX, n° 3554 (to G.J. Vossius, 30 April 1638), p. 248: "Nam si de magno synedrio capiendus is locus, cujus authoritati parendum in omnibus controversae interpretationis aut consuetudinis fuerit ad evitandum schisma, quod velle videtur Maimonides, [. . .]."
[203] *VRC*, V 8.2; 18.2, 3.
[204] *BW* VII, n° 2885, p. 581: "Bona accessio erit filii Maimonides, Iudaeorum prope solus sani judicii."
[205] *VRC*, V 8.3; 15.4; 16.12; 17.16; 19.11; 21.10, 11.
[206] *Ibid.*, 17.16: "Tam Jonathan quam Hierosolymitanae paraphraseos scriptor."
[207] Cf. *VRC*, V 19.11; and Emp. *ComJes.*, p. 50.
[208] Eyff, *Handschr.* ff. 59–21: "Hebreeuwse wetgeving, extracten uit Joodse auteurs";

5) Unlike Mornay Grotius had little knowledge or appreciation of the Cabbala.[209] But the Frenchman had belonged to an earlier generation of humanists, who praised the cabbalists for their philosophical and mystical profundity, and even honoured them above all the rabbis.[210] In Grotius' time Christian humanists were more interested in medieval Jewish biblical commentaries and systematic works, and had hardly any interest in the Cabbala. Grotius had little occasion to refer to it. In only one note does he refer to a cabbalistic work, which he cites erroneously.[211] In the text of §21, as we have seen, he followed Mornay in referring to the cabbalists, who distinguished three lights in the deity.[212] This reference was too explicit not to demand a note, but in that note Grotius refers to the polyglot lexicon of the Christian orientalist Valentin Schindler, probably because he could not find a suitable cabbalistic work.[213]

6) Grotius repeatedly cites the hellenistic Jewish authors Flavius Josephus and Philo Judaeus, to whom he also refers frequently in the other books.[214]

Book 6

The shortest book in this apologetic work is suitably equipped with the shortest apparatus of notes. The various types of literature to which Grotius refers in these notes can be distinguished as follows: I) literature of and about Islam; II) ancient classical works; III) early Christian and patristic literature; IV) the Bible; and V) Byzantine history.

2^r: "Pentateuchum Chaldaicum et Fagius"; 2^v: "Fagius ad Pentateuchum." This must mean Paul Fagius, *Thargum hoc est Paraphrasis Onkeli Chaldaica in Sacra Biblia, ex Chaldaico in latinum fidelissime versa, additis in singula fere capita succintis annotationibus* [. . .], Argentorati [= Strasbourg] 1546.

[209] Cf. *BW* VII, n° 2554 (to J. de Voisin, 14 April 1636), p. 92: "Cavalae pleraque somnia otiosorum."

[210] For this see J.L. Blau, *The Christian Interpretation of the Cabala in the Renaissance*, New York 1944, pp. 95–102.

[211] *VRC*, V 18.3: "Messiae res fore coelestes, ait liber cabbalisticus Nezaël Israël." For the correction see Bergman, 'Suppl. Annot.', p. 272.

[212] *VRC*, V.21, pp. 221–2.

[213] *Ibid.*, 21.7. The reference is to Valentin Schindler, *Lexicon pentaglotton Hebraicum, Chaldaicum, Syriacum, Thalmudico-Rabbinicum et Arabicum post auctoris obitum in lucem prolatum*, Hannover 1612.

[214] *VRC*, V 3.4; 9.2; 14.1, 5, 12, 13; 15.1; 19.9, 10; 20.12, 13 (Josephus); *Ibid.*, 9.3; 14.10; 21.1, 2, 3, 4, 5 (Philo).

I) Apart from a work by Euthymius Zigabenus, all the literature of and about Islam to which Grotius refers can be found in the collection compiled by Theodor Bibliander. This work, which has rightly been described as the first Christian encyclopaedia of Islam, consists of three parts.[215] The first part contains the first Latin translation of the Koran, dating from the twelfth century; the second offers the most important Christian refutations of Islam from the middle ages; and the third part gathers together a number of works on the history of the Turks.[216]

The greatest part of Grotius' references to Islam consists of references to the Koran. He states that, for the reader's benefit, he is using the first Latin edition of the Koran.[217] This is the translation made between 1141 and 1143 by the English scholar Robertus Ketenensis for Peter the Venerable, which first appeared in print in Bibliander's compilation.[218] In his references to the Koran Grotius follows the chapter division of this edition.[219] He also makes sporadic references to three other Islamic works in the *Corpus Toletanum*, included in the first part of Bibliander's collection: *Doctrina Mahumet*, *Liber generationis Mahumet* and *Fabulae Sarracenorum*.[220]

---

[215] For Bibliander's work see P. Manuel, 'Une encyclopédie de l'Islam. Le recueil de Bibliander 1543 et 1550', *En terre d'Islam*, 21 (1946), 31–7; R. Pfister, 'Die Zürcher Koranausgabe von 1542/43', *Evangelisches Missionsmagazin*, 99 (1955), 37–43; and H. Bobzin, 'Über Theodor Biblianders Arbeit am Koran (1542/3)', *Zeitschrift der deutschen morgenländischen Gesellschaft*, 136 (1986), 347–63.

[216] Grotius must have made use of the second edition of this work, which appeared under the title *Machumetis Saracenorum principis, eiusque successorum vitae, doctrina ac ipse Alcoran, [. . .] His adiunctae sunt confutationes multorum et quidem probatiss. authorum, Arabum, Graecorum, et Latinorum, [. . .]. Adiuncti sunt etiam de Turcarum sive Saracenorum [. . .] origine et rebus gestis, [. . .]. Haec omnia in unum volumen redacta sunt, opera et studio Theodori Bibliandri,* Basel 1550 [= Bibl. *Mach.*] This second edition added to the first a number of writings, some of which are mentioned in Grotius' notes: *Joannis Cantacuzeni Contra sectam Mahumeticam, Christiana et orthodoxa assertio:* Bibl. *Mach.* II, pp. 193–385, and *Bartholomaei Georgevitii De afflictione tam captivorum quam etiam sub Turcae tributo viventium Christianorum,* Bibl. *Mach.* III, pp. 174–91.

[217] *VRC*, VI 2.1: "Alcoranus Azoara XIII, ut habet prima editio Latina, quam hic in lectoris gratiam sequimur."

[218] Bibl. *Mach.* I, pp. 8–199: "Lex Saracenorum, quam Alcoran vocant, id est collectionem praeceptorum." On the translation of Robertus Ketenensis (= Robert of Ketton), see M. Th. D'Alveny, 'Deux traductions latines du Coran au Moyen-Age', *Archives d'histoire doctrinale et litteraire du Moyen-Age*, 22–23 (1947–8), 69–131; and on Bibliander's share in this publication, H. Bobzin, 'Über Theodor Biblianders Arbeit am Koran', *Zeitschrift der deutschen morgenländischen Gesellschaft*, 136 (1986), pp. 347–63.

[219] For the chapter division of Robertus Ketenensis see Kritzeck, *Peter the Venerable*, pp. 97–100.

[220] Bibl. *Mach.* I, pp. 189–200: 'Doctrina Mahumet'; pp. 201–12: 'Liber de generatione Machumet et nutritia eius'; pp. 213–23: 'Chronica mendosa et ridiculosa

Grotius also relies on a number of works from the second part of
Blbliander's collection, such as the *Disputatio Saraceni et Christiani a
Petro Abbate Cluniacensi edita*.[221] He refers to a very old Arabic dialogue included in Latin translation in the *Corpus Toletanum*,[222] and
makes a few references to Ricoldo da Montecroce's *Confutatio Alcorani*,
mentioned above,[223] to the apologetic work *Contra sectam Mahumeticam*
of the Byzantine emperor John VI Cantacuzene,[224] and to the *Cribratio
Alcorani* of the famous cardinal Nicolas of Cusa.[225]

Finally he refers to one work in the third volume of Bibliander's collection, the *De afflictione tam captivorum quam etiam sub Turcae tributo viventium Christianorum* of the Hungarian pilgrim Bartholomej Georgijevic.[226]

Grotius gives no citations from the Koran or the other works in
Bibliander's collection, probably because they were all translations,
but he does cite the polemical work *Disputatio de fide cum philosopho*

Saracenorum, de vita Mahumetis et successorum eius'. This last title is inaccurate
and should be 'Fabulae Sarracenorum' (see Kritzeck, *Peter the Venerable*, p. 75). The
first two works were translated by Hermannus Dalmata and the last by Robertus
Ketenensis. For these translations see Kritzeck, pp. 75–96.

[221] *VRC*, VI 4.7 and 4.8.

[222] Bibl. *Mach.* II, pp. 1–20: 'De haeresi et principatu ex lege Mahumeti disputatio
Christani eruditissimi [. . .] et Sarraceni sodalis ipsius, adversus doctrinam et flagitia
Mahumetis dignissima visa est, quae ex XXIIII libro Speculi historialis huc adjicere-
tur. Bibliander took this text from the well known *Speculum historiale* (ca. 1250, first
printed in 1473) of Vincent of Beauvais. He also reprinted Vincent's introduction,
which stated that this book had been translated from Arabic by Peter of Toledo
on the instructions of Peter the Venerable (Bibl. *Mach.* II, p. 2). The text appears
to be a partial translation of an Islamic-Christian dialogue between Al-Hashimi and
Al-Kindi, of the ninth century: see G. Tartar, *Dialogue islamo-chrétien sous le calife Al
Ma'mun (813–834). Les épitres d'Al-Hashimi et d'Al-Kindi*, Paris 1955, p. 17. The Latin
translation made by Peter of Toledo for the *Corpus Toletanum* is entitled 'Epistola
Sarraceni et Rescriptum Christianum'; see Kritzeck, *Peter the Venerable*, pp. 101–7.

[223] Bibl. *Mach.* II, pp. 121–84: 'Richardi Confutatio legis latae Saracenis a male-
dicto Mahumeto'. Bibliander gave Bartholomaeus de Monte Arduo's Latin version
of the Greek translation of Demetrios Kydones.

[224] Bibl. *Mach.* II, pp. 193–385: 'Joannis Cantacuzeni Contra sectam Mahumeticam,
Christiana et orthodoxa assertio.' This detailed work was written according to the
emperor's own statement in 1360, and consists of four apologies and four diatribes
against Muhammad. For this work see H.G. Beck, *Kirche und theologische Literatur im
byzantinischen Reich*, Munich 1959, pp. 731–2.

[225] Bibl. *Mach.* II, cols. 31–121: 'Cribratio Alcorani Nicolao de Cusa cardinale
autore'. (Bibliander changed from pagination to columns at this point.) For this
work see Ludwig Hagemann, *Der Kur'an in Verständnis und Kritik bei Nikolaus von Kues*,
Munich 1976.

[226] Bibl. *Mach.* III, pp. 174–91: *Bartholomaei Georgevitii De afflictione tam captivorum
quam etiam sub Turcae tributo viventium Christianorum*. This is the account of the experiences of the pilgrim Bartholemej Georgijevic, who was captured and enslaved. See
Göllner, *Turcica*, p. 12 (n. 10).

saraceno in urbe Melitine of Euthymius Zigabenus (eleventh-twelfth century).[227] This Byzantine author wrote, at the request of emperor
Alexios I (1081–1118), a great work against all existing heresies, the
last part of which was an attack on Islam in the customary form of
a dialogue.[228] This part appeared separately in the compilation
Saracenica sive Moamethica (1595) of Fridrich Sylburgius, which may
have been used by Grotius.[229]

Not all of Grotius' references to literature of and about Islam give
appropriate support to the argument in the body of the text. That
is not surprising. His method of work entailed a certain superficiality,
as we have been able to see on several occasions. Undoubtedly he
had not used the works he cites in the notes when was writing his
text. That causes a certain tension between the text and the notes. Some
of the references are only tenuously relevant, others cannot be used
to prove the argument in the text, and Grotius also failed to mention in the notes many suitable passages in the literature that was
available to him.[230] As we saw he drew exclusively from secondary
literature, which naturally limited his understanding of Islam greatly.

II) The first six notes of the first section contain no fewer than
five extensive citations from Ammianus Marcellinus.[231] The texts he
cites from this stoic historian fit in very well with the text, so that it
appears permissible to assume that Grotius was in fact citing a source
of his argument. The only other classical author he names is Plato.[232]

III) Grotius refers sporadically to early Christian literature. He cites
from such well known authors as Jerome,[233] Origen[234] and Lactantius.[235]
He gives one citation from the *De gubernatione Dei* of Salvianus.[236]

---

[227] *VRC*, VI 4.2; 9.4. See also *ibid.*, 7.5; 8.1; 8.4; 8.6.

[228] For this work see M. Jugie, 'La vie et les oeuvres d'Euthyme Zigabène', *Echo d'Orient*, 15 (1912), 215–22; A. Th. Khoury, 'Gespräch über den Glauben zwischen Euthymios Zigabenos und einem sarazenischen Philosophen', *Zeitschrift für Missionswissenschaft und Religionswissenschaft*, 48 (1964), 192–203; and G. Podskalsky, 'Euthymios Zigebenos', in *TRE*, 10 (1982), pp. 557–8.

[229] F. Sylburgius, *Saracenica sive Moamethica*, [Heidelberg] 1595, pp. 1–55: *Ismaeliticae seu Moamethicae sectae praecipuorum dogmatum Elenchus, ex Euthymii Zigabeni Panoplia Dogmatica.*

[230] This is convincingly shown by Koecher and Bergman, see Bergman, 'Suppl. Annot.', pp. 276–80.

[231] See *VRC*, VI 1.1; 1.4; 1.6.

[232] *Ibid.*, 9.4.

[233] *Ibid.*, 1.4.

[234] *Ibid.*, 2.2.

[235] *Ibid.*, 7.4.

[236] *Ibid.*, 1.10.

This less famous fifth century priest evidently exerted a strong attraction for the eirenicists of the sixteenth and seventeenth centuries. Grotius had already closed his *Meletius* with a lengthy citation from this work of Salvianus.[237] He reveals his preference for Tertullian by choosing him as the only author to be cited in his *peroratio*.[238]

IV) The *peroratio*, in which Grotius developed his own ideas, is provided with more notes than all the other sections of this book put together. Apart from two citations from Tertullian they contain exclusively brief references to passages in the Bible.

V) In the notes to the first section he gives a few citations from the Byzantine historians Procopius of Caesarea,[239] Joannes Zonaras[240] and Nicephorus Gregoras.[241] It is remarkable that the translation of part of the text of Procopius cited in the sixth note agrees exactly with the translation in his posthumously published *Historia Gothorum*.[242] A single note refers to contemporary works on the history of the Turks (*Turcica*).[243]

Finally he appeals once to his old teacher Scaliger, to support his argument that the word 'Saracens' actually means robbers.[244]

---

[237] *Mel.* 91.48–59.

[238] *VRC*, VI 11.1 and 11.10.

[239] *Ibid.*, 1.6.

[240] *Ibid.*, 1.3.

[241] *Ibid.*, 1.6 (3 citations). For these authors see G. Ostrogorsky, *Geschichte des byzantinischen Staates*, 2nd ed., Munich 1952; and M.E. Colonna, *Gli storici byzantini del IV al XV secolo. I. Storici profani*, Naples 1956.

[242] Cf. *VRC*, VI 1.3 and *Hist. Gotth.*, pp. 145–6.

[243] *VRC*, VI 1.13: "Vide Turcica Leunclavii et Laonicucm Chalcocondylam." He probably meant the following works: J. Leunclavius, *Historiae Musulmanae Turcarum, de monumentis ipsorum exscriptae libri XVIII*, Frankfurt 1591; and Laonicus Chalcocondyle Atheniensis, *De origine et rebus gestis Turcarum libri X*, Basel 1556 (translated into Latin by Konrad Klauser). For these works see Göllner, *Turcica*, pp. 247–9.

[244] *VRC*, VI 6.1. See Scal. *Emend. temp.* II [not III!]: 'De Periodo Arabum', p. 108. In his addition to Grotius' note Clericus pointed out the inaccuracy of this etymology; see *VRC* (Koecher, 1740), p. 555.

CHAPTER SEVEN

RECEPTION

Grotius' apologetic work became one of the most famous and most often reprinted works in the history of Christian apologetics. It enjoyed a certain fame during the author's lifetime, but it did not become an overwhelming success until after his death, as the number of editions and translations shows. In the eighteenth century a new edition appeared nearly every year. An entire study could easily be devoted to the work's reception. In this chapter we shall confine ourselves necessarily to some aspects of its *Wirkungsgeschichte*. We shall consider first (a) the attitude that Grotius took to the criticisms his work provoked; and (b) the translations that appeared in the author's lifetime. Finally, by way of an appendix, we shall give (c) a survey of the editions and translations published after his death.

a) *Criticism*

The criticisms of his work that Grotius had to bear during his lifetime were largely dictated by the tension between remonstrants and contra-remonstrants. Grotius had sided with the remonstrants and could therefore count on the certain enmity of the contra-remonstrants. But his Dutch didactic poem provoked virtually no reaction. How is this to be explained?

Grotius' earlier theological writings, the *Ordinum Pietas* (1613) and *De satisfactione* (1618), had raised storms of protest among the contra-remonstrants, as a result of which the author was stigmatised for good as a remonstrant and crypto-Socinian.[1] After his political fall and the Synod of Dordrecht the pressure was eased, and the mood of the contra-remonstrants appeared for the time being to be calmed by the sweet taste of victory. It was also fortunate for Grotius that his poem appeared at the same time as the remonstrant confession

---

[1] See E. Rabbie, *Sat.* Introd., pp. 40–8.

of faith, on which the contraremonstrants' attention was concentrated.[2] This confession had been drafted by the remonstrant leader Simon Episcopius and formed the most important target of contraremonstrant criticism in the following years; this certainly helped to draw their fire away from the work of Grotius.[3]

Yet Grotius had been warned by those he trusted, at a very early stage, of the criticisms that his apologetic work would provoke. His brother Willem warned him, directly after the work was conceived, that omitting the central Christian doctrines of the trinity and the divinity of Christ would be taken ill, because his ill-wishers would conclude that he doubted these dogmas.[4] In fact Willem was alluding to the charge of Socinianism, which was indeed often brought against Grotius' work later.

Hugo answered laconically that no one had ever managed to please everybody. He was very well aware that objections would be raised, but he was convinced that his work did not need much defence before honest judges. It was self-evident that he had not dealt with Christian doctrines; no one had ever been converted to Christianity in that way. First the authority of the Scriptures had to be proved, and after that the Christian doctrines could be derived from them, according to Grotius.[5]

Later in 1620, when Vossius pointed out a certain resemblance to Socinus, Grotius was irritated and remarked that his friend would do better to notice what was true and not what would please the critics. He declared that he would prefer to put off publication, if necessary until after his death, rather than be the slave of others.[6]

---

[2] *Confessio sive declaratio sententiae pastorum, qui in foederato Belgio Remonstrantes vocantur, super praecipuis articulis religionis christianae*, [n.p.] 1621.

[3] *Apologia pro confessione sive declaratio sententiae eorum, qui in foederato Belgio vocantur Remonstrantes, super praecipuis articulis religionis christianae. Contra censuram quatuor professorum Leidensium, inscripta nobil., pud. ac potent. d.d. deput. et consil. ordinum Hollandiae et West-Frisiae*, [n.p.] 1629. For a survey of the many reactions to this defence see A.H. Haentjens, *Simon Episcopius als apologeet van het remonstrantisme in zijn leven en werken geschetst*, Leiden 1899, pp. 90–109, 154–8.

[4] ARA, 1911, XXIII, n° 32 (from W. de Groot, 2 April 1620): "Non dubito etiam, quin aliqui institutum tuum calumniantes dicturi sint in scripto tuo non probari trinitatem neque divinitatem Christi, imo ne eius quidem, si bene memini, mentionem fieri: nec sufficiet malignis istis hominibus, si respondeamus id alienum a tuo proposito esse, neque enim perfectum a te christianum describi sed eius elementa adumbrari, nam omnia in pejorem sumere consueti, si quid tale a te praeteritum vident, id pro eo ac si de ipso dogmate dubites habituri sunt."

[5] *BW* II, n° 600 (to W. de Groot, 12 April 1620), pp. 30–1.

[6] *BW* II, n° 608 (to G.J. Vossius, [November 1620]), p. 37: "Tu non quid cen-

Grotius thus showed himself stubbornly unwilling to concede to possible criticisms, even before his work appeared.

When the Latin version appeared he said sceptically "we shall see what judgement this rather fastidious age passes".[7] Grotius was thus prepared for anything, but for the time being no criticism was heard and the opinions were largely favourable. The laudatory reactions to the work reached the author before the work itself. Vossius, who arranged for publication, wrote to Grotius, as we saw, that whenever he read his friend's work he felt that he was dining at a heavenly banquet with the gods themselves.[8] Two months later Grotius heard from his brother in law Nicolaas van Reigersberch that his defence of the faith had been highly praised by the Venetian nobleman Domenico da Molino.[9] His work was well received in wide circles. The author was soon able to note that his book was appreciated not only by Protestants but also by Catholics, among them the famous cardinal Francesco Barbarini.[10]

The success of the work meant, indirectly, a success for the remonstrants. The author himself made this connection explicitly. On 11 March 1628 he reported to Van Reigersberch: "my little book de veritate religionis christianae is doing good not just for me, but for the remonstrants in general".[11] Grotius did not distance himself from the remonstrants, as friends in Holland and France advised him; clearly he felt no call to give up for opportunist reasons the beliefs he had championed for years.[12] In 1641 he even decided that the

---

soribus placiturum sit, sed quid verum maxime putes tecum et cum aliis cogita. Id enim sequi certum est; ac potius differre editionem, vel ad mortem usque, quam aliorum captui servire."

[7] *BW* III, n° 1189 (to G.J. Vossius, 16 October 1627), p. 187: "Latina mea de Veritate christianae religionis nondum accepi. Videbimus quae futura sint fastidiosi satis saeculi iudicia."

[8] *BW* III, n° 1167 (from G.J. Vossius, 23 August 1627), p. 161: "Excusus jam liber tuus de Religionis christianae veritate. Quem cum lego in coelesti coenaculo cum dis mihi epulari videor."

[9] *BW* III, n° 1192 (from N. van Reigersberch, 23 October 1627), p. 193: "Molina, een aansienelijck persoon te Venetiën, heeft gesien uE. boucxken de Veritate religionis christianae, prijst seer het werck ende autheur aen de heer van der Myle."

[10] *BW* III, n° 1278 (to W. de Groot, 24 June 1628), p. 332: "Libri de Veritate religionis christianae cardinali Barbarino aliisque Romae probantur. Hic paene omnibus romanensibus et protestantibus."

[11] *BW* III, n° 1240, p. 264.

[12] See H.J.M. Nellen, 'Grotius' Relations with the Huguenot Community of Charenton (1621–1635)', *Lias*, 12 (1985), 150–3.

proceeds of this apologetic work would be used for the benefit of the remonstrants.[13]

For the time being the less favourable reactions were confined to rumours. In the autumn of 1628 he heard from his brother Willem that Heinsius and Thysius were accusing him of Socinianism. Grotius replied calmly that he was not worried by the 'gossip' of the Leiden scholars. He proudly pointed out that there was not a single Protestant or Catholic to be found in Paris who did not praise the work. Perhaps Heinsius and Thysius felt, like Voetius, that anyone who saw the commandments as the most important part of the Christian faith must be a Socinian. Grotius declared that he gave the priority to ethics, but added that in this he agreed with all the Christians of the earliest centuries.[14]

This answer reveals Grotius' imperturbable self-confidence. The charge of Socinianism, which had previously led him to compose an entire work against Socinus, now left him cold. If necessary, he would endure being called a Socinian, if that meant that ethics were given priority over doctrine in religion, for that agreed with the general view of the early Church. The accusation of Socinianism against the remonstrants, which was intended as a theological death sentence, had gradually become a commonplace.[15] Many Calvinist theologians regarded anyone who deviated a hairsbreadth from the line laid down at Dordrecht as a Socinian. Since their demonstration of sympathy for Vorstius, the remonstrants had continually been exposed to the charge. Among the contra-remonstrants Grotius had long been considered a crypto-Socinian, and so he was not surprised when the charge was now repeated by Heinsius and Thysius.

---

[13] *BW* XII, n° 5400 (to W. de Groot, 5 October 1641), p. 553.

[14] *BW* III, n° 1325 (to W. de Groot, 28 October 1628), pp. 301–2: "Heinsii et Thysii rumusculos non curo. Hic nemo est romaniensium, nemo protestantium, qui non probet. Sed forte illi cum Voetio sentiunt socinianum esse praecipuam religionis partem in observatione mandatorum Christi ponere. Ego vero ita sensisse video primorum saeculorum christianos, coetus, doctores, martyres, pauca esse, quae sciri opus sit, ceterum ex animi obsequentis proposito nos apud Deum aestimari. Hujus ego quoque sum sententiae neque ejus unquam me poenitebit."

[15] On Socinians and remonstrants see W.J. Kühler, *Het socinianisme in Nederland.* Voorzien van een inleiding van A. de Groot en vermeerderd met een register samengesteld door Dirk Visser, Leeuwarden 1980 [= reissue of the first edition, Leiden 1912], pp. 69–80; J.C. van Slee, *De geschiedenis van het socinianisme in Nederland,* Haarlem 1914, pp. 105–35; and W.J. Kühler, 'Remonstranten en socinianen', in G.J. Heering (ed.) *De remonstranten. Gedenkboek bij het 300-jarig bestaan der Remonstrantsche Broederschap,* Leiden [1919], pp. 137–58.

Antonius Thysius, who had previously criticised Grotius' *De satis-factione*,[16] had been a professor in the faculty of theology at Leiden since 1619 and was one of the signatories of a manifesto against the remonstrant confession of faith, in which all remonstrants were accused of Socinianism.[17] Daniel Heinsius, Grotius' former bosom friend, had been known since his appearance at the synod of Dordrecht as a fierce contra-remonstrant, who accused his religious adversaries in turn of atheism and Socinianism.[18] Heinsius and Thysius did not elaborate their charge against Grotius, at least not in writing, so that it remained 'gossip'. In a letter to Willem de Groot Grotius also made a passing reference to Gisbertus Voetius, who earlier that year had attracted his attention as a grim adversary of his Arminian friend Daniel Tilenus, and who was later also to cause Grotius himself a great deal of annoyance.[19]

---

[16] See E. Rabbie, *Sat.* Introd., p. 43.

[17] *Censura in confessionem sive declarationem sententiae eorum qui in foederato Belgio remon-strantes vocantur, super praecipuis articulis christianae religionis a. S.S. theologiae Profess. Academiae leydensis instituta*, Leiden 1612. The dedication of this work is signed by the four professors in the Leiden faculty of theology: Johannes Polyander (1568–1646), André Rivet (1572–1651), Anthonius Thysius (1565–1640) and Anthonius Walaeus (1573–1639).

[18] In 1620 Heinsius published a letter from Simon Episcopius to Paulus Stochius, found during a search of a house in Leiden, entitled *Simonis Episcopii brief. Inde welcke de gront van de remonstranten aengaende hare Belijdenis ende eenstemminge in het gheloove, naer-stelick ontdekt wort. Met een voorreden aende Hoog. mog. Heeren Staten Generael der Vereenighde Nederlanden*, The Hague 1620. In the foreword, written by Heinsius, the remon-strants are accused of Socinianism (p. 17). In 1621 Heinsius wrote an anonymous treatise in which he accused his religious opponents of an atheistic attitude: *Cras credo hodie nihil, sive modus tandem sit ineptiarum. Satyra Menippea*, Leiden 1621. When Heinsius in turn was accused of Socinianism by the remonstrants, he defended him-self in a short work, *Monsterken van de ontrouwicheyt ende notoire leugenen der genoemde remonstranten, nu onlancx in seker schrift genoemt Antwoorde op de Extracten, etc. uytgestroyt tegens den Hoochgeleerden ende wijtberoemden Daniel Heinsius*, Leiden 1629. In this Heinsius declares that he considers himself far above such infamous accusations. In the fol-lowing years he continued to act as an agitator against the remonstrants. See for example *Praestantium ac eruditorum virorum epistolae* [. . .], 3rd ed., Amsterdam 1704, n° 477 (C. Barlaeus to S. Episcopius, 8 June 1634), p. 746: "Heinsius magnus causae vestrae insectator, quique modo atheismum, modo cum mitius loqui vult socinia-nismum vobis impingit, tam foede circa trinitatis dogma lapsus est, ut expediat plures hoc scire".

[19] *BW* III, n° 1318 (to W. de Groot, 30 September 1628), p. 385. On Voetius see A.C. Duker, *Gisbertus Voetius*, 3 vols with index vol., Leiden 1897–1915. A photo-graphic reprint of Duker's work with a foreword by A. de Groot was published in 1989 at Leiden. See also *De onbekende Voetius. Voordrachten wetenschappelijk symposium Utrecht, 3 maart 1989*, ed. J. van Oort, C. Graafland, A. de Groot and O.J. de Jong, Kampen 1989.

While the remonstrants and contra-remonstrants continued their
intellectual struggle, Grotius calmly forged ties of friendship with
leading Socinian theologians, at the very time when his remonstrant
kindred spirits were doing everything in their power to distance themselves from Socinianism.[20] On 10 May 1631 Grotius wrote in passionately friendly terms to the prominent Socinian Johannes Crellius,
who had published a refutation of his *De satisfactione* in 1623.[21] Grotius
did not not blame his correspondent; on the contrary he acknowledged that he had learned a great deal from him. He was grateful
that there were still men in his century who were not so concerned
with controversies about subtleties as with the improvement and
sanctification of life. Grotius wrote very modestly of his apologetic
work, and considered that its chief merit was its conciseness. He
assured Crellius that if there was anything in it that pleased him
and those who shared his views, that was more than he had dared
to hope.[22]

This pronouncement appears even more revealing when one recalls
how much Grotius owed to Socinus in this work. In this letter Grotius
unambiguously revealed his interest in and even his adherence to
the Socinian cause. His next letter to Crellius made this even clearer,
for in it he declared that he hoped to have the strength, as he had
the will, to defend the common cause of Christendom.[23] Grotius' letters to Ruarus are written in the same tone of warm friendship.[24]
He continued to correspond with Socinians even after his friends in
the Netherlands warned him of the risks that this entailed.[25]

---

[20] See Kühler, *Het socinianisme*, pp. 86–90; and van Slee, *De geschiedenis van het socinianisme*, pp. 108–17.

[21] J. Crellius, *Ad librum Hugonis Grotii quem de satisfactione Christi adversus Faustum Socinum Senensem scripsit responsio* [. . .] in *J. Crellii Operum tomus quartus scripta eiusdem didactica et polemica complectens* [. . .], Irenopoli [= Amsterdam] ca. 1656, [*BsG* n° 295].

[22] *BW* IV, n° 1633 (to J. Crellius, 10 May 1631), p. 392: "Liber de Veritate religionis christianae magis ut esset nobis solatio quam ut aliis documento scriptus, non
video quid post tot aliorum labores utilitatis afferre possit, nisi ipsa forte brevitate.
Si quid tamen in eo est, quod tibi tuique similibus placeat, id mihi supra spem
eveniet."

[23] *BW* IV, n° 1769, (to J. Crellius, 20 June 1632), p. 49: "Quare Deum precor,
ut et tibi et similibus vitam det et quae alia ad istiusmodi labores necessaria. Mihi
ad juvandam communem christianismi causam, utinam tam adessent vires, quam
promptus est animus."

[24] See for example *BW* IV, n°ˢ 1635, 1696; *BW* V, n°ˢ 1732, 1855, 1873, 1907.

[25] *BW* V, n° 1732 (to M. Ruarus, 19 January 1632), p. 11: "Quas ad me in
Galliam destinaveras litteras, Ruare doctissime, eae me in patria deprehenderant,
quo veneram amicorum vocatu existimantium et tempore et meae in patriam fidei

It was not until ten years after the appearance of the Latin version of his apologetic work that Grotius began to be troubled by criticisms. These came from Gisbertus Voetius and Martinus Schoockius. Immediately after his appointment as professor at the Illustrious School in Utrecht in 1634, Voetius launched a lengthy polemic against several remonstrants.[26] His comprehensive work *Thersites heautontimorumenos* (1635) is a violent but thorough indictment of the remonstrants, whom he considered to be penetrated by the pernicious tendencies of Roman Catholicism, scepticism and Socinianism.[27] Voetius showed himself a capable polemicist, who coupled a great parade of learning with an exceptionally sharp tone, which sometimes degenerated into vulgar invective.[28] His work provoked indignant reactions from the remonstrants.[29] Voetius did not take on the task of replying to it himself, but left it to his pupil and kindred spirit Martinus Schoockius, who in 1637 published a brief defence, entitled *Remonstranto-libertinus.*[30] The pupil's work, which was probably largely inspired by the master, again provoked the remonstrants to a counter-attack.[31]

---

haud dubiis experimentis mitigatos esse animos eorum, qui per nostram ruinam in potentatum reipublicae viam sibi fecerant."

[26] For this polemic see Duker, *Gisbertus Voetius*, II, pp. 1–70.

[27] G. Voetius, *Thersites heautontimorumenos, hoc est remonstrantium hyperaspistes, catechesi, et liturgiae Germanicae, Gallicae et Belgicae denuo insultans, retusus; idemque provocatus ad probationem mendaciorum et calumniarum quae in illustr. dd. ordd. et ampliss. magistratus Belgii, religionem reformatam, ecclesias, synodos, pastores etc. sine ratione, sine modo effudit,* Utrecht 1635.

[28] He called his adversary J.J. Batelier, for example, 'a stinking abscess': see Duker, *Voetius*, II, p. 48.

[29] S. Naeranus, *Propulsatio contumeliaraum quibus G. Voetius in Thersite suo petit,* [n.p.] 1636; and J.J. Batelier, *Confutatio insulsi et maledici libri, quem adversus remonstrantes edidit Gisbertus Voetius theologiae in academia Ultrajectina professor, titulo Thersites heautontimorumenos* [n.p.] 1637.

[30] Martinus Schoockius, *Remonstranto-libertinus, a cl. d. Gisberto Voetio th. d. et prof. in acad. Ultrajectina in Thersite heautontimorumenos autokatakritos deprehensus in blasphemiis in Deum ac religionem, in calumniis et mendaciis in illustr. ordd. ampliss. magistratus etc. indicante ac provocante eum ad tribunal societatis Sociniano-Remonstranticae,* Utrecht 1637. On Martinus Schoockius (1614–69) see *BL,* II (1983), pp. 394–5; and *NNBW,* X, cols. 889–91.

[31] [J.J. Batelier], *Gisberti Voetii doctoris et professoris theologiae academiae anti-Remonstrantico-libertinica, seu methodus in disputandi adversus remonstrantes; exhibita in tractatu cui titulus 'Remonstranto-libertinus',* Utrecht 1637; and Timotheus Philopatris [= Carolus Niëllius], *Proeve van de conscientieuse oprechtigheydt ende wijsheydt Gisberti Voetii, ende van eenighe sijne medestanders. Waerinne uyt enighe harer schriften aenghewesen wordt, hoe onchristelijck ende ontrouwelijck van haer teghen de Remonstranten wordt gehandelt, ende met wat onwaerheyden sy sommighe aensienlijcke personen soecken te onteeren. In 't Neder-duytsch uytgheheven, tot waerschouewinghe van alle vrome Christenen, op dat sy sulcke luyden niet al te veel gheloofs gheven, ende wel toesien aen wien sy hare zielen toevertrouwen* [n.p.] 1637 [= Niëllius, *Proeve*].

On 12 August 1637 Willem de Groot sent his brother Hugo a
book of remonstrant origin, which challenged Voetius' attack on
remonstrantism and at the same time defended Grotius against the
calumnies of ill-wishers.[32] This must have been the *Proeve van de
Conscientieuse oprechtigheyd ende wijsheydt Gisberti Voetii, ende van eenighe sijne
medestanders* by Timotheus Philopatris, a pseudonym of the Amsterdam
remonstrant preacher Carolus Niëllius.[33] This book is a reply to the
Remonstranto-libertinus, which its author was firmly convinced was a
co-production of Voetius and his straw man Schoockius.[34] Niëllius
was especially indignant that Schoockius had not spared even Grotius
his false accusations of Socinianism, and he devoted a whole chapter to an attempt to clear Grotius from this charge.[35]

Voetius and Schoockius, however, had made only sporadic mention of Grotius in their attack on remonstrantism. Voetius had only
named Grotius occasionally in his *Thersites heautontimorumenos*, and in
more or less neutral terms.[36] Schoockius, however, in his *Remonstranto-
libertinus*, had remarked that Grotius' much-translated apologetic work
had cunningly led readers of all inclinations to the bases of Socino-
remonstrantism.[37] Niëllius was incensed by this accusation, for Grotius
was the jewel in the crown of remonstrantism, and he devoted a
whole chapter to refuting it.[38]

No wonder that Grotius was rather indignant when he heard of
this work. In a letter to his brother Willem he admits that he only
knows the criticisms of Voetius and Schoockius from the replies they

---

[32] *BW* VIII, n° 3205 (from W. de Groot, 12 August 1637), p. 488: "Et vicissim
mitto libellum recenter hic contra Voetium ejusque asseclas editum, in quo et te
defensum invenies et a malevolorum calumniis vindicatum."

[33] See *BW* VIII, n° 3205, p. 488 n. 2. Grotius' reply (*BW* VIII, n° 3310, pp.
665–8), of which more in a moment, shows unmistakeably that Willem had sent
him Niëllius' book. Batelier's work entirely passes over Schoock's charge of Socinianism
against Grotius, which so enraged Niëllius and disturbed Grotius. On Niëllius see
C.D. Sax jr, *Carolus Niëllius*, Amsterdam 1896.

[34] Niëllius, *Proeve*, p. 9.

[35] *Ibid.*, pp. 40–50: "Caput 5: Waer in de Heer Grotius cortelijck wort ghesuyvert
van de valsche blamen die sijne religie aengaen."

[36] Voetius, *Thersites heautontimorumenos*, pp. 73, 78, 240, 276.

[37] Schoockius, *Remonstranto-Libertinus*, p. 11: "Magnus est Grootius [sic!], stupen-
dae eruditionis, celebris, et honoratus, et tamen homo est, ac non satis defecatus a
fermento Socino-Remonstrantismi. [. . .] Cum ipse velut ἀλλοτριο-επίσκοποσ inquirat
in alienum, et subdole libello de Veritate christianae religionis, in omnes linguas
pene translato, apud cuiuscumque religionis hominis fundamenta Socino-Remon-
strantismo moliatur."

[38] Niëllius, *Proeve*, pp. 40–1.

had provoked, but he is surprised at the malicious machinations of his opponents.[39] He clearly regards Voetius as the *auctor intellectualis* of the charge of Socinianism, and bitterly observes that there can be little hope of Christian unity as long as men like Voetius set the tone in the churches.[40] He states that his apologetic work is read with pleasure and profit in many languages. Is it not surprising, he wonders, that the doctors of the Sorbonne, who judged the work before it was published, have overlooked the Socinianism that Voetius professed to detect in it? The same applies, says Grotius, to cardinal Barbarini, who always had the work with him and recommended it to others, to the English bishops who were pressing for a translation, to the Calvinist Huguenots of Charenton who agreed with it, and finally to the Lutheran (Köler) who had translated the work into German.[41] Which English bishops he refers to is not known, nor do we know if his appeal to the theologians of Charenton had any basis in fact.[42]

He also believes that his book *De satisfactione* had sufficiently proven that he was not a Socinian. If he has said certain things that Socinus had said before him, why should he be denied a right that Augustine and Jerome had enjoyed, namely the right to adopt certain opinions of heretics? For heretics would not be heretics if their assertions did not contain some truth, and if they did not have some common ground with us. Let those who cause or foment schism in the Church look to it, warned Grotius, that they do not give occasion to deviate much further from Christianity than Socinus had.[43]

In this typically Grotian answer, as reasonable as it was elusive, Grotius did not deny the possibility of agreements between his work and Socinus, though he did not openly admit them. He considered that he was entirely within his rights to take a hint from heretics,

---

[39] *BW* VIII, n° 3310 (to W. de Groot, 22 October 1637), p. 665.

[40] *BW* VIII, n° 3310, p. 665.

[41] *BW* VIII, n° 3310, p. 667.

[42] Cf. H.J.M. Nellen, *Hugo de Groot. De loopbaan van een geleerd staatsman*, Weesp 1985, pp. 150–3.

[43] *BW* VIII, n° 3310, p. 666: "Socinianus quam non sim, ostendit liber de Satisfactione [. . .]. Caeterum si quaedam mihi dicta etiam Socini in mentem venere, non dicam cum illo apud Senecam, pereant qui ante nos nostra dixerunt, sed mihi licuisse quod Augustino, qui ex Tychino, Hieronymo, qui ex Apollinari, hominibus alterius communionis sententiarum multa transcripsere. Haeretici, nisi aliquid haberent veri ac nobiscum commune, iam haeretici non essent. Videant illi, qui in ecclesia scissuras aut faciunt aut alunt, ne occasionem multis dent longius abeundi a christianismo quam abiit Socinus."

and appealed in his defence to the fathers of the Church, who were beyond all suspicion. On the one hand he let Socinus be stigmatised as a heretic, but on the other he warned his contra-remonstrant opponents not to fall into even more serious heresies.

A few weeks later Grotius remarked that both his apologetic work and his poem on baptism had been translated into Swedish, undoubtedly, he added sarcastically, to the great dismay of Voetius and such 'buffoons'.[44]

In the same year (1637) Grotius received reports of accusations voiced by André Rivet.[45] This theologian of French origin had been appointed a professor at Leiden and was also chosen by Frederick Henry as the tutor of prince William II. Rivet was a particularly authoritative and influential man among the Calvinist theologians. In December 1637 Grotius received from his brother in law Van Reigersberch an account of a conversation that Van Reigersberch had had with Rivet at the house of Andreas Rey, the Polish ambassador to the Republic. When the relationship between remonstrants and Socinians came up for discussion, Rivet had remarked that Grotius, according to some, inclined towards Socinianism, because he was said to have used the translation of the Bible by Castellio and was supposed to have interpreted some biblical passages in Socinian terms in *De iure belli*.[46]

When Van Reigersberch heard that after this conversation Rivet was telling everyone who would listen that Grotius was preaching Socinianism, he sought a second interview with Rivet at the house of the Polish ambassador.[47] Over dinner Van Reigersberch asked Rivet to explain his charge against Grotius more fully, and the court

[44] *BW* VIII, n° 3342 (to W. de Groot, 14 November 1637), p. 720: "Liber de Veritate religionis christianae meus et de baptismo etiam in Suedicam transfertur linguam, quo magis doleat Voetius eique similes sanniones."
[45] On André Rivet (1572–1651): *NNBW*, VII, cols 1051–2; H.J. Honders, *Andreas Rivetus als invloedrijk gereformeeerd theoloog in Holland's bloeitijd*, The Hague 1930; A.G. van Opstal, *André Rivet, een invloedrijk Hugenoot aan het hof van Frederik Hendrik*, Harderwijk 1937.
[46] *BW* VIII, n° 3366 (from N. van Reigersberch, 1 December 1637), pp. 760–1: "Het gesprek in't vervolg gevallen synde op de remonstranten en socinianen, zoo zeide de heer Rivet, dat eenigen meenden De Groot te hellen naar de socinianen; om dat hij doorgaans, zoo hy zeide, de overzetting gebruikte van Castellio in 't boek wegens 't recht van oorlog en vrede het V. en XIX. cap. van Matth. met Socinus verstont, en Socinus uitvluchten niet had beantwoordt."
[47] For a report of this conversation see *BW* VIII, n° 3375 (from N. van Reigersberch, 7 December 1637), pp. 773–8.

preacher replied by restating his previous points in detail and adding as a new argument that Grotius spoke of God in very general terms in his apologetic work.[48]

Although Van Reigersberch vigorously championed his brother in law in this conversation, Grotius was so irritated that he defended himself against Rivet's criticisms in no fewer than three subsequent letters to Van Reigersberch.[49] He emphatically denied that he had used Castellio's Bible translation in his apologetic work, and remarked that in any case it was hard to link Castellio with Socinus, who had lived after his time.[50] He could not help it if he had sometimes reached the same conclusions as Socinus, and he felt it was unfair to demand that he should believe that Socinus could never have hit on a true idea.[51] In passing he demonstrated that his translation of Is. 53 in De veritate was flatly contrary to Socinus' exegesis.[52] As for Rivet's charge that he spoke of God in too general terms, Grotius answered that one could simply go no further on the basis of natural reason. He appealed for this to his teacher Junius, who had accused Mornay of having tried to prove the trinity from natural reason, whereas this doctrine could not be deduced from any source but revelation.[53]

This was a telling argument, which he was to repeat several times in the following years. In one of his letters Grotius did not fail to point out that Rivet was well known in Paris to be as mediocre in his judgement as in his learning.[54]

---

[48] BW VIII, n° 3375, p. 775: "Soo geraeckten wij vast voort met verscheyde atteinten, die ick en passant daeronder lardeerde, sonder dat Rivet vergat, want hij socht te astrueren de redenen van sijn ender sijner suspiciën voort te brengen, dat in libro de Veritate religionis christianae uEd. spreeckt in seer generale termen De Deo, [. . .]."

[49] BW VIII, n° 3382 (12 December 1637), pp. 787–8; n° 3390 (19 December 1637), pp. 802–4; n° 3397 (26 December 1637), pp. 813–17.

[50] BW VIII, n° 3382, p. 787, n° 3390, p. 801.

[51] BW VIII, n° 3390, p. 802: "Quam vero iniquum est id a nobis exigere, ut credamus nihil Socino veri in mentem venire potuisse?"

[52] BW VIII, n° 3390, p. 803: "In Veritate vero religionis christianae contra iudaeos disputans verba Esaiae capite LIII ita verti ut sententiam Socini sententiae contrariam aperte exprimant." Cf. VRC, V 19, pp. 214–16.

[53] BW VIII, n° 3397, p. 814: "Dat ick de Deo niet en heb bewesen dan generalia is waer, omdat ick houde, dat men ex naturalibus rationibus niet verder en can gaen. Ende staet mij voor, dat doctor Junius in 't boeck van Plessis quaed vond, dat hij meende trinitatem te bewijsen met naturlijcke redenen, quod ille putabat esse causam prodere, cum ea res probari nequeat, nisi ex revelatione."

[54] BW VIII, n° 3397, p. 814: "Rivet wert hier gehouden pro homine mediocris

In autumn 1638 Grotius was again confronted with the criticism
of Schoockius. His brother Willem told him that Schoockius had
published a short book in Dutch, which announced a forthcoming
study that would accuse Grotius of Socinianism, because in his apologetic work he had passed over many things that others had discussed.[55] The book of Schoockius to which Willem referred was his
Claere en oprechte ontdeckinge [Clear and honest discovery].[56] In it the
author repeats the claim that Niëllius had rejected, that Grotius'
apologetic work had cunningly helped to propagate Socinianism, and
goes on to promise a Latin treatise in which he will investigate
Grotius' theology in detail.[57]

By way of a foretaste, Schoockius gives his readers some hints on
the proper approach to Grotius' apologetic work. His chief point is
that one will seek in vain in the *De veritate* for the doctrines of the
trinity, the divinity of Christ and satisfaction. These doctrines, which
undoubtedly form the core of Christian belief and have been demonstrated by Christian apologetes of all tendencies, are denied by the
Socinians and neglected by Grotius.[58] Grotius' Socinianism is even
more evident in his characterisation of the promises of Moses as

---

admodum judicii et eruditionis." Cf. *BW* X, n° 4181 (to W. de Groot, 25 June
1639), p. 423: "Rivetum autem tam exigui puto judicii, ut in quo cardine versentur illae quaestiones, non intelligat."

[55] *BW* IX, n° 3764 (from W. de Groot, 13 September 1638), p. 571: "Martinus
Schoockius e discipulis Voetii libellum Belgice edidit, in quo scriptum Latinum
promittit, quo tu socinianismi arguaris et quidem ex tractatu de Veritate religionis
christianae, in quo multa ab aliis tractata a te omitti queritur."

[56] M. Schoockius, *Claere en oprechte ontdeckinge der genaemder remonstranten leugenen en
lasteringen, tegen de hooge en laage overigheden, gereformeerde kercken, en haere yeverighe voorstanders. Als oock een bondich vertooch van harere sociniaensche grouwelen, alles vergadert uyt drie
naemloose boecxkens geintituleert: I. Proeve van de conscientieuse oprechtigheydt Gisberti Voetii. II.
Academia Gisberti Voetii. II. Den rechten remonstrantsche theologant*, Utrecht 1638 [= Schoockius,
Ontdeckinge]. On Grotius see pp. 111–14.

[57] Schoockius, *Ontdeckinge*, pp. 111–12: "Ick hadde in mijn tractaetgen in passant
gheseyt dat de heere Grotius niet 't eenemael vry waer van de afgrijselicke socini-
anisterije, maer die selve bedecktelick trachte te propageren en verspreyden in zijn
boecxken van de waerheydt der christelicke religie; [...] Maer heb ick hem ongelijck ghedaen dat ick gheseyt hebbe dat zijn boecxken de veritate religionis christianae, 't welck nu in verscheyden taelen wort gelesen nae socinianistery ruyckt?
Geensins. Godt lof, so ver is het van daer, dat ick geseyt hebbe segge ick alsnoch,
en sal eerstganghs in 't openbaer bewijsen in een Latijns tractaet waer in ick wijt-
loopigh Grotii theologie, voorgestelt in zijn boecxken van de waerheyt der christelijcke religie, en van 't recht van den oorlogh en vrede, examineere. Ick bidde
dat de socen [sc. remonstrants] so lang patientie willen hebben tot dat mijn boeck
ghedruckt is." The work that Schoockius announced, however, was never published.

[58] Schoockius, *Ontdeckinge*, pp. 112–13.

earthly and temporal, and of the commandments of Christ as the fulfilment of the moral law of Moses.[59] Schoockius dismisses Grotius' defence of the idea of Christ as the son of God against the Muslims in the sixth book, as unchristian.[60] Finally he remarks, not without some venom, that if Grotius had once written a work against Socinus, this does not excuse his present heresy. Grotius had gone the way of all the remonstrants: the heresies that they had long dissimulated had gradually come to the surface through despair. As long as they had hoped to keep their hold on the town halls and the Church, they kept up a semblance of Christianity, but now that this hope had vanished they let their true religious beliefs appear plainly, according to Schoockius.[61]

Grotius' reply to his brother's warning was calm and self-assured. He said that he was not worried about criticism from Schoockius and his like, for his apologetic work would continue to live and flourish. He had deliberately refrained from discussion of the trinity and other controversial matters. He believed that those who sought to prove these things from natural reason or by Platonic arguments had done more to harm Christianity than to help it.[62]

A few months later Vossius again drew Grotius' attention to Schoockius' book. He was careful to list the points on which Schoockius thought he had grounds to stigmatise Grotius' apologetic work as Socinian: he had only given minimal attention to the trinity, dismissed Moses' promises to his people as only temporarily valid, presented Christ's commandments as new, and called Christ God's son because of the virgin birth.[63]

---

[59] Schoockius, *Ontdeckinge*, p. 113. Cf. *VRC*, II 10, p. 86; and V 6, pp. 182–4.

[60] Schoockius, *Ontdeckinge*, pp. 113–14. Cf. *VRC*, VI 9, pp. 237–8. Schoockius' sponsor was also disturbed by this passage in the Grotius's work: see G. Voetius, *Selectarum disputationum fasciculus*. Recognovit et praefatus est Abr. Kuyper, Amsterdam 1887, Disputatio quarta: de necessitate et utilitate dogmatis de SS. Trinitate, p. 76.

[61] Schoockius, *Ontdeckinge*, p. 114.

[62] *BW* IX, n° 3775 (to W. de Groot, 25 September 1638), p. 589: "Schokium hominesque similes non multum curo. Liber ille de veritate religionis illis ringentibus vivet et florebit. De trinitate et alias controversias directe ibi tractare non debui et qui eas ex naturali ratione aut Platonicis scitis tractarunt antehac plus laeserunt quam adiuverunt causam christianismi."

[63] *BW* IX, n° 3887 (from G.J. Vossius, 15 December 1638), p. 751: "Hic [sc. Schoockius] Ultrajecto iam in Daventriensem scholam concessit ac opere postremo, quod vernacula scripsit lingua minatur librum iustum, quo comprobet te quoque in castris militare Socini. Nam illa de satisfactione Christi tantum temporum illorum gratia, quo facilius falleres, scripsisse; ubi illa via non processit, te larva deposita ostendisse, quis fores, in libris de Veritate religionis christianae. Ubi minime sacrae

In his embittered reply Grotius remarked that Schoockius must indeed be a bad man, who would still not grant him, the much vexed Grotius, any rest.[64] He answered the criticisms as follows: he justified his refusal to go into the dogma of the trinity with a combination of the arguments he had already employed in his previous letters. His teacher Junius had taught him that the trinity could not be proven from unreliable natural reasoning or Platonic arguments, as Mornay and others had wrongly believed. This dogma, which must remain incomprehensible without divine revelation, had to be omitted when engaging in discussion with atheists, pagans, Jews and Muslims, who all had to be led towards the holy Scriptures.[65] Grotius was brief about the promises of Moses and Christ's commandments: he considered that it was simply obvious that his opinions were wholly in agreement with the teaching of the early Church and the Scriptures. Finally, and rather surprisingly, he defended his notion of God's son by an appeal to Thomas Aquinas.[66]

Grotius makes an astonishing remark in the postscript to this letter: whoever wishes to know his opinion of the trinity will find it adequately expressed in his recently published poems.[67] This was undoubtedly intended to show that he did not reject the dogma of the trinity, and therefore could not be called a Socinian. At that time Socinianism was virtually equated with anti-trinitarianism.[68]

In March 1638 Grotius heard from his son Pieter that Rivet had repeated the charges of Socinianism against him during a conversation with the English theologian Samuel Johnson, who took up Grotius' cause.[69] Johnson, court preacher to the Bohemian royal

triados mysterium tradas, dicas Mosem populo tantum temporalia promittere, Christi praecepta nova esse ac perfectiora Mosaicis; Christum dici filium Dei, quia natus sit a virgine, conceptus e spiritu sancto."

[64] *BW* X, n° 3917 (to G.J. Vossius, 1 January 1639), p. 12: "Schoockius homo sit malus oportet, qui me tamdiu a popularibus meis vexatum nihil ipsis debentem nondum quiescere patiatur."

[65] *BW* X, n° 3917, p. 12: "Triados probationem in eo libro directe aggressus non sum memor ejus, quod a viro magno socero tuo [sc. F. Junius sr.] audieram, peccasse Plessaeum et alios, quod rationibus a natura petitis et Platonicis saepe non valde appositis testimoniis astruere voluissent rem, non ponendam in illa cum atheis, paganis, judaeis, mahumetistis disputatione, qui omnes ad Sacras Literas ducendi sunt, ut inde talia hauriant, quae nisi Deo semet patefaciente cognosci nequeunt."

[66] *BW* X, n° 3917, pp. 12–13.

[67] *BW* X, n° 3917, p. 14: "Illud addam, siquis meam de summa trinitate sententiam scire cupiat, reperturum quod satis sit in poematis nuper editis."

[68] See Kühler, *Het socinianisme*, pp. 86–90.

[69] *BW* X, n° 4039 (from P. de Groot, [28] March 1638), p. 207: "Est ille [sc.

house, was well known for his Arminian sympathies, and later in that year got into difficulties in The Hague, where he was staying at the time, because he was suspected of Socinianism. Rivet was even supposed to have asked the king of Bohemia to remove Johnson as a Socinian.[70]

Grotius in his turn defended Johnson, with whom he had become friends in Hamburg. He wrote to Van Reigersberch that he shared Johnson's critical opinion of Calvin's view of Christ's divinity. But he added that he was careful not to go too deeply into a matter that was so far above his understanding. He had become increasingly convinced that those who did not pay enough attention to the consensus of the early Church every day nourished new opinions such as that of Socinus.[71] Everyone who knew him knew how he had always remained inside the limits of the ancient Church, and not only on such dogmas as the trinity and the nature of Christ's satisfaction, which Socinus and his followers attacked.[72] By these pronouncements he distanced himself from Socinianism, taking his refuge in the early Church as the beacon of religious truth.

On 23 May 1639 Willem de Groot again reported to his brother that the Johnson affair had revived the suspicions of Socinianism against Grotius, because the English preacher had appealed to Grotius in a conversation with Rivet.[73] Grotius assured him that he was not too worried by this accusation, which was voiced by 'such bad men'. He could not help it if Socinus' opinion, that dogmas ought to serve as guides to action and not for contemplation, agreed with the old and true opinions of the early Church. For his part he wished to hold fast to the early Church in any case. He knew very well that

---

Johnson] pacis ecclesiasticae, ut video, amantissimus habuitque, ut narravit mihi, verba cum D. Riveto super tuo libro de Veritate religionis christianae, praesertim quod socinianismi te accusaret; cui ille paucis respondit se crediturum ei posthac, si aliquid magis christianum posset reperire, quod non in illo libro contineretur."

[70] *BW* X, nᵒ 4094 (from N. van Reigersberch, 2 May 1639), p. 303.

[71] *BW* X, nᵒ 4113 (to N. van Reigersberch, 14 May 1639), p. 328.

[72] *BW* X, nᵒ 4156 (to Th. Graswinckel, 11 June 1639), p. 392: "Quantopere ego intra pactos ab antiquitate fines me semper tenuerim, non in sententiis modo de summa trinitate, de utraque Christi natura, de satisfactione Christi et aliis, quae Socinus et sociniani oppugnant, norunt omnes, qui me norunt."

[73] *BW* X, nᵒ 4124, p. 345: "Nunc hoc addam ab amicis mihi relatum iterum recrudescere in te socinismi suspicionem, cui jam novum incrementum dedit Jonsonius, qui Riveto ea de re suspectus dixit se tecum saepe iis de quaestionibus disseruisse, atque ex te ea intellexisse argumenta, quae adversus Rivetum urgebat; [. . .]." Cf. *BW* X, nᵒ 4125 (from N. van Reigersberch, 23 May 1639), p. 347.

he would never be able to satisfy Rivet and other ill-wishers, nor did he think them worth the effort.[74]

Early in 1640 the annotated version of Grotius' apologetic work appeared. The author sent copies to his friends, who were almost unanimous in their praise. The edition had royal approval and its reception was generally so favourable that Grotius could not forbear to remark triumphantly that Voetius must be ashamed to brand his work as Muhammadan or Socinian.[75] He only received sporadic further criticism of his work. Grotius sent his friend, the French lawyer Claude Sarrau, a copy almost as soon as the book appeared.[76] Sarrau at first reacted with delight when he received this 'golden book'.[77]

Later in the same year, however, Sarrau began to raise objections. He wrote to Grotius on 18 December 1640 that the author's reply had entirely removed the difficulties he felt about the absence of any treatment of Christ's divinity and satisfaction.[78] Evidently Sarrau and Grotius had previously exchanged thoughts on these topics. But there was one problem left, which Sarrau brought to his friend's attention. In his apologetic work Grotius had stated that

---

[74] *BW* X. n° 4143 (to W. de Groot, 4 June 1639), pp. 373–4: "Calumnias, quae in me a pessimis hominibus de socinianismi sparguntur, non multum curo. Facile refutabuntur apud aequos judices scriptis meis, quae edidi quaeque sum editurus. In dogmatibus ad actus magis quam ad contemplationes pertinentibus evenit Socino, ut in veras veteresque sententias incideret. Eas non deseram et puto de iis me contulisse cum D. Iohnsono Hamburgi. [. . .] Riveto et aliis destinato malignis saepe et eas ipsas quaestiones, de quibus agunt non intelligentibus, satisfacere me non posse scio nec eos tanti habeo, ut aut in id laborem aut ab aliis laborari velim." Cf. *BW* X, n° 4181 (to W. de Groot, 25 June 1639), pp. 422–3: "Ego, mi frater, inimicos quidem meos non cessare insidiari mihi rebusque meis certus sum. Caeterum conscientia fretus optimarum sententiarum illis de socinianismo calumniis nihil plane moveor scioque multo probabilius Calvinum arianismi accusatum quam me socinianismi; Rivetum autem tam exigui puto judiciii, ut in quo cardine versentur illae quaestiones, non intelligat."

[75] *BW* XI, n° 4561 (to W. de Groot, 27 March 1640), p. 144: "Virorum doctissimorum hic et senatorum et aliorum favens de libro nostro pro veritate religionis christianae judicium et adsecuta regia auctoritas efficient, puto, ut Voetium pudeat eum librum habere pro mahumetistico aut sociniano."

[76] *BW* XI, n° 4547 (to C. Sarrau, 5 March 1640), p. 124. Earlier, in 1628, Grotius had presented Sarrau with a copy of his *Sensus*; see *BW* III, n° 1238, pp. 263–4. On Claude Sarrau (1603–51) see J. Andrieu, *Bibliographie générale de l'Agenais*, Paris/Agen 1886, III, pp. 277–8; and Peter J. Rott, *Les Lettres Jean Calvin de la collection Sarrau*, Paris 1972, pp. 10–19.

[77] *BW* XI, n° 4559 (from C. Sarrau, 15 March 1640), p. 141.

[78] *BW* XI, n° 4840 (from C. Sarrau, 18 September 1640), p. 520: "Plenissime nuper coram satisfaciebas dubiis, quae tibi proponere ausus eram circa divinitatem et satisfactionem D.N. Iesu Christi, de quibus extare nihil in aureo tuo libello de

Christ's apostles and Paul expected the world to end very soon.[79] Sarrau wondered if this did not strip the Scriptures of all their authority; for if the apostles had really believed this they would have been the victims of a delusion, and would immediately lose all their authority.[80]

Grotius answered Sarrau courteously and concisely, being content to refer his friend to the passages in his work where he could find an answer to the questions he raised. He acknowledged that the question of the reliability of the apostles had surprised him, but he was apparently unwilling to give a serious answer to it.[81] Everything suggests that Grotius, on the whole, was no longer interested in discussing his work. A year later Sarrau again asked for information about Grotius' apologetic work,[82] but this time the author replied even more briefly.[83]

Criticism of *De veritate* had fallen silent for some time. Grotius' adversaries had long lost sight of his apologetic work and had turned their fire on the eirenic programme that the author had presented in 1640.[84] Grotius had dared to attack two central tenets of the

---

Veritate religionis christianae nonnulli male feriati falso criminabantur, eoque nomine quodque mihi tela suppeditaveris, quibus eos confecero, ingentes habeo agoque gratias."

[79] Cf. *VRC*, II 6, p. 82.

[80] *BW* XI, n° 4840, p. 520: "Aliud superest, de quo quia tunc non succurrit—iterum veniam dabit summa tua humanitas—te interpello. Pagina 14 novissimae editionis dicis: Deum consilium suum celasse apostolos de mundi exitio; quinimo illos eum quasi imminentem expectasse et in scriptis suis docuisse, citatis in hanc rem pag. 369 in notis I Cor. XV: 54, et I Thessal. IV: 15–16, quibus ex locis probare intendis credidisse Paulum diem Domini esse in proximo. Haec autem opinio attentius ad calculos revocata omnem scripturae sacrae authoritatem elevare videtur. Si enim istud crediderint apostoli et docuerint, certe in eo falsi sunt. Si autem in hoc perperam nos docuerunt, in quo procul dubio, quemadmodum in reliquis, eos a Deo afflatos credere par est, qui constabit in aliis religionis capitibus, quae non fortius ab illis affirmantur, eos non esse hallucinatos?"

[81] *BW* XI, n° 4842 (to C. Sarrau, 20 September 1640), p. 522.

[82] *BW* XII, n° 5516 (from C. Sarrau, 22 December 1641), p. 686: "Accepi litteras ab amico, viro docto tuique studiosissimo, Maximiliano Langlaeao, Rothomagensi ecclesiaste, quibus me rogat, ut a te quaeram, quis sit ille magister Hebraeus Nehumias, qui quinquaginta annis ante Christi adventum aperte iactabat non posse ultra quinquagesimum annum Messiae adventum differri; cuius mentionem facis pagina 170 de relig. christ." Cf *VRC*, V 14, p. 203.

[83] *BW* XII, n° 5518 (to C. Sarrau, 23 December 1641), p. 688: "Nehumiae illius magistri Hebraei, vir amplissime, mentio fit in Thalmudicis; ni fallor est in titulo de Synedrio, ostendit istum mihi locum olim Hagae Stoctoxus. Puto eius fieri mentionem et in Abenada [= Abenesdra?] ad Danielem."

[84] On this see Posthumus Meyjes (1983) pp. 61–2; and Nellen, *Hugo de Groot*, pp. 107–9.

Reformation: 1) the identification of the Pope with Antichrist; and
2) justification by faith alone.[85] This not only aroused the wrath of
his Calvinist enemies but also alienated his most important friends
and kindred spirits.[86] But Grotius cared very little for criticism, and
persisted in his ambitious eirenical programme, which aimed at nothing short of the reunion of Protestants and Roman Catholics. In his
view the Reformation had missed its mark and degenerated into a
great schism. His ideal was the early Church of the first centuries,
which he admired for what he assumed to be its inviolate unity.[87]

His efforts to bring about peace immediately brought down on
him the suspicion of papism from his contra-remonstrant opponents.
Grotius was deluged with pamphlets and books, but his distaste for
Calvinism had by now grown so much that it did not deter him,
but rather encouraged him to continue on the path he had taken.
He made light of the various accusations against him, declaring that
those who called him a Socinian because he followed the early
Church en bloc whereas Socinus had only agreed with parts of it,
could themselves be more properly called Socinians, since, like Socinus,
they regarded the Pope as Antichrist.[88]

Although popery was the chief charge brought against Grotius in
the last years of his life, his opponents did not cease to confront him
with the old charge of Socinianism. One heresy by no means excluded
the other. Samuel Maresius, who in 1640 had savagely attacked
Grotius' work on the Antichrist,[89] remarked in his inaugural lecture
as professor at Groningen (1643) that Grotius had borrowed a great
deal from Socinus in his apologetic work.[90] We have already remarked

---

[85] *BG* n[os] 1100, 1109, 1117.
[86] See *BG* n° 1100, rem. 5.
[87] See Haentjens, *Simon Episcopius*, pp. 123–47.
[88] *BW* XI, n° 4693 (to W. de Groot, 15 June 1640), p. 332: "Qui me socinianum vocant, quod totius antiquitatis sententiam defenderim, in cuius partem aliquam Socinus incidit, eos ego justius socinianos vocabo, quod papam esse credant
Antichristum. Nam id siquis alius, Socinus et sociniani pro certissimo haberi volunt."
[89] *BsG* n° 299. On the polemic between Maresius and Grotius see D. Nauta,
Samuel Maresius, Amsterdam 1935, pp. 168–72.
[90] S. Maresius, *Oratio inauguralis de usu et abusu rationis in rebus theologicis et fidei*,
Groningen 1643, C2: "Eo spectant Summa Thomae contra gentes, Raymundi à
Sabunde, et Georgii Pacardi Theologia Naturalis, Hieronymi Savanarolae Triumphus
crucis; Veritas Christiana Ludovici Vivis, Philippi Mornaei, Hugonis Grotii hanc
ita in compendium redigentis ut multa insperserit ex Socino."

that Rivet in 1644 assumed that Grotius was indebted to Socinus' *De auctoritate Sacrae Scripturae* in his apologetic work.[91]

Summarising, we can say that the criticism of Grotius' apologetic work during the author's lifetime remained remarkably limited. His other theological writings provoked considerably more resistance and polemics, while *De veritate* enjoyed wide praise. The criticism that eventually raised its head above the parapet concentrated on the charge of Socinianism. That accusation was made by Calvinist contra-remonstrants who now stigmatised all remonstrants as Socinians. Grotius at first had no reason to be disturbed, for the charge was a cliché. But he lost his imperturbability when Schoockius and Rivet took up arms against him. Their most important accusation was that Grotius had totally neglected such central doctrines of Christianity as the trinity, the divinity of Christ and his satisfaction.

The most elaborate assault came from Schoockius, who in a short book against the remonstrants devoted a separate chapter to Grotius' Socinianism. Schoockius named a few concrete points of resemblance between Socinus and Grotius, and announced another book in which he would investigate Grotius' theology in particular. This promise was not fulfilled. Rivet voiced his rather general accusations in conversation, but did not put his criticisms on paper. Later Grotius' eirenic works would give Rivet the occasion to take up his pen against him.[92]

Grotius did not reply to his accusers directly. He felt a deep contempt for such theologians as Voetius, Schoockius and Rivet, and was averse to public polemics in pamphlets. He did, however, feel obliged to justify himself to his friends, and to offer a defence against the allegations. To do so he used four regular arguments:

1) He contrasted the great success of his apologetic work with the marginal criticism.
2) He appealed to his apologetic method, which necessarily entailed a non-dogmatic treatment.
3) He did not deny possible agreements with Socinus, but said that they were wholly fortuitous. Heretics might say some things that were true.
4) He referred to the 'early Church' as the norm for religious truth.

---

[91] H. Bots, P. Leroy, *Correspondance intégrale d'André Rivet et de Claude Sarrau*, II, Amsterdam 1980, n° 273 (Rivet to Sarrau, 5 September 1644), p. 370.
[92] *BsG* n° 305.

Schoockius and Rivet, however, had a good deal of right on their side. We saw that much of the argument of Grotius' apologetic work was derived from Socinus' *De auctoritate*. But Grotius was not a Socinian in the then usual sense of the word, that is an anti-trinitarian. He did not reject the dogmas of the trinity and the divinity of Christ, as Socinus had; he merely did not consider it appropriate to deal with them in his apology. He declared that such dogmas were beyond human understanding—a moderate sceptical humanist viewpoint, as we have seen, but one that the Calvinists could not comprehend.[93] Socinus and Grotius also took different views of natural theology. Grotius condemned Socinus' denial of natural theology, a view he called Epicurean and one which, in his opinion, had to be attacked with every weapon.[94]

Grotius occupied a very individual position in the theological battleground of his time, somewhere between remonstrantism and Socinianism. He reveals his sense of a close relationship with the latter in his friendly letters to Crellius and Ruarus. Grotius did not consider himself a full-blooded Socinian, but he did feel that he had every right to borrow from Socinus when it suited him. He wondered why he should not be free to do what Augustine and Jerome had done, namely to make use of heretical works. He had no message for partisans, for he felt that the truth was far above them. He believed in his right to seek advice from everyone. No one had seen the whole truth, just as no one must be regarded as entirely deprived of it.[95] It took a certain courage for Grotius to refuse to be denied this freedom of choice.

b) *Translations*

German translations

When Grotius sent the Latin edition of his apologetic work to his friend Georg Lingelsheim in March 1628, he assured him that he

---

[93] See chap. 4, pp. 000–000.
[94] *BW* IX, n° 3603 (to G.J. Vossius, 28 May 1638), p. 334: "Socinum sectae eiusdem principes, nuper Vogelius, nunc Ruarus non probant in eo, quod circa Dei cognitionem petita e natura rerum argumenta abdicaverit. Contra talem feram, qualis est Epicuri insania, omnibus armis dimicandum est."
[95] Cf. *IBP*, Prol. 42, p. 15: "Ego et hic alibi veterum christianorum sequor liber-

would have no objection if his work were reprinted or translated in Germany.[96] A few months later Lingelsheim had apparently found a willing translator in his household tutor, the poet Balthasar Venator. Grotius was delighted by the news and thanked his friend for his mediation.[97] In June the same year he wrote to Wtenbogaert: "At Strasbourg my book *De veritate religionis christianae* is being printed in High German, translated by Venator, formerly the secretary of the Count Palatine".[98] On 27 April 1629, however, Lingelsheim had to inform Grotius that Venator had still not been able to put the finishing touches to his translation.[99] After this date no more is heard of this translation, so that we may assume that Venator ultimately abandoned his project.[100]

The first German translation of Grotius' work to appear was by the great German poet Martin Opitz. Opitz was an enthusiastic and expert translator; his oeuvre includes more translations than poems of his own composition.[101] In 1620 he spent some time in Leiden, where he probably learned Dutch. A few years later he translated two great Dutch poems of Daniel Heinsius into German as *Lobgesang Jesu Christi* (1621) and *Lobgesang Bacchi* (1622).[102] Opitz probably became

---

tatem, qui in nullius philosophorum sectam iuraverant, non quod eis assentirentur qui nihil percipi posse dicebant, quo nihil est stultius; sed quod nullam esse sectam putarent quae omne verum vidisset, et nullam quae non aliud ex vero."

[96] *BW* III, n° 1237 (to G.M. Lingelsheim, 10 March 1628), p. 262: "Si qui apud vos avent recudere aut etiam vertere, non impedio, dum aliquid tuae sollicitudinis accedat, quam scio pro me ac meis semper esse maximam."

[97] *BW* III, n° 1257 (to G.M. Lingelsheim, 13 May 1628), p. 300: "Sed te iam spero omnium bonorum votis, quae nunquam tibi desunt, utinam et meis, restitutum meliori valetudini, cuius spem bonam Venator tuus mihi fecit, cui ego plurimum debeo, primum quod tui, id est hominis mei amantissimi, vices obire, deinde quod libellum meum, utinam tam utilem quam honesto proposito scriptum, etiam ab illis popularibus tuis, qui latine nesciunt, intelligi voluit. Gratulor mihi tam faventis iudicii benignitate." Cf. *BW* III, n° 1258 (to N. van Reigersberch, 13 May 1628), p. 304; "Mijn bouck de Veritate religionis christianae wordt in het hoog-duytsch overgeset tot Straesburgh."

[98] *BW* III, n° 1277 (to J. Wtenbogaert, 23 June 1628), p. 331.

[99] *BW* IV, n° 1387 (from G.M. Lingelsheim, 17 April 1629), p. 40: "Venator noster lentus est nactus discipulos Rehlingeros Augustanos, quos iam induxit Sedanum; non potuit extremum manum aureolo libello tuo de Veritate religionis in Germanicam linguam converso [. . .]."

[100] On Balthasar Venator (1594–1664) see E. Volkmann, *Balthasar Venator*, Berlin 1938.

[101] Cf. A. Gülich, *Opitz' Übersetzungen aus dem Französischen*, Kiel 1972, chap. 1: 'Die Funktion der Übersetzungen in Opitz' Werk', pp. 1–5.

[102] For these see U. Bornemann, *Anlehnung und Abgrenzung. Untersuchungen zur Rezeption der niederländischen Literatur in der deutschen Dichtungsreform des siebzehnten Jahrhunderts*, Assen/Amsterdam 1976, pp. 18–29, 62–85.

acquainted with Grotius' work in the years 1619 and 1620. At that time, like his later fellow-poet Venator, he was tutor in the household of Lingelsheim, and therefore in close touch with him.[103] In 1628 he published a German translation of Grotius' Latin paraphrase of the tale of Jonah, but without naming Grotius in the title.[104] In 1630 the German poet spent four months in Paris, where he was introduced to Grotius on Lingelsheim's recommendation. Grotius gave him a friendly and courteous reception.[105] The two authors became firm friends and mutual admirers over the following months.[106]

In October Opitz was recalled to Silesia by his employer, the president of the Silesian Estates, burgrave Karl Hannibal von Dohna [= Dohna].[107] A few months later the poet began the translation of Grotius' *Bewijs*, probably on Dohna's instructions.[108] Opitz asked his friend and pupil Christoph Köler to undertake the correction of the proofs.[109] When Grotius heard of this plan, he wrote to Opitz that his work did not deserve such a translator, and impressed on him that he must feel free to express things better than the author him-

---

[103] M. Szyrocki, *Martin Opitz*, 2nd ed. Munich 1974, pp. 35–6.

[104] Martin Opitz, *Jonas*, [Breslau 1628]; see *BG* n° 201. Grotius' Latin text, on which this translation is based, is in his *PC*, pp. 1–12.

[105] A. Reifferscheid, *Briefe G.M. Lingelsheims, M. Berneggers und ihrer Freunde*, [Quellen zur Geschichte des geistigen Lebens in Deutschland während des siebzehnten Jahrhunderts, I], Heilbronn 1889 (M. Opitz to G.M. Lingelsheim, 31 May 1630), p. 398: "Summus vir Grotius noster, cum aliis quibuscumque potest officiorum modis amorem erga me suum, tua commendatione partum, ostendit, tum heri ipse salutatum me accessit."

[106] *BW* IV, n° 1533 (to G.M. Lingelsheim, 22 August 1630), p. 250: "Opitii, quem mihi commendaris, Lingelshemi optime, et ingenium et eruditio et mores, quantopere mihi se probent, haud facile dixero, sed tu ex te de me judicium facito, nec falleris."

[107] *BW* IV, n° 1546 (to C. Saumaise, 5 October 1630), p. 273: "Opitius et literas tuas accepit et gratias tibi jussit agi maximas, subito revocatus in Silesiam a Barone Donaviensi, qui ibi in summa re ac potentia floret, Caesarianus adeo ut et religionem domini induerit." Opitz was in Dohna's service from 1626 to 1632 as secretary and head of the privy chancellery. On Opitz and Dohna see H. Palm, *Beiträge zur Geschichte der Deutschen Literatur des XVI. und XVII. Jahrhunderts*, Breslau 1876 [Fotomechanischer Neudruck der Originalausgabe, Leipzig 1977], pp. 189–214.

[108] Reifferscheid, *Briefe*, M. Opitz to G.M. Lingelsheim, 8 November 1630), p. 421: "Initia studiorum erunt de vera religione christiana libri communis magnique amici."

[109] *Ibid.* (M. Opitz to C. Köler, 2 February 1631), p. 434: "Primum Grotii de Veritate religionis christianae librum ad Gründerum nunc transmisi, idem statim facturus et cum reliquis. [. . .] A te impense rogo, ut et bono publico et operis dignitati et amicitiae nostrae tantum concedas, ut accurata perlectione tua opus hoc procederat quam correctissime."

self.[110] Opitz completed his translation on 12 April the same year,[111] and it was published a few weeks later.[112]

The translation is equipped with a long introduction and a short afterword by Opitz.[113] The introduction takes the form of a letter to the magistrates of the city of Breslau, where the work was published. In it Opitz places Grotius on the same level as the great classical apologetes Justin Martyr, Clement of Alexandria and Tertullian.[114] In his afterword he justifies his translation, and claims that he has kept as close to Grotius' Dutch text as possible.[115] Grotius wrote a lengthy letter of thanks to his friend, praising the elegance and beauty of his translation, and even admitted that the work had pleased him more in its German guise than in the original. He also thanked Opitz for making his name known in Germany.[116] Grotius' words of

---

[110] *BW* IV, n° 1597 (to M. Opitz, 1 March 1631), pp. 350–1: "Librorum nostrorum pro Veritate religionis christianae quod a scriptore est non meretur tantum interpretem: de ipso argumento idem dicere sine impietate non possim. Sed tamen hic quoque memineris, suadeo, liberum te esse, nec ita alligatum praeeuntibus verbis, ut non liceat tibi res easdem melius dicere."

[111] Reifferscheid, *Briefe* (M. Opitz to C. Köler, 14 April 1631), p. 449.

[112] *Ibid.* (M. Opitz to G.M. Lingelsheim, 5 May 1631), p. 453: "Nova ex iis leges quas ad magnum, quem iam dixi, amicum hodie dedi, quibus et exemplar adiunxi libellorum Grotianorum, quos male typographi oscitantia excepit."

[113] H. Grotius, *Von der Warheit der Christlichen Religion. Auss Holländischer Sprache Hochdeutsch gegeben durch Martin Opitzen*, [Breslau] 1631 [= *BG* n° 152].

[114] *Ibid.*, "Denen Edlen Bestrengen Ehrenvesten und Wohlbeambten Herren, Herren Hauptmannen und Rhatmannen der Stadt Bresslaw", p. xxj: "Dieses schöne Werk, wie er der Scribent die Meinung daraus selber in Latein gefasst, so das es nun von vielen Nationen und allerhand Religions verwandten, hohen und fürnehmen Leuten lieb und werth gehalten wird, also habe ich es unserer Sprache, weil auch gedachter mein groser Freund gern hierein gewilligt, länger nicht fürhalten wollen."

[115] *Ibid.*, 'An den Leser', p. 158: "Er [sc. Opitz] bekennet auch, das er in den Reimen bisweilen entweder wegen des Autorn, der sie selbst also gestellt, oder der Niederländischen Sprache halben, die er mit Versetzung der Wörter offtmals zimliche Freiheit nimmt, seine eigene Gesetze, welche er in vorigen Schriften in acht genommen, etwas überschritten hat."

[116] *BW* IV, n° 1664 (to M. Opitz, 24 July 1631), pp. 426–7: "Nunc demum, clarissime Opiti, me vitae in carcere actae non poenitet, cum video illius aerumnae meae fructus te tam fideli interprete quam felici poeta ad populum populorum principem pervenire. Minime mihi blandiri solitus illud tamen opus meum semper minime contemsi ideo, quod cum in materia versetur omnium optima, ad eam tractandam rationes dilegi, quas optimas existimavi. Nunc autem etiam qua parte meum est illud opus, multo plus quam antea placere mihi incipit, ex quo Germanicae gravitatis more cultum procedit. Non tantum tibi Germanos tuos debere arbitror, qui quae a me collecta sunt, alibi saltem sparsa legere poterant, quantum ego debeo, qui tuo munere Germaniae, antiquae parenti nostrae, innotescam. Elegantiam et nitorem ubique miror, nec ex alio libro Germanice loqui aut facilius discam aut lubentius."

praise were probably more than mere rhetorical courtesies. Opitz's
translation is indeed distinguished by its elegance, and its balance
allows the seriousness of the apologetic work to appear more clearly
than the Dutch text, as the author himself admitted.[117] Opitz also
showed a great affinity for Grotius' religious thinking.[118]

We saw that Opitz asked Christoph Köler to correct the proofs
of his translation.[119] On 5 March Köler told Opitz that while proof
reading Grotius' apologetic work he had come to appreciate it so
much that he would be glad to see the prose version translated into
German as well.[120] Opitz did not see his pupil's plan as a trouble-
some competitor of his own translation, but warmly encouraged him
to produce his own version.[121] Köler could also count on the support of burgrave Karl Hannibal von Dohna. On 21 March Köler
reported that he had already begun the translation, which he hoped
to complete within two weeks.[122] But to the great irritation of Opitz
and Dohna it was not a few weeks but half a year before Köler's
translation was ready.[123] In August 1631 Opitz was able to present
it to the burgrave.[124] Dohna had an interest in the early appearance
of Köler's translation, for in this year, on the instructions of the
Austrian emperor, the Catholic burgrave tried to negotiate a peace
with the Protestant Swedes. As a gesture of peace and religious tol-

---

[117] *BW* IV, n° 1664, p. 427.
[118] This has been convincingly shown by R.D. Hacken, *The Religious Thought of
Martin Opitz as the Determinant of his Poetic Theory and Practice* [Stuttgarter Arbeiten zur
Germanistik, n° 18], Stuttgart 1976, pp. 85–105: "Appendix: The Impact of Hugo
Grotius' Works on Martin Opitz' Religious Thought."
[119] Reifferscheid, *Briefe* (M. Opitz to C. Köler, 2 February 1631), p. 434.
[120] *Ibid.* (C. Köler to M. Opitz, 5 March 1631), p. 439: "In tuis corrigendis con-
stantem adhibebo diligentiam, adeo lectio operis prodest et delectat. Vellem sensum quoque VI librorum illorum verti. Nam poema non nisi eruditum et poetica
imbutum lectorem intime admittet. Scribe, quid velis fieri, et vale."
[121] *Ibid.* (M. Opitz to C. Köler, 8 March 1631), p. 439: "Müllerus [sc. the pub-
lisher] libellum ad te misit, bonae sane notae. Eum si Germanice per otium red-
des, magnopere virum hunc tibi devincies, et de gratitudine non dubitandum est."
[122] *Ibid.* (C. Köler to M. Opitz, 21 March 1631), p. 441: "Versionem autem,
quam hodie auspicatus sum, cum bono Deo intra duas hebdomadas absoluturum
me puto. Interea gratias ago tibi maximas, quod me illustrissimo tuo Maecenati,
raro hac aetate ingeniorum aestimatori, optime commendaveris, rogoque te per
communes nostras Musas, a quibus merito tuo in sublimi loco positus, illi diligen-
tiae meae ac prompti obsequii fidem facias."
[123] For the correspondence between the two translators Opitz and Köler, see
Reifferscheid, *Briefe*, pp. 439–72.
[124] *Ibid.* (M. Opitz to C. Köler, 28 August 1631), p. 473: "Libellos Grotianos
hero meo tradidi, et spero laborem tuum non prorsus irritum fore."

erance he wished to present the Swedes with two German translations of the apologetic work of the famous eirenist Hugo Grotius.[125]

Köler's translation was published in a particularly plain and cheap
edition, without a foreword or dedication.[126] Whatever the title might
suggest, the translation was not based on the first but on the second Latin edition of Grotius' apologetic work. Köler's translation is
a careful rendering of Grotius' text, but it has none of the elegance
of Opitz's work. It is not known if Grotius ever saw this version; in
any case he never reacted to it, though from 1637 he was aware of
its existence.[127]

French translations

Shortly after the appearance of the first Latin edition of his apologetic work Grotius and his friends were already investigating the possibilities of a French translation.[128] On 13 May 1628 Grotius told
his brother in law Nicolaas van Reigersberch that many, both Roman
Catholics and Protestants, had offered to translate it into French,
but that he did not wish to get involved.[129] A month later, however,
he could report that Etienne de Courcelles was translating the work
into French, because Daniel Tilenus was not interested and François
D'Or had no time.[130] One can infer from this Grotius was indeed

---

[125] For this dedication see Szyrocki, *Martin Opitz*, pp. 89–93.

[126] The title page reads: *Die Meinung der Bücher Hugonis Grotii Von der Warheit der
Christlichen Religion. Von ihm selbst auss dem Hollandischen inn Latein, und auss diesem inn
das Deutsche gezogen durch Christoph Colerum. In Vorlegung David Müllers 1631* [= *BG* n°
1008]. There is a copy of this edition in the library of the University of Amsterdam
(495 G 5).

[127] *BW* VIII, n° 3310 (to W. de Groot, 22 October 1637), p. 666: "Nec Latine
tantum, Gallice et Germanico carmine et oratione soluta, cum voluntate et fructu
legitur, sed et in Anglicum sermonem traductus a viro illustri multum ei genti probatur." Cf. *BW* X, n° 3917 (to G.J. Vossius, 1 January 1639), p. 12.

[128] *BW* III, n° 1246 (from J. Wtenbogaert, 5 April 1628), p. 277: "Waere uE.
boeck de Veritate religionis christianae van yemandt der bij uE. genoemden overgeset, het soude veel goeds doen."

[129] *BW* III, n° 1258 (to N. van Reigersberch, 13 May 1628), p. 304: "Mijn bouck
de veritate religionis christianae wordt in het hoogduytsch overgeset tot Straesburgh.
Veele presenteren haer dyenst om 't in 't Fransch te doen oversetten, catholycken
ende van de religie. Ick laet haer doen sonder het mij aen te trecken."

[130] *BW* III, n° 1277 (to J. Wtenbogaert, 23 June 1628), p. 331: "Tot Straesburch
wordt mijn boecxken de veritate religionis christianae in't hoogduytsch gedruckt,
overgeset door Venator, voor desen secretaris van den Paltsgraeff. Cocellus set het
over in het Fransch, also Tilenus geen lust en heeft, d'Or geen tijdt. Het sal mij
overgesonden worden. Mij wordt geseyt dat oock een catholyck besich is met de

involved in the French translation. The three French theologians he named had all been removed from their posts as preachers because of their Arminian sympathies, and had become more or less close friends of Grotius. In his first isolated years in Paris Grotius must have felt closely attached to them; he lived for some time in the same house as Tilenus, met D'Or regularly and also knew De Courcelles.[131] Étienne de Courcelles had been removed from his post after the synod of Alais in 1622, because he refused to agree to the synod's resolution to adopt the decisions of the synod of Dordrecht. Later, however, he signed an anti-Arminian declaration in order to be reinstated in his office, but he remained under suspicion among his French colleagues.[132] Even so, Grotius entrusted him with the French translation of his apologetic work.

On 2 December 1628 De Courcelles had completed a first draft of his translation, which he sent to Grotius for his opinion, giving the author the opportunity to make changes and improvements.[133] The translator stated in all modesty that he had not been able to match the elegant style of the Latin original, but that he had deliberately kept as close as possible to the author's words, to avoid weakening the content in any way. He was convinced that the arguments in the work were in themselves so solid that readers would pardon the unpolished style of the translation.[134] He added that he did not insist on his name appearing on the title page if the translation were published.[135]

---

oversetting, vrese op eenige plaetsen voor depravatie van sin." Nothing is known of a Catholic translation produced at this time.

[131] For Grotius' relationship with Tilenus, D'Or and De Courcelles see Nellen, *Hugo de Groot*, pp. 153, 171.

[132] On Étienne de Courcelles (1586–1659) see Haag, IV, pp. 791–5; J. Tideman, *De Remonstrantsche Broederschap. Biografische naamlijst van hare professoren, predikanten en proponenten* [. . .] Bewerkt door H.C. Rogge en B. Tideman, 2nd ed. Amsterdam 1905, pp. 14–15; *BWPGN*, II, pp. 337–40.

[133] *BW* III, n° 1345 (from E. de Courcelles, 2 December 1628), p. 425: "Ayant seu que vous desires de voir en françois le livre que vous avez compose pour la défense de nostre religion, afin qu'il profitast à tant plus de personnes, j'en ai entrepris la traduction, laquele je vous envoye la submettant du tout à vostre jugement pour y changer et corriger ce que vous verres estre à propos; [. . .]."

[134] *Ibid.*, p. 425: "Je sais bien que je n'ai point esgalé l'élegance de vostre stile latin; mais j'ai tellement peur d'affaiblir vos argumens en m'esloignant de vos paroles, que je les ai suivi de près par tout, autant que la propriété de nostre langue l'a pu permettre. [. . .] Les raisons contenues en vostre livre sont si solides et nerveuses, qu'elles contenteront en telle sorte le jugement des lecteurs, qu'ils ne s'arresteront pas à la rudesse du stile auquel je les répresente."

[135] *Ibid.*, pp. 425–6: "Pourtant si ma traduction ne vous desplait pas entièrement,

But it was to be several years before this translation appeared, since De Courcelles could not find a Paris publisher willing to publish it. In 1634 he left France to settle in Amsterdam, where he was given a friendly welcome by the remonstrant leader Simon Episcopius. De Courcelles made his living in the following years as a translator and corrector of proofs. In 1643 he was to succeed Episcopius as professor at the remonstrants' Seminary.[136]

On 5 November 1636 De Courcelles reported to Grotius that his translation had appeared. He had finally managed to find a publisher, for which he had sought in vain in Paris. He repeated what he had said eight years earlier: he could not equal the elegant Latin style of Grotius, but that need be no problem because the work's content was sufficient recommendation.[137]

De Courcelles' translation was published by Blaeu of Amsterdam without any mention of the translator's name on the title page, as already proposed by the translator in 1628.[138] The edition included a foreword by the translator, who explained to his readers that he had sought to give as faithful a rendering as possible of the author's intention, so that the arguments could appear in their full force.[139] De Courcelles recommends Grotius' work as a summary of what all Christians must believe.[140] Finally he assures them that the transla-

---

il sera bon d'en procurer l'impression, mais sans qu'elle porte mon nom en son front, car ma profession l'empescheroit d'estre si bien receuë."

[136] Haag, IV, pp. 791–5.

[137] *BW* VII, n° 2826, p. 488.

[138] Hugo Grotius, *Traicté de la verité de la religion chrestienne. Traduit du Latin de l'auteur*, Amsterdam 1636 [= *BG* n° 1060]. Ter Meulen and Diermanse doubt the identity of the translator and name Jean de Cordes as a possible translator. For this misunderstanding see *BW*, VII n° 2897 (to W. de Groot, 12 December 1636), p. 567 n. 4.

[139] H. Grotius, *Traicté de la verité de la religion chrestienne*, "Préface du traducteur", A2v: "Si vous trouvéz, que cette version ne respond point à la beauté de l'original latin, vous considereréz s'il vous plait qu'il est impossible de si bien tourner aucun escrit d'une langue en une autre, qu'il ne perde toujours quelque chose de sa grace. Aussi pour dire vrai, je ne me suis pas tant étudié à la parer d'un beau langage qu'à exprimer fidelement l'intention de l'auteur et vous representer ses raisons avec toute leur force, estimant qu'il falloit beaucoup mieux, que vous trouvassiez quelque chose à redire en la polisseure des armes, dont le christianisme est ici defendu, qu'a leur trempe et solidité."

[140] *Ibid.*, A2r–v: "Vous y avez aussi un petit sommaire de la doctrine en laquelle conviennent tous les chrétiens, quoique divisés en plusieurs sectes, mais tel toutefois (si on en veut juger sans passion) qu'il est suffisant pour nous apprendre le chemin du ciel. Car quant aux autres choses dont on dispute aujourd'hui avec tant d'animosité, ou bien ce sont des points subtils et difficiles à entendre, dont la connaissance ne rend personne meilleur, ou cérémonies et accessoires de la religion, a

tion includes the new matter added by the author, so that his read-ers will not miss anything.[141]

The translation appears to be based on the text of the third edi-tion of *De veritate* (1633), as a comparison of the two editions reveals. This means that De Courcelles must have revised the translation he had submitted to Grotius in 1628. Grotius' own contribution to this translation cannot be identified. The fact that De Courcelles addressed the author in almost identical terms after eight years suggests that Grotius probably left the translation entirely to the Frenchman. De Courcelles' careful rendering keeps closely to the Latin text. Although the translator repeatedly spoke modestly of his stylistic gifts, his trans-lation is by no means stilted. We do not know when Grotius saw the translation or what his first reaction was, but we form the impres-sion that he was satisfied with it. When a French nobleman offered himself as translator in 1640, Grotius referred him to the version of De Courcelles. But Grotius could not dissuade the new translator from his plans, and he suggested to his brother that De Courcelles would do well to translate the notes, which were now ready, into French, so that he could remain ahead of his competitor.[142] The plan was not realised.[143]

The French nobleman who wished to make a new translation of Grotius' apologetic work in 1640, against the author's wishes, must have been the historian François Eudes de Mézeray.[144] Despite Grotius' opposition, De Mézeray had completed his translation by 1641, and

---

l'occasion desquelles c'est une chose honteuse de s'entredéchirer les uns les autres, étant d'accord du principal."

[141] *Ibid.*, A2ᵛ.

[142] *BW* XI, n° 4599 (to W. de Groot, 14 April 1640), p. 205: "Est hic nobilis quidam qui vertit librum de Veritate christianae religionis in Gallicum sermonem, quanquam a me monitus ab alio iam versum esse in sermonem eundem. Impedire eum non potui. Sed Corcellius recte facturus est, si statim ut acceperit exemplar, vertat et annotationes; ita ipsius versio altera fiet vendibilior. Hac de re certiorem eum fieri non abs re erit." Grotius several times repeated the request to send De Courcelles a copy of the annotated edition: see *BW* XI, n° 4845, p. 526; and *BW* XII, n° 5324, p. 458.

[143] Later in the year there were difficulties between Grotius and De Courcelles. The latter worked as corrector of the works that Grotius was about to publish, but the author was dissatisfied with the results and even distrusted the Frenchman. Nevertheless Grotius remained grateful to him for translating his apologetic work. See *BW* XI, n° 4847 (to W. de Groot, 22 September 1640), pp. 525–6.

[144] On François Eudes de Mézeray (1610–83) see D. de Larroque, *Vie de Fr. Eudes de Mézeray*, Paris 1720; S. Combet, *Notice sur Mézeray*, Alais 1844.

it was published three years later.[145] This translation was particularly handsomely printed, in a cursive typeface like handwriting, and provided with royal approval. De Mézeray dedicated his translation to Bignon, whom he praised in a lengthy foreword as a model of erudition and piety. De Mézeray's translation, based on Grotius' text of 1633, is rather more elegant than that of De Courcelles, but also much more careless. Grotius was rather indignant at the result, and remarked peevishly in a letter to the Swedish chancellor Axel Oxenstierna that the translator had indeed paid him a visit but had not shown him the translation or the foreword. He emphatically disowned the translation, which in his opinion strayed from the sense of his text on a number of points.[146]

The English translation

In October 1636 Grotius heard from his nephew Johan Van Reigersberch of an English translation of his apologetic work.[147] A few months later he told his brother Willem that it had been produced by a son of Lord Thomas Coventry.[148]

He was undoubtedly referring to the translation published at London in 1632.[149] The translator's name is not given on the title page

[145] H. Grotius, *La vérité de la religion chrestienne*, Paris [1644] [= *BG* n° 1061].

[146] H. Grotius, *Epistolae ad Axelium Oxenstierna*, Tomus posterior 1640–1645, [Rikskansleren Axel Oxenstiernas Skrifter och Brefvexling] Stockholm 1891, n° 538 (Paris 15/25 June 1644), p. 440: "Prodiit hic versio gallica libri a me pridem facti pro Veritate religionis christianae. Qui eam fecit me adiit, sed neque versionem neque praefationem, quam addidit, mihi ostendit unquam. In quibusdam a meo sensus aberrat, quod ideo scribo, ne aliena dicta pro meis accipiantur." It is not clear which points of difference Grotius had in mind.

[147] *BW* VII, n° 2812 (to N. van Reigersberch, 24 October 1636), p. 461: "De jonge neeff Reigersberg heeft in Engelant veel vrundschap ontfangen van veele heeren, dye mij goed gunnen. Mijn boeck, De Satisfactione, werdt daer zeer gepresen, mijne Sacra Poemata zijn te Oxford nagedruckt ende liber de veritate christianae religonis is overgeset in 't Engelsch [...]." Cf. *BW* VII, n° 2813 (to W. de Groot, 25 October 1636), p. 465.

[148] *BW* VII, n° 2907 (29 December 1636), p. 616: "Coventrii, viri illustris apud Anglos, filius vertit Anglica nostra pro religione christiana." Cf. *BW* VIII, n° 2912 (1 January 1637), p. 3: "Librum meum de Veritate religionis christianae transtulit in Anglia viri praenobilis D. Coventrii filius." *BW* VIII, n° 3310 (22 October 1637), p. 666: "Nec. [sc. *VRC*] Latine tantum, Gallice et Germanico carmine et oratione soluta, cum voluntate et fructu legitur, sed et in Anglicum sermonem traductus a viro illustri multum ei genti probatur."

[149] *True Religion explained and defended against the archenemies thereof in these times. In six bookes. Written in Latin by Hugo Grotius, and now done in English for the common good,*

of this edition, but it was officially registered under the name of F. Coventry.[150] The translator must indeed have been Francis Coventry, the second son of Thomas Coventry, keeper of the Great Seal, by his second marriage.[151] It has been suggested that the translation was by the Franciscan Christopher Davenport, who employed the pseudonyms Franciscus a Santa Clara and Francis Coventrie,[152] but we have found nothing to suggest that this assumption is plausible.[153]

Coventry's translation goes back to the second edition of Grotius' Latin text (1629). It is written in fluent English and offers a good rendering of the work's contents. The translator did not prefix any foreword or introduction, but only a sober prayer for the opponents of the true religion. Grotius repeatedly expressed his satisfaction with this translation, which he probably saw in 1639.[154]

Greek, Swedish and Persian translations

On 24 October 1636 Grotius made his first mention of a Greek translation, which was said to have been made on the suggestion of his friend John Scudamore, the English ambassador in Paris.[155] A

London 1632 [= *BG* n° 1015]. In 1971 this edition was reprinted in facsimile: H. Grotius, *True Religion. London 1632* [The English Experience, its record in early printed books published in facsimile, n° 318], Amsterdam/New York 1971.

[150] See A.W. Pollard and G.R. Redgrave, *A Short-Title Catalogue of Books Printed in England, Scotland and Ireland and of English Books Printed Abroad, 1475–1640*, 2nd ed. London 1986, I, n° 12400, p. 532. The translation was registered on 28 January 1631 under the name F. Coventry.

[151] Unfortunately almost nothing is known of Francis Coventry; see *DNB*, XII, pp. 357–9, 362–4.

[152] See *BW* VII, n° 2812, p. 461 n. 8; *BW* VII, n° 2907, p. 616 n. 6; *BW* VIII, n° 2912, p. 3 n. 4. These notes are by C.M. Schulten.

[153] The name of F. Coventry is given in the official registration of the translation, and will therefore not be a pseudonym. Furthermore, Grotius had good contacts in England, who guaranteed reliable reports. On Christopher Davenport (1598–1680), see J.B. Dockery O.F.M., *Christopher Davenport. Friar and Diplomat*, London 1960. See also *DNB*, XIV, pp. 108–9 and *DHGE*, XIV, pp. 109–11.

[154] *BW* X, n° 4259 (to W. de Groot), p. 531: "Liber noster de Veritate religionis christianae pulchre versus et editus est in Anglia." Cf. *BW* X, n° 4262 (to J. Wtenbogaaert, 20 August 1639), p. 540: "Mijn boeck van de waerheit van de christelijcke religie is seer wel overgeset ende gedruckt in 't Engelsch." *BW* X, n° 4301 (to M. Casaubonus, 19 September 1639), p. 612: "Anglicana versio libri nostri pro Veritate religionis christianae valde mihi placet, [. . .]."

[155] *BW* VII, n° 2812 (to N. van Reigersberch, 24 October 1636), pp. 461–2: "Mijn boeck De satisfactione werdt daer [sc. in England] zeer gepresen, mijne Sacra Poemata zijn te Oxford nagedruckt ende liber de Veritate christianae religionis is overgeset in 't Engelsch alsoock in 't Gryecksch door den predictie van mijnheer den ambassadeur ordinaris van Engelant alhier."

year later he wrote to his brother Willem that his apologetic work had already been translated into Greek, but had not yet been published.[156] A year later still he said that it was Scudamore's chaplain who was translating the work into Greek.[157] As far as we know no Greek version of Grotius' work was ever published. Grotius' report is extremely vague and inconsistent, so that we are forced to assume that he was misinformed.[158]

In November 1637 Grotius noted that both his apologetic work and his poem on baptism had been translated into Swedish.[159] A month later he noted with satisfaction that his apologetic work was already being read in Swedish.[160] The basis for these reports is not clear, since the first Swedish translation was not to be published until the eighteenth century.[161]

In December 1638 Grotius reported to his brother Willem that Roman Catholic clergy were translating his apologetic work into Persian, with a view to the conversion of the Muhammadans.[162] He repeated this news in a letter to Vossius.[163] Later he again mentioned

---

[156] *BW* VIII, n° 3310 (22 November 1637), p. 666: "Etiam [sc. *VRC*] Graece versus est, sed nondum editus."

[157] *BW* X, n° 3917(to G.J. Vossius, 1 January 1639), p. 12: "Vertit eum Graece pastor legati hic Anglicani." In a note Matthias Turner and Thomas Lockey are named as possible translators. But the latter is not eligible, since he did not serve as Scudamore's chaplain. On Thomas Lockey see *DNB*, XXXIV, pp. 43–4. Matthias Turner was Scudamore's chaplain at the time, and moreover so learned in Greek that he often wrote his sermons in that language. But Grotius knew Turner personally and repeatedly mentioned him in his letters to Scudamore, without making a single allusion to the Greek translation. This makes it unlikely that Turner made a Greek translation of the work. On 20 August 1640 Grotius made his last reference to a Greek translation, again without naming the translator: *BW* X, n° 4262 (to J. Wtenbogaert), p. 540.

[158] It is possible that some work was already done in these years on a Greek translation of his *T'samensprake over den doop*, which was to be published in 1747 [= *BG* n° 80]. The translator of this was Christopher Wase, an English pedagogue who, as far as we know, was never in John Scudamore's service.

[159] *BW* VIII, n° 3342 (to W. de Groot, 14 November 1637), p. 720: "Liber de veritate religionis christianae meus et de Baptismo etiam in Suedicam transfertur linguam, quo magis doleat Voetius eique similes sanniones."

[160] *BW* VIII, n° 3390 (to N. van Reigersberch, 19 December 1637), p. 801.

[161] *BG* n° 1082.

[162] *BW* IX, n° 3874 (to W. de Groot, 4 December 1638), p. 730: "Liber meus de Veritate religionis christianae, mi frater, qui socinianus est Voetianis, adeo hic pro tali non habetur, ut studio religiosorum pontificorum vertatur in sermonem Persicum ad convertendos, si Deus coepto annuat, ejus imperiii mahumetistas."

[163] *BW* X, n° 3917 (to G.J. Vossius, 1 January 1639), p. 12: "Pontificii autem nunc Persice vertunt, ut mahumetistas, si Deus aspiret, faciant christanos."

a Persian translation,[164] but never referred to it after that. It is not known if any work was in fact done on a Persian translation, and if so by whom.[165] It appears virtually certain that no such translation was ever published.

Summary

During Grotius' lifetime five translations of his apologetic work appeared: one English, two German and two French. Four of these translations were based on one of the Latin versions of the work, while the Dutch *Bewijs* was only translated once, albeit by no less a person than the famous poet Martin Opitz. Grotius was exceptionally pleased with this translation, but he took scarcely any notice of the prose translation made by the less well-known Christoph Köler from the Latin version of his work. Grotius was more involved with the French translation of his work than with the others, probably because he lived in Paris and had many friends there. He showed a distinct preference for a translator who would sympathise with the remonstrants, and found one in the person of Etienne de Courcelles. In 1644 he was indignant when a second French translation was produced, without his explicit consent, by De Mézeray.

The English translation was made without his knowledge, and he did not become aware of it until four years after its publication, but this version did meet with his approval. It is doubtful if all the information that reached Grotius was equally reliable. Occasionally he mentioned Greek and Persian translations, which in all probability were never realised. He also referred to a Swedish translation, although the first rendering into that language known to us did not appear until the eighteenth century.

---

[164] *BW* X, n° 4262 (to J. Wtenbogaert, 10 August 1639), p. 540: "Is [sc. *VRC*] oock overgeset in 't Griecx ende in 't Persisch."

[165] Cf. H.C. Millies, 'Over de Oostersche vertalingen van het beroemde geschrift van Hugo Grotius, *De veritate religionis christianae*', *Verslagen en Mededeelingen der Koninklijke Akademie van Wetenschappen*, afd. Letterkunde, vol. 7, Amsterdam 1863, 108–34. On p. 126 Millies mentions the possibility that the order of the discalced Carmelites, which at that time was very active in missions, worked on the Persian translation of Grotius' apologetic work.

c) *Editions and translations after 1645*

Grotius was delighted to find that his apologetic work became a great success in his own lifetime. The only criticism came from the Calvinists, but he had expected this and was not dismayed by it. The author had felt that his work would survive his own death, but he cannot have guessed the extent of its posthumous success. No other work of his was to be so often reprinted and translated.

Seventeen editions or translations of the apologetic work were published in the author's lifetime:

2 editions of the *Bewijs*
1 translation of the *Bewijs*
10 editions of *De veritate*
4 translations of *De veritate*

The number of posthumous editions and translations amounted to 144:

7 editions of the *Bewijs*
2 translations of *Bewijs*
55 editions of *De veritate*
80 translations of *De veritate*.

The success of the Latin version far surpassed that of the original poem. One can say that Grotius' *De veritate* appeared in an almost uninterrupted stream of editions and translations between 1650 and 1850. As we shall see, the work was often presented with pronounced theological intentions, two of them being particularly obvious: 1) in the eighteenth century, as the forewords and additions to the text showed, it was seen as a suitable weapon against atheism and agnosticism, which were gaining ground; 2) it was employed well into the nineteenth century in Christian missions, as the various translations into eastern languages make clear. To be of most use for these goals the work had to be adapted somewhat: in the first case, Grotius' apologetic work was supplemented by additional text and notes, and in the second text or notes were suppressed, even the name of the author.

Grotius' apology was free from a too specific confessional colouring, so that Christians of diverse confessions could find common ground in it. The result was that various groups claimed it as their own. In Catholic editions Grotius was depicted as a crypto-Catholic,

and many English editions and translations included testimonies of
Grotius' admiration for the Anglican church. It was the remonstrants
Gerard Brandt (*Bewijs*) and Johannes Clericus (*De veritate*) above all
whose editions set the tone and largely determined the posthumous
influence of the apologetic work.

Bewijs

The Dutch poem was reissued several times very soon after Grotius'
death, in combination with his other Dutch poems (1648, 1652).[166]
In 1683 the well known remonstrant preacher and historian Gerard
Brandt produced an edition that was to be the basis of all subsequent editions.[167] Brandt added to Grotius' text a modest apparatus
of notes, consisting of scriptural references and brief explanations,
which he took chiefly from *De veritate*. He was following a suggestion of the author himself, who in a letter to his brother Willem
had stated a preference for a new edition of the *Bewijs* with notes
over a Dutch translation of the Latin version.[168] Grotius' Dutch poems
were twice reprinted in the eighteenth century and last reissued in
the mid-nineteenth century in the edition of Jeronimo de Vries (1849).
De Vries added a few explanatory notes of his own to Brandt's notes
on the *Bewijs*.[169] The German translation by Opitz was twice reprinted
(1690 and 1746).[170]

De veritate

Editions

After Grotius' death no fewer than 55 editions of his *De veritate*
appeared, 16 of them in the second half of the seventeenth century,
22 in the eighteenth, 16 in the nineteenth and 1 edition in the twentieth century.[171] Most of them contained both the text and Grotius'
notes.

---

[166] *BG* n°s 145, 146.
[167] *BG* n° 147.
[168] *BW* XI, n° 4823 (to W. de Groot, 8 September 1640), p. 501.
[169] *BG* n° 151.
[170] *BG* n°s 153, 154.
[171] *BG* n°s 955–1007.

The first posthumous edition (Paris 1650) included, by way of introduction, the letter Grotius had written to Bignon on 28 August 1639, when he presented him with his apparatus of notes.[172] This example was followed in many later editions, among them that in Grotius' *Opera theologica* (1679).[173] This well known edition, which agrees with the last impression authorised by Grotius, was the first to print the *annotata* as footnotes.[174] Grotius' apologetic work was included in the first edition of the famous compilation *Critici sacri* (1660),[175] but omitted from the third edition (1698) because—the editors declared—virtually everyone had access to a copy of the work.[176] Nevertheless the work continued to be reprinted many times in the following centuries, albeit mostly in combination with other texts.

In 1709 the remonstrant professor Johannes Clericus produced an edition in which he added his own notes, consisting of additions and corrections, to Grotius' text and notes. Clericus also added a short discussion of the necessity to choose between various Christian views, clearly intended as a supplement to Grotius' argument.[177] Nine years later Clericus issued a second edition almost identical to the first, but with a few additional notes.[178] In 1724 Clericus brought out his third edition, which contained both new notes and a second treatise on religious indifference.[179] The remonstrant Clericus undoubtedly felt that he was adapting Grotius' work to the needs of the new age. Clericus' last edition was reissued thirteen times in the eighteenth and nineteenth centuries.

In 1709 the scholar E.S. Cyprianus produced an edition, which he also provided with additional commentary.[180] In 1726 Cyprianus published a second edition, to which he added an argument of his

---

[172] *BG* n° 95. Cf. *BW* X, n° 4270, p. 554.

[173] *BG* n°ˢ 965–965A. Reprints of the *Opera theologica*, Basel 1732 (*BG* n° 980) and Stuttgart 1972.

[174] H. Grotius, *De veritate religionis christianae. Editio novissima in qua eiusdem annotationes textui suis quaeque locis atque paginis ad faciliorem usum subjectae sunt*, in *Hugonis Grotii Operum theologicorum tomus tertius, continens opuscula diversa*, Amsterdam 1679, pp. 1–96.

[175] *BG* n° 958. See also the unrevised reprint of *Critici Sacri* (Frankfurt 1695).

[176] *Critici sacri, sive annotata doctissimorum virorum in Vetus ac Novum Testamentum. Quibus accedunt tractatus varii theologico-philologici. Editio nova in novem tomos distributa, multis anecdotis commentariis, ac indice ad totum opus locupletissimo, aucta*. Amsterdam/Utrecht 1698, "Praefatio ad lectorem", [fol. V].

[177] *BG* n° 971.

[178] *BG* n° 972.

[179] *BG* n° 974.

[180] *BG* n° 970.

own composition against Clericus' discussion of the need to choose
between various Christian views.[181] More synthetic and above all
much more thorough was the work of J.C. Koecher, who in 1726
presented what can be regarded as the first critical edition of *De veri-*
tate.[182] Koecher corrected Grotius' notes and text, adding his own
explanatory notes. He published a second expanded and improved
edition in 1734.[183] Koecher also composed two solid studies of *De*
veritate. The first appeared in 1727 and was a compilation of all the
published commentaries on Grotius' work; the second, which appeared
in 1739, comprised a number of treatises by Koecher, one of them
the first account of the history of *De veritate*.[184]

The collected works of the seventeenth century scholar H. Conring,
which were published in 1730, included an edition of *De veritate* provided with Conring's notes, which had been collected a few years
earlier by Koecher.[185] Koecher's notes in their turn were incorporated in several nineteenth century editions (1845, 1852).[186] The third
and until now the last critical edition appeared in 1831, and was
edited by the then librarian of Leiden University, J.T. Bergman.[187]
This edition is largely based on the work of Koecher, but contains
the necessary improvements and additions, chiefly in the references
to literature. After a century and a half Bergman's edition is of course
capable of improvement but it can still be described as acceptable.
A new critical edition is now in preparation.

Most editions of the *De veritate* appeared in England. The last edition prepared by Clericus was reprinted ten times in that country.
In the nineteenth century specially adapted editions appeared for use
in schools and universities. Clearly Grotius' work formed a regular
part of the curriculum at this time. To make things easier for students editions with the Latin text and notes translated into English
were produced.[188]

---

[181] *BG* n° 976.
[182] *BG* n° 975.
[183] *BG* n° 982.
[184] *BG* n° 975, rem. 5.
[185] *BG* n° 979. A reprint appeared in 1971: H. Conring, *Opera*. Herausgegeben
und mit Anmerkungen von W. Göbel, [Neudruck der Ausgabe Braunschweig 1730],
vol. 5, Aalen 1971, pp. 1–105: "Grotius' De veritate religionis christianae cum annotationibus Hermanni Conringii."
[186] *BG* n°s 1003, 1005.
[187] *BG* n° 1000.
[188] *BG* n°s 1004, 1006.

The number of editions in Roman Catholic countries was limited. The Church of Rome had reservations about Grotius' work, though by comparison with most other Protestant authors Grotius came off lightly. His apologetic work was not forbidden in the Index of 1667, but permitted with a few minor corrections.[189] In the eighteenth century therefore it was possible to reprint Grotius' work eight times in Italy with the official approval of the Church.[190] Several of these editions were provided with eulogies to Grotius, which made the most of the author's Catholic leanings and above all praised his acknowledgement of the Pope's authority.[191] No more than three editions appeared in France (1650, 1845, 1852)[192] and only one in Spain (1788).[193]

Translations

After Grotius' death no fewer than 80 translations of his work appeared in 12 languages: English, French, German, Dutch, Arabic, Urdu, Swedish, Danish, Celtic, Hungarian, Polish and Italian. Twenty two translations were published in the second half of the seventeenth century, 34 in the eighteenth, 21 in the nineteenth and finally 2 in the twentieth century.

English

The majority of these translations appeared in England (45 items). After the translation by Coventry the English public had to wait some time for the second complete translation. Clarke Barksdale published a translation of the first two books of Grotius' apologetic work in 1652, with a partial translation of his *Votum*.[194] To the edition of 1658 he added a translation of the third book,[195] and in 1676 he produced a separate translation of the last three books of *De veritate*.[196]

---

[189] F.H. Reusch, *Der Index der verbotenen Bücher. Ein Beitrag zur Kirchen- und Literaturgeschichte*, Bonn 1885, II, p. 105.
[190] *BG* nos 978, 983, 986–8, 990.
[191] *BG* nos 986, 988.
[192] *BG* nos 955, 1003, 1005.
[193] *BG* no 991.
[194] *BG* no 1016.
[195] *BG* no 1018.
[196] *BG* no 1020.

In 1680 Simon Patrick translated all six books, adding a seventh book of his own, an attack on the Church of Rome.[197] Patrick went back to Coventry's translation, but like Barksdale he omitted Grotius' notes. His translation was reprinted five times in the following years.[198]

The fourth translator, John Clarke, relied entirely on the editions of Johannes Clericus. In 1711 he produced a translation of Clericus' first edition of *De veritate*, including Grotius' notes and the remonstrant editor's additions. The fourth edition of Clarke's translation was entirely revised in accordance with Clericus' third edition; it was sixteen times reprinted between 1754 and 1860, and thus became the most current English translation.[199]

Yet not everyone was satisfied with it. Clarke's translation, which was equipped with a double system of notes and two extra treatises, appeared to be addressed chiefly to a public of theologians and laymen with theological interests. In 1782 Spender Madan presented a "familiar translation" without notes and additions, intended "for the lower ranks of people".[200] But Madan was just as unable to resist the urge to add extra matter. In 1814 he produced a translation that followed Clarke's example by including both Grotius' text and notes, and the annotations and treatises of Clericus.[201]

In the seventeenth and eighteenth century *De veritate* was twice translated into English verse. The first version was produced by William Atwood and appeared at the instigation of the famous scientist Robert Boyle in 1686.[202] Charles l'Oste made a second verse translation in 1776, to which he added his own notes.[203] In the mid-nineteenth century a literal translation was published with the aim of encouraging students of theology to read Grotius' work in Latin.[204] This translation, by T. Sedger, was twice reprinted and evidently met a need.[205] Finally the first English translation by Coventry was reprinted in 1971.[206]

---

[197] *BG* n° 1022.
[198] *BG* n°ˢ 1023, 1025–8.
[199] *BG* n°ˢ 1033, 1035–6, 1039, 1042–3, 1045–6, 1048–50, 1051–5, 1058.
[200] *BG* n° 1041. A reprint appeared in 1797: *BG* n° 1044.
[201] *BG* n° 1047.
[202] *BG* n° 1024.
[203] *BG* n° 1038.
[204] *BG* n° 1056.
[205] *BG* n° 1057, 1059.
[206] H. Grotius, *True Religion; London 1632*. [The English Experience, its record in early printed books published in facsimile, n° 318], Amsterdam/New York 1971.

French

The first French translation to appear after the death of Grotius was that by the oratorian Jacques Talon (1659), and was clearly Roman Catholic in inspiration.[207] Talon dedicated his version to no less a person than Jesus Christ himself, and assured his readers in a separate foreword that even if Grotius had not been born a Roman Catholic, he had shown Catholic leanings in his thought. Of course the Dutchman had made mistakes, but Talon corrected these in the margins of the translated text.[208] The Huguenot exile in the Netherlands P. Le Jeune produced a translation in 1692. Le Jeune incorporated Grotius' notes, adding his own, and explained in a lengthy introduction that Grotius' work was a useful weapon against the spread of atheism, even if Grotius' philosophy was antiquated. In the second edition of this translation (1728) Le Jeune also included the two treatises by Clericus.[209]

But Catholic interest in Grotius' work had not yet disappeared. In 1724 the Catholic historian C.P. Goujet published a translation with the approval of the Church. This translator omitted Grotius' notes but included his own.[210] The same procedure was followed by the famous J.P. Migne in his translation of Grotius' work, included in a great compilation of Christian apologies (1845).[211]

German

The German translation that appeared in 1656 was by the Lutheran Valentinus Musculus. Besides the text he also incorporated Grotius' notes. In his foreword Musculus warned his readers against some of Grotius' theological errors on the relationship of the Old and New Testaments.[212] This translation was reprinted three times.[213] In the eighteenth century two further German translations appeared, the first without notes (1746) and the second with those of Grotius (1768).[214]

---

[207] *BG* n° 1062.
[208] See Laplanche, *L'Évidence*, p. 35.
[209] *BG* n° 1065.
[210] *BG* n° 1066.
[211] *BG* n° 1067.
[212] *BG* n° 1009.
[213] *BG* n°s 1010–12.
[214] *BG* n°s 1013, 1014.

Dutch

On 27 August 1640 Willem de Groot informed his brother Hugo that there were some who felt that a Dutch translation of the Latin version of his apologetic work with notes would be particularly useful.[215] Grotius did not think this a good idea. He replied that a Dutch translation of work that was itself translated from Dutch, would not be to his liking. He believed it would be more satisfactory to reissue the *Bewijs*, if necessary adding clarifications from the Latin prose version and the notes.[216] Willem asked his brother to reconsider the matter and suggested adding both notes and extra lines of verse to the text of the Dutch poem.[217] But Grotius rejected this idea. In his opinion there could be no changes to the text of his poem, and the additions from the Latin text could if necessary be incorporated in the form of footnotes.[218]

The author's emphatic words appear to have nipped any such initiative in the bud for the time being, and no Dutch translation of the Latin apologetic work appeared in Grotius' lifetime. But after his death several Dutch translations of the *De veritate* were produced. Nothing is known of the first, said to have been made by the remonstrant preacher Nicolaes Borremans (1650).[219] The second translation was by I.D. Volder, who did not include Grotius' notes (1653).[220] In 1667 the third Dutch translation appeared, the work of an anonymous translator.[221] This translation was reissued in 1686 in a version improved and expanded by the poet Joachim Oudaen. This edition included both Grotius' notes and a translation of the seventh book of Simon Patrick.[222] The fifth edition of this translation (1728)

---

[215] *BW* XI, n° 4805, p. 481: "Sunt qui putent e re esse publica, ut et liber ipse [sc. *VRC*] in Belgicum sermonem prosa, ut Latine scriptus est, vertatur eique auctuarii loco accedant Notae, magni apud omnis generis homines usus futurae."

[216] *BW* XI, n° 4823 (to W. de Groot, 8 September 1640), p. 501: "Cum librorum illorum versio ex Belgico sit sumta, ex isto Latino iterum in Belgicum transfundi mihi non placeat. Sed possent mei versus Belgici recudi et, siquid obscurum est, ex prosa Latina breviter illustrari, deinde addi testimonia."

[217] *BW* XI, n° 4860 (from W. de Groot, 1 October 1640), p. 545.

[218] *BW* XI, n° 4876 (to W. de Groot, 13 October 1640), p. 563: "In carmine Belgico nihil mutandum censeam, sed siquid amplius in latinis est, id oratione pedestri interspargi annotatis."

[219] *BG* n° 1068.

[220] *BG* n° 1069.

[221] *BG* n° 1071.

[222] *BG* n° 1072.

was quite bulky, for besides Patrick's book it also included the notes and two treatises by Clericus.[223]

Arabic

The English scholar Edward Pocock, who in 1636 became the first professor of Arabic at Oxford, paid Grotius a visit in Paris in December 1640, on his return from three years of study in Constantinople.[224] Grotius reported on the meeting in a letter to his brother on 16 February 1641. Pocock had told him that he was translating his apologetic work into Arabic, since he knew no book better fitted to convert the Muslims in the east.[225] Pocock's translation was published in 1660.[226] The edition contained both Grotius' Latin text and notes, and the Arabic translation, and was provided with a dedication and foreword by the translator.[227] Pocock dedicated his work to the famous Robert Boyle, who had borne the whole cost of publication. Besides his scientific interests Boyle was also an enthusiast for Christian missions.[228]

In the dedication Pocock expresses his gratitude to Boyle, for he had not found a publisher willing to print a work from which no profit could be expected, since it was to be distributed free in the east. He states that his translation had no other purpose than to bring Muslims to Christianity, and to educate converts to Christianity who were still uninformed about Christian doctrine.[229] In a separate foreword Pocock warns the reader that in his translation, with the

---

[223] *BG* nº 1074.

[224] On Pocock see *DNB*, XLVI, pp. 7–12; and J.G. Fück, *Die arabischen Studien in Europa bis in den Anfang des 20. Jahrhunderts*, Leipzig 1955, pp. 85–90.

[225] *BW* XII, nº 5061 (to W. de Groot, 16 February 1641), p. 103: "Fuit apud me his diebus Anglus vir doctissimus, qui diu in Turcico vixit imperio, et meum librum de veritate religionis christianae in Arabicum vertit sermonem; curabitque si potest typis in Anglia edi. Is nullum librum putat esse utiliorem aut instruendis illarum partium Christianis, aut etiam convertendis Mahumetistis, qui sunt in Turcico imperio, aut Persico, aut Tartarico, aut Punico, aut Indiano."

[226] H. Grotius, *De veritate religonis christianae. Editio nova cum annotationibus, cui accessit versio Arabica*, Oxford 1660.

[227] *BG* nº 957.

[228] See J. van den Berg, *Constrained by Jesus' Love. An Inquiry into the Motives of the Missionary Awakening in Great Britain in the Period between 1698 and 1815*, Kampen 1956, pp. 28–9.

[229] See *VRC* [*BG* nº 957], A 5ʳ·ᵛ, Epistola dedicatoria honoratissimo, eruditione, virtute et nobilitate generis, clarissimo Domino Roberto Boyle."

author's consent, he had omitted certain things that were wrongly ascribed to Muslims.[230]

The Arabic translation is based on the text of 1640, and does not translate the notes. Pocock replaced the dedication to Bignon with his own introduction, in which he explains the object of the work.[231] The copies intended for the east omitted the Latin text, the dedication and foreword, as well as the names of the author, translator and publisher, and the date and place of publication.[232] Pocock was evidently afraid of encountering obstruction from Roman Catholic missionaries if it should become known from what quarter his work came. Later the missionary Robert Huntington, who distributed the work between 1671 and 1682, even thought it necessary for his own safety to cut the sixth book out of the copies he disseminated.[233] All these omissions and excisions gave rise to misunderstandings. A look at the anonymous Arabic text later convinced the Scots traveller Watson that Grotius had stolen the contents of his apologetic work from an unnamed Arabic author.[234]

Pocock's translation was repeatedly used in the eighteenth and nineteenth centuries for missionary purposes. The sixth book, intended to convert the Muslims, was translated into Arabic and published at Halle, the centre of pietism and evangelisation, in 1731.[235] A few years later separate editions of the translated third and fifth books were also published at Halle.[236] Finally, about a century later, an abbreviated version of the Arabic translation, anonymous but with the intriguing title 'Book of the key to the treasure chests and the explanation of the mysteries', was published under the auspices of the Society for the Propagation of Religious Knowledge (ca. 1833).[237]

---

[230] *VRC* [*BG* n° 957], A6ᵛ: "Monendus est lector, si pauca quaedam de libro sexto (de operis totius praefatione nil opus est hoc monere) in versione arabica omissa vel mutata repererit, ideo hoc factum ne quid de mohammedorum rebus et sententia affirmaretur, quod non authorum apud ipsos omni exceptione maiorum, fide et testimonio constaret; idque authorem ipsum, dum in vivis esset, ea de re consultum, faciendum censuisse, e.g. quod de columba ad aurem Mohammedis advolante a nostris asseritur, etc."

[231] See *BG* n° 1075, rem. 6.

[232] *BG* n° 1075.

[233] See Millies, 'Oostersche vertalingen', 120.

[234] *Ibid.*, 119.

[235] *BG* n° 1076.

[236] *BG* nᵒˢ 1077, 1078.

[237] *BG* n° 1079.

Other languages

Grotius' apologetic work was twice translated into Danish (1678, 1747),[238] and once into Swedish (ca. 1712).[239] In the eighteenth century translations into Hungarian (1732) and Polish (1766) also appeared.[240] The Welsh translation of 1712 was twice reprinted in the nineteenth century (1820, 1854).[241] In 1839 the English missionary Robert Cotton Mather produced a translation into Urdu, the language of what is now Pakistan.[242] The first Italian translation appeared in the early nineteenth century (1806–07).[243] The second Italian translation, which is also the latest translation to be produced to date, was published in 1971.[244]

---

[238] *BG* n[os] 1081, 1084.

[239] *BG* n[os] 1082, 1083 (reprint).

[240] *BG* n[os] 1088, 1089.

[241] *BG* n[os] 1085–7.

[242] *BG* n° 1080.

[243] *BG* n° 1090.

[244] H. Grotius, *Della vera religione cristiana*. A cura di Fiorella Pintacuda de Michelis, [Piccola biblioteca filosofica Laterza, 86], Milan 1973. The translation is based on the Latin edition of 1679 (*Opera Theologica*, III, *BG* n° 965). De Michelis not only incorporated Grotius' notes but added explanatory notes of her own.

CONCLUSION

Grotius' apologetic work must be described as traditional, because the author took all his arguments from existing apologetic literature. He showed his originality by presenting in a new order the material he had found in his predecessors. But his really innovative contribution was his *reduction* of that material: he refrained from discussing Christian doctrines and thereby detached apologetics from dogmatics. This detachment is significant for Grotius' primarily ethical view of the Christian religion.

Grotius wished to offer a remedy for the 'sickness' of his time, which in his opinion was plagued by dogmatic disputes that had driven out the truth. A victim of these disputes himself, in his cell in Loevestein he sought 'passionately' for the vanished truth. Here he wrote his apologetic work, in which he reminded all Christians of what they had in common and what distinguished them from the rest of humanity.[1] The truth, in his opinion, was indissolubly bound up with peace and unity; discussions of doctrines represented a threat to peace and therefore to truth. To determine the truth of the Christian religion he considered it neither desirable nor necessary to discuss matters of doctrine.

This undogmatic method of marshalling the evidence was very unusual in Christian apologetics at that time. Grotius' preference for this method was not merely the result of his particular situation when he wrote the work. A theologically trained author would never have gone so far. In fact this method was juridical. Grotius was an amateur theologian and felt completely unconstrained by all theological traditions. He allowed himself unrestricted freedom to choose from the works of such disparate authors as the Protestant Mornay, the Roman Catholic Vives and the anti-trinitarian Socinus.

Surprisingly, almost all of the historical-juridical argument in the central parts of Grotius' apologetic work can be found in Socinus' *De auctoritate Sacrae Scripturae*. The conclusion that Grotius used this work in producing his own apologetic work appears unavoidable. It

---

[1] Cf. *BW* II, n° 662 (to A. Schottus, 8 April 1622), p. 102.

is, however, possible that the imprisoned politician received an anonymous edition of this work in Loevestein, and was in fact unaware
of its author. We cannot be certain of this. Grotius was to deny the
charge of Socinianism most emphatically, but he could hardly do
otherwise: to admit it would in fact have been to sign his own theological death warrant.

He differed from Socinus in upholding 'natural theology'. Grotius
had more, though not unbounded confidence in the deductive powers of right reason (*recta ratio*). He was convinced that man was forced
to rely on God's revelation for absolute certainty in religion. In his
apologetic work, however, he was unwilling to appeal to divine revelation and the deductions that could be drawn directly from it: the
Christian dogmas and the testimony of the Holy Spirit. Instead of
a 'vertical' construction he chose a 'horizontal' method: he tried to
prove the truth of the Christian religion from purely rational arguments and historical testimonies. His strategy was to use these universally valid means of proof to lead all non-Christians to the Bible,
so that they could themselves derive the contents of the Christian
faith from it. Grotius attached special importance to the testimony
of miracles, and saw them as the decisive proof of the supernatural
truth of the Christian religion.

The number of editions and translations shows that Grotius' apologetic work continued to enjoy enormous popularity in the eighteenth
and nineteenth centuries. The work owed part of this great success
to its non-denominational character. Christians of many confessions,
among them remonstrants, anglicans, Lutherans and Roman Catholics
could all find something to agree with in the golden book. Only
orthodox Calvinists rejected it as Socinian-remonstrant heresy. But
the revival of Christian apologetics at the end of the seventeenth
century also contributed to the work's success. Grotius' undogmatic
method of proof found imitators among the rationalist apologetes of
the early Enlightenment. His work was very often presented, above
all in the eighteenth century, as a weapon in the battle against atheism and religious agnosticism, both of which were gaining ground.
A third reason for its success was the suitability of Grotius' work,
abbreviated or in full, for use in missionary activity.

Grotius' golden little book was—as we have already remarked—
the characteristic expression of late humanist classicism. This classicism lost its lustre and value in the seventeenth century, through the
appearance of such innovators as Bacon, Hobbes, Descartes, Spinoza

and Pascal, all of whom stood outside the established academic culture of their times.[2] Grotius was not an innovator but as a leading citizen of the Republic of Letters he was very closely linked with this conservative academic culture. Huizinga made a telling remark about Grotius: 'His gaze was directed at an ideal that reflected an imaginary past. The obsession with antiquity blinkered his view.'[3]

For the modern reader the apologetic work of Grotius, in both its Dutch and Latin versions, has lost virtually all of the charm that former generations evidently found in it. It may be going too far to say, with Busken Huet, that Grotius' philosophy was 'petty bourgeois thought itself.'[4] Grotius' so-called rational arguments often strike us as trivial and arbitrary. However, this reflection takes nothing away from the merits and historical significance of this work as a golden link in the chain between late humanism and the early Enlightenment.

---

[2] See J. Huizinga, 'Grotius' plaats in de geschiedenis van den menschelijken geest,' in *Tien Studiën*, Haarlem 1926, pp. 117–25; and Laplanche, *L'Évidence*, pp. 232–6.
[3] J. Huizinga, 'Hugo de Groot en zijn eeuw', *Tien Studiën*, Haarlem, 1926, p. 111.
[4] C. Busken Huet, *Het land van Rembrand*, 5th ed., Haarlem [n.d.], II 2, p. 110.

SOURCES AND LITERATURE

A) Sources

I. *The Bible*

Old Testament
Gen. = Genesis
Exod. = Exodus
Deut. = Deuteronomy
Pss. = Psalms
Dan. = Daniel

New Testament
Matt. = Matthew
Luke
John
Heb. = Epistle to the Hebrews
Jas. = Epistle of James
2 Pet. = Second Epistle of Peter
2–3 John = Second and Third Epistles of John
    Jude
Rev. = Revelation

II. *Classical and Patristic Works*

Aristot. – Aristotle
  Eth. Nic. = *Ethica Nicomachea*
  Metaphys. = *Metaphysica*
  Phys. = *Physica*
  Rhet. = *Rhetorica*
  Top. = *Topica*
Aug. = Augustine
  Civ. = *De civitate Dei*
Cic. = Cicero
  ND = *De Natura deorum*
  Top. = *Topica*
  Tusc. = *Tusculanae disputationes*
Clem. Al. = Clement of Alexandria
  Strom. = *Stromateis*
Eus. = Eusebius
  PE = *Praeparatio Evangelica*
Ios. = Flavius Josephus
  Ant. Iud. = *Antiquitates Iudaicae*
  Ap. = *Contra Apionem*
Iust. Ma. = Justin Martyr
  1 Apol. = *Prima Apologia*
  Dial. Tryph. = *Dialogus cum Tryphone*

Philo = Philo Judaeus
   Vit. Mos. = De vita Mosis
Proc. = Proclus
   Theol. Plat. = Theologia Platonica
Tert. = Tertullian
   Adv. Iud. = Adversus Iudaeos
   Apol. = Apologeticum

III. *Medieval and Humanist Works*

Agric. = Rudolphus Agricola
   DID = De inventione dialectica libri omnes et integri & recogniti, qui iam olim quidem in publicum prodierunt, sed trunci ac mutili nec minus item depravati, nunc demum ad autographi exemplaris fidem, Cologne 1539.
Bib. = Theodorus Bibliander
   Mach. = *Machumetis Saracenorum principis, eiusque successorum vitae, doctrina, ac ipse Alcoran, [. . .]. His adiunctae sunt confutationes multorum et quidem probatiss. authorum, Arabum, Graecorum et Latinorum, [. . .]. Adiuncti sunt etiam de Turcarum sive Saracenorum [. . .] origine ac rebus gestis, [. . .]. Haec omnia in unum volumen redacta sunt, opera et studio Theodori Bibliandri*, Basel 1550.
Calv. = Jean Calvin
   Inst. = Institutio Christianae Religionis, Geneva 1559.
Emp. = Constantijn L'Empereur van Oppijck
   ComJes = D. Isaaci Abrabanielis et R. Mosis Alschechi Comment. in Esaiae prophetiam, cum additamento eorum quae R. Simeon e veterum dictis collegit. Subjuncta [. . .] refutatione et textus nova versione ac paraphrasi, Leiden 1631.
   ParaDan. = Paraphrasis Josephi Iachiadae in Danielem, cum versione et annotationibus, Amsterdam 1633.
Gennebr. = Gilbert Gennebrard
   Albonis argumenta = R. Iosephi Albonis, R. Davidis Kimhi et alius cuiusdam Hebraei anonymi argumenta quibus nonnullos fidei christianae articulos oppugnant, G. Genebrardo interprete, Paris 1566.
Gerson = Christian Gerson
   Thal. = Des jüdischen Thalmuds Auslegung und Widerlegung, Neu bearbeitet von J. Deckert, Vienna 1895.
Menasseh = Menasseh ben Israel
   Concil. = Conciliator, sive de convenientia locorum S. Scripturae, quae pugnare inter se videntur, Francofurti [= Amsterdam] 1633.
Mornay = Philippe du Plessis Mornay
   Ver. = De la vérité de la religion chrestienne contre les athées, epicuriens, payens, juifs, mahumédistes, et autres infidèles, Antwerp 1581.
Ramus = Petrus Ramus
   Dial. = Dialectique (1555) Édition critique avec introduction, notes et commentaires de Michel Dassonville, Geneva 1964.
Sabundus, R., *Theologia naturalis seu liber creaturarum*, [Faksimile-Neudruck der Ausgabe Sulzbach 1852, mit literargeschichtlicher Einführung und kritischer Edition des Prologs und des Titulus I von F. Stegmüller], Stuttgart/Bad Cannstatt 1966.
Scal. = Josephus Justus Scaliger
   Emend. temp. = Opus de emendatione temporum, castigatius et auctius. Item veterum Graecorum fragmenta selecta cum notis eiusdem Scaligeri, Leiden 1598 (first edition Paris 1583).
   Thes. temp. = Thesaurus temporum. Eusebii Pamphili Chronicorum Canonum omnimodae historiae libri duo, interprete Hieronymo . . . Opera ac studio Josephi Justi Scaligeri, editio altera, Amsterdam 1658 (first edition Leiden 1606).

Soc. = Faustus Socinus

ASS = De auctoritate Sacrae Scripturae liber, in *Opera omnia in duos tomos distincta. Tomus primus continens eius Opera Exegetica et Didactica . . .*, [Bibliotheca fratrum Polonorum quos unitarios vocant, I, [Irenopoli = Amsterdam] 1656, pp. 265–80.

Thomas = Thomas Aquinas

ScG = Summa contra Gentiles.

Sth = Summa Theologica.

Valla = Laurentius Valla

DD = Dialecticae Disputationes in *Opera Omnia*, Scripta in editione Basilensi anno MDXL collecta, Turin 1962, pp. 643–761.

Van. = Julio Cesare Vanini

Amph. = Amphitheatrum aeternae providentiae, divino-magicum, christiano-physicum, nec non astrologo-catholicum. Adversus veteres philosophos, atheos, epicureos, peripateticos et stoicos, Lugduni [= Lyon] 1615.

Vives = Juan Luis Vives

Ver. = De veritate fidei christianae, in *Opera*, vol. II, Basel 1555, pp. 286–496.

IV. *Works of Grotius*

Animadv. in animadv. Riv. = Animadversiones in animadversiones Andreae Riveti [= *BG* n° 1175] in *OT* IV, pp. 639–50.

Annot. in NT = Annotationes in Novum Testamentum [= *BG* n°ˢ 1135 sqq.] in *OT* II–III.

Annot. in VT = Annotationes in Vetus Testamentum, [*BG* n°ˢ 1137 sqq.] in *OT* I.

Ant. = Liber de antiquitate reipublicae Batavicae, Leiden 1610 [= *BG* n° 691].

Baptiz. = Baptizatorum puerorum institutio alternis interrogationibus et responsionibus, Amsterdam 1635 [= *BG* n°ˢ 78 sqq.] in *OT* IV, pp. 629–32.

Bewijs = Bewijs van den waren godsdienst met zijn overige Nederlandsche gedichten, ed. J. de Vries, Amsterdam 1844 [= *BG* n° 151], pp. 1–167.

BW = Briefwisseling van Hugo Grotius, ed. P.C. Molhuysen, B.C. Meulenbroek, P.P. Witkam, H.J.M. Nellen and C.M. Ridderikhoff, 17 vols. [RGP], The Hague 1928– 2001 [= *BG* n° 1212].

Chr. Pat. – Tragoedia Christus Patiens [– *BG* n° 31] in *Dichtwerken*, I 2a/b 3.

Dichtwerken = De Dichtwerken van Hugo Grotius. Oorspronkelijke dichtwerken, ed. B.L. Meulenbroek et al., Assen 1971–88.

Disq. = Disquisitio an Pelagiana sint Dogmata quae nunc sub eo nomine traducuntur, Paris 1622 [= *BG* n° 937].

Eur. Trag. Phoen. = Euripidis tragoedia Phoenissae, Emendata ex manuscriptis, & latina facta ab Hugone Grotio, Paris 1630 [= *BG* n° 496].

GV = 'Geloofs Voorberecht', Ms. in Bibliothèque Nationale Paris, Fonds Néerlandais n° 34.

Hist. Gotth. = Historia Gotthorum, Vandalorum et Longobardorum, ab Hugone Grotio partim versa, partim in ordinem digesta, Amsterdam 1655 [= *BG* n° 735].

IBP = De iure belli ac pacis libri tres. In quibus ius naturae & gentium, item iuris publici praecipua explicantur, ed. B.J.A. de Kanter—Van Hettinga Tromp, Leiden 1939; facsimile reprint with 'annotationes novae', ed. R. Feenstra et al., Aalen 1939.

Imp. = De imperio summarum potestatum circa sacra [= *BG* n° 907], critical edition with introduction, English translation and commentary by H.J. van Dam [Studies in the History of Christian Thought, 102], Leiden etc. 2001.

IPC = De iure praedae commentarius, ed. H.G. Hamaker, The Hague 1868 [= *BG* n° 684].

Luc. Phars. = M. Annaei Lucani Pharsalia, sive de bello civili Caesaris et Pompeii Libri X. Ex emendatione Hugonis Grotii, cum eius ad loca insigniora notis, Leiden 1626 [= *BG* n° 425].

Mel. = *Meletius sive de iis quae inter christianos conveniunt epistola.* Critical edition with translation, commentary and introduction by G.H.M. Posthumus Meyjes, [Studies in the History of Christian Thought, 40], Leiden etc. 1988.

ML = *Mare Liberum, sive de iure quod Batavis competit ad Indicana commercia dissertatio,* Leiden 1609 [= *BG* n° 54].

Mort. J. Arm. = *In Mortem Jacobi Arminii,* in *PC* [= *BG* n° 1], pp. 304–7.

Orat. = *Oratio habita in Senatu Amstelredamensi* [= *BG* n° 847] in *OT* IV, pp. 75–94.

Ordin. Pietas = *Ordinum Hollandiae ac Westfrisiae pietas ab improbissimis multorum calumniis [. . .] vindicata* [= *BG* n° 817 sqq.] (1613), Critical edition with English translation and commentary by E. Rabbie, [Studies in the History of Christian Thought, 66], Leiden etc. 1995.

Orig. gent. = *De origine gentium Americanarum dissertatio altera* [= *BG* n° 731].

OT = *Opera Theologica,* vols. I–IV, Basel 1732; facsimile reprint Stuttgart, Bad Cannstatt 1972.

Pac. Ecc. = *Via ad pacem ecclesiasticam* [= *BG* n° 1150] in *OT* IV, pp. 535–49.

Parall. = *Parallelon rerumpublicarum liber tertius. De moribus ingeniorumque populorum Atheniensium, Romanorum, Batavorum,* ed. J. Meerman, Haarlem 1801–03 [= *BG* n° 750].

PC = *Poemata Collecta & magnam partem nunc primum edita a fratre Guilielmo Grotio,* Leiden 1617 [= *BG* n° 1].

Remonst. = *Remonstrantie nopende de ordre die in de landen van Hollandt ende Westvrieslandt dijent gestelt op de joden,* ed. J. Meijer, Amsterdam 1949 [= *BG* n° 816].

Riv. Apol. Disc. = *Rivetiani Apologetici pro schismate contra Votum pacis facti discussio* [= *BG* n° 1195] in *OT* IV, pp. 679–745.

Sacra = *Sacra in quibus Adamus Exul* [= *BG* n° 21] in *Dichtwerken* I 1a–1b.

Sat. = *Defensio fidei catholicae de satisfactione Christi adversus Faustum Socinum Senensem,* ed. E. Rabbie, English transl. H. Mulder (Hugo Grotius, Opera theologica, I), Maastricht/Assen 1990.

Sensus = *Sensus librorum sex quos pro veritate religionis Christianae Batavice scripsit Hugo Grotius,* Leiden 1627 [= *BG* n° 944].

Stob. Dicta Poetarum = *Dicta Poetarum quae apud Io. Stobaeum exstant,* Paris 1623 [= *BG* n° 458].

Uytl. = *Uytlegginghe van het Gebedt ons Heeren Iesu Christi, ghenaemt het Vader-ons* [n.p.] 1619 [= *BG* n° 121].

Verantw. = *Verantwoordingh van de wettelijcke regieringh van Hollandt ende West-Frieslandt,* Hoorn 1622 [= *BG* n° 872].

Votum = *Votum pro pace ecclesiastica, contra examen Andreae Riveti et alios irreconciliabiles,* [= *BG* n° 1183] in *OT* IV, pp. 653–76.

Vraghe = *Vraghe en antwoordt over den doop, Ghestelt in zijn gevanckenisse voor zijn dochter Cornelia de Groot* [n.p.] 1618 [= *BG* n° 59].

VRC = *De veritate religionis christianae,* ed. J.T. Bergman, Leiden 1831 [= *BG* n° 1000].

VRC² = *De veritate religionis Christianae. Editio secunda, priore auctior et emendatior,* Leiden 1629 [= *BG* n° 946].

VRC³ = *De veritate religionis christianae. Editio tertia, prioribus auctior, et emendatior,* Leiden 1632 [= *BG* n° 947].

VRCⁿ = *De veritate religionis christianae. Editio nova, additis annotationibus in quibus testimonia,* Paris 1640 [= *BG* n° 950].

V. *Contemporary Works*

Apologia pro confessione sive declaratio sententiae eorum, qui in foederato Belgio vocantur remonstrantes, super praecipuis articulis religionis christianae. Contra censuram quatuor professorum Leidensium, [n.p.] 1629.

Batelier, J.J., *Confutatio insulsi et maledici libri, quem adversus remonstrantes edidit Gisbertus Voetius theologiae in academia Ultrajectina professor, titulo Thersites heautontimorumeni,* [n.p.] 1637.

——, *Gisberto Voetii doctoris et professoris theologiae academia anti-remonstrantico-libertinica seu methodus disputandi adversus remonstrantes; exhibita in tractatu cui titulus 'Remonstranto-Libertinus'*, Utrecht 1637.

Brandt, G., *Historie der reformatie en andere kerkelyke geschiedenissen in en omtrent de Nederlanden*, vol. 4, Rotterdam 1704.

Broughton, H. *Commentarius in Danielem, primum anglice scriptus ab Hughone Broughton, nunc latinitate donatus per Johannem Boreel*, Basel 1599.

Casaubonus, I., *De rebus sacris et ecclesiasticis exercitationes XVI ad Cardin. Baronii Prolegomena in Annales et primam eorum partem de Jesu Christi nativitate, vita, passione, assumtione*, London 1614.

Castellio, S., *De arte dubitandi et confitendi, ignorandi et sciendi*, ed. E. Feist-Hirsch [Studies in Medieval and Reformation Thought, 29], Leiden 1981.

Censura in confessionem sive declarationem sententiam eorum qui in foederato Belgio remonstrantes vocantur, super praecipuis articulis christianae religionis a S.S. theologiae profess. academiae Leydensis instituta, Leiden 1626.

Chalcocondyle Atheniensis, L., *De origine et rebus gestis Turcarum libri X*, Basel 1556.

Chelec oder thalmudischer Jüdenschatz, ist ein Capittel des jüdischen Thalmuds dessen fürnehmster Inhalt in der Vorrede an den Leser und im letzten Register zu finden ist. Der werthen Christen zu einer Probe fürgestellet und frewlich verdeutschet durch Christianum Gerson, Helmstadt 1610.

Confessio sive declaratio sententiae pastorum qui in foederato Belgio remonstrantes vocantur, super praecipuis articulis religionis christianae, [n.p.] 1621.

Crellius, F., *Isagoge logica in duas partes distributa, in communem et propriam*, Neustadt 1581.

Crellius, J., *Ad librum Hugonis Grotii quem de satisfactione Christi adversus Faustum Socinum Senensem scripsit responsio . . .*, in *J. Crellii Operum tomus quartus scripta eiusdem didactica et polemica complectens*, Irenopoli [= Amsterdam] after 1656.

Critici Sacri, sive annotata doctissimorum virorum in Vetus ac Novum Testamentum. Quibus accedunt tractatus varii theologico-philologici. Editio nova in novem tomos distributa, multis anecdotis commentariis ac indice ad totum opus locupletissimo, aucta, Amsterdam/Utrecht 1698.

Episcopius, S., *Brief inde welcke de gront van de remonstranten aengaende hare Belijdenis ende eenstemminge in het gheloove, naerstelick ontdekt wort. Met een voorreden aende Hoog. mog. Heeren Staten General der Vereenighde Nederlanden*, The Hague 1620.

Erasmus, D., *Paraclesis*, in *Ausgewählte Werke*, ed. A. Holborn – H. Holborn, Munich 1933, pp. 139–49.

——, *De libero arbitrio DIATRIBE sive collatio*, in *Opera omnia*, vol 9, Hildesheim 1962 [photomechanical reprint of the edition of J. Clericus, Leiden 1706], pp. 1215–48.

Everardus, N., *Topicorum, seu de locis legalibus liber*, Leuven 1516.

Fagius, P., *Thargum hoc est Paraphrasis Onkeli Chaldaica in Sacra Biblia, ex Chaldaico in Latinum fidelissime versa, additis in singula fere capita succintis annotationibus*, Argentorati [= Strasbourg] 1546.

Gammarus, P.A., *Legalis dialectica, in qua de modo argumentandi et locis argumentorum legaliter disputatur*, Bologna 1507.

Heinsius, D., *Nederduytsche Poemata*. Bij een vergadert en uytgegeven door Petrus Scriverius, Amsterdam 1616.

——, *Cras credo hodie nihil sive modus tandem sit ineptiarum, Satyra Menippea*, Leiden 1621.

——, *Monsterken van de ontrouwicheyt ende notoire leugenen der genoemde remonstranten, nu onlancx in seker schrift genoemt Antwoorde opde Extracten etc. uytgestroyt tegens den Hoochgeleerden ende wijtberoemden Daniel Heinsius*, Leiden 1629.

——, *Bacchus en Christus*. Twee lofzangen van Daniel Heinsius. Opnieuw uitgegeven door L.Ph. Rank, J.D.P. Warner en F.L. Zwaan, [Zwolse drukken en herdrukken voor de Maatschappij der Nederlandsche Letterkunde te Leiden], Zwolle 1965.

Hotman, F., *Franco-Gallia sive tractatus isagogicus de regimine regum Galliae*, Paris 1574.

Junius, F., *Eirenicum de pace ecclesiae catholicae inter christianos, quamvis diversos sententiis, religiose procuranda, colenda atque continuanda . . .*, in *Opuscula theologica selecta*. Recognovit et praefatus est Abr. Kuyperus, Amsterdam 1882, pp. 395–494.

Leunclavius, J., *Historiae musulmanae Turcarum, de monumentis ipsorum exscriptae libri XVIII*, Frankfurt 1594.

Maimonides, M., *Constitutiones de fundamentis legis Rabbi Mosis fil. Maüemon, Latine redditae per G. Vorstium*, Amsterdam 1638.

Maresius, S., *Oratio inauguralis de usu et abusu rationis in rebus theologicis et fidei*, Groningen 1643.

Melanchthon, Ph., *Loci communes rerum theologicarum seu hypotyposes theologicae*, in *Philippi Melanchthonis Opera quae supersunt omnia* [Corpus Reformatorum, 21, ed. C.G. Bretschneider – H.E. Bindseil], Braunschweig 1854.

Meursius, J., *Illustris academia Lugd. batava, id est virorum clarissimorum icones, elogia ac vitae, qui eam scriptis suis illustrarunt*, Leiden 1613.

———, *Athenae Batavae, sive de urbe Leidensi et academia, virisque claris qui utramque ingenio suo atque scriptis illustrarunt*, Leiden 1625.

Molinaeus, P., *Elementa logica*, Leiden 1607.

Mornay, Ph. Duplessis, *L'Advertissement aux juifs sur la venue du Messie*, Saumur 1607.

Naeranus, S., *Propulsatio contumeliarum quibus G. Voetius in Thersite suo petit*, [n.p.] 1636.

Philopatris, T. [= C. Niëllius], *Proeve van de conscientieuse oprechtigheydt ende wijsheydt Gisberti Voetii, ende van eenighe sijne medestanders. Waerinne uyt eenighe harer schriften aenghewesen wordt, hoe onchristelijck ende ontrouwelijck van haer tegen de remonstranten wort gehandelt, ende met wat onwaerheyden sy sommighe aensienlijcke personen soecken te onteeren. In 't Nederduytsch uytghegeven, tot waerschouwinghe van alle vromen christenen, opdat sy sulcke luyden niet al te veel gheloofs gheven ende wel toesien aen wien sy hare zielen toevertrouwen*, [n.p.] 1637.

Pocock, E., *Specimen historiae Arabum*, Oxford 1806.

Postel, G., *De originibus seu de Hebraicae linguae et gentis antiquitate deque variarum linguarum affinitate liber*, Paris 1538.

———, *Linguarum duodecim characteribus differentium alphabetum, introductio ac legendi modus longe facilimus*, Paris 1538.

———, *Des histoires orientales et principalement des Turcs*, Paris 1575.

Praestantium ac eruditorum virorum epistolae ecclesiasticae et theologicae quarum longa pars scripta est a Jac. Arminio, Joan. Uytenbogardo, Conr. Vorstio, . . . ed. C. Hartsoeker, Ph. a Limborch, 3rd ed., Amsterdam 1704.

Reifferscheid, A., *Briefe G.M. Lingelsheims, M. Berneggers und ihrer Freunde*, [Quellen zur Geschichte des geistigen Lebens in Deutschland während des siebzehnten Jahrhunderts, 1] Heilbronn 1889.

Sandius, C.C., *Bibliotheca anti-trinitariorum*, Freistadt [= Amsterdam] 1684.

Schindler, V., *Lexicon pentaglotton Hebraicum, Chaldaicum, Syriacum, Thalmudico-rabbinicum et Arabicum post auctoris obitum in lucem prolatum*, Hanover 1612.

Schoockius, M., *Remonstranto-libertinus a cl. d. Gisberto Voetio th. d. et prof. in acad. Ultrajectina in Thersite heautontimorumeno autokatakritos deprehensus in blasphemiis in Deum ac religionem, in calumniis et mendaciis in illustr. ordd. ampliss. magistratus etc. indicante ac provocante eum ad tribunal societatis sociniano-remonstranticae*, Utrecht 1637.

———, *Claere en oprechte ontdeckinge der genaemder remonstranten leugenen en lasteringen, tegen de hooge en laage overigheden, gereformeerde kercken, en haere yeverighe voorstanders. Alsoock een bondich vertooch van haere sociniaensche grouwelen, alles vergadert uyt die naemloose boecxkens geintituleert: I. Proeve van de conscientieuse oprechtigheydt Gisberti Voetii. II. Academia Gisberti Voetii. III. Den rechten remonstrantsche theologant*, Utrecht 1638.

[Socinus, F.], *De auctoritate S. Scripturae. Opusculum his temporibus nostris utilissimum, quemadmodum intelligi potest ex praecipuis rerum, quae in ipso tractantur, capitibus. Ea vero proxime seqq. pagellis notata sunt. In praefatione ad lectorem ratio huius editionis exponitur*, Steinfurt 1611 [= Petit, n° 19].

Sylburgius, F., *Saracenica sive Moamethica*, Heidelberg 1595.

Thou, J.A. de, *Historiarum sui temporis pars prima*, Paris 1604.

Voetius, G., *Thersites heautontimorumenos, hoc est remonstrantium hyperaspistes, catechesi, et liturgiae Germanicae, Gallicae, et Belgicae denuo insultans, retusus: idemque provocatus ad probationem mendaciorum, et calumniarum, quae in illustr. dd. ordd. et ampliss. magistratus Belgii, religionem reformatam, ecclesias, synodos, pastores etc. sine ratione, sine modo effudit*, Utrecht 1635.
——, *Selectarum disputationum fasciculus*, Recognovit et praefatus est Abr. Kuyper, Amsterdam 1887.

B) LITERATURE

Albertsen, L.L., *Das Lehrgedicht. Eine Geschichte der antikisierenden Sachepik in der neueren deutschen Literatur mit einem unbekannten Gedicht Albrecht von Hallers*, Aarhus 1967.

Andrieu, J., *Bibliographie générale de l'Agenais*, 3 vols. Paris – Agen 1886.

Arnim, H. von, 'Das Ethische in Aristoteles' Topik', *Sitzungsberichte der Akademie der Wissenschaften*, 205 (1934), 325–57.

Atkinson, G., *Les Nouveaux Horizons de la renaissance française*, Paris 1935.

Baldwin, C.S., *Renaissance Literary Theory and Practice. Classicism in the Rhetoric and Poetic of Italy, France and England 1400–1600*, New York 1939.

Barth, H.M., *Atheismus und Orthodoxie. Analysen und Modelle christlicher Apologetik im 17. Jahrhundert*, Göttingen 1971.

Baumgarten, A.I., *The Phoenician History of Philo of Byblos. A Commentary*, Leiden 1981.

Beck, H.G., *Kirche und theologische Literatur im byzantinischen Reich*, Munich 1959.

Berg, J. van den, *Constrained by Jesus' Love. An Inquiry into the Motives for the Missionary Awakening in Great Britain in the Period between 1698 and 1815*, Kampen 1956.

Berkel, K. van, 'Universiteit en natuurwetenschap in de 17de eeuw, in het bijzonder in de Republiek', in *Natuurwetenschappen van Renaissance tot Darwin. Thema's uit de wetenschapsgeschiedenis*, ed. H.A.M. Snelders and K. van Berkel, The Hague 1981, pp. 107–30.

Betz, O. 'Miracles in the Writings of Flavius Josephus', in *Josephus, Judaism and Christianity*, ed. L.H. Feldman and G. Hata, Leiden 1987, pp. 212–35.

Blau, J.L., *The Christian Interpretation of the Cabala in the Renaissance*, New York 1944.

Blumenkranz, B., *Juifs et chrétiens dans le monde occidental, 430–1096*, Paris/The Hague 1960.

——, 'Vie et survie de la polémique antijuive', *Studia Patristica*, 1 (1957), 460–76.

Bobzin, H., 'Martin Luthers Beiträge zur Kenntnis und Kritik des Islam', *Neue Zeitschrift für systematische Theologie und Religionsphilosophie*, 27 (1985), 262–89.

——, 'Islam und Christentum (7.–19. Jahrhundert)', *TRE*, XVI pp. 336–49.

——, 'Über Theodor Biblianders Arbeit am Koran (1542/3)', *Zeitschrift der deutschen morgenländischen Gesellschaft*, 136 (1986), 347–63.

Bornemann, U., *Anlehnung und Abgrenzung. Untersuchungen zur Rezeption der niederländischen Literatur der deutschen Dichtungsreform des siebzehnten Jahrhunderts*, Assen/Amsterdam 1976.

Borst, A., *Der Turmbau von Babel. Geschichte der Meinungen über Ursprung und Vielfalt der Sprachen und Völker*, 6 vols., Stuttgart 1957–63.

Bots, H. and Leroy, P., *Correspondance intégrale d'André Rivet et de Claude Sarrau, 1641–1650*, 3 vols., Amsterdam 1978–82.

Boxer, C.R., *The Dutch Seaborne Empire 1600–1800*, London 1965.

Breugelmans, R., 'Maire's Editions of Grotius' De veritate religionis christianae from 1627 to 1640', *Quaerendo*, 22 (1992), 191–6.

Bruyère, N., *Methode et dialectique dans l'oeuvre de La Ramée*, Paris 1984.

Buck, A., *Machiavelli*. [Erträge der Forschung, 226] Darmstadt 1985.

Busken Huet, C., *Het land van Rembrand. Studiën over de Noordnederlandsche beschaving in de zeventiende eeuw*, 5th ed., Haarlem [n.d.].

Camporeale, S.I., 'Lorenzo Valla. "Repastinatio liber primus, retorica e linguaggio"', in *Lorenzo Valla e l'umanesimo Italiano. Atti del convegno internazionale di studi umanistici, Parma 18–19 ottobre 1984*, Padua 1986, pp. 217–40.

Cantimori, D., *Italienische Haeretiker der Spätrenaissance*, Basel 1949.

Cioranesco, A., *Bibliographie de la littérature française du XVIe siècle*, Paris etc. 1959.

Cohen. G., *Ecrivains français en Hollande dans la première moitié du XVIIe siècle*, Paris 1920.

Colish, M.L., *The Stoic Tradition from Antiquity to the Early Middle Ages*, 2 vols., Leiden 1985.

Colonna, M.E., *Gli storici bizantini del iv al xv secolo*, Naples 1956.

Combet, S., *Notice sur Mézeray*, Alais 1844.

Curtius, E.R., *Europäische Literatur und lateinisches Mittelalter*, 6th ed., Bern/Munich 1967.

D'Alverny, M.Th., 'Deux traductions latines du Coran au Moyen Age', *Archives d'histoire doctrinale et littéraire du Moyen-Age*, 22–3 (1947–8), 69–131.

Daniel, N.A., *Islam and the West. The Making of an Image*, Edinburgh 1960.

Daniélou, H., *Message évangélique et culture hellénistique aux IIe et IIIe siècles*, Paris 1961.

Dannenfeldt, K.H., *The Renaissance Humanists and the Knowledge of Arabic*, New York 1955.

Davidson, H.A., *Proofs for Eternity, Creation and the Existence of God in Medieval Islamic and Jewish Philosophy*, New York/London 1987.

De onbekende Voetius. Voordrachten wetenschappelijk symposium Utrecht 3 maart 1989, ed. J. van Oort, C. Graafland, A. de Groot and O.J. de Jong, Kampen 1989.

Deppe, F., *Niccolò Machiavelli. Zur Kritik der reinen Politik*. [Kleine Bibliothek, Wissenschaft: 445], Cologne 1987.

Dibon, P., *L'Enseignement philosophique dans les universités néerlandaises à l'époque pré-cartésienne (1575–1650)*, Leiden 1954.

——, 'L'Influence de Ramus aux universités néerlandaises du 17e siècle', in *Actes du XIeme congrès international de philosophie Bruxelles, 20–26 Aout 1953*, 14 [Volume complémentaire et communications du colloque de logique], Amsterdam/Leuven 1953, pp. 307–11.

Dienstag, J.I., 'Christian translators of Maimonides' Mishneh Torah into Latin', in *Salo Wittmayer Baron Jubilee Volume on the Occasion of his eightieth Birthday*, English section, Jerusalem 1974.

Dockery, B., *Christopher Davenport. Friar and Diplomat*, London 1960.

Droetto, A., *Studi Groziani*, Turin 1968.

Dubois, C.G., *Mythe et langage au seizième siècle*, Bordeaux 1970.

——, *La Conception de l'histoire en France au XVIeme siècle (1560–1610)*, Paris 1977.

Duker, A.C., *Gisbertus Voetius*, 3 vols. with index volume, Leiden 1897–1915.

Dulles, A., *A History of Apologetics*, London 1971.

Eekhof, A., 'Heeft Hugo de Groot Arabisch gekend?', *Nederlands Archief voor Kerkgeschiedenis*, new series, 17 (1924), 231–4.

Erasmus in Hispania, Vives in Belgio. Acta colloquii Brugensis 23–26, IX 1985, ed. J. IJsewijn and A. Losada, Colloquia Europalia 11, Leuven 1986.

Etter, E.L., *Tacitus in der Geistesgeschichte des 16. und 17. Jahrhunderts*, Basel/Stuttgart 1966.

Europäische Lehrdichtung. Festschrift für Walter Naumann zum 70. Geburtstag. Herausgegeben von H.G. Rötzer – H. Walz, Darmstadt 1981.

Eyffinger, A., 'Some marginal notes', *Grotiana*, new series 2 (1981), 115–22.

——. and Vermeulen, B.P., *Hugo de Groot; denken over oorlog en vrede* (Geschiedenis van de wijsbegeerte in Nederland, 81), Baarn 1991.

Eysinga, W.J.M. van, *Huigh de Groot. Een schets*, Haarlem 1945.

——, 'Iets over de Groots jongelingsjaren', *De Gids*, 105, 4 (1941), 36–67.

Fabian, B., 'Das Lehrgedicht als Problem der Poetik', in *Die nicht mehr schönen Künste, Grenzphänomenen des Aesthetischen.* [Poetik und Hermeneutik, 3], Munich 1968, pp. 67–89.

Feenstra, R., 'La systématique du droit dans l'oeuvre de Grotius', in *La sistema giuridica. Storia, teori e problemi attuali.* [Biblioteca internazionale di cultura, 122], Rome 1991, 333–43.

———, 'Quelques remarques sur les sources utilisées par Grotius dans ses travaux de droit naturel', in *The World of Hugo Grotius (1583–1645)*, Proceedings of the International Colloquium Organized by the Grotius Committee of the Royal Netherlands Academy of Arts and Sciences Rotterdam 6–9 April 1983, Amsterdam/Maarssen 1984, 65–81.

Fikentscher, W., *De fide et perfidia. Der Treuegedanke in den Staatsparallelen des Hugo Grotius aus heutiger Sicht*, Munich 1979.

Fraenkel, P., *Testimonia Patrum. The Function of the Patristic Argument in the Theology of Philip Melanchthon*, Geneva 1961.

Fück, J., *Die arabischen Studien in Europa vom 12. bis in den Anfang des 19. Jahrhunderts.* [Beiträge zur Arabistik, Semitistik und Islamswissenschaft], Leipzig 1944.

Fumaroli, M., *L'Age de l'éloquence. Rhétorique et 'res literaria' de la Renaissance au seuil de l'époque classique*, Geneva 1980.

Gerl, H.B., *Rhetorik als Philosophie. Lorenzo Valla*, Munich 1974.

Gerlach, H., *Het proces tegen Oldenbarnevelt en de 'Maximen in den staet'*, Haarlem 1965.

Goethe, J.W. von, *Werke.* Herausgegeben im Auftrag der Grossherzogin Sophie von Sachsen, vol. 41, 2, Weimar 1903.

Göllner, C., *Turcica: III. Band. Die Türkerfrage in der öffentlichen Meinung Europas im 16. Jahrhundert*, Bucharest/Baden-Baden 1978.

Graf, P., *Ludwig Vives als Apologet.* [Inaugural dissertation der theologischen Fakultät Freiburg], Freiburg 1932.

———, *Luis Vives como apologeta. Contribución a la historia de la apologetica por el Dr Pablo Graf.* Tradución directa del alemán por J.M. Millas Vallicrosa, Madrid 1943.

Grafton, A., 'Joseph Scaliger and Historical Chronology: the Rise and Fall of a Discipline', *History and Theory*, 14 (1975), 156–85.

———, 'Protestant versus Prophet. Isaac Casaubon on Hermes Trismegistus', *Journal of the Warburg and Courtauld Institutes*, 46 (1983), 78–93.

———, *Joseph Scaliger. A Study in the History of Classical Scholarship, I: Textual Criticism and Exegesis*, Oxford 1983.

———. and de Jonge, H.J., *Joseph Scaliger. A Bibliography 1852–1982*, The Hague 1983.

———, *Defenders of the Text. The Traditions of Scholarship in an Age of Science, 1450–1800*, London/Cambridge Massachusetts 1991.

Grant, R.M., *Miracle and Natural Law in Graeco-Roman and Early Christian Thought*, Amsterdam 1952.

Groenveld, S., 'De loop der gebeurtenissen 1609–1650', in *De bruid in de schuit. De consolidatie van de Republiek 1609–1650*, Zutphen 1985, pp. 10–140.

Groot, W. de, *Broeders gevangenisse. Dagboek van Willem de Groot betreffende het verblijf van zynen broeder Hugo op Loevestein.* Uit echte bescheiden aangevuld en opgehelderd door H. Vollenhoven, The Hague 1842.

Gülich, A., *Opitz' Übersetzungen aus dem Französischen*, Kiel 1972.

Güterbock, C., *Der Islam im Lichte der byzantinischen Polemik*, Berlin 1912.

Guy, A., *Vives ou l'humanisme engagé*, Paris 1972.

Hacken, R.D., *The Religious Thought of Martin Opitz as the Determinant of his Poetic Theory and Practice*, [Stuttgarter Arbeiten zur Germanistik, n° 18], Stuttgart 1976.

Haentjens, A.H., *Simon Episcopius als apologeet van het remonstrantisme in zijn leven en werken geschetst*, Leiden 1899.

———, *Hugo de Groot als godsdienstig denker*, Amsterdam 1946.

Hagemann, L., *Der Kuran im Verständnis und Kritik bei Nikolaus von Kues*, Munich 1976.

Haggenmacher, P., *Grotius et la doctrine de la guerre juste*, Paris 1983.

Harrie, J., 'Du Plessis Mornay, Foix-Candale and the Hermetic Religion of the World', *Renaissance Quarterly*, 31 (1978), 495–514.

Heim, K., *Das Gewissheitsproblem in der systematischen Theologie bis zu Schleiermacher*, Leipzig 1911.

Heppe, H. and Bizer, E., *Die Dogmatik der evangelisch reformierten Kirche*, Neukirchen 1958.

Herzog, I., 'John Selden and Jewish Law', *Journal of Comparative Legislation and International Law*, 13 (1931), 236–45.

Holte, R., 'Logos spermatikos, Christianity and Ancient Philosophy according to St Justin's Apologies', *Studia Theologica*, 12 (1958), 109–68.

——, *Béatitude et sagesse. Saint Augustine et la problème de la fin de l'homme dans la philosophie ancienne*, Paris 1962.

Honders, H.J., *Andreas Rivetus als invloedrijk gereformeerd theoloog in Holland's bloeitijd*, The Hague 1930.

Hove, A. van, *La Doctrine du miracle chez Saint Thomas et son accord avec les principes de la recherche scientifique*, Paris 1927.

Huizinga, J., 'Hugo de Groot en zijn eeuw', *Tien Studiën*, Haarlem 1926, pp. 99–116.

——, 'Grotius' plaats in de geschiedenis van den menschelijken geest, *Tien Studiën*, Haarlem 1926, pp. 117–25.

——, *Patriottisme en nationalisme in de Europeesche geschiedenis tot het einde der 19e eeuw*, Haarlem 1940.

Jäger, H.W., 'Zur Poetik der Lehrdichtung in Deutschland', *Deutsche Vierteljahrschrift für Literaturwissenschaft und Geistesgeschichte*, 44 (1970), 544–76.

Jonge, C. de, *De irenische ecclesiologie van Franciscus Junius (1542–1602)*. Onderzoek naar de plaats van het geschrift *Le Paisible Chrestien* (1593) in zijn theologische denken, Nieuwkoop 1980.

——, 'The Study of the New Testament' in *Leiden University in the Seventeenth Century. An Exchange of Learning*, ed. Th. H. Lunsingh Scheurleer and G.H.M. Posthumus Meyjes, Leiden 1975, 65–109.

——, 'Hugo Grotius exégète du Nouveau Testament', in *The World of Hugo Grotius (1583–1645)*, Proceedings of the International Colloquium Organized by the Grotius Committee of the Royal Netherlands Academy of Arts and Sciences Rotterdam 6–9 April 1983, Amsterdam/Maarssen 1984, pp. 97–115.

Jugie, M., 'La Vie et les oeuvres d'Euthyme Zigabène,' *Echo d'Orient*, 15 (1912), 215–225.

Juynboll, W.M.C., *Zeventiende-eeuwse beoefenaars van het Arabisch in Nederland*, Utrecht 1931.

Kantorowicz, E.H., *The King's Two Bodies. A Study in Medieval Political Theory*, Princeton 1970.

Katchen, A.L., *Christian Hebraists and Dutch Rabbis. Seventeenth Century Apologetics and the Study of Maimonides' Mishneh Torah*, Cambridge Massachusetts/London 1984.

Kelley, D.R., *Foundations of Modern Historical Scholarship. Language, Law and History in the French Renaissance*, New York/London 1970.

Khoury, A.Th., 'Gespräch über den Glauben zwischen Euthymios Zigabenos und einem sarazenischen Philosophen', *Zeitschrift für Missions-wissenschaft und Religionswissenschaft*, 48 (1964), 192–203.

——, *La Controverse byzantine avec l'islam*, Paris 1969.

——, *Polémique byzantine contre l'islam (VIIIe–XIIIe siècle)*, Leiden 1972.

Koecher, J.C., 'Historia libri Grotiani de Veritate religionis Christianae', in Hugo Grotius, *De veritate religionis Christianae*. Variis dissertationibus illustratus, Opera ac studio Io. Chr. Koecheri, Halle 1739, pp. 1–192.

Kossmann, E.H., 'The Dutch Case. A National or Regional Culture', *Transactions of the Royal Historical Society*, 29 (1979), 155–69.

Krauss, S., *Das Leben Jesu nach jüdischen Quellen*, Berlin 1902.

Kristeller, P.O., *Renaissance Thought. The Classic, Scholastic and Humanist Strains* [a revised and enlarged edition of *The Classics and Renaissance Thought*], New York etc. 1961.

Kritzeck, L., *Peter the Venerable and Islam*, Princeton 1964.

Krusche, W., *Das Wirken des heiligen Geistes nach Calvin*, Berlin 1957.

Kühler, W.J., 'Remonstranten en socinianen', in G.J. Heering (ed.), *De remonstranten. Gedenkboek bij het 300-jarig bestaan der Remonstrantsche Broederschap*, Leiden 1919, pp. 137–58.

———, *Het socinianisme in Nederland*. Voorzien van een inleiding van A. de Groot en vermeerderd met een register samengesteld door D. Visser, Leeuwarden 1980 [= reprint of the first edition, Leiden 1912].

Kuiper, E.J., 'Hugo de Groot en de remonstranten', *NTT*, 37 (1983), 111–25.

Kümmel, W.G., *Das Neue Testament. Geschichte der Erforschung seiner Probleme*, Freiburg 1970.

Lachs, Ph.S., 'Hugo Grotius' use of Jewish Sources in On the Law of War and Peace', *Renaissance Quarterly*, 30 (1977), 181–200.

Lang, A., *Die Entfaltung des apologetischen Problems in der Scholastik des Mittelalters*, Freiburg 1962.

Laplanche, F., *L'Évidence du Dieu chrétien. Religion, culture et société dans l'apologétique protestante de la France classique (1576–1670)*, Strasbourg 1983.

Larroque, D., *Vie de Fr. Eudes de Mézeray*, Paris 1720.

Lausberg, H., *Handbuch der literarischen Rhetorik*, 2nd ed., Munich 1970.

Lecler, J., *Histoire de la tolérance au siècle de la Réforme*, vol. 1, Paris 1955.

Leipoldt, J., *Geschichte des neutestamentlichen Kanons*, vol. II, Leipzig 1908.

Liebs, D., *Lateinische Rechtsregeln und Rechtssprichwörter*, Darmstadt 1986.

Looten, C., *De Grotio christianae religionis defensore*, Insulis [= Lille] 1889.

Maffei, D., *Gli inizi dell' umanesimo giuridico*, Milan 1956.

Mallinckrodt, W., 'Grotius' gedicht op het sterven van Arminius (1609 19 oktober)', *Geloof en Vrijheid* 40 (1906), 29–80.

Mann, U., *Das Wunderbare. Wunder-Segen und Engel*, [Handbuch systematischer Theologie, Bd. 17], Gütersloh 1979.

Manuel, P., 'Une Encyclopédie de l'islam. Le recueil de Bibliander 1543 et 1550', *En terre d'islam*, 21 (1946), 31–7.

Meeks, W.A., 'The Divine Agent and his Counterfeit in Philo and the Fourth Gospel',in *Aspects of Religious Propaganda in Judaism and Early Christianity*, ed. E. Schüssler Fiorenza, London 1976, pp. 43–50.

Meijer, H., *Geschichte der Lehre von den Keimkräften von der Stoa bis zum Ausgang der Patristik nach den Quellen dargestellt*, Bonn 1914.

Mesnard, P., *L'Essor de la philosophie politique au XVIᵉ siècle*, Paris 1969.

Meter, J.H., *The Literary Theories of Daniel Heinsius*, Assen 1984.

Millies, H.C., 'Over de Oostersche vertalingen van het beroemd geschrift van Hugo Grotius, *De veritate religionis christianae*', *Verslagen en Mededeelingen der Koninklijke Akademie van Wetenschappen, Afdeeling Letterkunde*, 7, Amsterdam 1863, 108–34.

Molhuysen, P.C., *Bronnen tot de geschiedenis der Leidsche universiteit (1574–1610)*, [RGP 20] The Hague 1913.

Moltmann, J., 'Zur Bedeutung des Petrus Ramus für Philosophie und Theologie im Calvinismus', *Zeitschrift für Kirchengeschichte*, 68 (1957), 295–318.

Monneret de Villart, U., 'La vita, le opere e i viaggi di fratre Ricoldo da Montecroce O.P.', *Orientalia christiana periodica*, 10 (1944), 227–74.

Nauta, D., *Samuel Maresius*, Amsterdam 1935.

Nellen, H.J.M., 'Le Rôle de la correspondance de Grotius pendant son exil', in *The World of Hugo Grotius (1583–1645)*, Proceedings of the International Colloquium

Organised by the Grotius Committee of the Royal Netherlands Academy of Arts and Sciences Rotterdam 6–9 April 1983, Amsterdam/Maarssen 1984, pp. 133–59.
——, 'In strict confidence: Grotius' correspondence with his Socinian friends', *Self presentation and social identification. The rhetoric and pragmatics of letter writing in early modern times*, ed. T. van Houdt et al., Louvain 2002, pp. 227–45.
——, *Hugo de Groot (1583–1645). De loopbaan van een geleerd staatsman*, Weesp 1985.
——, 'Grotius' Relations with the Huguenot Community of Charenton (1621–1635)', *Lias*, 12 (1985), 147–77.
——. and Rabbie, E., eds., Hugo Grotius theologian. Essays in honour of G.H.M. Posthumus Meyjes, [Studies in the History of Christian Thought, 55], Leiden etc. 1994.
Noreña, C.G., *Juan Luis Vives*, The Hague 1970.
Oehler, K., 'Der consensus omnium als Kriterium der Wahrheit in der antiken Philosophie und der Patristik', *Antike und Abendland*, 10 (1961), 103–29.
Ogonowksi, Z., 'Faustus Socinus 1539–1604', *Shapers of Religious Traditions in Germany, Switzerland and Poland 1560–1600*, ed. J. Raitt, New Haven/London 1981, pp. 643–65.
Oliver, J.H., 'The Civilizing Power. A Study of the Panathenaic Discourse of Aelius Aristides', *Transactions of the American Philosophical Society*, new series, 58 (1968), 5–36.
Ong, W.J., *Ramus, Method and the Decay of Dialogue. From the Art of Discourse to the Art of Reason*, Cambridge Massachusetts 1958.
Opstal, A.G. van, *André Rivet. Een invloedrijk Hugenoot aan het hof van Frederik Hendrik*, Harderwijk 1937.
Ostrogorsky, G., *Geschichte des byzantinischen Staates*, 2nd ed., Munich 1952.
Palm, H., *Beiträge zur Geschichte der Deutschen Literatur des XVI. und XVII. Jahrhunderts*, Breslau 1877.
Pérau, G.L.C., *Vie de Jérôme Bignon, advocat-général et conseiller d'état*, Paris 1757.
Peter, R. and Rott, J., *Les Lettres à Jean Calvion de la collection Sarrau*, Paris 1972.
Pfister, R., 'Die Zürcher Koranausgabe von 1542/43', *Evangelisches Missions-Magazine*, 99 (1955), 37–43.
Pintard, R., *Le Libertinage érudit dans la première moitié du XVIIe siècle*, Paris 1983 [= unrevised reprint of Paris 1943].
Pioli, G., *Fausto Socino. Vita—Opere—Fortuna. Contributo alla storia del liberalismo religioso*, Guanda 1952.
Places, E. des, 'Un Thème platonicien dans la tradition patristique: le juste crucifié, (Platon République 361 e4–362 a2)', *Studia Patristica*, 9 (1966), 30–40.
Plato, *Timaeus. A Calcidio translatus commentarioque instructus*. In societatem operis coniuncto P.J. Jensen edidit J.H. Waszink [Corpus Platonicum Medii Aevi, 4: ed. R. Klibansky], editio altera, London/Leiden 1975.
Pollard, A.W. and Redgrave, G.R., *A Short-Title Catalogue of Books Printed in England, Scotland and Ireland, and of English Books Printed Abroad 1475–1640*, second edition revised and enlarged, begun by W.A. Jackson and F.S. Ferguson, completed by K.F. Pantzer, I, London 1986.
Popkin, R.H., *The History of Scepticism from Erasmus to Descartes*, Assen 1964.
Posthumus Meyjes, G.H.M., *Jean Gerson. Apostle of Unity. His Church Politics and Ecclesiology* [Studies in the History of Christian Thought, vol. 94], Leiden 1999.
——, 'Protestants irenisme in de 16de en eerste helft van de 17de eeuw', *NTT*, 36 (1982), 205–22.
Rademaker, C.S.M., 'Books and Grotius at Loevestein', *Quaerendo*, 2 (1972), 2–29.
——, *Life and Work of Gerardus Joannes Vossius (1577–1649)*, Assen 1981.
Rijk, L.M. de, *Middeleeuwse wijsbegeerte*, 2nd ed. Assen 1977.
Risse, W., *Logik der Neuzeit*, 2 vols. Bad Cannstatt, 1964–70.
Roellenbleck, G., *Das epische Lehrgedicht Italiens im fünfzehnten und sechzehnten Jahrhundert: ein Beitrag zur Literaturgeschichte des Humanismus und der Renaissance* [Münchener romanistische Arbeiten, 43], Munich 1975.

Roldanus, C.W., *Hugo de Groot's Bewijs van den waren godsdienst*, Arnhem 1944.

Romein, J. and Romein, A., 'Huig de Groot, het Delfts orakel', in *Erflaters van onze beschaving. Nederlandse gestalten uit zes eeuwen*, 5th ed., Amsterdam 1979, pp. 231–56.

Rooden, P.T. van, *Theology, Biblical Scholarship and Rabbinical Studies in the Seventeenth Century. Constantijn L'Empereur (1591–1648), Professor of Hebrew and Theology at Leiden* (Studies in the History of Leiden University, 6), Leiden etc. 1989.

Rosenberg, A.W., 'Hugo Grotius as Hebraist', *Studia Rosenthaliana*, 12 (1978), 62–90.

Roy, C., *Hugo Grotius considéré comme apologète*, Colmar 1855.

Sassen, F., 'Grotius philosophe aristotélicien', *Grotiana*, 9 (1941–42), 38–53.

——, 'Het oudste wijsgeerig onderwijs te Leiden (1575–1619)', *Mededeelingen der Nederlandsche Akademie van Wetenschappen*, n° 4, (1941), 1–45.

Sax, D., *Carolus Niëllius*, Amsterdam 1896.

Scheibe, S., 'Zu einigen Grundprinzipien einer historisch-kritischen Ausgabe', in G. Martens and H. Zeller, eds., *Texte und Varianten. Probleme ihrer Edition und Interpretation*, Munich 1971, pp. 1–44.

Schnabel, E., *Inspiration und Offenbarung. Die Lehre vom Ursprung und Wesen der Bibel*, Wuppertal 1986.

Schnur, R., *Die französische Juristen im Konfessionellen Bürgerkrieg des 16. Jahrhunderts. Ein Beitrag zur Entstehungsgeschichte des modernen Staates*, Berlin 1962.

Schöffer, I., 'De crisis van de jonge Republiek, 1609–1625', in *Algemene Geschiedenis der Nederlanden*, vol. 6, Utrecht/Antwerp 1953, pp. 1–51.

——, 'The Batavian Myth during the Sixteenth and Seventeenth Centuries', in P.A.M. Geurts and A.E.M. Janssen, eds., *Geschiedschrijving in Nederland*, vol. 2, The Hague 1981, pp. 85–109.

Scholder, K., *Ursprung und Probleme der Bibelkritik im 17. Jahrhundert. Ein Beitrag zur Entstehung der historisch-kritischen Theologie* [Forschungen zur Geschichte und Lehre des Protestantismus, 33], Munich 1966.

Sellin, P.R., *Daniel Heinsius and Stuart England*, Leiden/London 1968.

Shapiro, B.J., *Probability and Certainty in Seventeenth Century England. A study of the Relationships between Natural Science, Religion, History, Law and Literature*, Princeton 1983.

Slee, J.C. van, *De geschiedenis van het socinianisme in Nederland*, Haarlem 1914.

Soutendam, J., 'Een onbekend werk van Huig de Groot uit zijn vroege jeugd (Hugonis Grotii oratio in laudem navigationis)', *Oud Holland. Nieuwe Bijdragen*, 7 (1889), 293–7.

Southern, R.W., *Western Views of Islam in the Middle Ages*, Cambridge Massachusetts 1962.

Spaans, J.W., 'Het bewijs van de waarheid der christelijke religie, Hugo de Groot "teghen de Mahumetisterije"', [unpublished paper, University of Leiden, Faculty of Theology 1982].

Stolleis, M., *Arcana imperii und ratio status, Bemerkungen zur politischen Rhetorik des frühen 17. Jahrhunderts*, Göttingen 1980.

Stylianopoulos, T., *Justin Martyr and the Mosaic Law*, Missoula Montana 1975.

Szyrocki, M., *Martin Opitz*, 2nd ed., Munich 1974.

Taal, J., 'Het geestelijk milieu van Grotius te Leiden', *Jaarboekje voor geschiedenis en oudheidkunde van Leiden en Rijnland (Leids Jaarboekje)*, 36 (1944), 124–42.

Tartar, G., *Dialogue islamo-chrétien sous le calife Al-Ma'mun (813–834). Les Épitres d'Al-Hashimi et d'Al-Kindi*, Paris 1955.

Tavard, G.H., *Holy Writ or Holy Church*, New York 1959.

Tex, J. den, *Oldenbarnevelt*, 5 vols., Haarlem 1960–72.

Tideman, J., *De Remonstrantsche broederschap. Biografische naamlijst van hare professoren, predikanten en proponenten*. Bewerkt door H.C. Rogge en B. Tideman, 2nd ed., Amsterdam 1905.

Troje, H.E., 'Wissenschaftlichkeit und System in der Jurisprudenz des 16. Jahrhunderts', *Philosophie und Rechtswissenschaft: zum Problem ihrer Beziehung im 19. Jahrhundert*.

Herausgegeben von J. Blühdorn und J. Ritter, Frankfurt am Main 1969, pp. 63–88.

Tuynman, P., 'Petrus Scriverius (12 January 1576–30 April 1660)', *Quaerendo*, 7 (1977), 5–37.

Vasoli, C., *La dialettica e la retorica dell'Umanesimo. 'Invenzione' e 'metodo' nella cultura del XV e XVI secolo*, Milan 1968.

Verdonk, J.J., *Petrus Ramus en de wiskunde*, Assen 1966.

Viehweg, Th., *Topik und Jurisprudenz*, Munich 1953.

Vogel, C.J. de, *Greek Philosophy. A Collection of Texts with Notes and Explanations*, 3 vols., Leiden 1969–73.

Völker-Hetzel, B., 'Klassizismus', in *Handlexikon zur Literaturwissenschaft*, 2nd ed., Munich 1974, pp. 226–30.

Volkmann, E., *Balthasar Venator*, Berlin 1938.

Vollenhoven, C. van, *Verspreide Geschriften*, I Haarlem 1934.

Vollgraff, J.A., 'Pierre de la Ramée (1515–1572) et Willbrord Snel van Royen (1580–1626)', *Janus. Archives internationales pour l'histoire de la médecine et de la géographie médecinale*, Leiden 1913, 596–625.

Walker, D.P., *The Ancient Theology. Studies in Christian Platonism from the Fifteenth to the Eighteenth Century*, London 1972.

Weevers, T., *The Poetry of the Netherlands in its European Context 1170–1930*, London 1960.

Wijnmalen, T.C.L., *Hugo de Groot als verdediger des Christendoms beschouwd. Eene literarisch-apologetische proeve*, Utrecht 1869.

Wilbur, E.M., *A History of Unitarianism, Socinianism and its Antecedents*, Cambridge Massachusetts 1945.

Wilde, W.J. de, *De messiaansche opvattingen der middeleeuwse exegeten Rasji, Aben Esra en Kimchi vooral volgens hun commentaren op Jesaja*, Wageningen 1929.

Williams, A.L., *Adversus Judaeos. A Bird's Eye View of Christian Apologiae until the Renaissance*, Cambridge 1935.

Williams, G.H., *The Radical Reformation* [Sixteenth Century Essays and Studies, 15], Kirksville Missouri 1992.

——, *The Polish Brethren, Documentation of the History and Thought of Unitarianism in the Polish-Lithunian Commonwealth and in the Diaspora, 1601–1685*, I–II [Harvard Theological Studies, 30] Missoula, Montana 1980.

INDEX OF NAMES

INDEX OF SUBJECTS

Studies in the History
of Christian Thought

EDITED BY HEIKO A. OBERMAN

46. GARSTEIN, O. *Rome and the Counter-Reformation in Scandinavia.* 1553-1622. 1992
47. GARSTEIN, O. *Rome and the Counter-Reformation in Scandinavia.* 1622-1656. 1992
48. PERRONE COMPAGNI, V. (ed.). *Cornelius Agrippa, De occulta philosophia Libri tres.* 1992
49. MARTIN, D. D. *Fifteenth-Century Carthusian Reform.* The World of Nicholas Kempf. 1992
50. HOENEN, M. J. F. M. *Marsilius of Inghen.* Divine Knowledge in Late Medieval Thought. 1993
51. O'MALLEY, J. W., IZBICKI, T. M. and CHRISTIANSON, G. (eds.). *Humanity and Divinity in Renaissance and Reformation.* Essays in Honor of Charles Trinkaus. 1993
52. REEVE, A. (ed.) and SCREECH, M. A. (introd.). *Erasmus' Annotations on the New Testament.* Galatians to the Apocalypse. 1993
53. STUMP, Ph. H. *The Reforms of the Council of Constance (1414-1418).* 1994
54. GIAKALIS, A. *Images of the Divine.* The Theology of Icons at the Seventh Ecumenical Council. With a Foreword by Henry Chadwick. 1994
55. NELLEN, H. J. M. and RABBIE, E. (eds.). *Hugo Grotius – Theologian.* Essays in Honour of G. H. M. Posthumus Meyjes. 1994
56. TRIGG, J. D. *Baptism in the Theology of Martin Luther.* 1994
57. JANSE, W. *Albert Hardenberg als Theologe.* Profil eines Bucer-Schülers. 1994
59. SCHOOR, R.J.M. van de. *The Irenical Theology of Théophile Brachet de La Milletière (1588-1665).* 1995
60. STREHLE, S. *The Catholic Roots of the Protestant Gospel.* Encounter between the Middle Ages and the Reformation. 1995
61. BROWN, M.L. *Donne and the Politics of Conscience in Early Modern England.* 1995
62. SCREECH, M.A. (ed.). *Richard Mocket, Warden of All Souls College, Oxford, Doctrina et Politia Ecclesiae Anglicanae.* An Anglican Summa. Facsimile with Variants of the Text of 1617. Edited with an Introduction. 1995
63. SNOEK, G.J.C. *Medieval Piety from Relics to the Eucharist.* A Process of Mutual Interaction. 1995
64. PIXTON, P.B. *The German Episcopacy and the Implementation of the Decrees of the Fourth Lateran Council, 1216-1245.* Watchmen on the Tower. 1995
65. DOLNIKOWSKI, E.W. *Thomas Bradwardine: A View of Time and a Vision of Eternity in Fourteenth-Century Thought.* 1995
66. RABBIE, E. (ed.). *Hugo Grotius, Ordinum Hollandiae ac Westfrisiae Pietas (1613).* Critical Edition with Translation and Commentary. 1995
67. HIRSH, J.C. *The Boundaries of Faith.* The Development and Transmission of Medieval Spirituality. 1996
68. BURNETT, S.G. *From Christian Hebraism to Jewish Studies.* Johannes Buxtorf (1564-1629) and Hebrew Learning in the Seventeenth Century. 1996
69. BOLAND O.P., V. *Ideas in God according to Saint Thomas Aquinas.* Sources and Synthesis. 1996
70. LANGE, M.E. *Telling Tears in the English Renaissance.* 1996
71. CHRISTIANSON, G. and IZBICKI, T.M. (eds.). *Nicholas of Cusa on Christ and the Church.* Essays in Memory of Chandler McCuskey Brooks for the American Cusanus Society. 1996
72. MALI, A. *Mystic in the New World.* Marie de l'Incarnation (1599-1672). 1996
73. VISSER, D. *Apocalypse as Utopian Expectation (800-1500).* The Apocalypse Commentary of Berengaudus of Ferrières and the Relationship between Exegesis, Liturgy and Iconography. 1996
74. O'ROURKE BOYLE, M. *Divine Domesticity.* Augustine of Thagaste to Teresa of Avila. 1997
75. PFIZENMAIER, T.C. *The Trinitarian Theology of Dr. Samuel Clarke (1675-1729).* Context, Sources, and Controversy. 1997
76. BERKVENS-STEVELINCK, C., ISRAEL, J. and POSTHUMUS MEYJES, G.H.M. (eds.). *The Emergence of Tolerance in the Dutch Republic.* 1997
77. HAYKIN, M.A.G. (ed.). *The Life and Thought of John Gill (1697-1771).* A Tercentennial Appreciation. 1997
78. KAISER, C.B. *Creational Theology and the History of Physical Science.* The Creationist Tradition from Basil to Bohr. 1997
79. LEES, J.T. *Anselm of Havelberg.* Deeds into Words in the Twelfth Century. 1997
80. WINTER, J.M. van. *Sources Concerning the Hospitallers of St John in the Netherlands, 14th-18th Centuries.* 1998

81. TIERNEY, B. *Foundations of the Conciliar Theory*. The Contribution of the Medieval Canonists from Gratian to the Great Schism. Enlarged New Edition. 1998
82. MIERNOWSKI, J. *Le Dieu Néant*. Théologies négatives à l'aube des temps modernes. 1998
83. HALVERSON, J.L. *Peter Aureol on Predestination*. A Challenge to Late Medieval Thought. 1998.
84. HOULISTON, V. (ed.). *Robert Persons, S.J.: The Christian Directory (1582)*. The First Booke of the Christian Exercise, appertayning to Resolution. 1998
85. GRELL, O.P. (ed.). *Paracelsus*. The Man and His Reputation, His Ideas and Their Transformation. 1998
86. MAZZOLA, E. *The Pathology of the English Renaissance*. Sacred Remains and Holy Ghosts. 1998.
87. 88. MARSILIUS VON INGHEN. *Quaestiones super quattuor libros sententiarum*. Super Primum. Bearbeitet von M. Santos Noya. 2 Bände. I. Quaestiones 1-7. II. Quaestiones 8-21. 2000
89. FAUPEL-DREVS, K. *Vom rechten Gebrauch der Bilder im liturgischen Raum*. Mittelalterliche Funktionsbestimmungen bildender Kunst im *Rationale divinorum officiorum* des Durandus von Mende (1230/1-1296). 1999
90. KREY, P.D.W. and SMITH, L. (eds.). *Nicholas of Lyra*. the Senses of Scripture. 2000
92. OAKLEY, F. *Politics and Eternity*. Studies in the History of Medieval and Early-Modern Political Thought. 1999
93. PRYDS, D. *The Politics of Preaching*. Robert of Naples (1309-1343) and his Sermons. 2000
94. POSTHUMUS MEYJES, G.H.M. *Jean Gerson – Apostle of Unity*. His Church Politics and Ecclesiology. Translated by J.C. Grayson. 1999
95. BERG, J. VAN DEN. *Religious Currents and Cross-Currents*. Essays on Early Modern Protestantism and the Protestant Enlightenment. Edited by J. de Bruijn, P. Holtrop, and E. van der Wall. 1999
96. IZBICKI, T.M. and BELLITTO, C.M. (eds.). *Reform and Renewal in the Middle Ages and the Renaissance*. Studies in Honor of Louis Pascoe, S. J. 2000
97. KELLY, D. *The Conspiracy of Allusion*. Description, Rewriting, and Authorship from Macrobius to Medieval Romance. 1999
98. MARRONE, S.P. *The Light of Thy Countenance*. Science and Knowledge of God in the Thirteenth Century. 2 volumes. 1. A Doctrine of Divine Illumination. 2. God at the Core of Cognition. 2001
99. HOWSON, B.H. *Erroneous and Schismatical Opinions*. The Question of Orthodoxy regarding the Theology of Hanserd Knollys (c. 1599-169)). 2001
100. ASSELT, W.J. VAN. *The Federal Theology of Johannes Cocceius (1603-1669)*. 2001
101. CELENZA, C.S. *Piety and Pythagoras in Renaissance Florence the* Symbolum Nesianum. 2001
102. DAM, H.-J. VAN (ed.), *Hugo Grotius, De imperio summarum potestatum circa sacra*. Critical Edition with Introduction, English translation and Commentary. 2 volumes. 2001
103. BAGGE, S. *Kings, Politics, and the Right Order of the World in German Historiography c. 950-1150*. 2002
104. STEIGER, J.A. *Fünf Zentralthemen der Theologie Luthers und seiner Erben*. Communicatio – Imago – Figura – Maria – Exempla. Mit Edition zweier christologischer Frühschriften Johann Gerhards. 2002
105. IZBICKI T.M. and BELLITTO C.M. (eds.). *Nicholas of Cusa and his Age: Intellect and Spirituality*. Essays Dedicated to the Memory of F. Edward Cranz, Thomas P. McTighe and Charles Trinkaus. 2002
106. HASCHER-BURGER, U. *Gesungene Innigkeit*. Studien zu einer Musikhandschrift der Devotio moderna (Utrecht, Universiteitsbibliotheek, MS 16 H 94, olim B 113). Mit einer Edition der Gesänge. 2002
107. BOLLIGER, D. *Infiniti Contemplatio*. Grundzüge der Scotus- und Scotismusrezeption im Werk Huldrych Zwinglis. 2003
108. CLARK, F. *The 'Gregorian' Dialogues and the Origins of Benedictine Monasticism*. 2002
109. ELM, E. *Die Macht der Weisheit*. Das Bild des Bischofs in der *Vita Augustini* des Possidius und andere spätantiken und frühmittelalterlichen Bischofsviten. 2003
110. BAST, R.J. (ed.). *The Reformation of Faith in the Context of Late Medieval Theology and Piety*. Essays by Berndt Hamm. 2004.
111. HEERING, J.P. *Hugo Grotius as Apologist for the Christian Religion*. A Study of his Work *De Veritate Religionis Christianae* (1640). Translated by J.C. Grayson. 2004.
112. LIM, P.C.-H. *In Pursuit of Purity, Unity, and Liberty*. Richard Baxter's Puritan Ecclesiology in its Seventeenth-Century Context. 2004.
113. CONNORS, R. and GOW, A.C. (eds.). *Anglo-American Millennialism, from Milton to the Millerites*. 2004.
114. YARDENI, M. and ZINGUER, I. (eds.). *Les Deux Réformee Chrétiennes*. Propagation et Diffusion. 2004.